W9-AJQ-511

2 1982 02035 4944

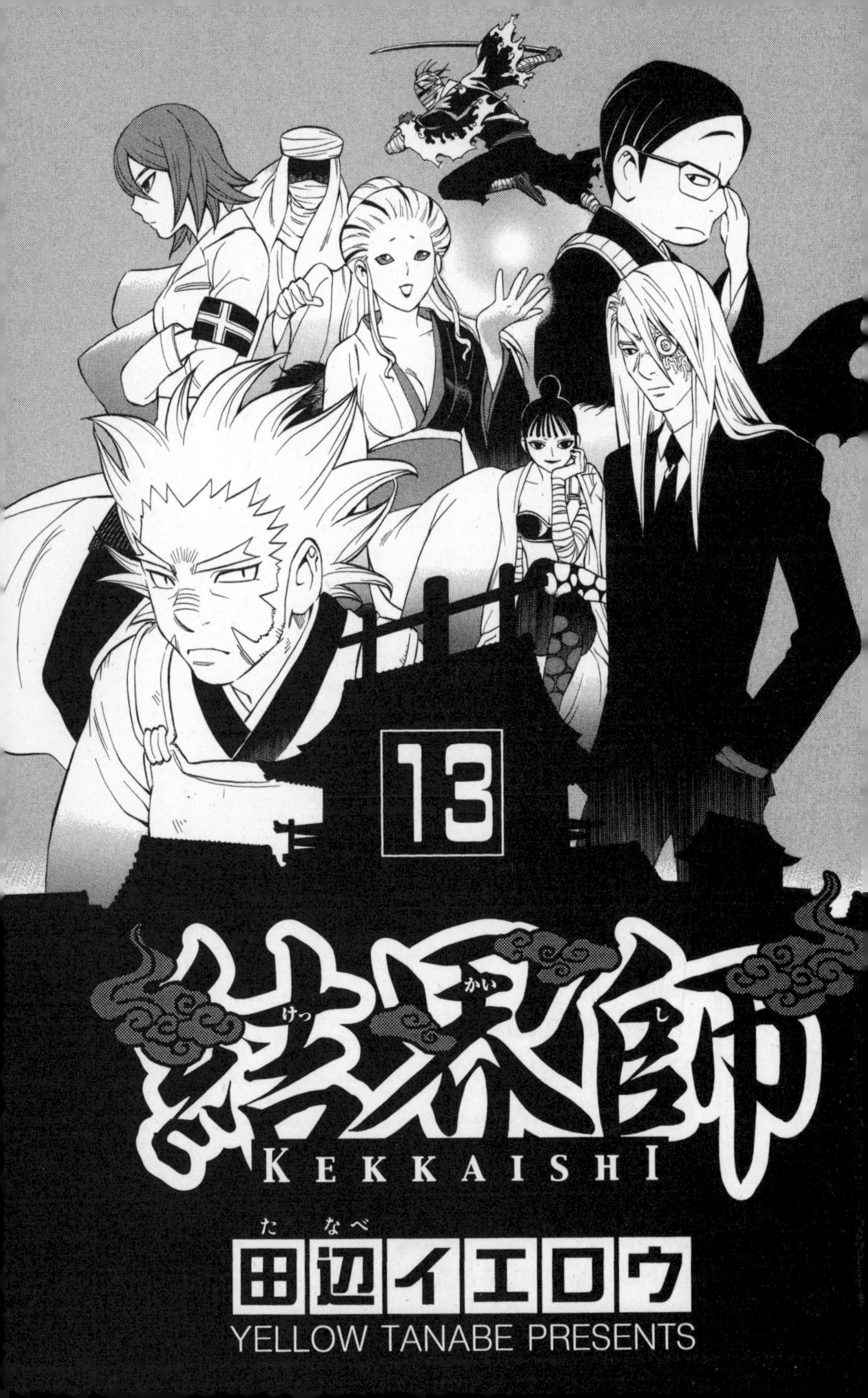
13

結界師

けっ かい し

KEKKAISHI

たなべ

田辺イエロウ

YELLOW TANABE PRESENTS

THE STORY THUS FAR

Yoshimori Sumimura and Tokine Yukimura have an ancestral duty to protect the Karasumori Forest from supernatural beings called *ayakashi*. People with their gift for terminating ayakashi are called *kekkaishi*, or "barrier masters."

Yoshimori infiltrates his enemy's lair, Kokuboro Castle, to avenge his friend, Gen Shishio, who fell in battle. First, he has to rescue Sen Kagemiya, a member of the "Night Troops," who followed him there only to be caught and held captive.

Meanwhile, Tokine, Masamori (Yoshimori's elder brother) and the rest of the Night Troops use Tokine's grandmother's magical passageway to Kokuboro Castle to try and rescue Yoshimori and Sen.

Just as Kokuboro Castle is beginning to completely disintegrate, Yoshimori finally locates Kaguro, Gen's murderer, and confronts him. At first, Kaguro tries to tempt Yoshimori to join his side. Then, armed with a powerful magical sword, he charges him at full force.

Kaguro's strength only increases as his fight with Yoshimori progresses. But just when Kaguro is about to defeat him, Yoshimori generates the most extraordinary kekkai he has ever produced…!

KEKKAISHI VOL. 13
TABLE OF CONTENTS

Chapter 116: Different

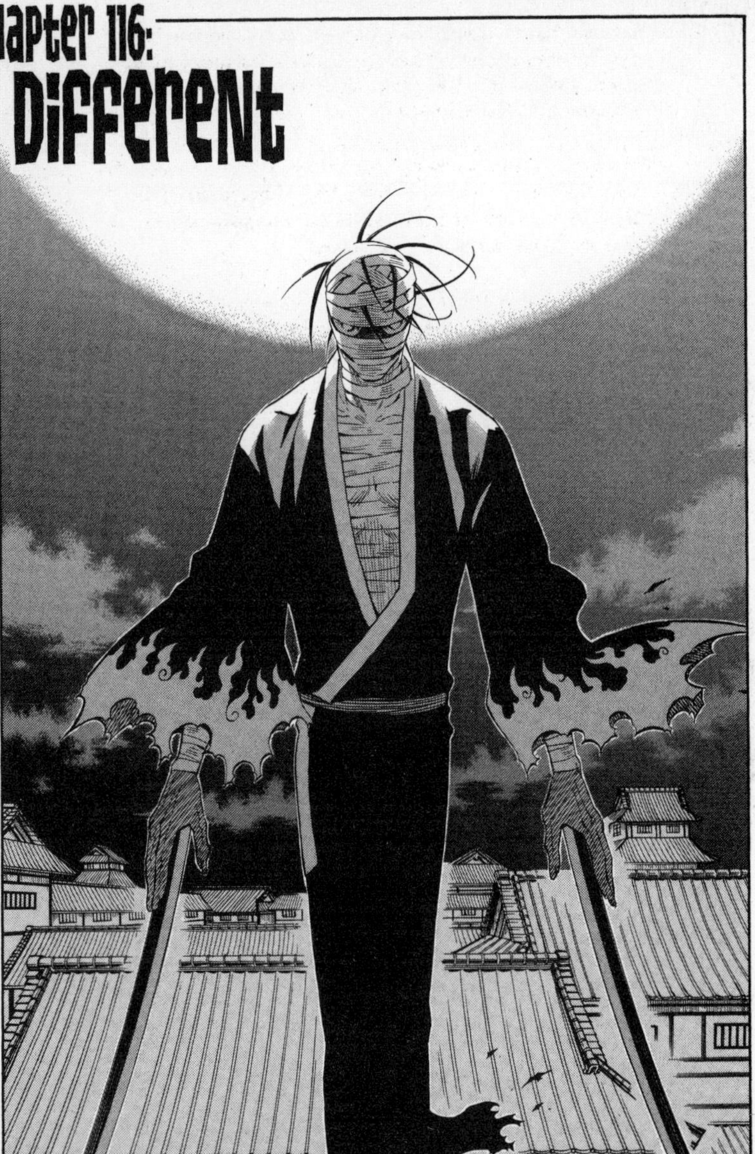

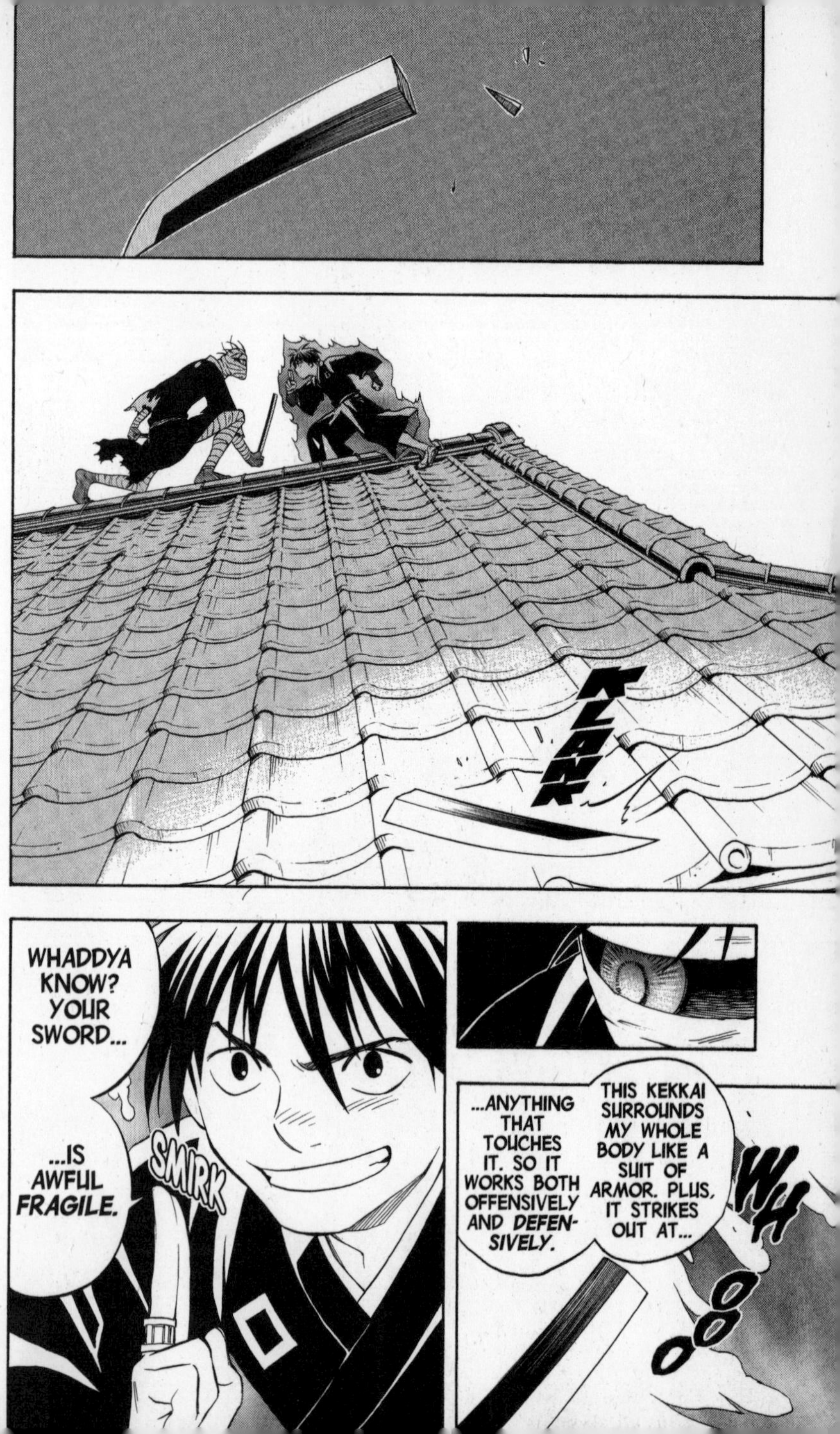
KLANK
THIS KEKKAI SURROUNDS MY WHOLE BODY LIKE A SUIT OF ARMOR. PLUS, IT STRIKES OUT AT...
...ANYTHING THAT TOUCHES IT. SO IT WORKS BOTH OFFENSIVELY AND DEFENSIVELY.
WHOOOO
WHADDYA KNOW? YOUR SWORD...
...IS AWFUL FRAGILE.
SMIRK

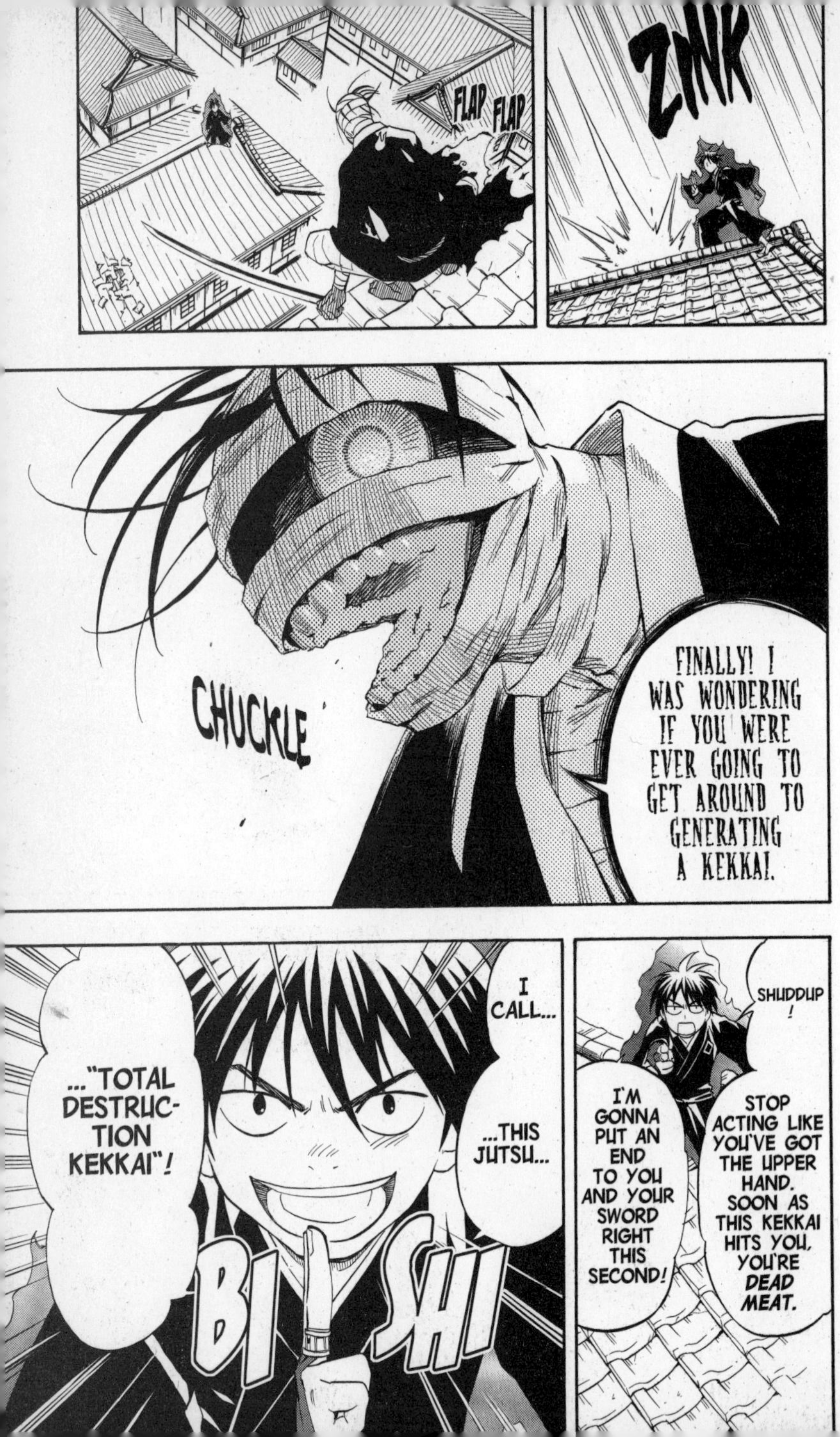
ZINK
FLAP FLAP
FINALLY! I WAS WONDERING IF YOU WERE EVER GOING TO GET AROUND TO GENERATING A KEKKAI.
CHUCKLE
SHUDDUP!
STOP ACTING LIKE YOU'VE GOT THE UPPER HAND. SOON AS THIS KEKKAI HITS YOU, YOU'RE *DEAD MEAT.*
I'M GONNA PUT AN END TO YOU AND YOUR SWORD RIGHT THIS SECOND!
I CALL...
...THIS JUTSU...
..."TOTAL DESTRUC-TION KEKKAI"!
BISHI

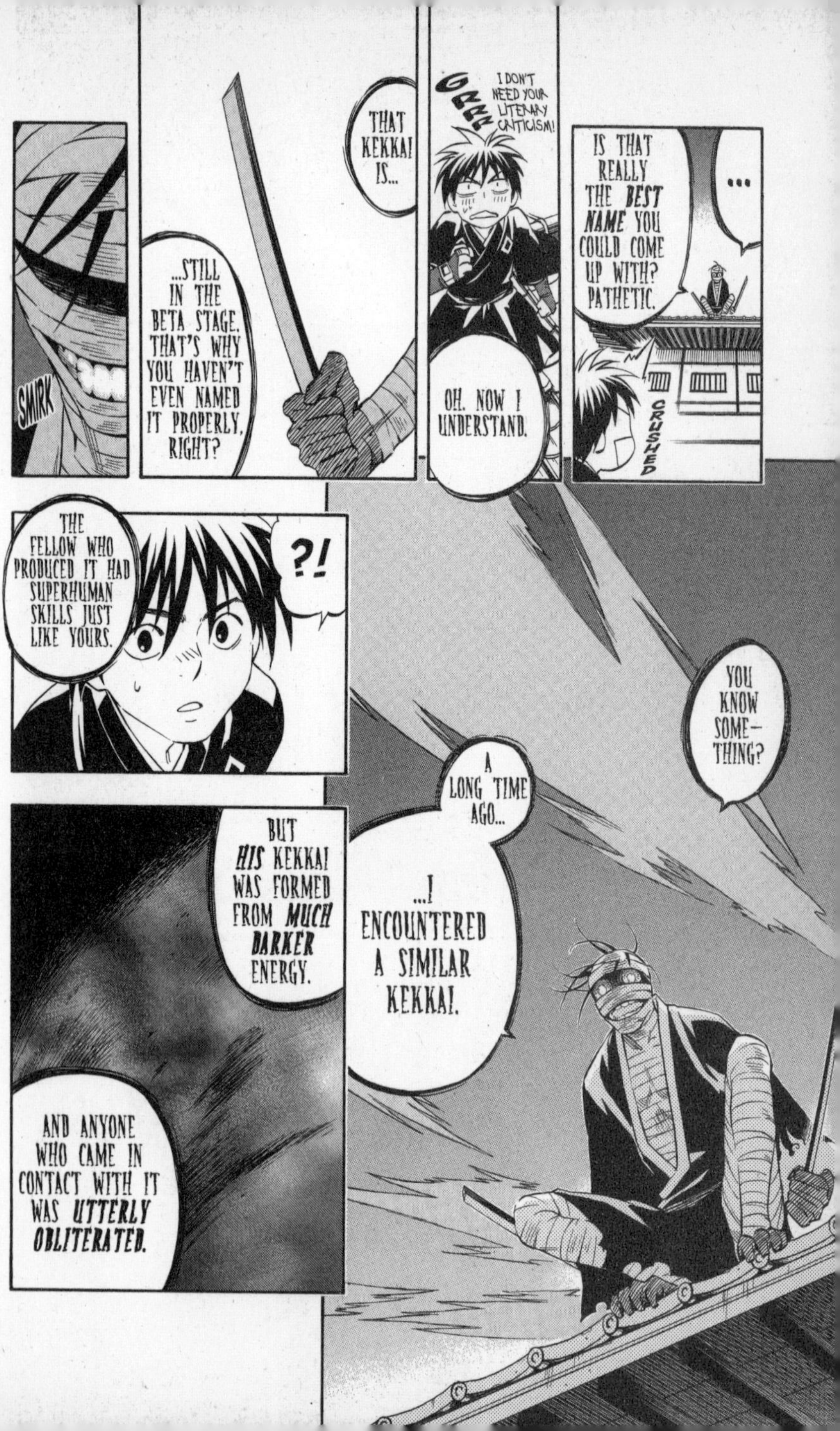
...
IS THAT REALLY THE BEST NAME YOU COULD COME UP WITH? PATHETIC.
CRUSHED
GRRR
I DON'T NEED YOUR LITERARY CRITICISM!
OH. NOW I UNDERSTAND.
THAT KEKKAI IS...
...STILL IN THE BETA STAGE. THAT'S WHY YOU HAVEN'T EVEN NAMED IT PROPERLY, RIGHT?
SMIRK
YOU KNOW SOME-THING?
A LONG TIME AGO...
...I ENCOUNTERED A SIMILAR KEKKAI.
?!
THE FELLOW WHO PRODUCED IT HAD SUPERHUMAN SKILLS JUST LIKE YOURS.
BUT HIS KEKKAI WAS FORMED FROM MUCH DARKER ENERGY.
AND ANYONE WHO CAME IN CONTACT WITH IT WAS UTTERLY OBLITERATED.

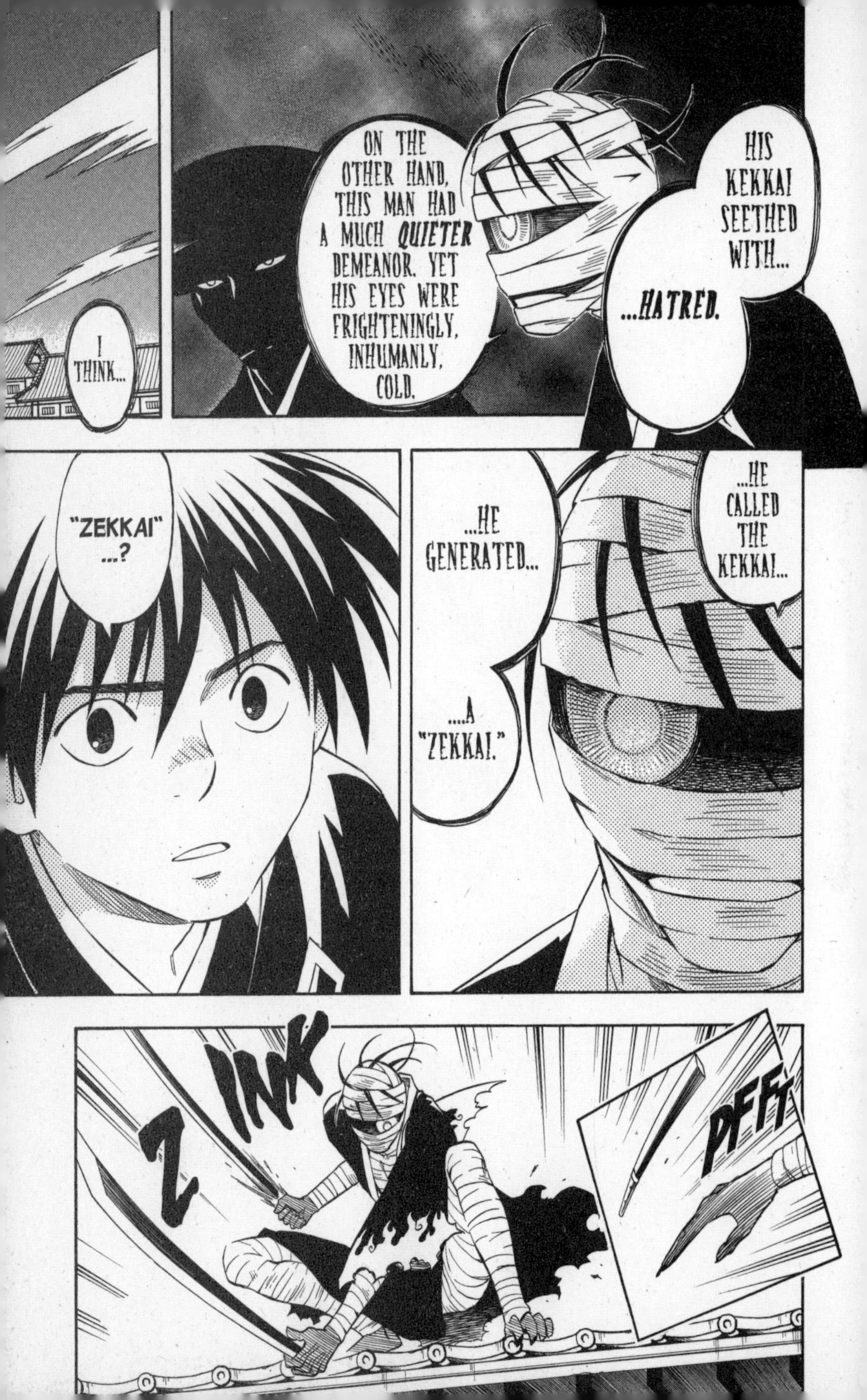
HIS KEKKAI SEETHED WITH...
...HATRED.
ON THE OTHER HAND, THIS MAN HAD A MUCH *QUIETER* DEMEANOR. YET HIS EYES WERE FRIGHTENINGLY, INHUMANLY, COLD.
I THINK...
...HE CALLED THE KEKKAI...
...HE GENERATED...
....A "ZEKKAI."
"ZEKKAI" ...?
PFFT
ZINK

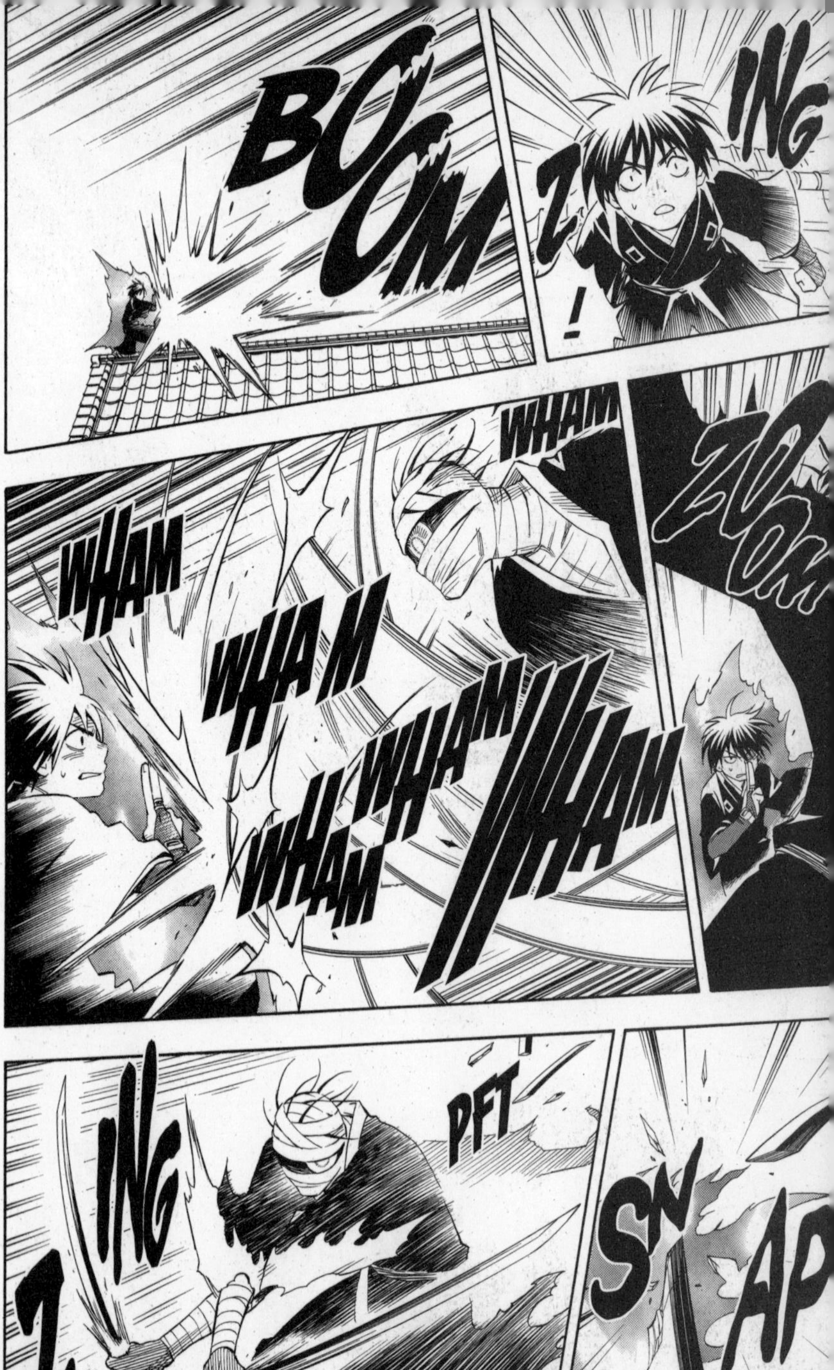
ZING
!
BOOM
ZOOM
WHAM
WHAM
WHAM
WHAM
WHAM
WHAM
WHAM
SNAP
PFT
ZING

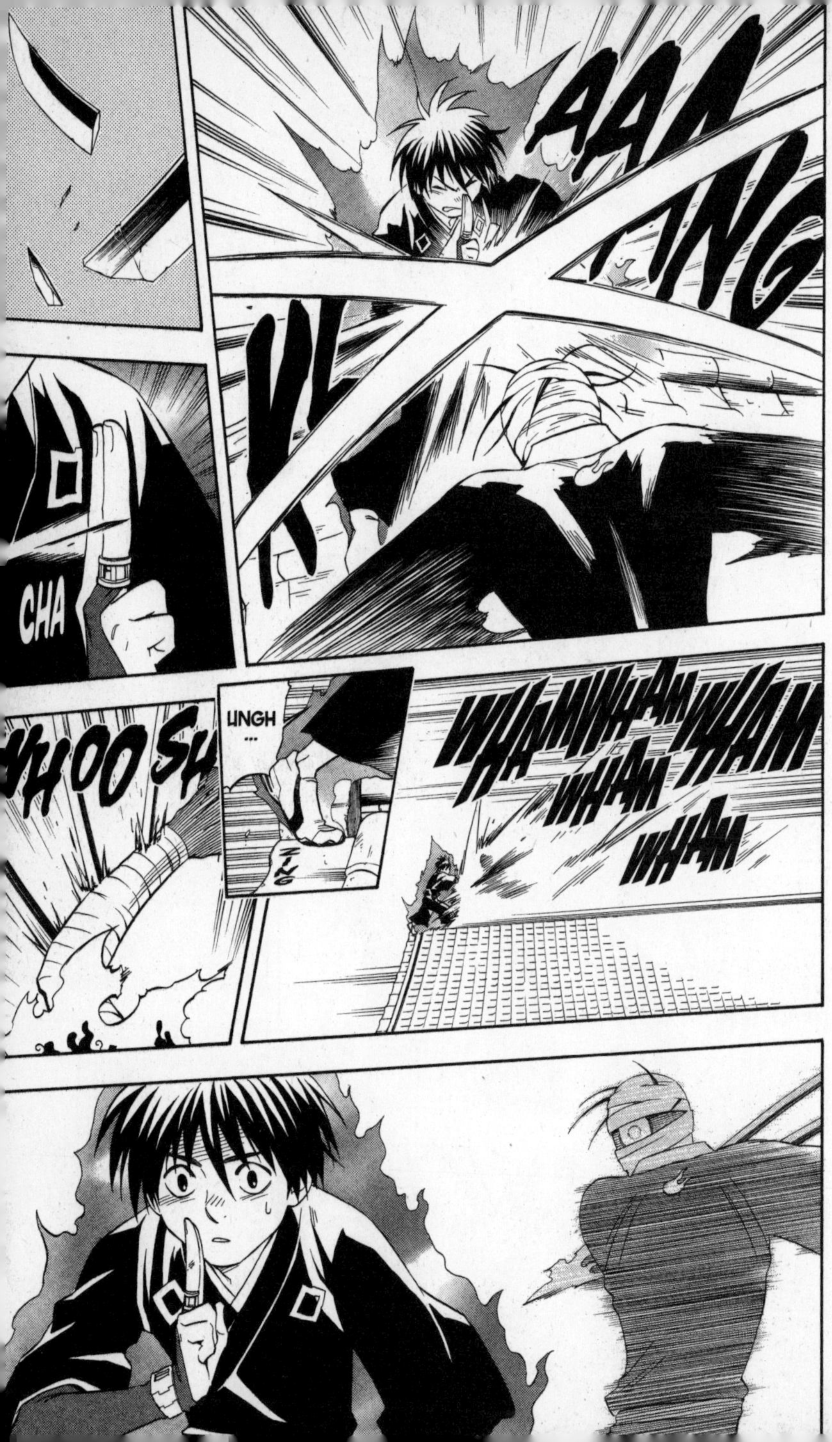

AAAN
ANG
KL
CHA
WHAM WHAM WHAM WHAM
WHAM WHAM
WHAM
UNGH...
TING
WHOOSH

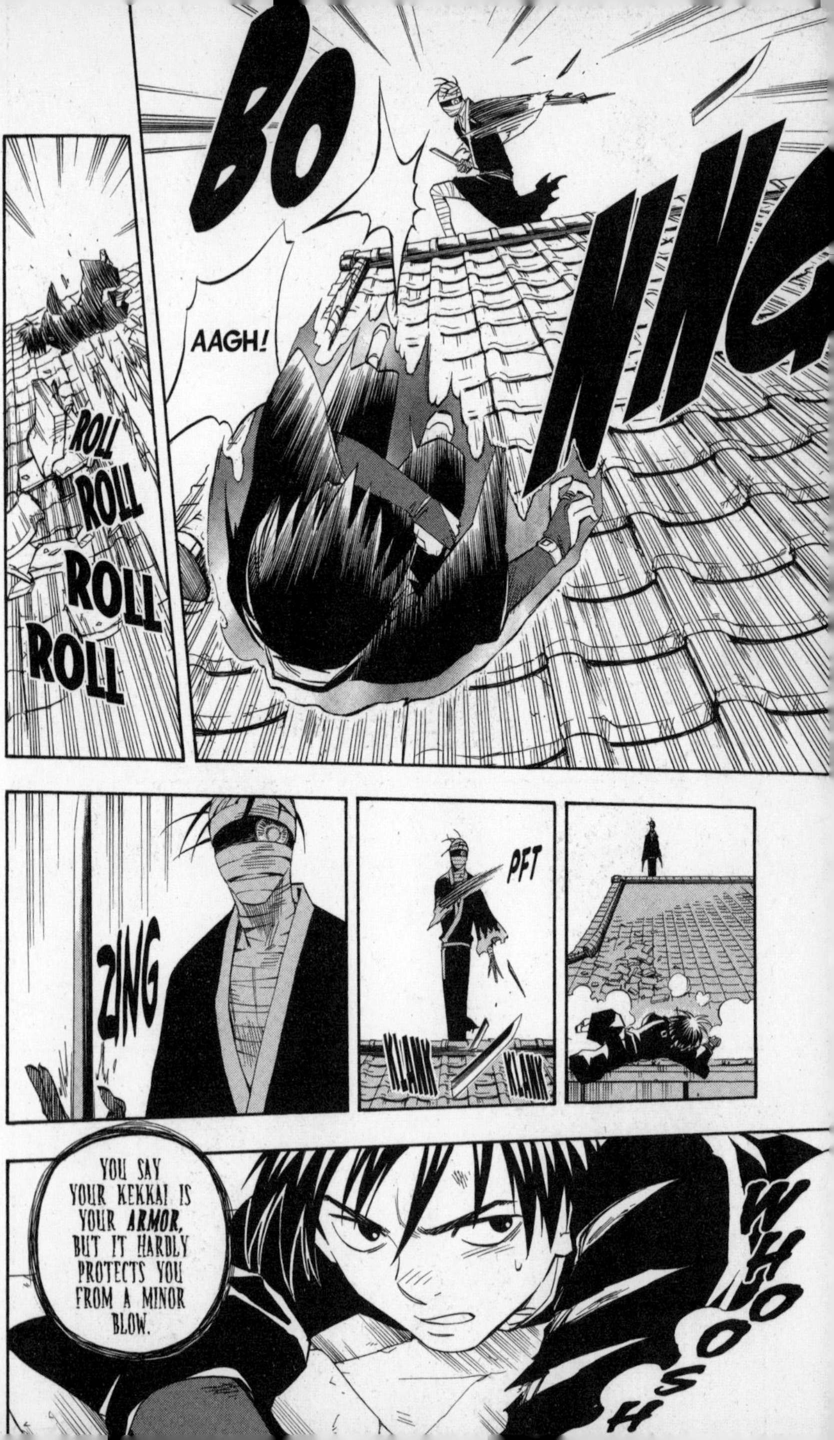
BONNG
AAGH!
ROLL
ROLL
ROLL
ROLL
PFT
KLANK
KLANK
ZING
YOU SAY YOUR KEKKAI IS YOUR *ARMOR*, BUT IT HARDLY PROTECTS YOU FROM A MINOR BLOW.
WHOOOSH

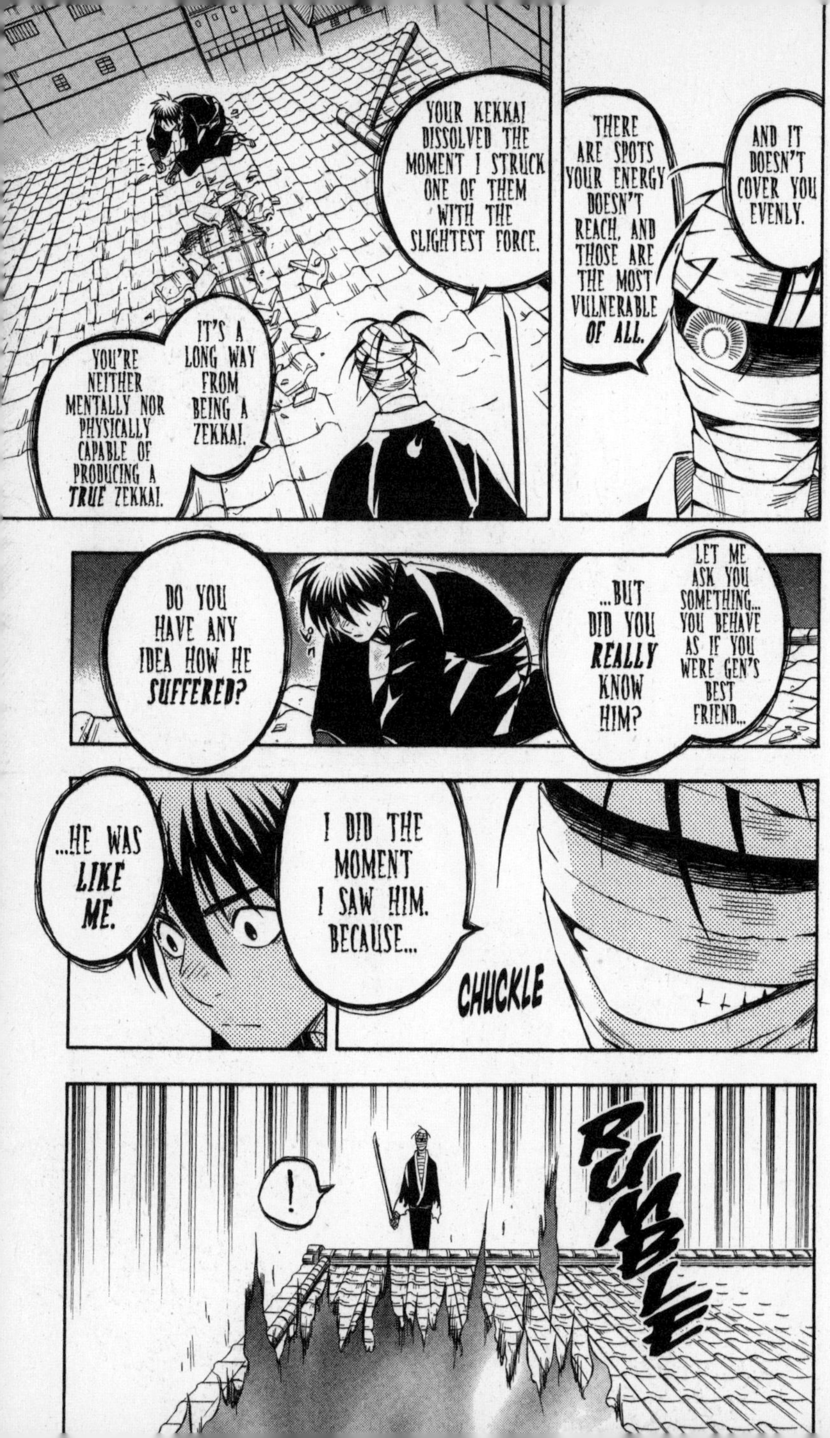
AND IT DOESN'T COVER YOU EVENLY.
THERE ARE SPOTS YOUR ENERGY DOESN'T REACH, AND THOSE ARE THE MOST VULNERABLE OF ALL.
YOUR KEKKAI DISSOLVED THE MOMENT I STRUCK ONE OF THEM WITH THE SLIGHTEST FORCE.
IT'S A LONG WAY FROM BEING A ZEKKAI.
YOU'RE NEITHER MENTALLY NOR PHYSICALLY CAPABLE OF PRODUCING A TRUE ZEKKAI.
LET ME ASK YOU SOMETHING... YOU BEHAVE AS IF YOU WERE GEN'S BEST FRIEND...
...BUT DID YOU REALLY KNOW HIM?
DO YOU HAVE ANY IDEA HOW HE SUFFERED?
CHUCKLE
I DID THE MOMENT I SAW HIM. BECAUSE...
...HE WAS LIKE ME.
RUMBLE
!

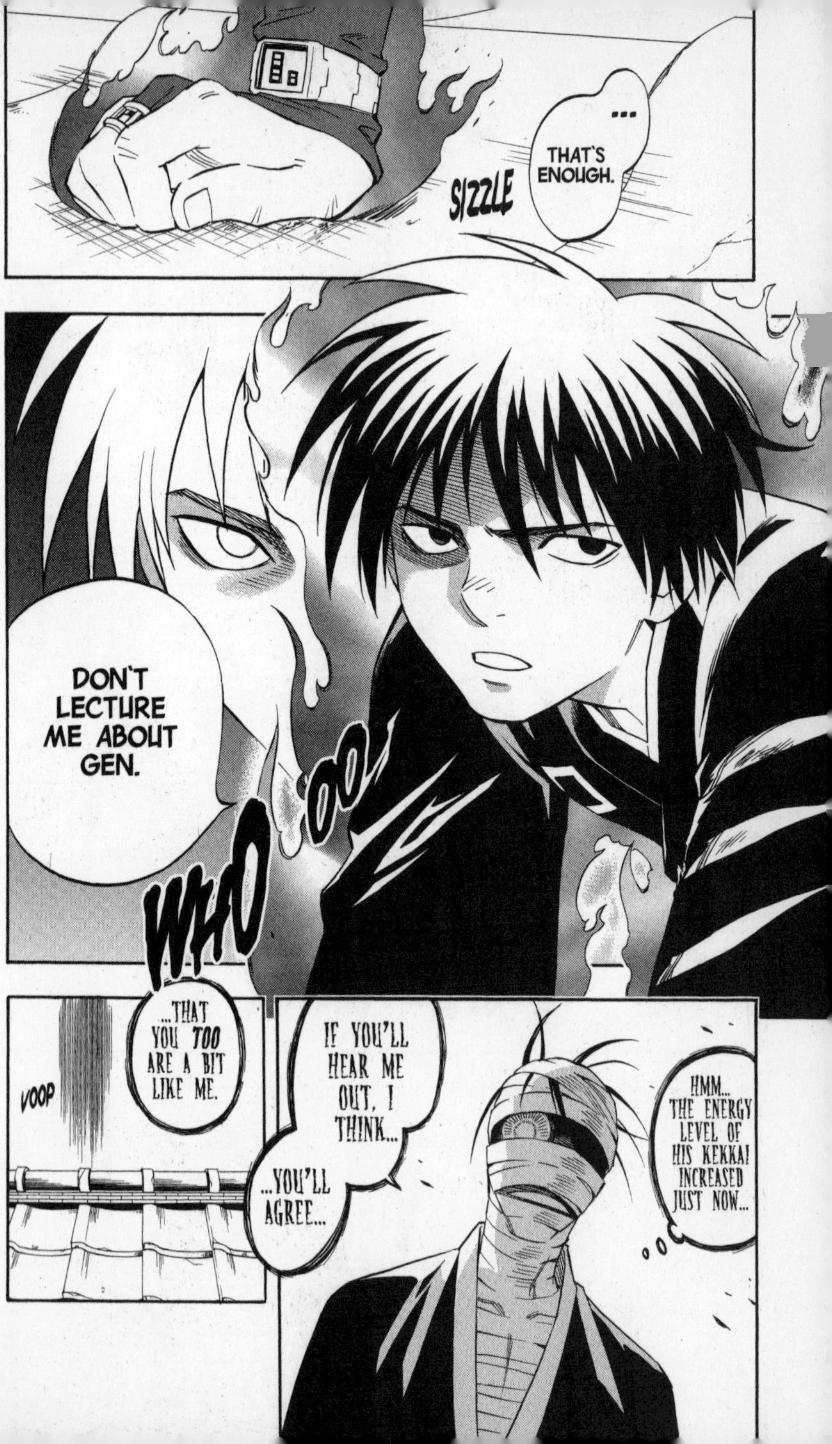
...
THAT'S ENOUGH.
SIZZLE
DON'T LECTURE ME ABOUT GEN.
WHOOO
HMM... THE ENERGY LEVEL OF HIS KEKKAI INCREASED JUST NOW...
IF YOU'LL HEAR ME OUT, I THINK...
...YOU'LL AGREE...
VOOP
...THAT YOU *TOO* ARE A BIT LIKE ME.

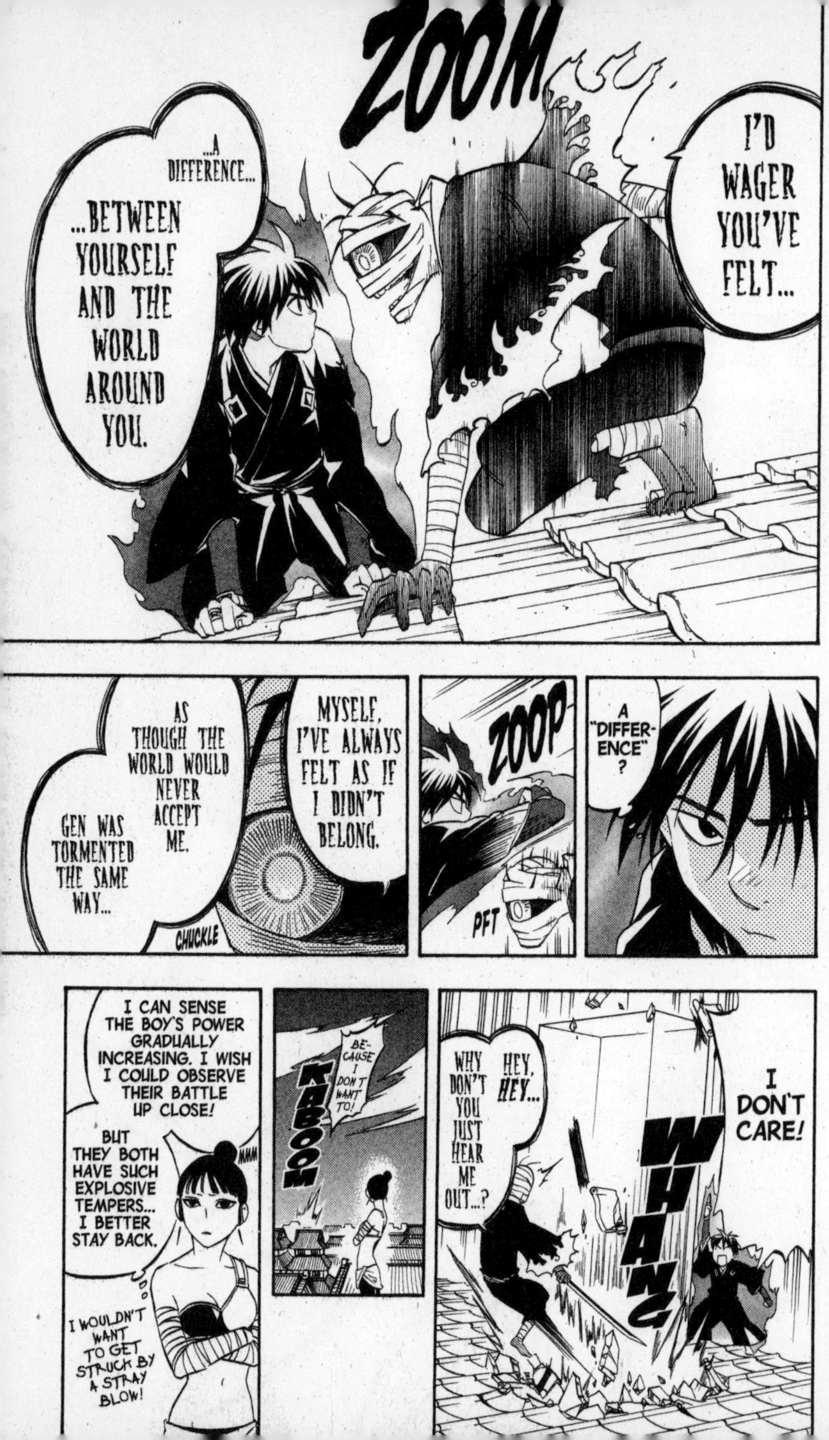
ZOOM
I'D WAGER YOU'VE FELT...
...A DIFFERENCE...
...BETWEEN YOURSELF AND THE WORLD AROUND YOU.
A "DIFFERENCE"?
ZOOP
PFT
MYSELF, I'VE ALWAYS FELT AS IF I DIDN'T BELONG.
AS THOUGH THE WORLD WOULD NEVER ACCEPT ME.
GEN WAS TORMENTED THE SAME WAY...
CHUCKLE
I DON'T CARE!
HEY, HEY...
WHY DON'T YOU JUST HEAR ME OUT...?
WHANG
BE-CAUSE I DON'T WANT TO!
KABOOM
I CAN SENSE THE BOY'S POWER GRADUALLY INCREASING. I WISH I COULD OBSERVE THEIR BATTLE UP CLOSE!
MMM
BUT THEY BOTH HAVE SUCH EXPLOSIVE TEMPERS... I BETTER STAY BACK.
I WOULDN'T WANT TO GET STRUCK BY A STRAY BLOW!

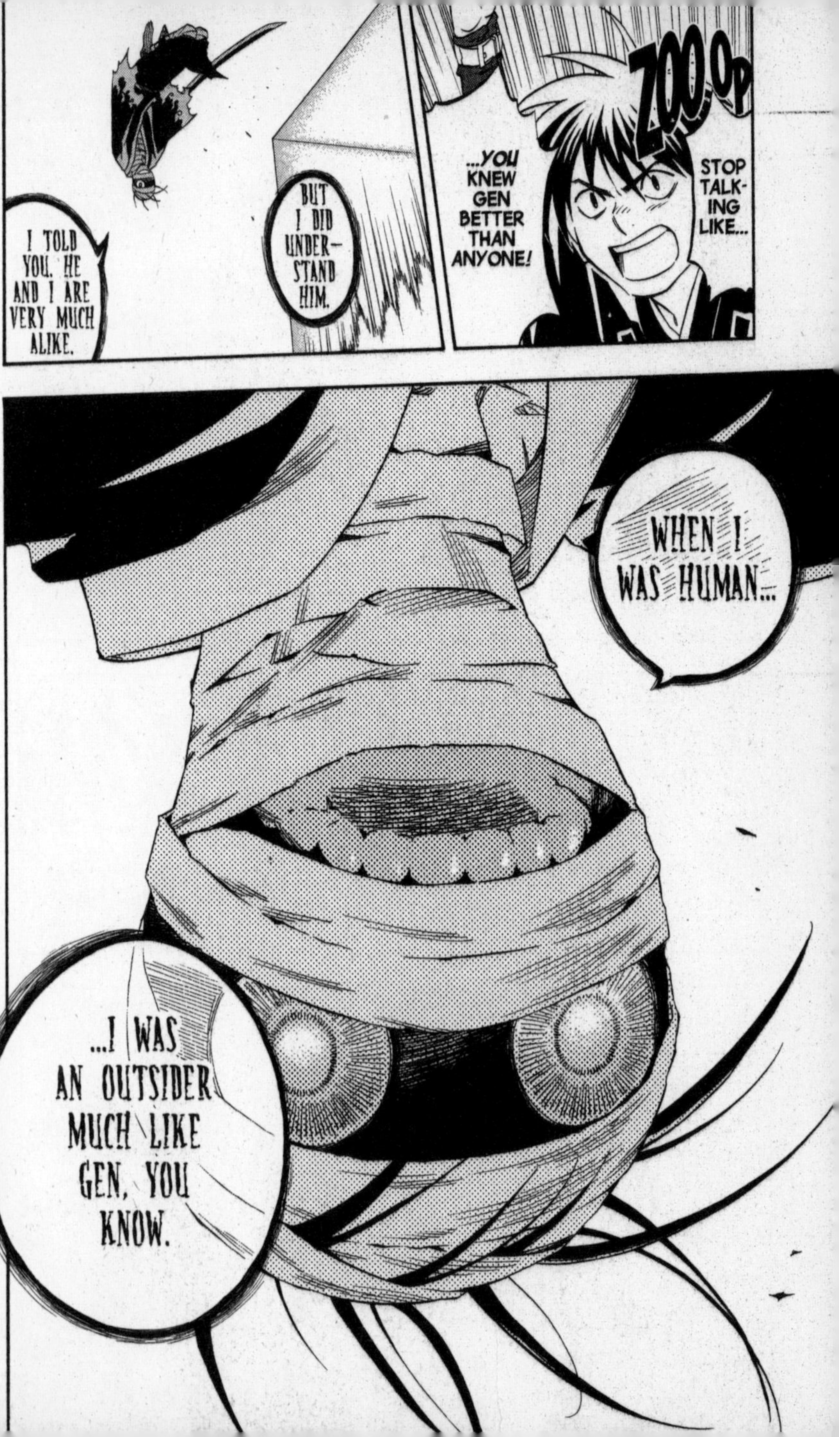
ZOOOP
STOP TALKING LIKE...
...YOU KNEW GEN BETTER THAN ANYONE!
BUT I DID UNDERSTAND HIM.
I TOLD YOU. HE AND I ARE VERY MUCH ALIKE.
WHEN I WAS HUMAN...
...I WAS AN OUTSIDER MUCH LIKE GEN, YOU KNOW.

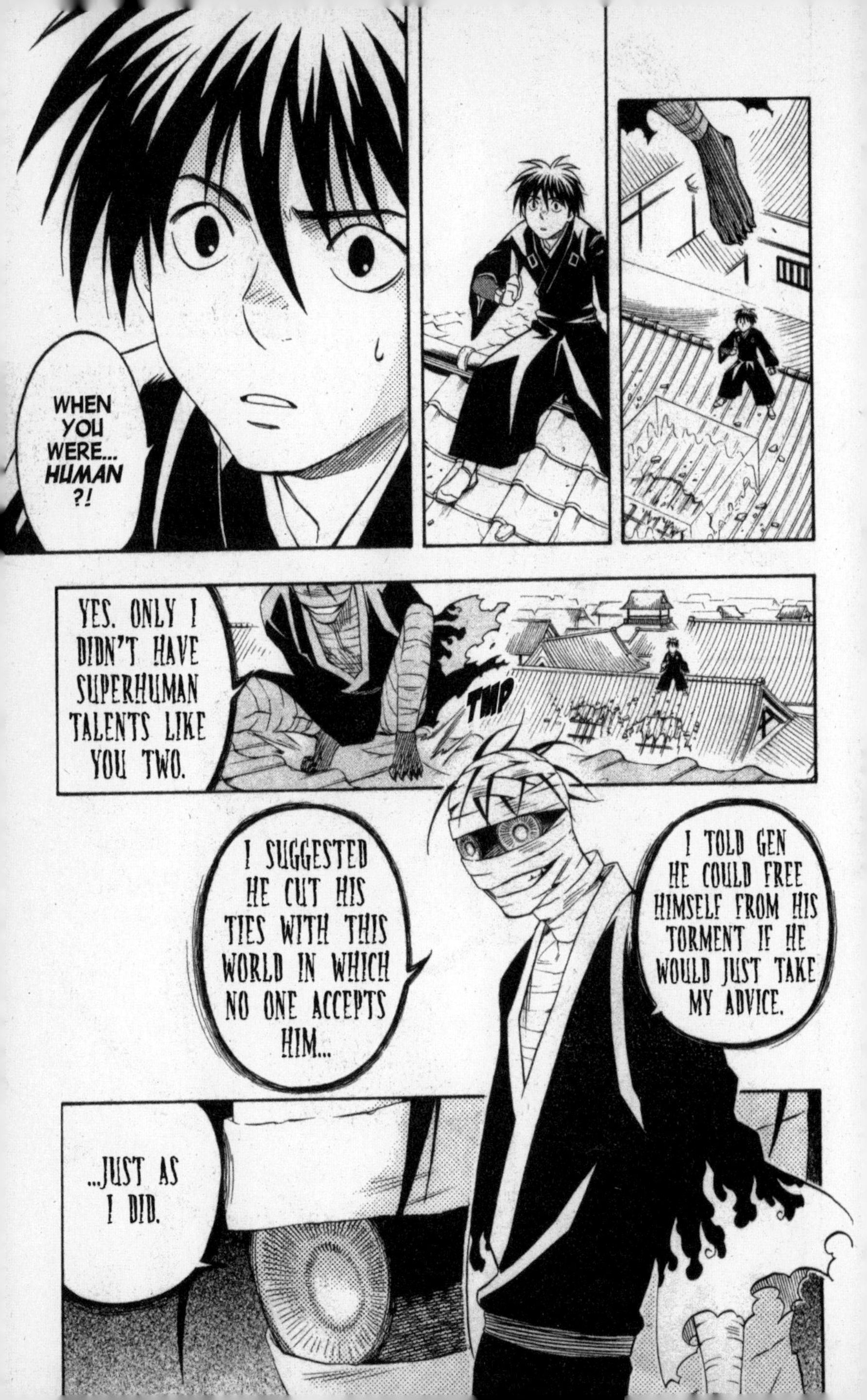
WHEN YOU WERE... HUMAN?!
YES. ONLY I DIDN'T HAVE SUPERHUMAN TALENTS LIKE YOU TWO.
TMP
I TOLD GEN HE COULD FREE HIMSELF FROM HIS TORMENT IF HE WOULD JUST TAKE MY ADVICE.
I SUGGESTED HE CUT HIS TIES WITH THIS WORLD IN WHICH NO ONE ACCEPTS HIM...
...JUST AS I DID.

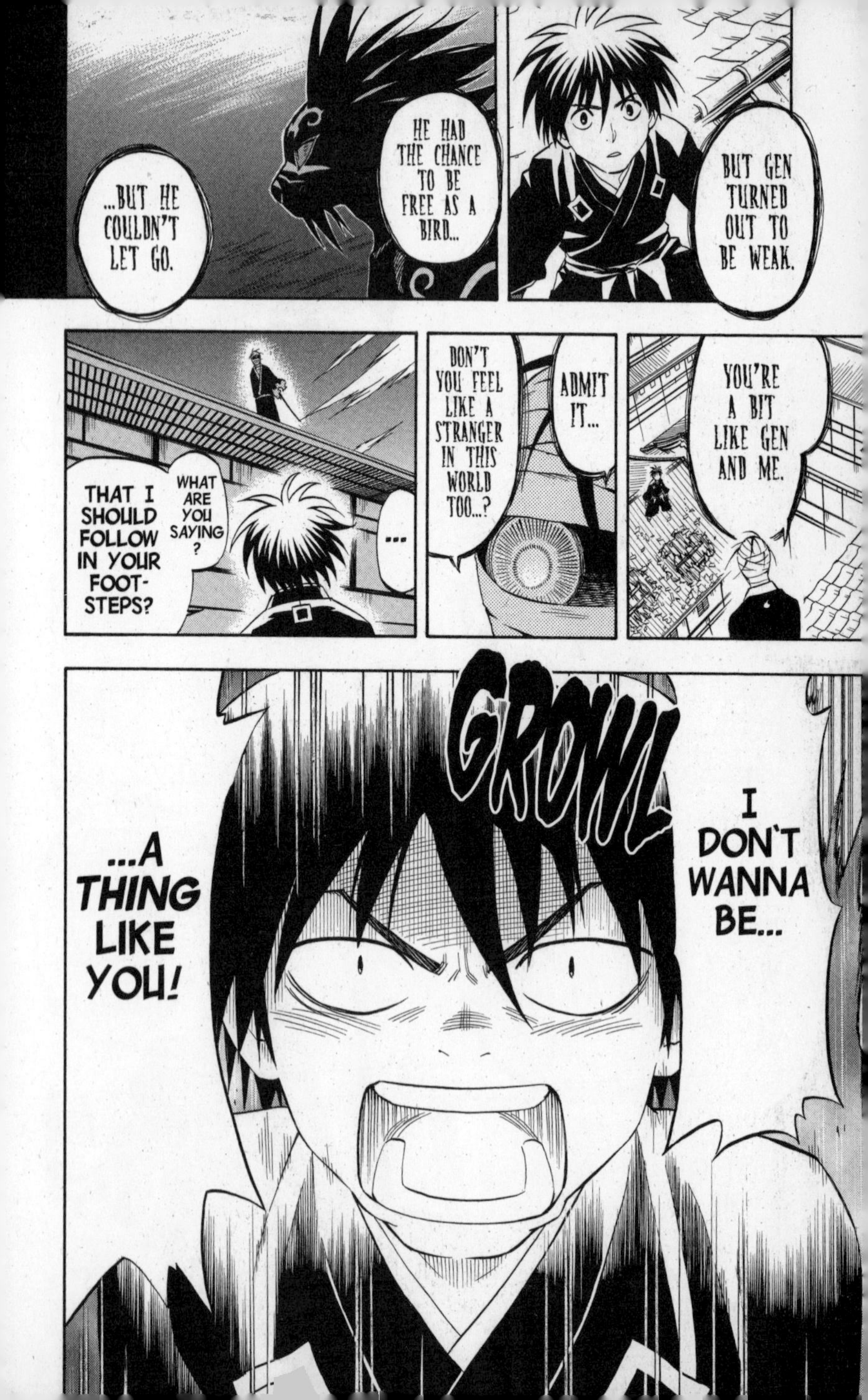
BUT GEN TURNED OUT TO BE WEAK.
HE HAD THE CHANCE TO BE FREE AS A BIRD...
...BUT HE COULDN'T LET GO.
YOU'RE A BIT LIKE GEN AND ME.
ADMIT IT...
DON'T YOU FEEL LIKE A STRANGER IN THIS WORLD TOO...?
...
WHAT ARE YOU SAYING?
THAT I SHOULD FOLLOW IN YOUR FOOT-STEPS?
GROWL
I DON'T WANNA BE...
...A THING LIKE YOU!

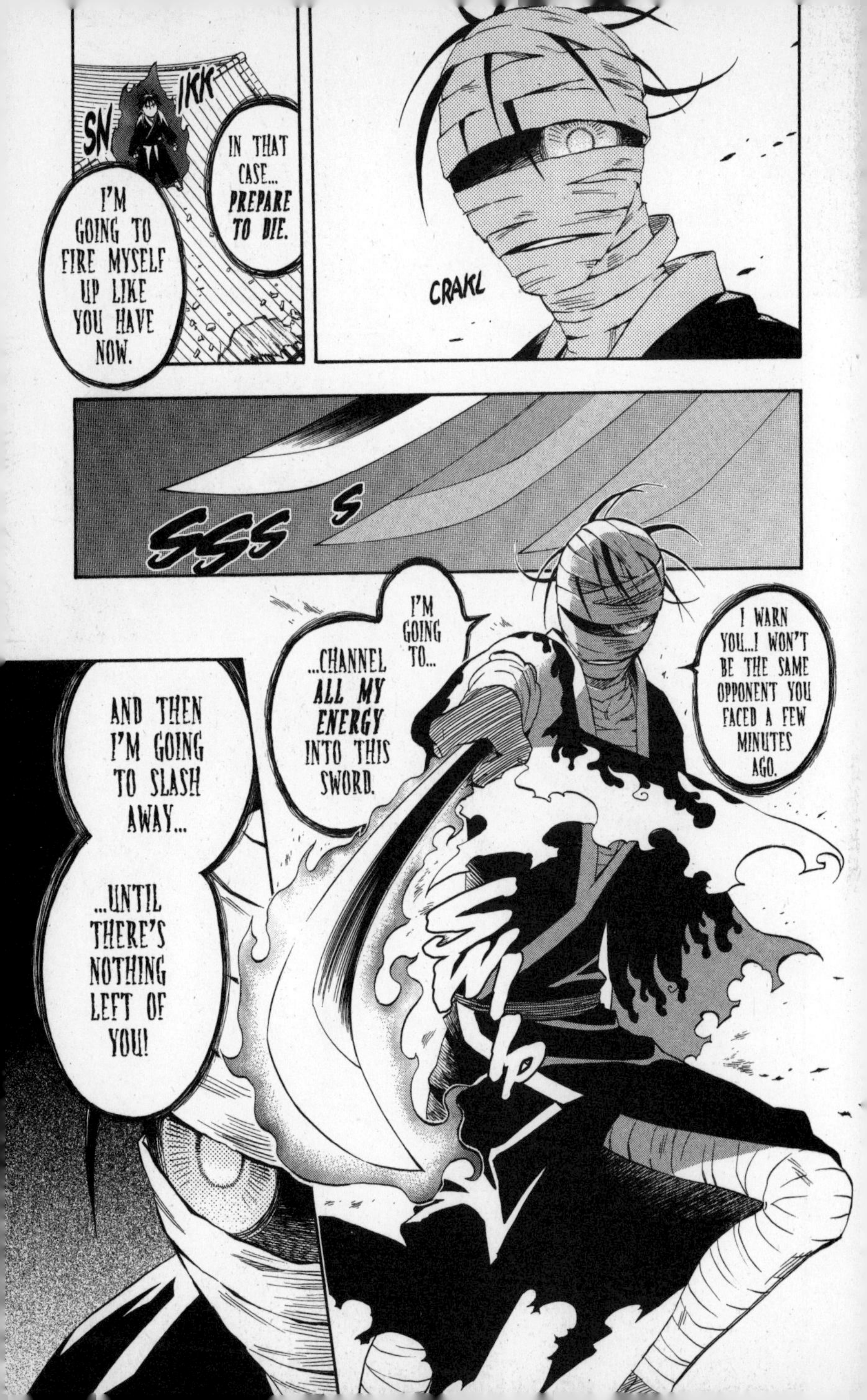
CRAKL
IN THAT CASE... PREPARE TO DIE.
SNIKK
I'M GOING TO FIRE MYSELF UP LIKE YOU HAVE NOW.
SSSS
I WARN YOU...I WON'T BE THE SAME OPPONENT YOU FACED A FEW MINUTES AGO.
I'M GOING TO...
...CHANNEL ALL MY ENERGY INTO THIS SWORD.
AND THEN I'M GOING TO SLASH AWAY...
...UNTIL THERE'S NOTHING LEFT OF YOU!
SWIP

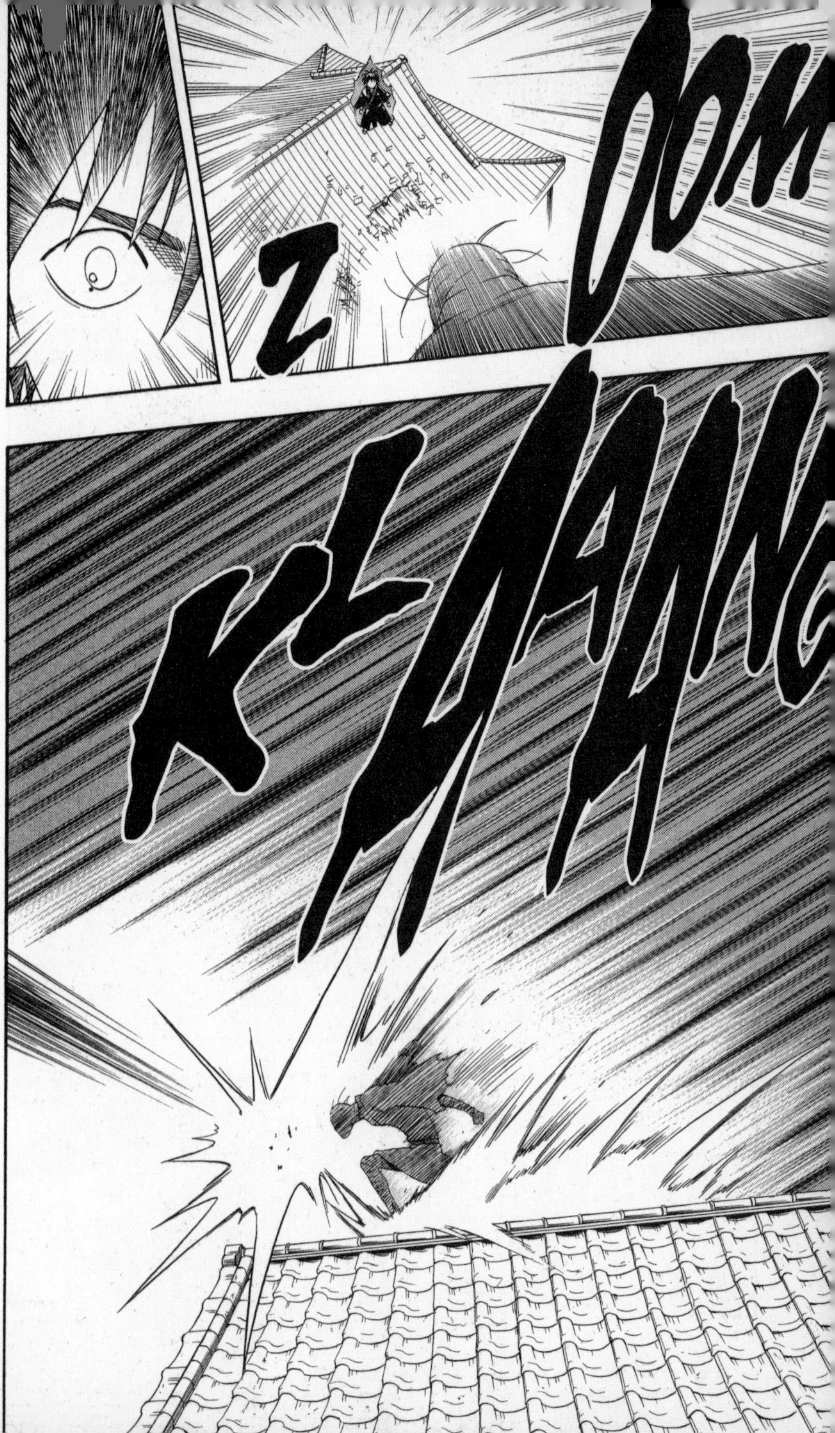
DON
Z

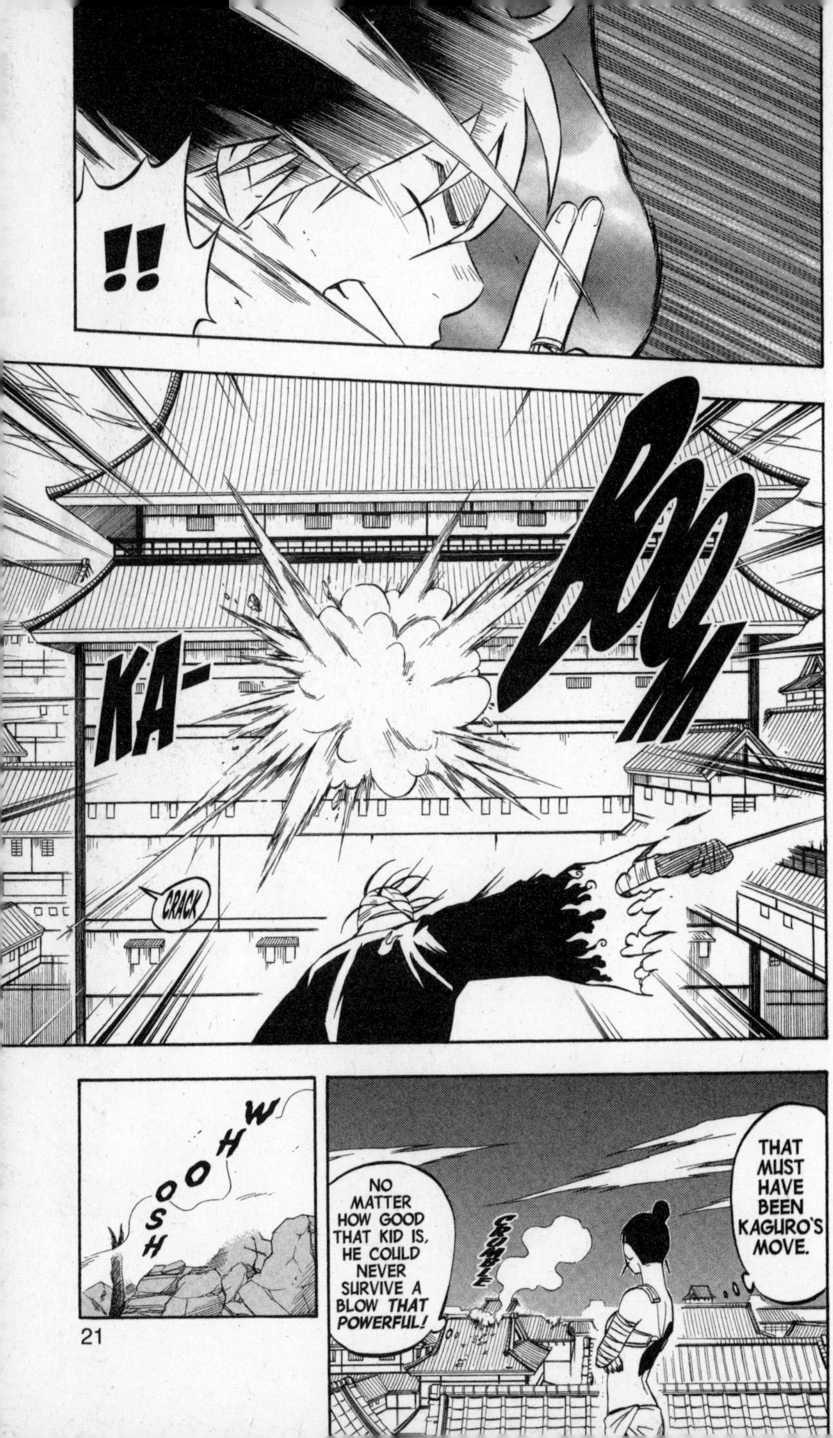
!!
KA-
BOOM
CRACK
THAT MUST HAVE BEEN KAGURO'S MOVE.
NO MATTER HOW GOOD THAT KID IS, HE COULD NEVER SURVIVE A BLOW THAT POWERFUL!
CRUMBLE
WHOOOSH

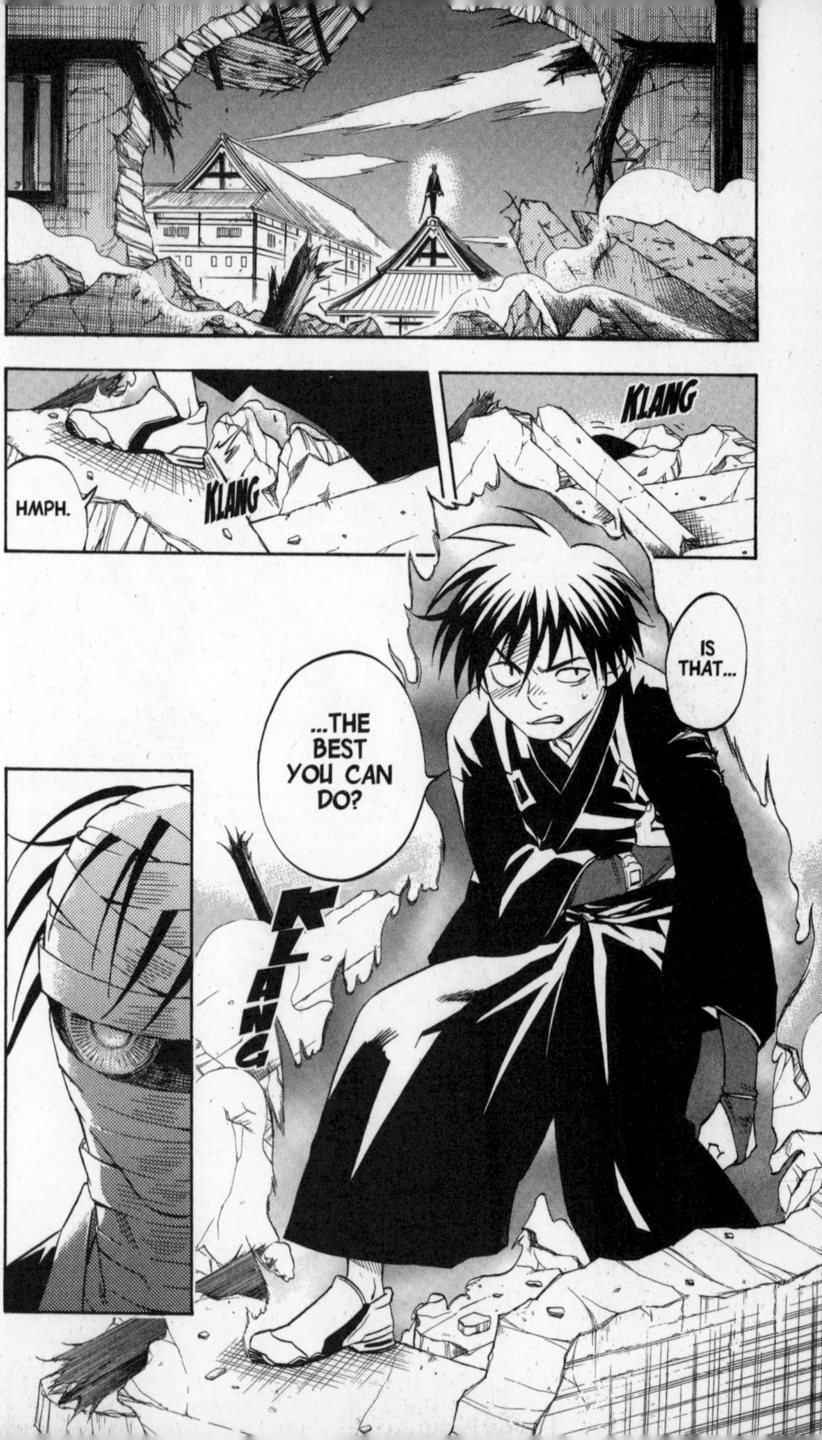
KLANG
HMPH.
KLANG
IS THAT...
...THE BEST YOU CAN DO?
KLANG

Chapter 117: Advice

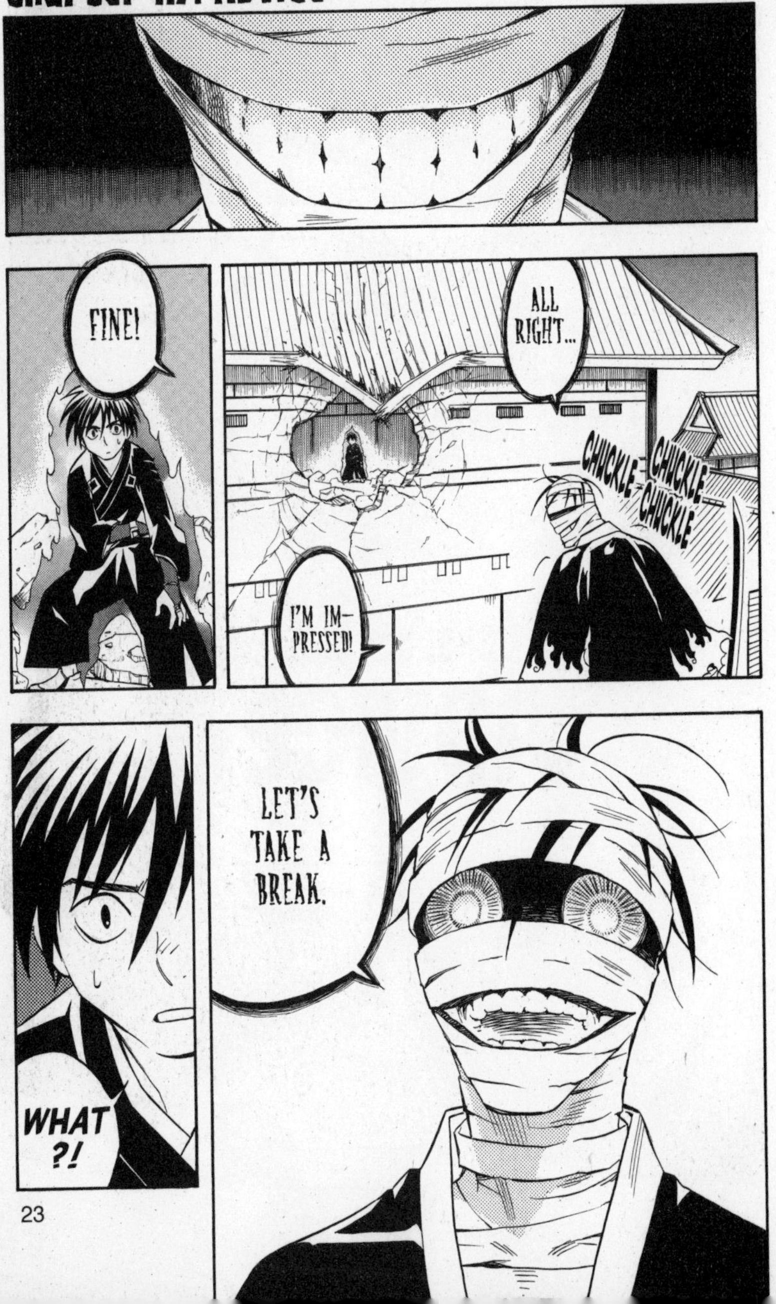
ALL RIGHT...
CHUCKLE CHUCKLE CHUCKLE
I'M IMPRESSED!
FINE!
LET'S TAKE A BREAK.
WHAT?!

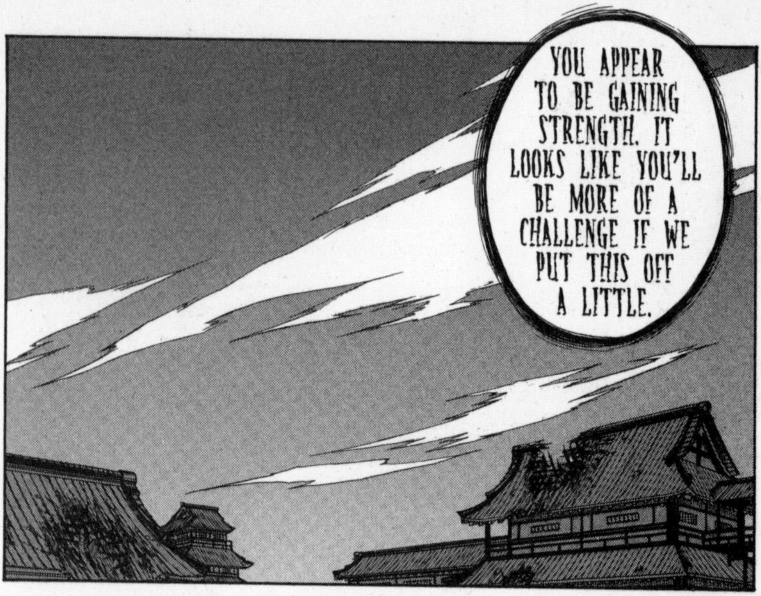
YOU APPEAR TO BE GAINING STRENGTH. IT LOOKS LIKE YOU'LL BE MORE OF A CHALLENGE IF WE PUT THIS OFF A LITTLE.

CHAPTER 117:
ADVICE

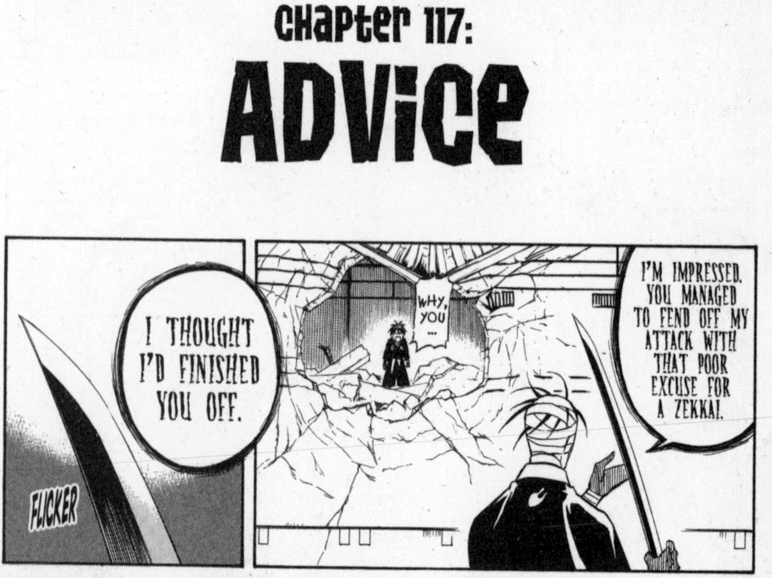
I'M IMPRESSED. YOU MANAGED TO FEND OFF MY ATTACK WITH THAT POOR EXCUSE FOR A ZEKKAI.
WHY, YOU ...
I THOUGHT I'D FINISHED YOU OFF.
FLICKER

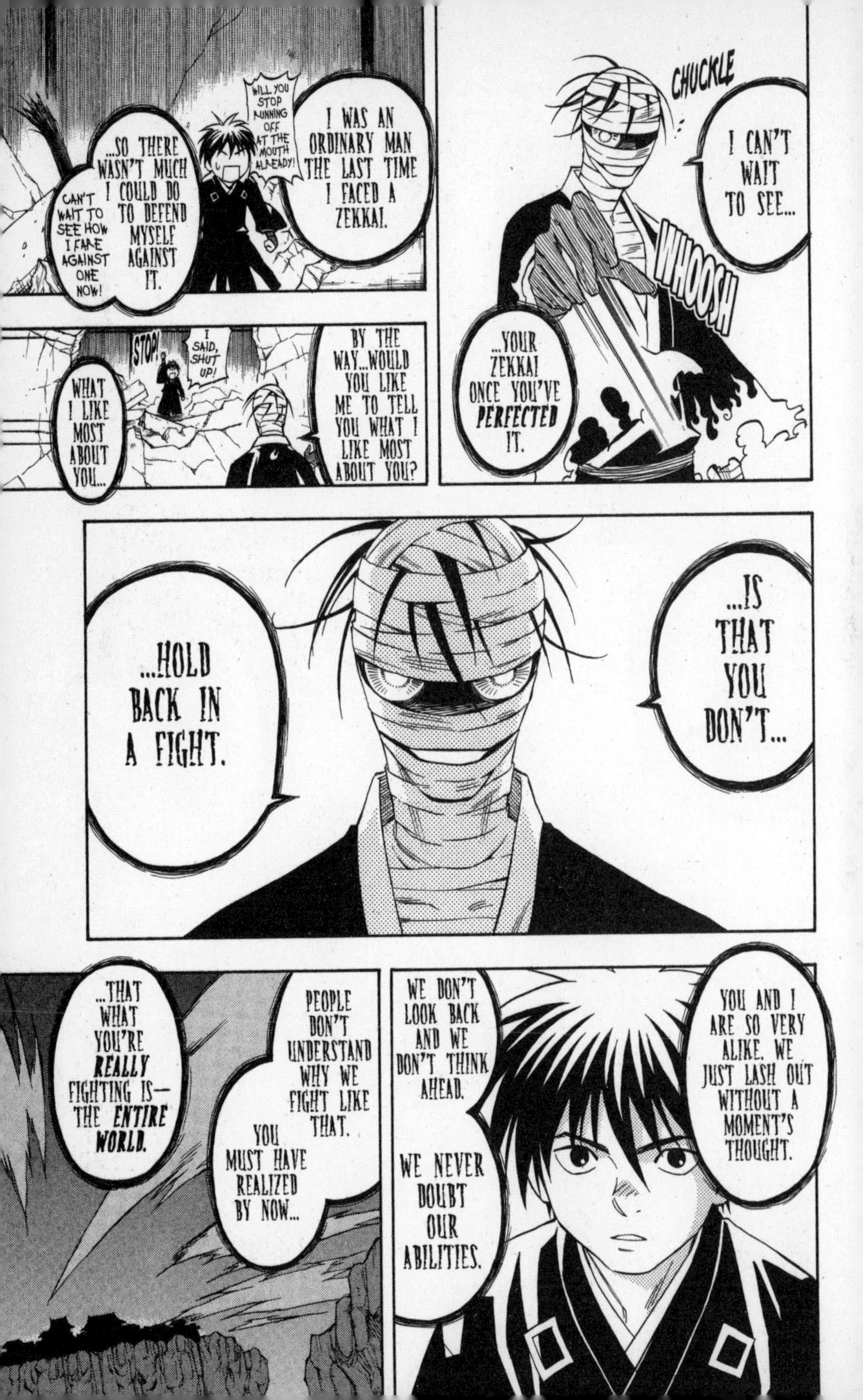
CHUCKLE
I CAN'T WAIT TO SEE...
WHOOSH
...YOUR ZEKKAI ONCE YOU'VE **PERFECTED** IT.
I WAS AN ORDINARY MAN THE LAST TIME I FACED A ZEKKAI.
WILL YOU STOP RUNNING OFF AT THE MOUTH ALREADY!
...SO THERE WASN'T MUCH I COULD DO TO DEFEND MYSELF AGAINST IT.
CAN'T WAIT TO SEE HOW I FARE AGAINST ONE NOW!
BY THE WAY...WOULD YOU LIKE ME TO TELL YOU WHAT I LIKE MOST ABOUT YOU?
I SAID, SHUT UP!
STOP!
WHAT I LIKE MOST ABOUT YOU...
...IS THAT YOU DON'T...
...HOLD BACK IN A FIGHT.
YOU AND I ARE SO VERY ALIKE. WE JUST LASH OUT WITHOUT A MOMENT'S THOUGHT.
WE DON'T LOOK BACK AND WE DON'T THINK AHEAD.
WE NEVER DOUBT OUR ABILITIES.
PEOPLE DON'T UNDERSTAND WHY WE FIGHT LIKE THAT.
YOU MUST HAVE REALIZED BY NOW...
...THAT WHAT YOU'RE **REALLY** FIGHTING IS—THE **ENTIRE WORLD.**

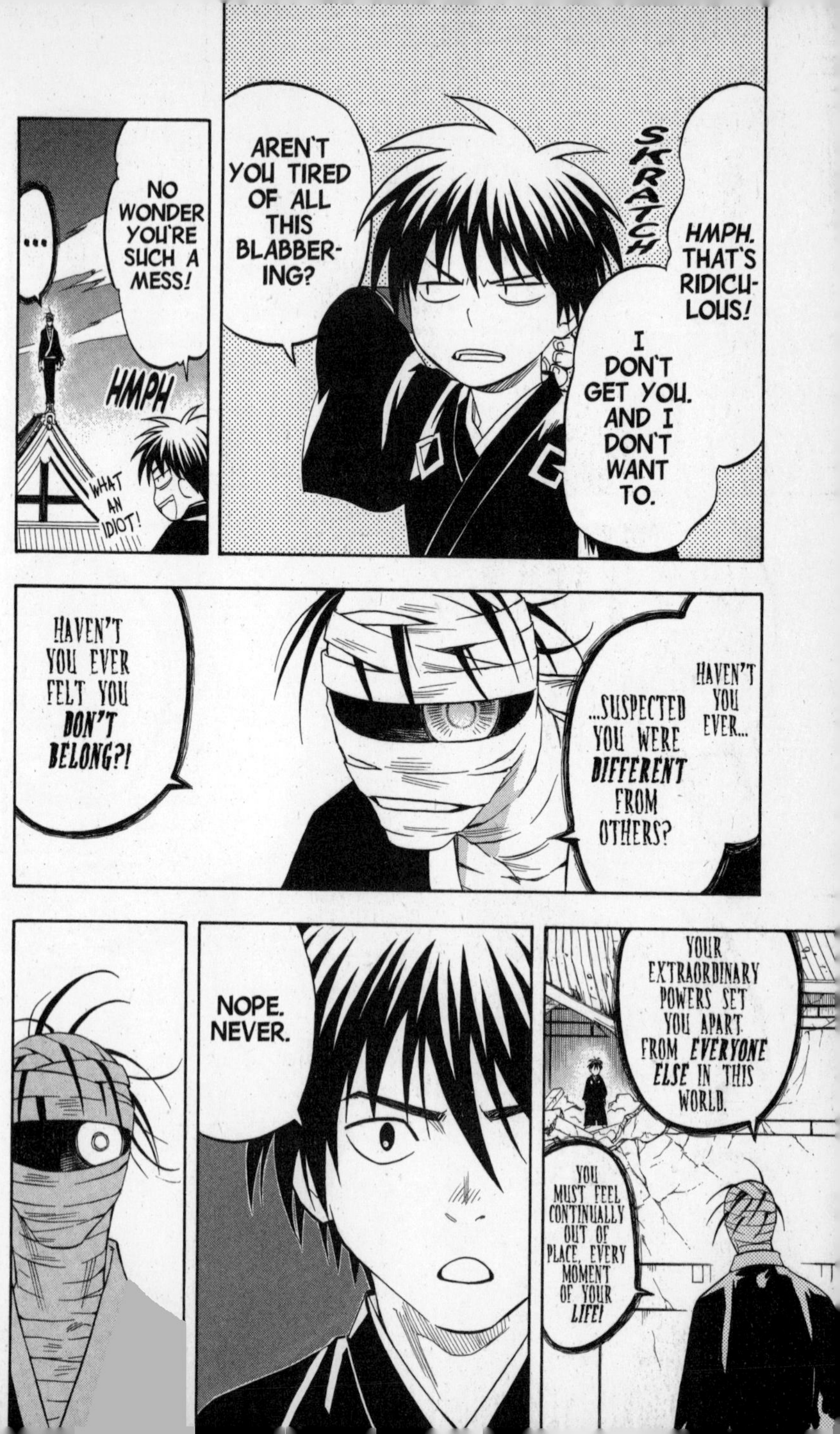
SKRATCH
HMPH. THAT'S RIDICULOUS!
I DON'T GET YOU. AND I DON'T WANT TO.
AREN'T YOU TIRED OF ALL THIS BLABBERING?
NO WONDER YOU'RE SUCH A MESS!
...
HMPH
WHAT AN IDIOT!
HAVEN'T YOU EVER...
...SUSPECTED YOU WERE DIFFERENT FROM OTHERS?
HAVEN'T YOU EVER FELT YOU DON'T BELONG?!
YOUR EXTRAORDINARY POWERS SET YOU APART FROM EVERYONE ELSE IN THIS WORLD.
YOU MUST FEEL CONTINUALLY OUT OF PLACE, EVERY MOMENT OF YOUR LIFE!
NOPE. NEVER.

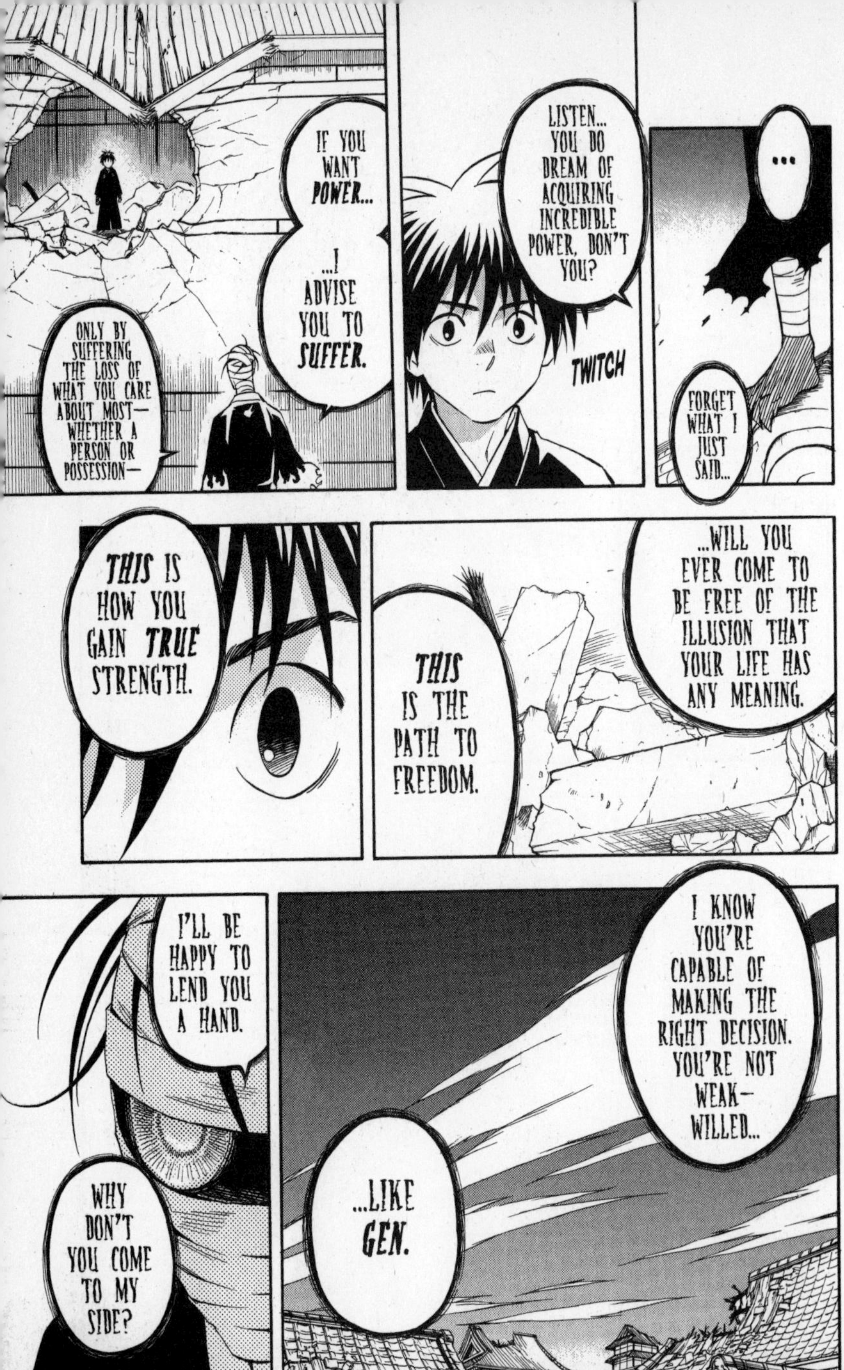
...
FORGET WHAT I JUST SAID...
LISTEN... YOU DO DREAM OF ACQUIRING INCREDIBLE POWER, DON'T YOU?
TWITCH
IF YOU WANT POWER...
...I ADVISE YOU TO SUFFER.
ONLY BY SUFFERING THE LOSS OF WHAT YOU CARE ABOUT MOST— WHETHER A PERSON OR POSSESSION—
...WILL YOU EVER COME TO BE FREE OF THE ILLUSION THAT YOUR LIFE HAS ANY MEANING.
THIS IS THE PATH TO FREEDOM.
THIS IS HOW YOU GAIN TRUE STRENGTH.
I KNOW YOU'RE CAPABLE OF MAKING THE RIGHT DECISION. YOU'RE NOT WEAK-WILLED...
...LIKE GEN.
I'LL BE HAPPY TO LEND YOU A HAND.
WHY DON'T YOU COME TO MY SIDE?

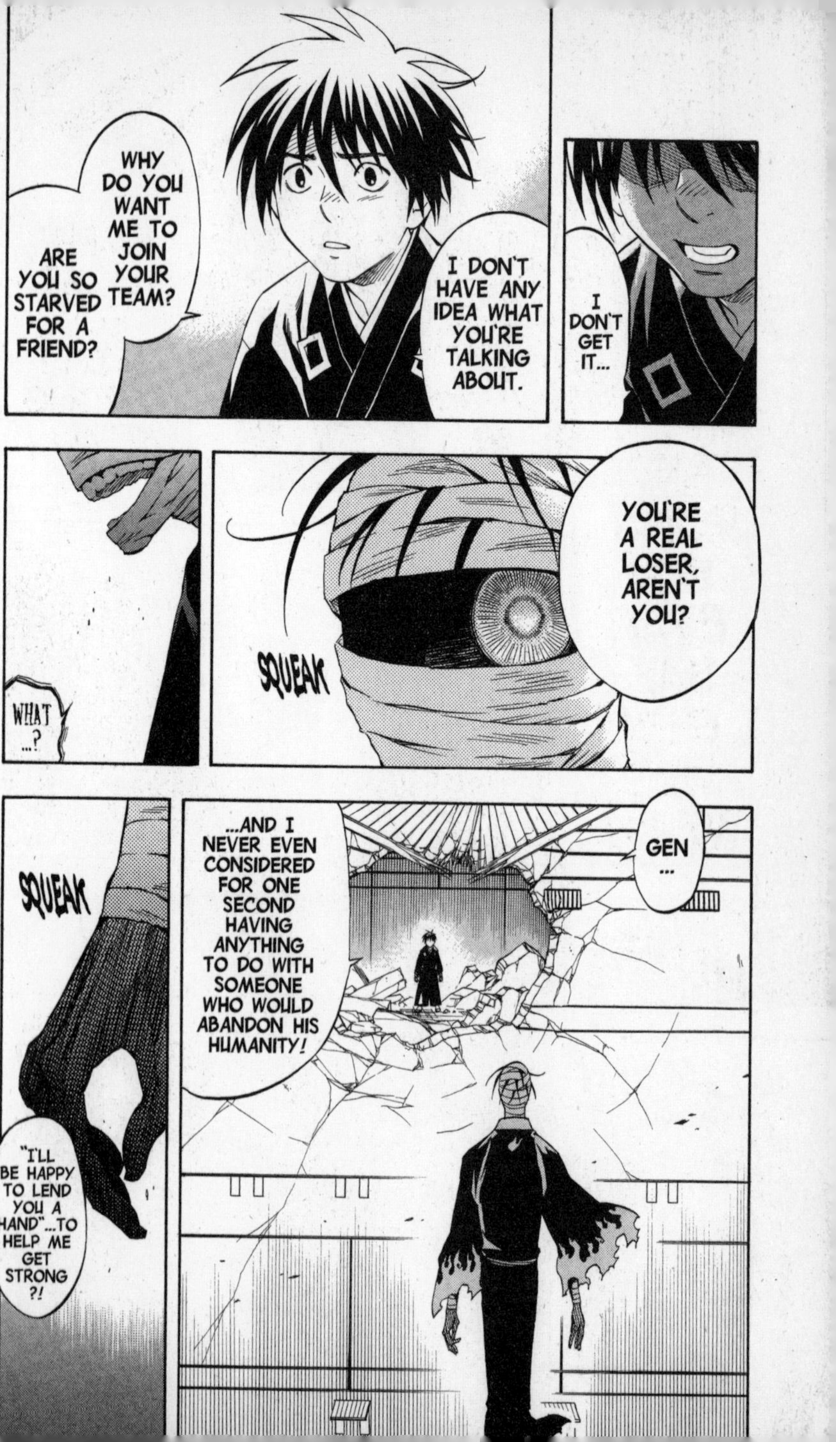
I DON'T GET IT...
I DON'T HAVE ANY IDEA WHAT YOU'RE TALKING ABOUT.
WHY DO YOU WANT ME TO JOIN YOUR TEAM?
ARE YOU SO STARVED FOR A FRIEND?
YOU'RE A REAL LOSER, AREN'T YOU?
SQUEAK
WHAT ...?
GEN ...
...AND I NEVER EVEN CONSIDERED FOR ONE SECOND HAVING ANYTHING TO DO WITH SOMEONE WHO WOULD ABANDON HIS HUMANITY!
SQUEAK
"I'LL BE HAPPY TO LEND YOU A HAND"...TO HELP ME GET STRONG ?!

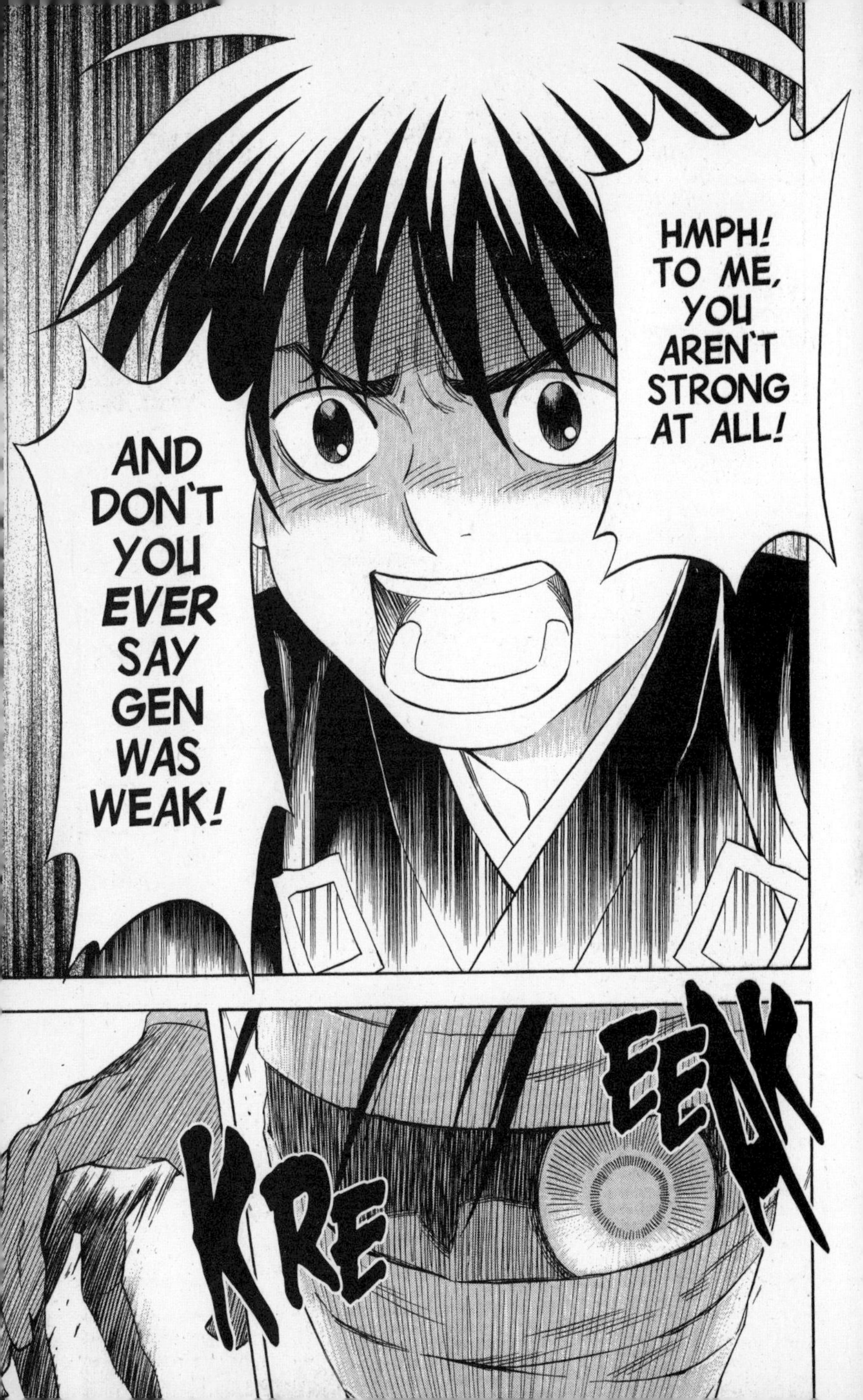
HMPH! TO ME, YOU AREN'T STRONG AT ALL!
AND DON'T YOU EVER SAY GEN WAS WEAK!
KREEEK

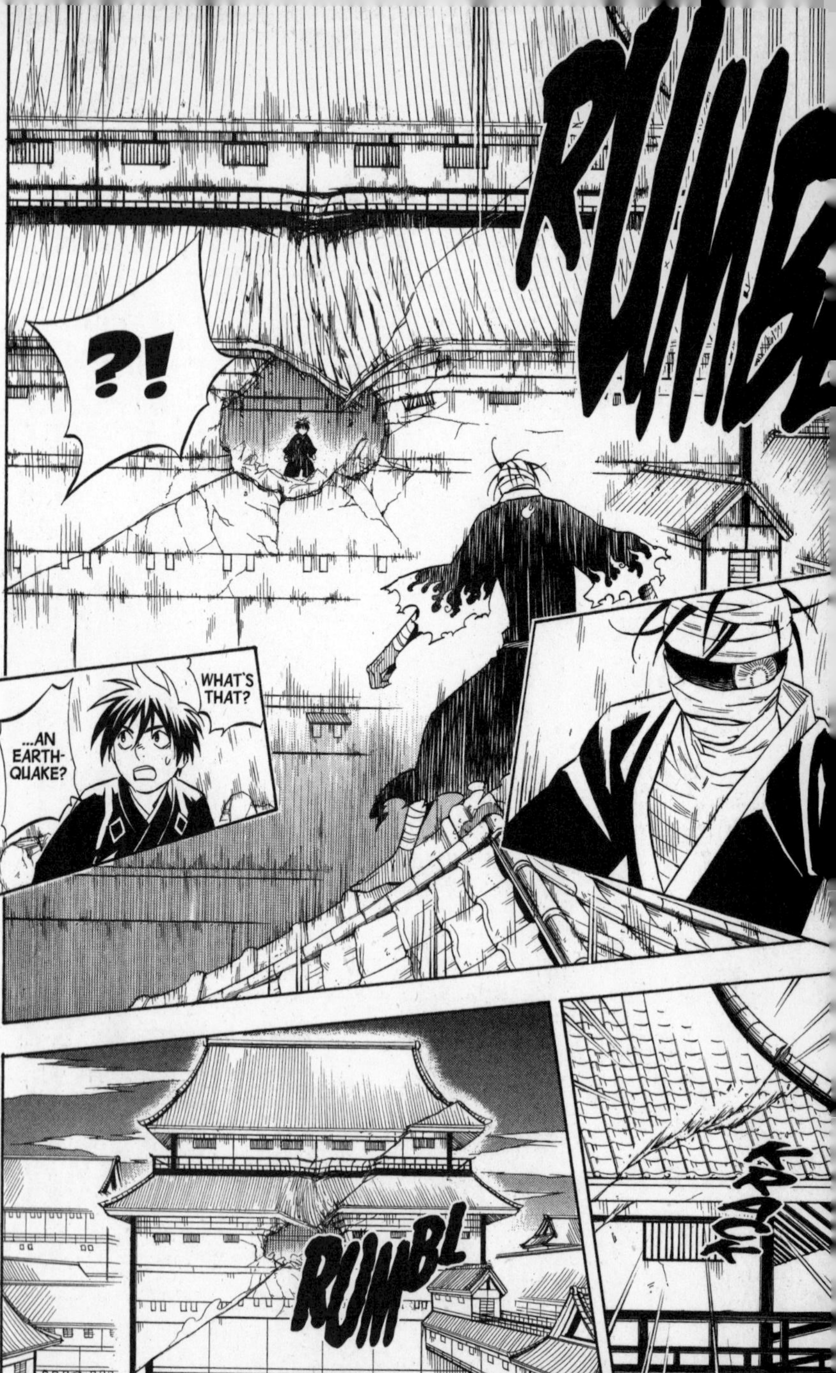
?!
WHAT'S THAT?
...AN EARTH-QUAKE?
RUMBL

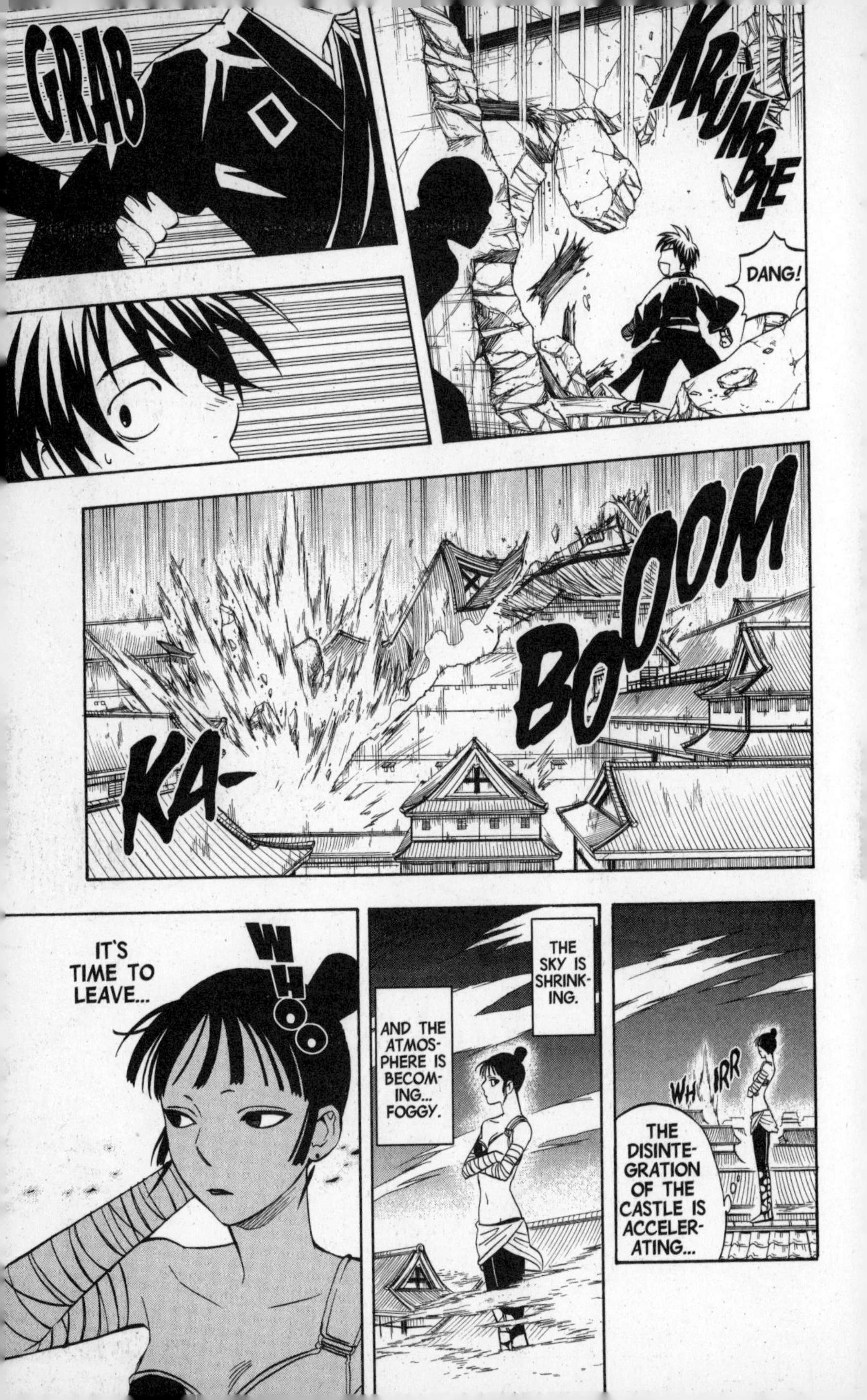
KRUMBLE
DANG!
GRAB
KA-BOOOOM
WHIRR
THE DISINTE-GRATION OF THE CASTLE IS ACCELER-ATING...
THE SKY IS SHRINK-ING.
AND THE ATMOS-PHERE IS BECOM-ING... FOGGY.
WHOOO
IT'S TIME TO LEAVE...

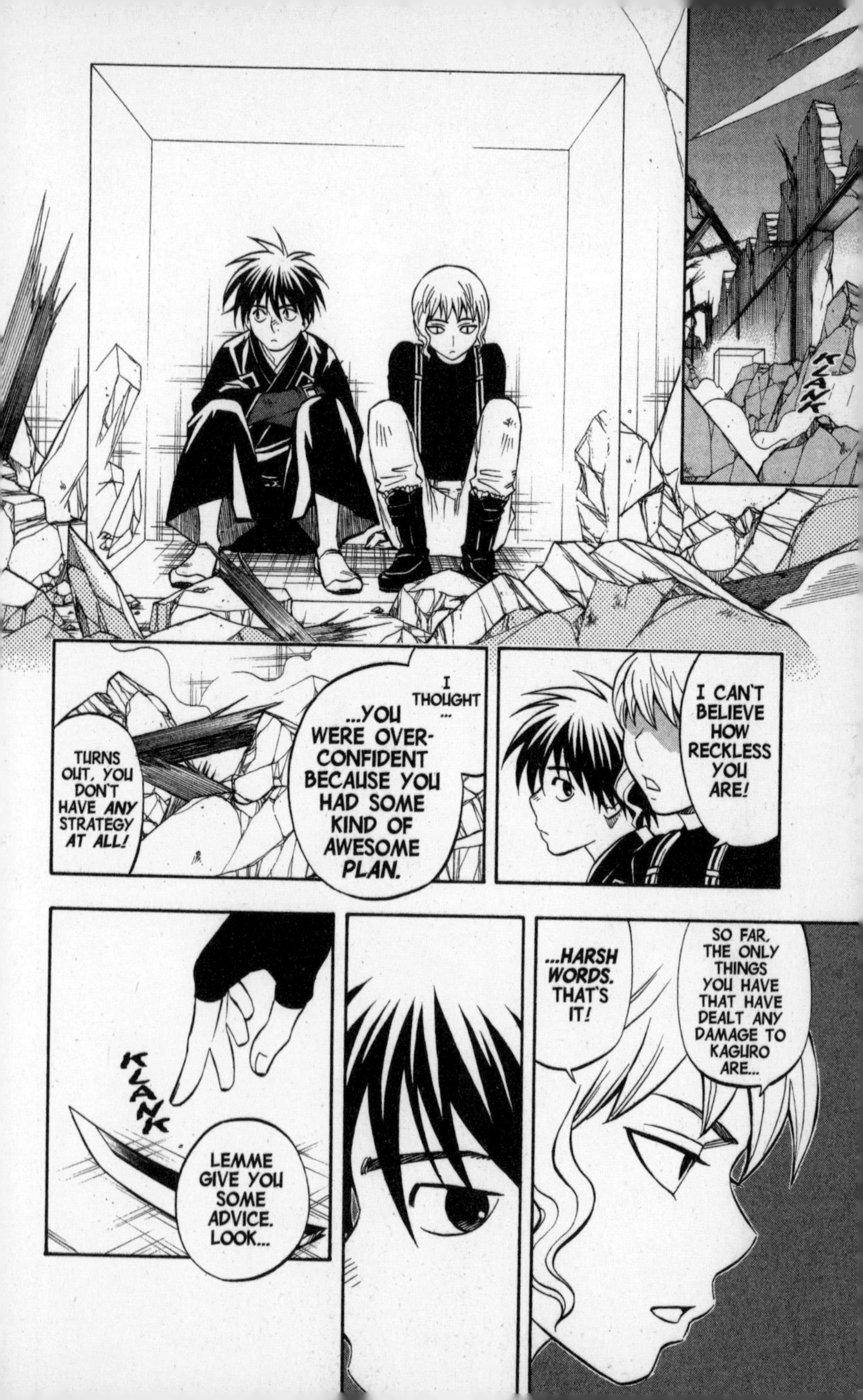
KLANK
I CAN'T BELIEVE HOW RECKLESS YOU ARE!
I THOUGHT ...
...YOU WERE OVER-CONFIDENT BECAUSE YOU HAD SOME KIND OF AWESOME PLAN.
TURNS OUT, YOU DON'T HAVE ANY STRATEGY AT ALL!
SO FAR, THE ONLY THINGS YOU HAVE THAT HAVE DEALT ANY DAMAGE TO KAGURO ARE...
...HARSH WORDS. THAT'S IT!
KLANK
LEMME GIVE YOU SOME ADVICE. LOOK...

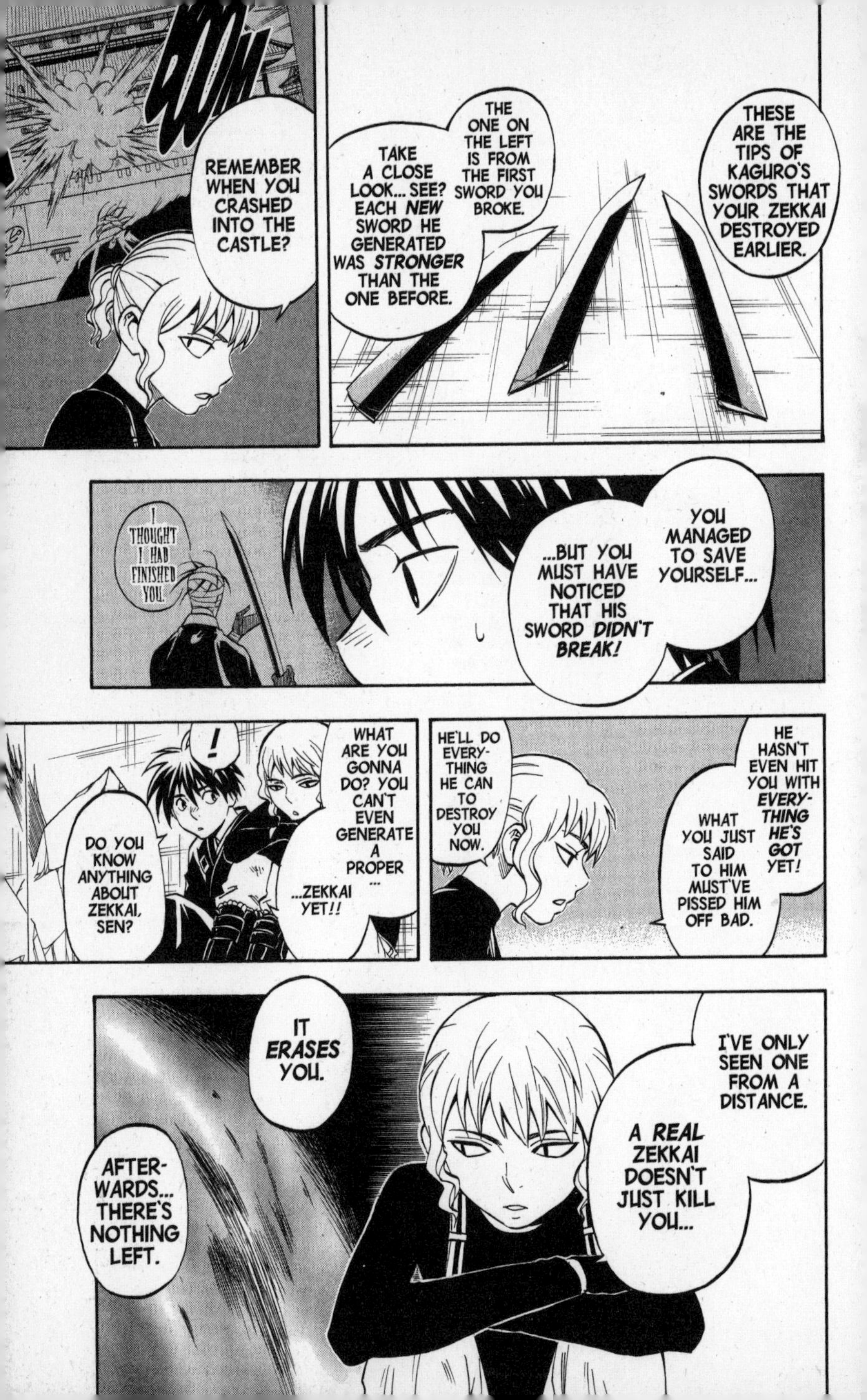
THESE ARE THE TIPS OF KAGURO'S SWORDS THAT YOUR ZEKKAI DESTROYED EARLIER.
THE ONE ON THE LEFT IS FROM THE FIRST SWORD YOU BROKE.
TAKE A CLOSE LOOK... SEE? EACH NEW SWORD HE GENERATED WAS STRONGER THAN THE ONE BEFORE.
BOOM
REMEMBER WHEN YOU CRASHED INTO THE CASTLE?
YOU MANAGED TO SAVE YOURSELF...
...BUT YOU MUST HAVE NOTICED THAT HIS SWORD DIDN'T BREAK!
I THOUGHT I HAD FINISHED YOU.
HE HASN'T EVEN HIT YOU WITH EVERYTHING HE'S GOT YET!
WHAT YOU JUST SAID TO HIM MUST'VE PISSED HIM OFF BAD.
HE'LL DO EVERYTHING HE CAN TO DESTROY YOU NOW.
WHAT ARE YOU GONNA DO? YOU CAN'T EVEN GENERATE A PROPER ...
!
...ZEKKAI YET!!
DO YOU KNOW ANYTHING ABOUT ZEKKAI, SEN?
I'VE ONLY SEEN ONE FROM A DISTANCE.
A REAL ZEKKAI DOESN'T JUST KILL YOU...
IT ERASES YOU.
AFTER-WARDS... THERE'S NOTHING LEFT.

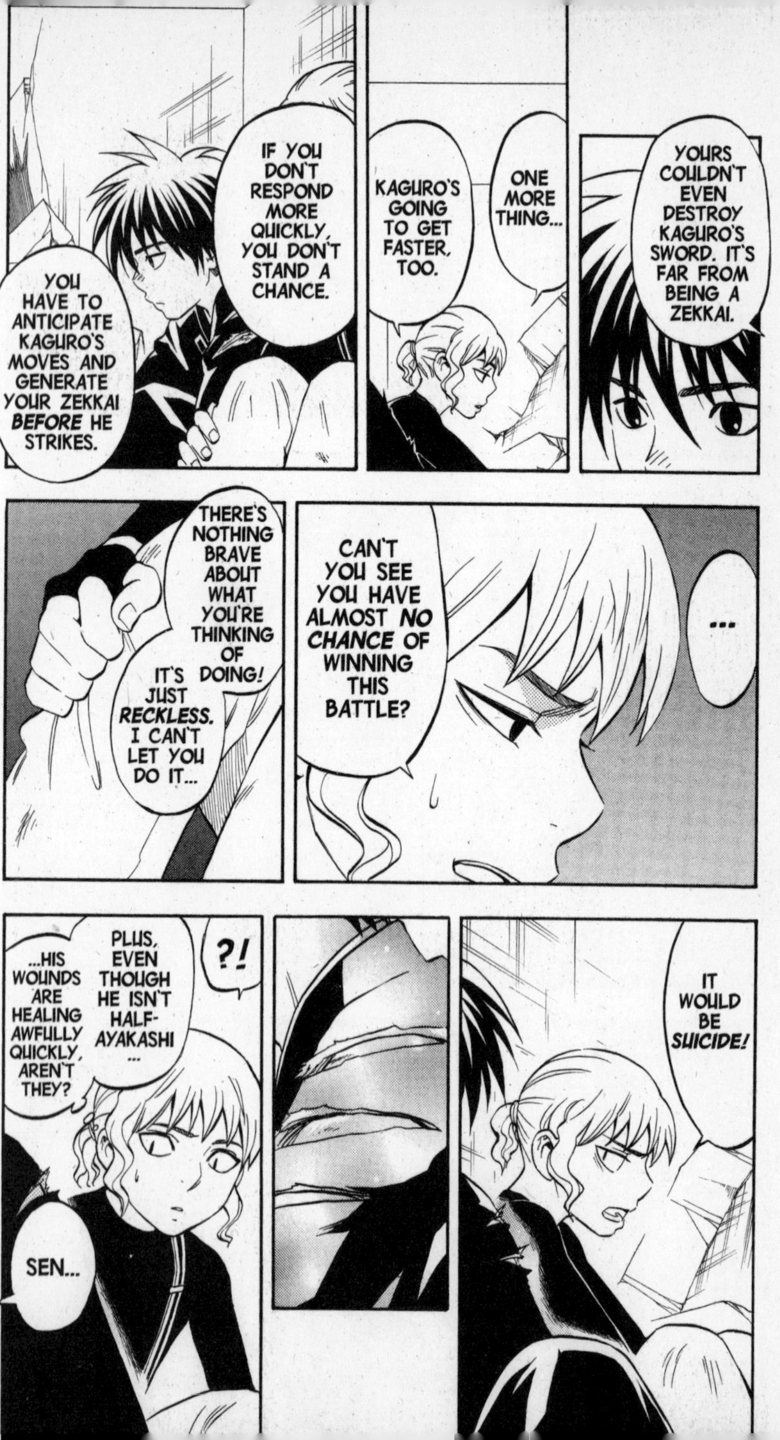
YOURS COULDN'T EVEN DESTROY KAGURO'S SWORD. IT'S FAR FROM BEING A ZEKKAI.
ONE MORE THING...
KAGURO'S GOING TO GET FASTER, TOO.
IF YOU DON'T RESPOND MORE QUICKLY, YOU DON'T STAND A CHANCE.
YOU HAVE TO ANTICIPATE KAGURO'S MOVES AND GENERATE YOUR ZEKKAI *BEFORE* HE STRIKES.
...
CAN'T YOU SEE YOU HAVE ALMOST *NO CHANCE* OF WINNING THIS BATTLE?
THERE'S NOTHING BRAVE ABOUT WHAT YOU'RE THINKING OF DOING!
IT'S JUST *RECKLESS.* I CAN'T LET YOU DO IT...
IT WOULD BE *SUICIDE!*
?!
PLUS, EVEN THOUGH HE ISN'T HALF-AYAKASHI...
...HIS WOUNDS ARE HEALING AWFULLY QUICKLY, AREN'T THEY?
SEN...

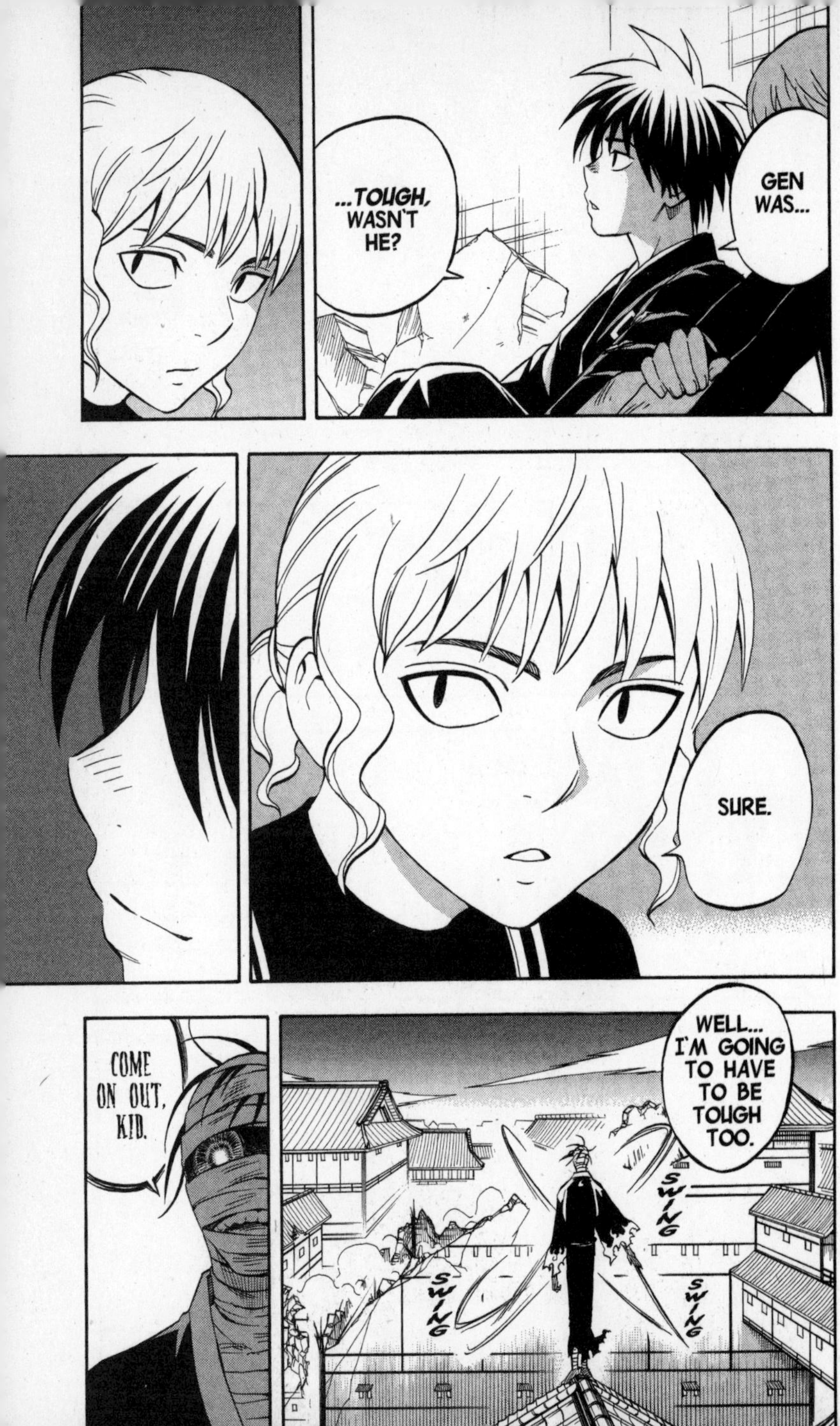
GEN WAS...
...TOUGH, WASN'T HE?
SURE.
WELL... I'M GOING TO HAVE TO BE TOUGH TOO.
SWING
SWING
SWING
COME ON OUT, KID.

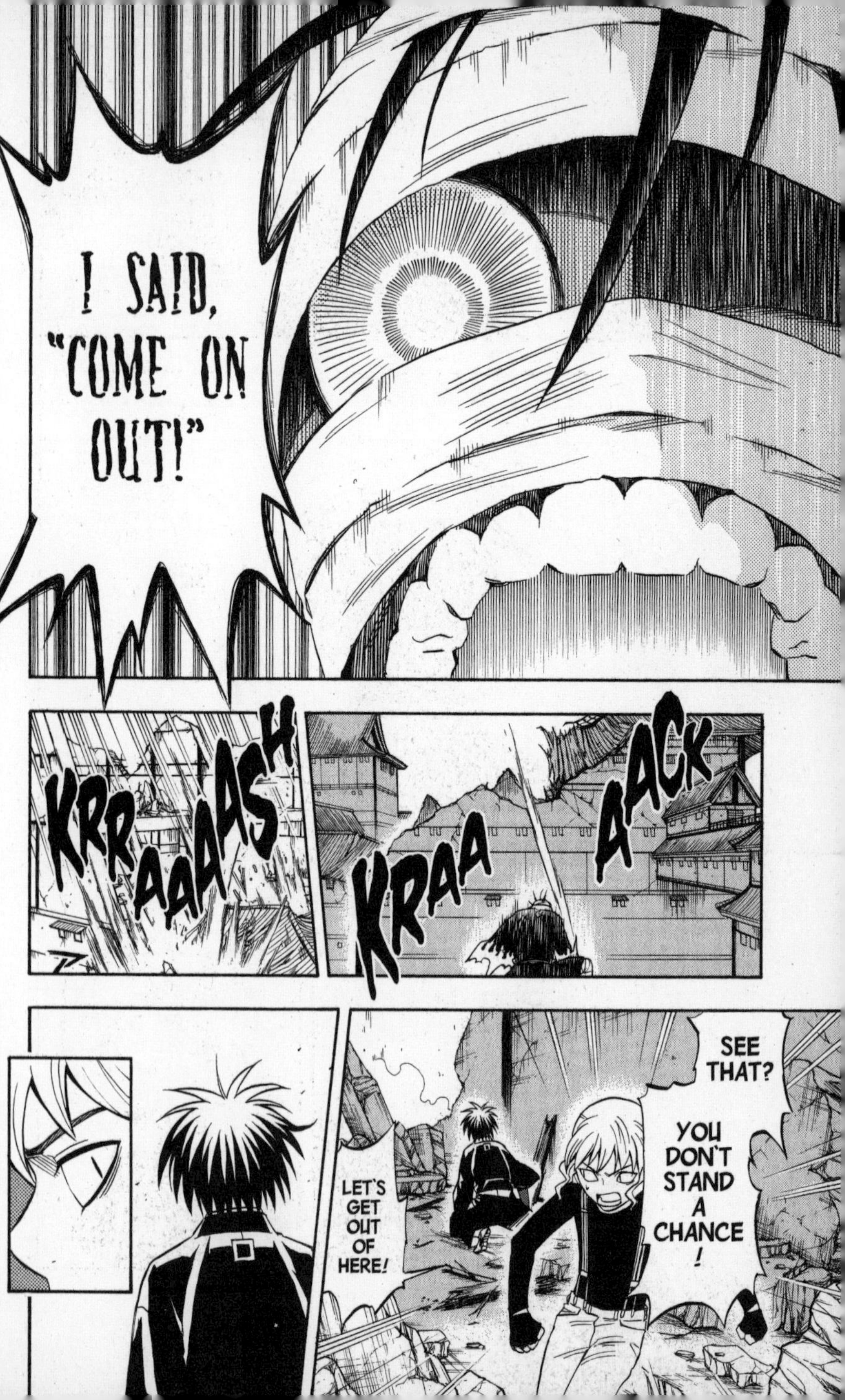
I SAID, "COME ON OUT!"
KRAA AACK
KRRAAAASH
SEE THAT?
YOU DON'T STAND A CHANCE!
LET'S GET OUT OF HERE!

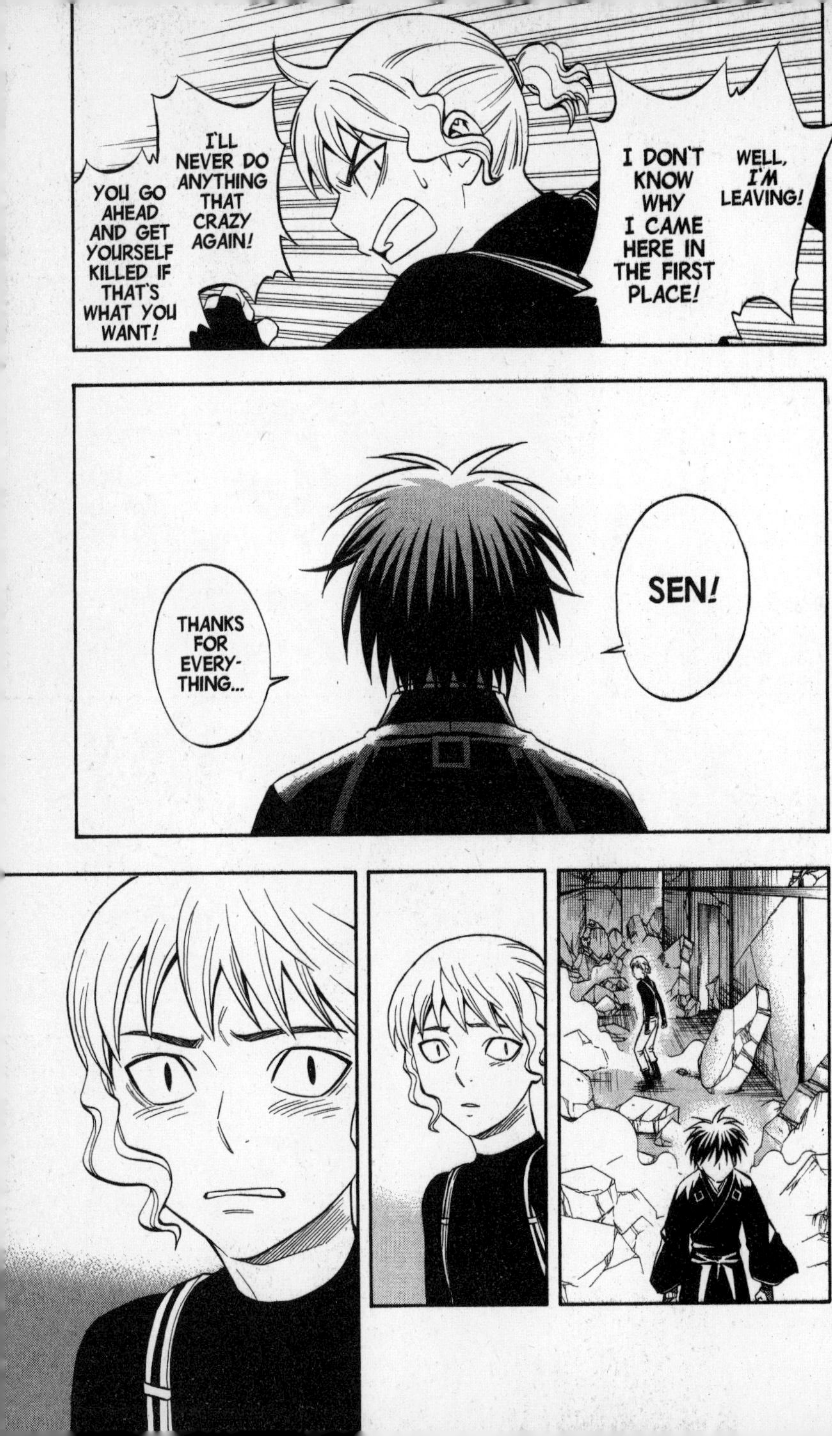
WELL, I'M LEAVING!
I DON'T KNOW WHY I CAME HERE IN THE FIRST PLACE!
I'LL NEVER DO ANYTHING THAT CRAZY AGAIN!
YOU GO AHEAD AND GET YOURSELF KILLED IF THAT'S WHAT YOU WANT!
SEN!
THANKS FOR EVERY-THING...

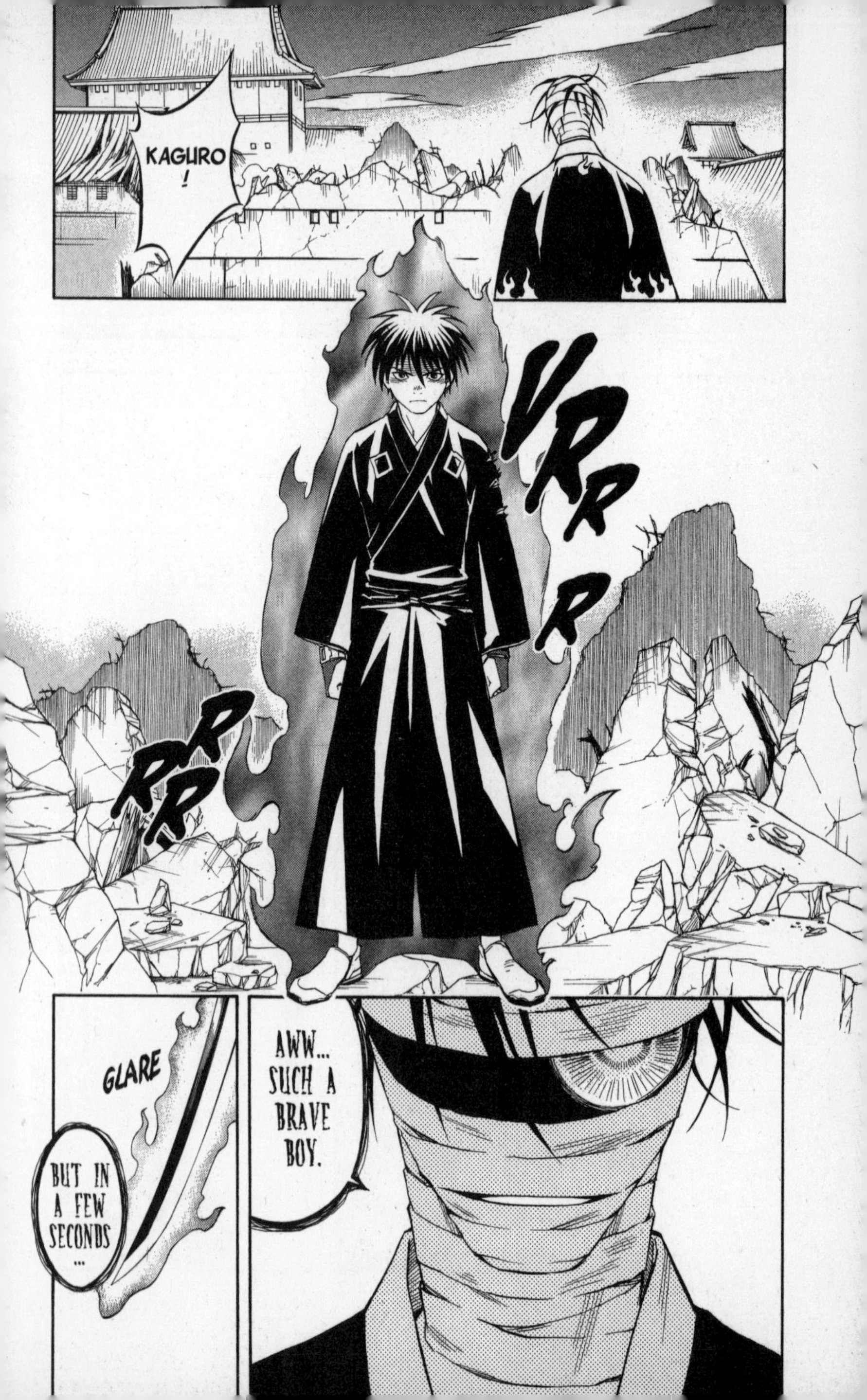
KAGURO!
VRRR
RRRR
AWW... SUCH A BRAVE BOY.
GLARE
BUT IN A FEW SECONDS...

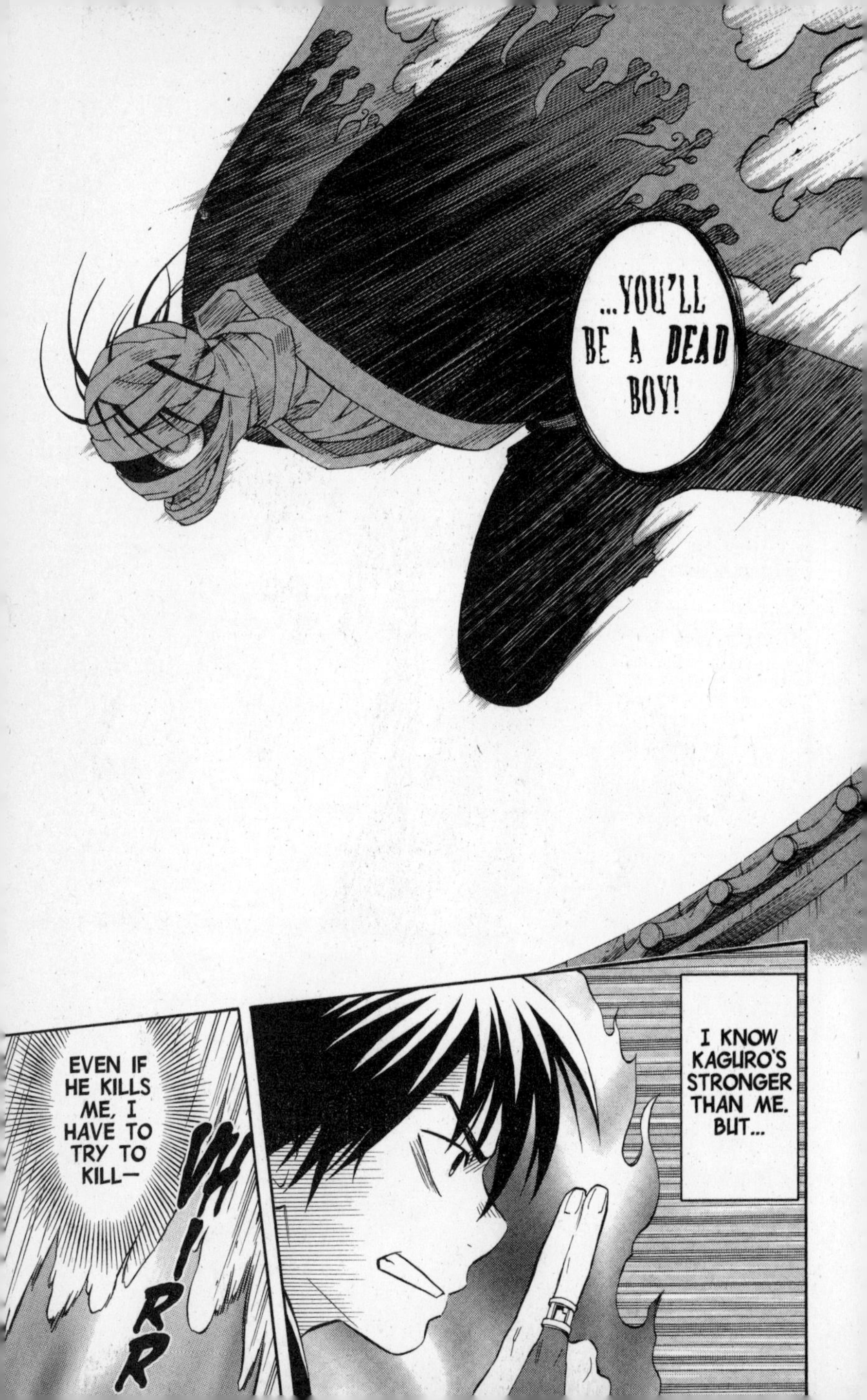
...YOU'LL BE A DEAD BOY!
I KNOW KAGURO'S STRONGER THAN ME. BUT...
EVEN IF HE KILLS ME, I HAVE TO TRY TO KILL—
WHIRR

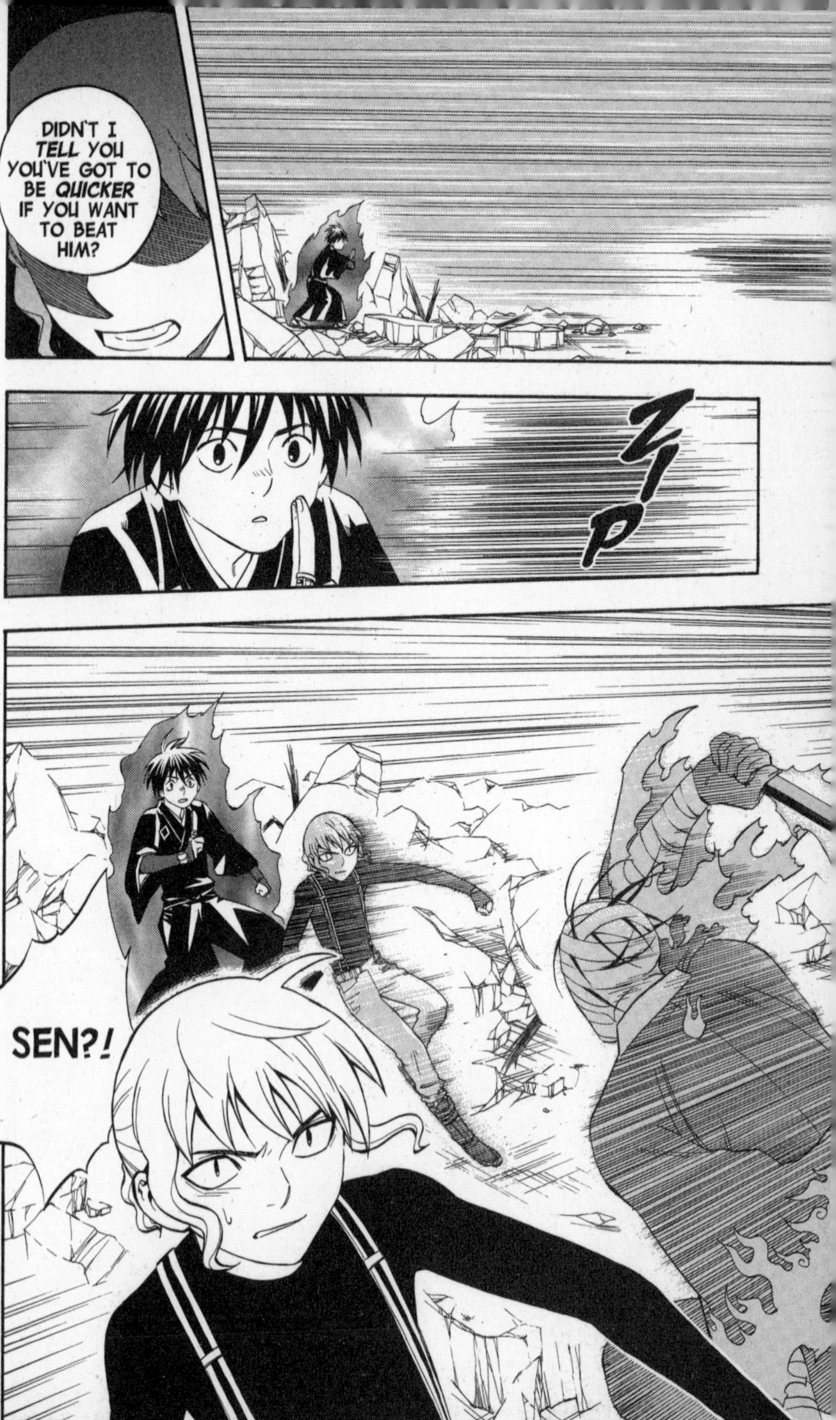
DIDN'T I TELL YOU YOU'VE GOT TO BE QUICKER IF YOU WANT TO BEAT HIM?
ZIP
SEN?!

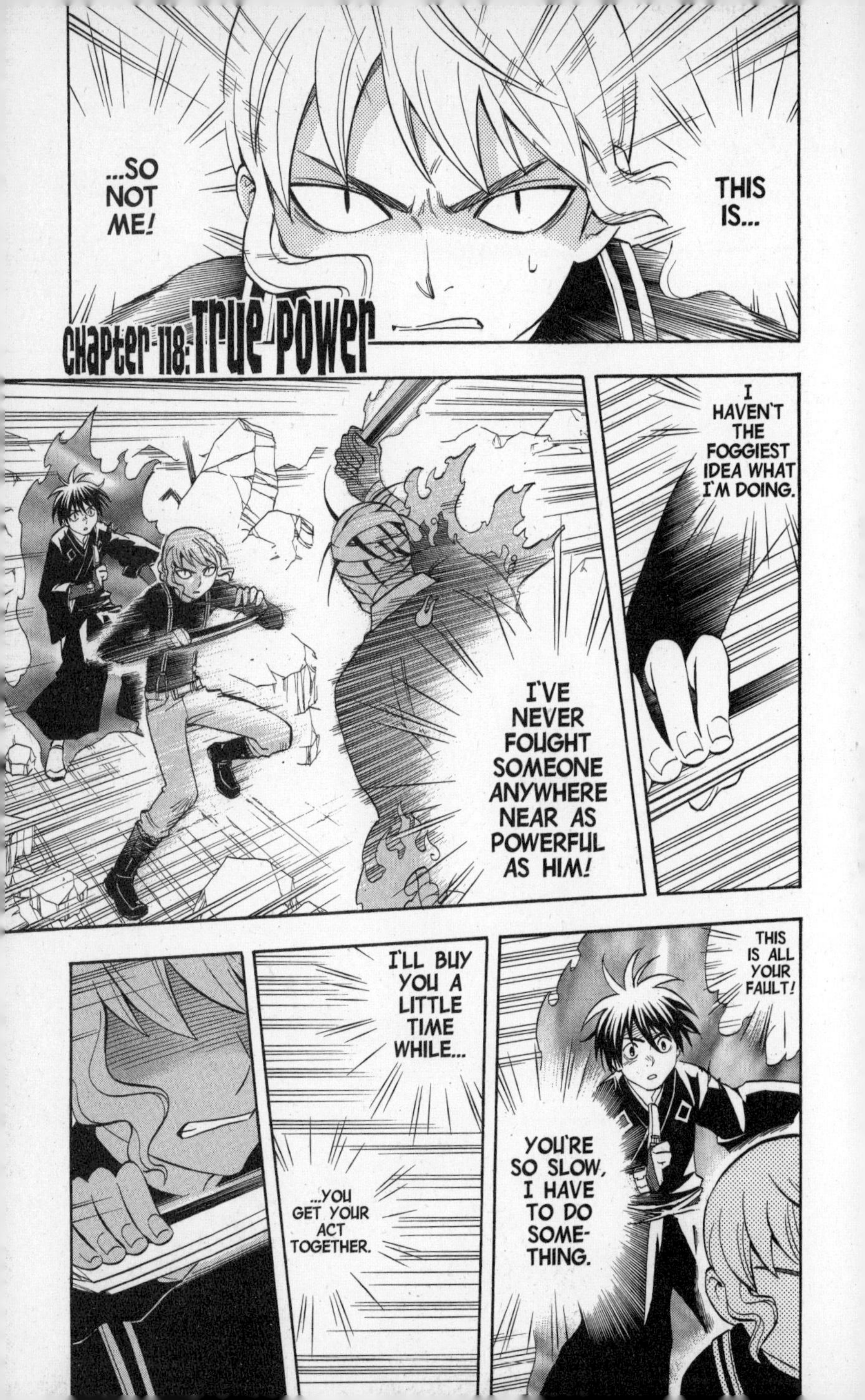
THIS IS...
...SO NOT ME!
Chapter 118: True Power
I HAVEN'T THE FOGGIEST IDEA WHAT I'M DOING.
I'VE NEVER FOUGHT SOMEONE ANYWHERE NEAR AS POWERFUL AS HIM!
THIS IS ALL YOUR FAULT!
YOU'RE SO SLOW, I HAVE TO DO SOME-THING.
I'LL BUY YOU A LITTLE TIME WHILE...
...YOU GET YOUR ACT TOGETHER.

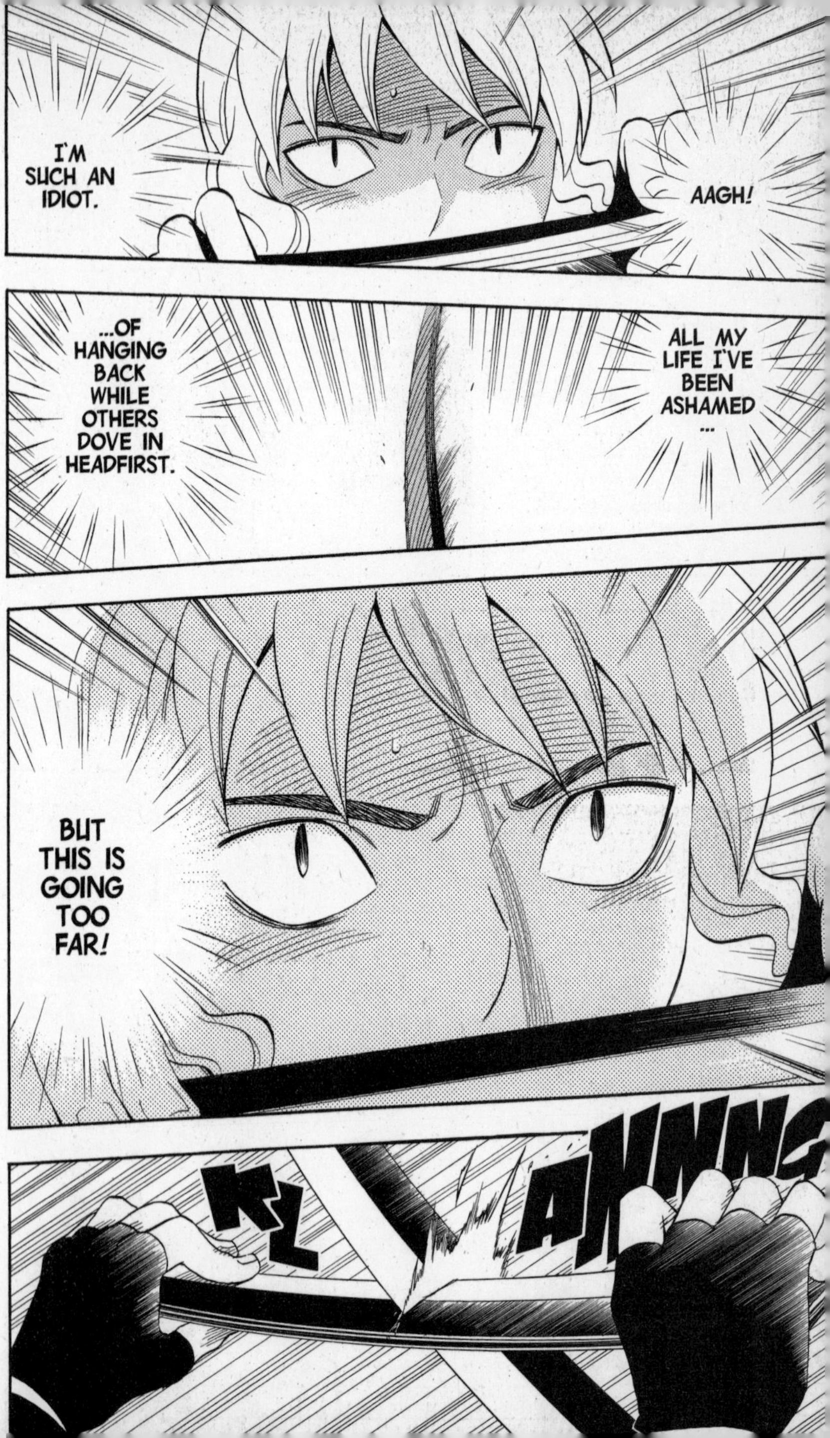
AAGH!
I'M SUCH AN IDIOT.
ALL MY LIFE I'VE BEEN ASHAMED...
...OF HANGING BACK WHILE OTHERS DOVE IN HEADFIRST.
BUT THIS IS GOING TOO FAR!
KLANNNG

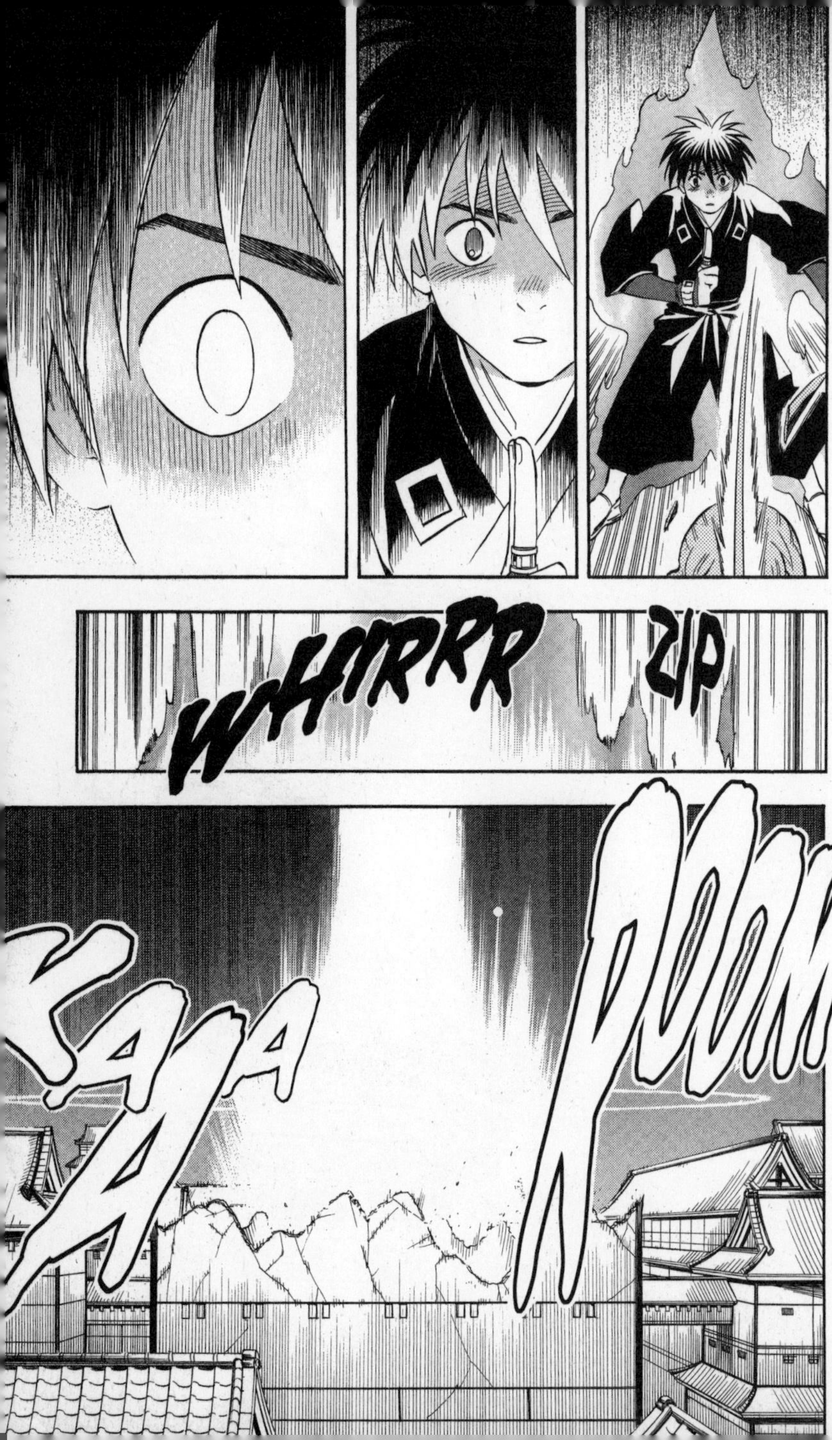
ZIP
WHIRRR

Chapter 118:
True Power

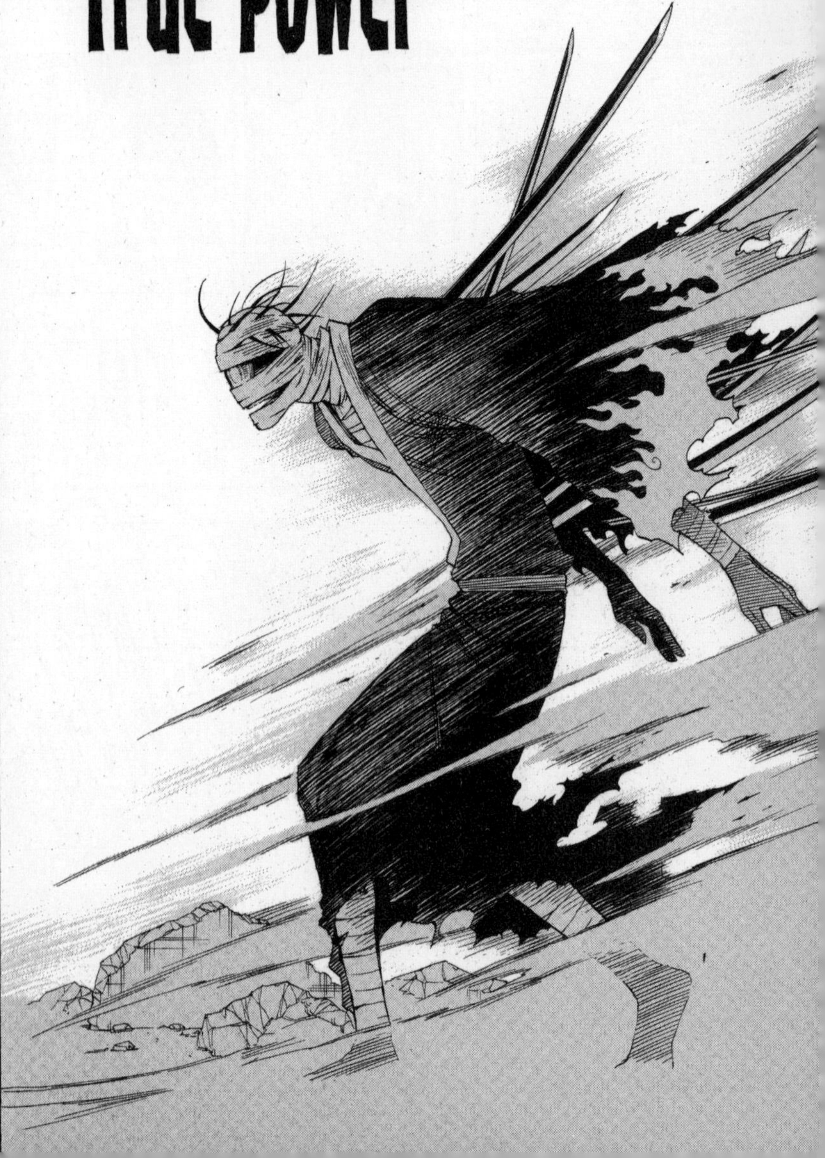

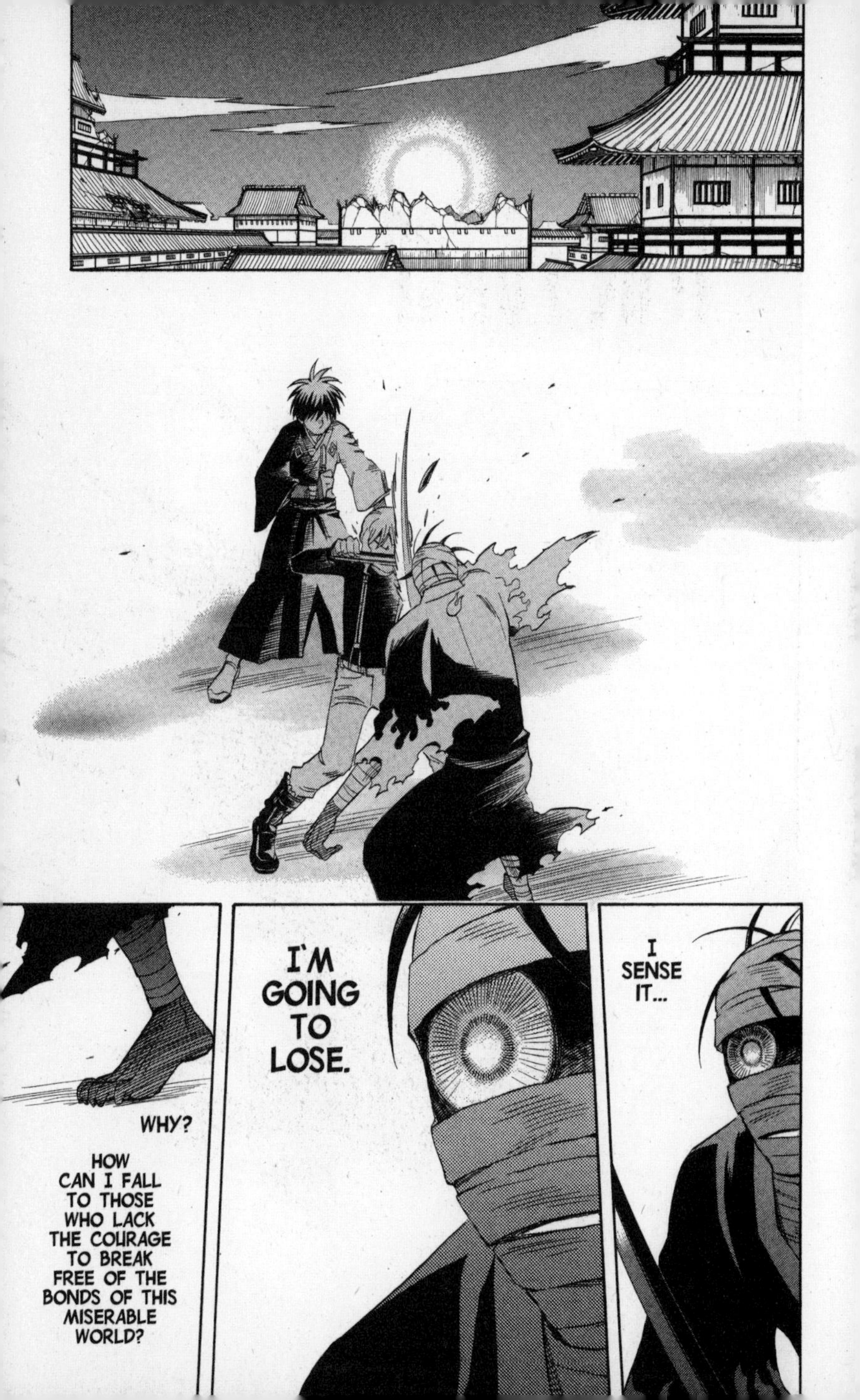
I SENSE IT...
I'M GOING TO LOSE.
WHY?
HOW CAN I FALL TO THOSE WHO LACK THE COURAGE TO BREAK FREE OF THE BONDS OF THIS MISERABLE WORLD?

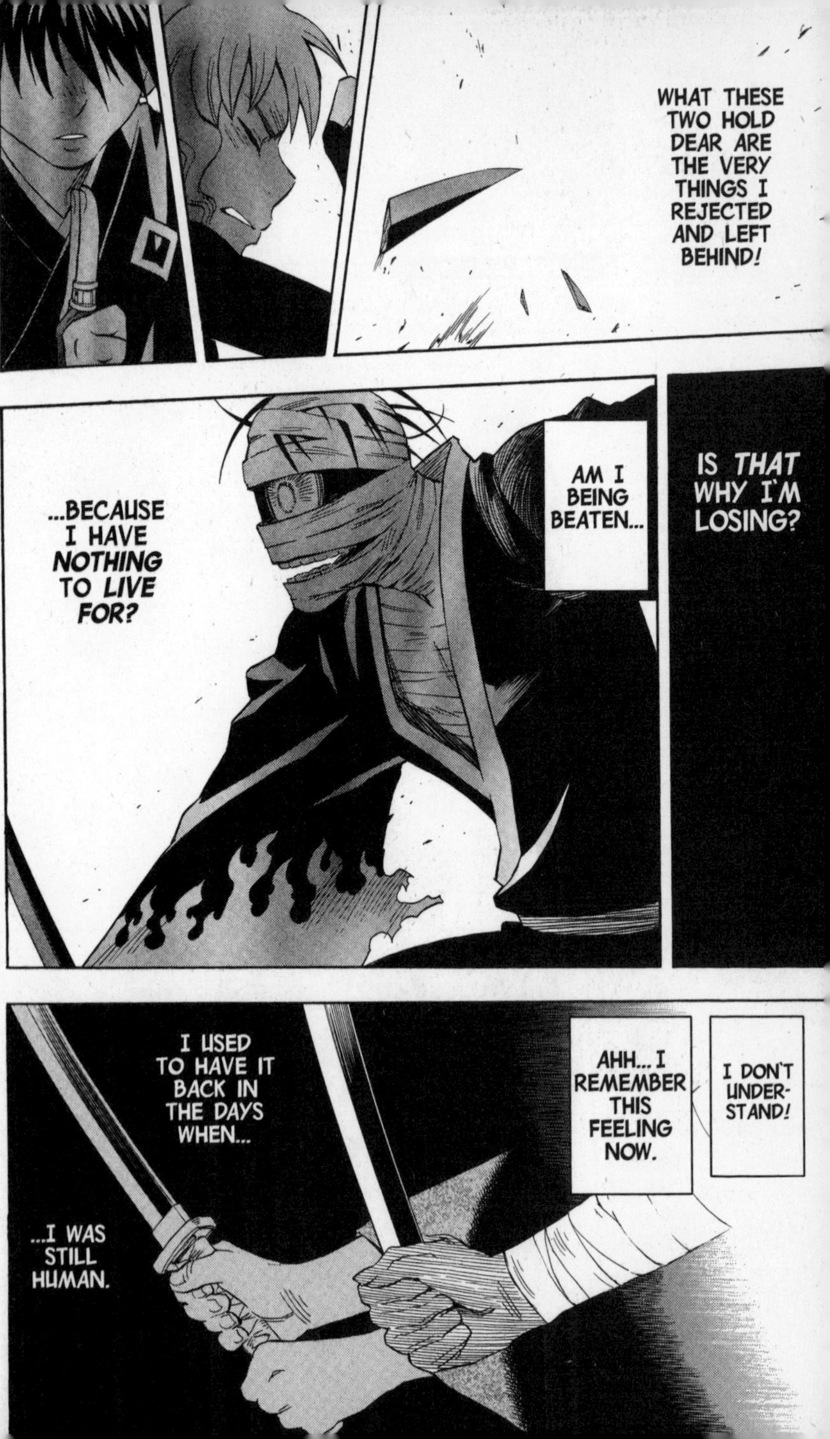
WHAT THESE TWO HOLD DEAR ARE THE VERY THINGS I REJECTED AND LEFT BEHIND!
IS *THAT* WHY I'M LOSING?
AM I BEING BEATEN...
...BECAUSE I HAVE *NOTHING* TO *LIVE* FOR?
I DON'T UNDER-STAND!
AHH... I REMEMBER THIS FEELING NOW.
I USED TO HAVE IT BACK IN THE DAYS WHEN...
...I WAS STILL HUMAN.

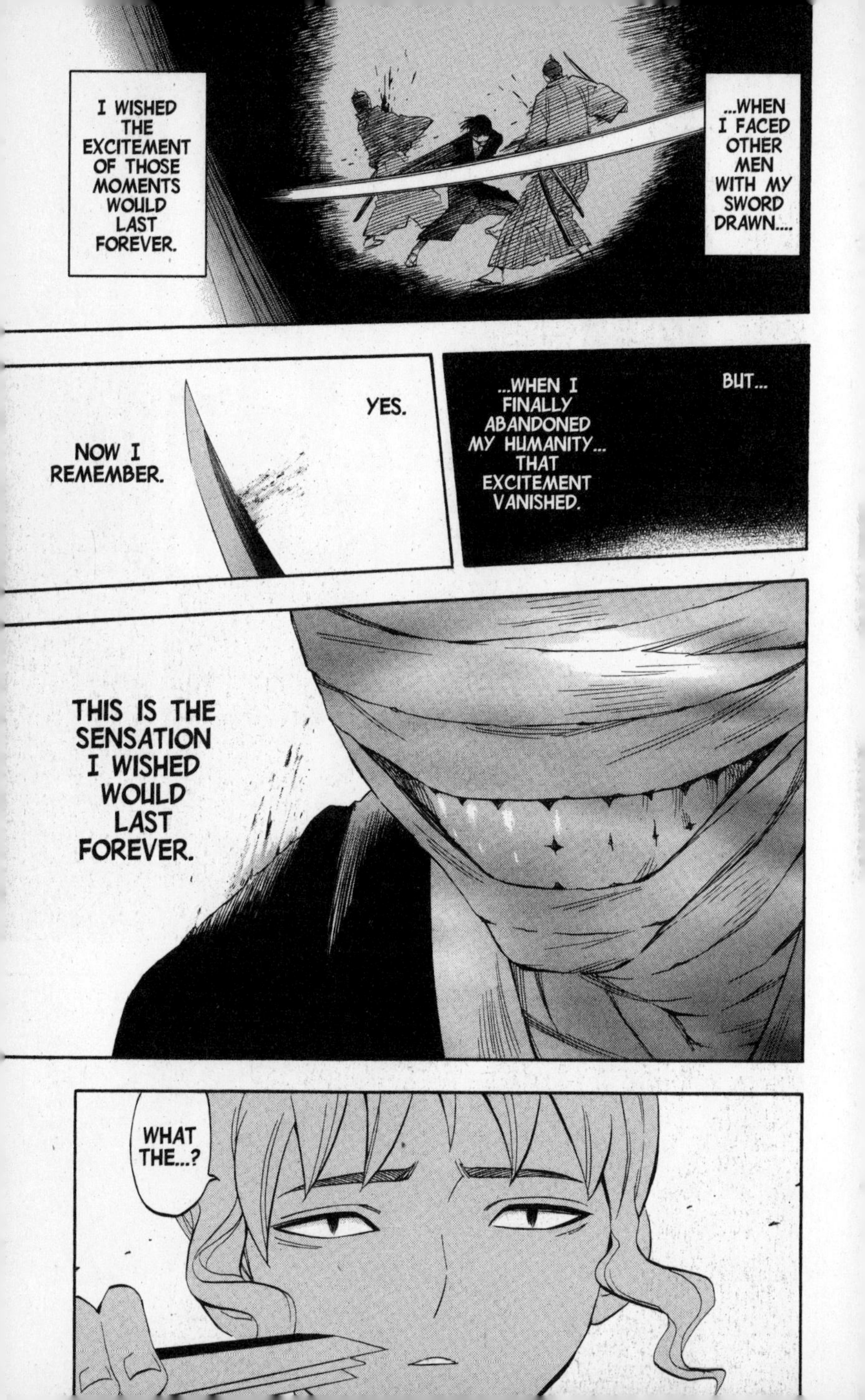
...WHEN I FACED OTHER MEN WITH MY SWORD DRAWN....
I WISHED THE EXCITEMENT OF THOSE MOMENTS WOULD LAST FOREVER.
BUT...
...WHEN I FINALLY ABANDONED MY HUMANITY... THAT EXCITEMENT VANISHED.
YES.
NOW I REMEMBER.
THIS IS THE SENSATION I WISHED WOULD LAST FOREVER.
WHAT THE...?

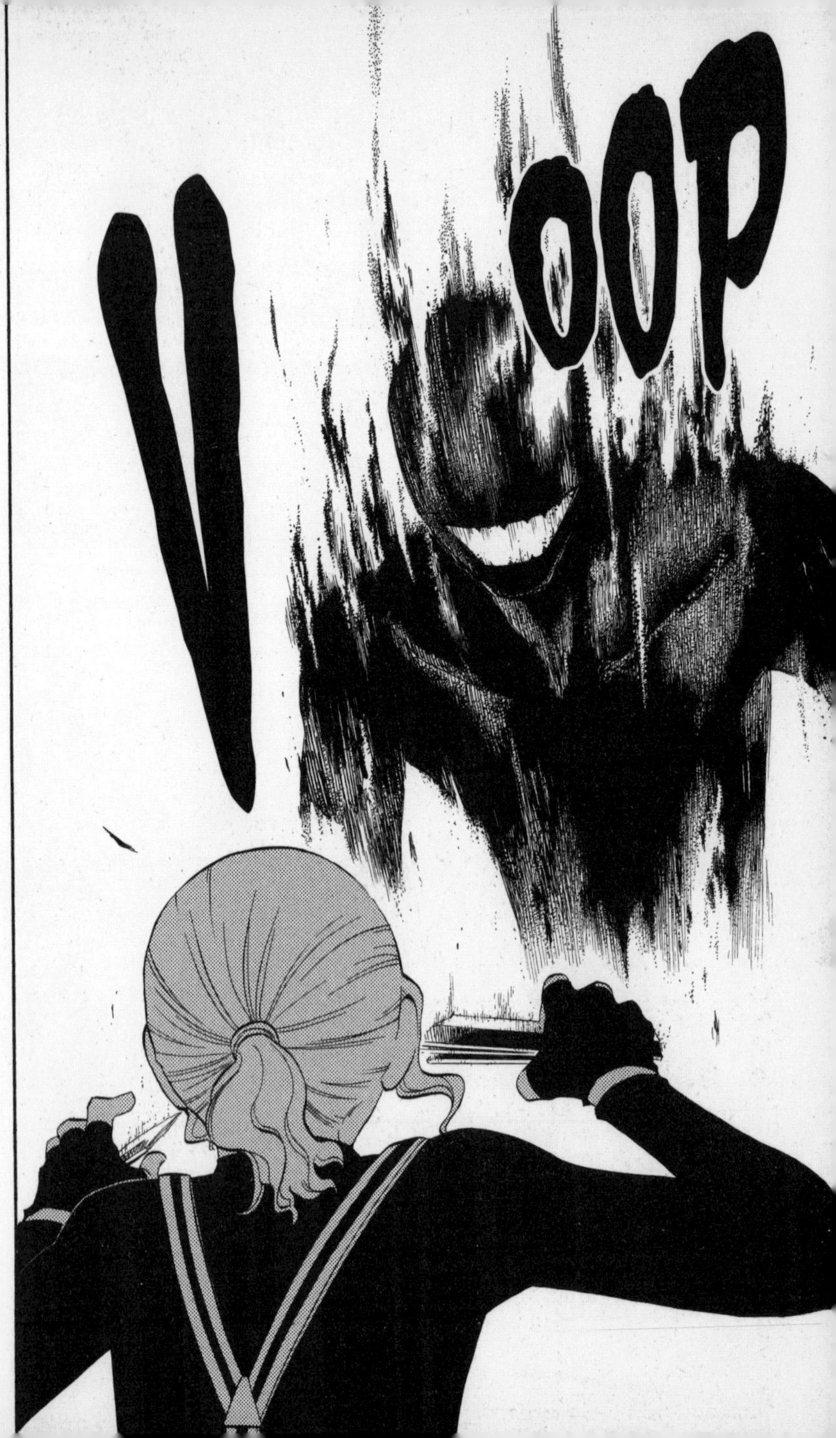
VLOOP

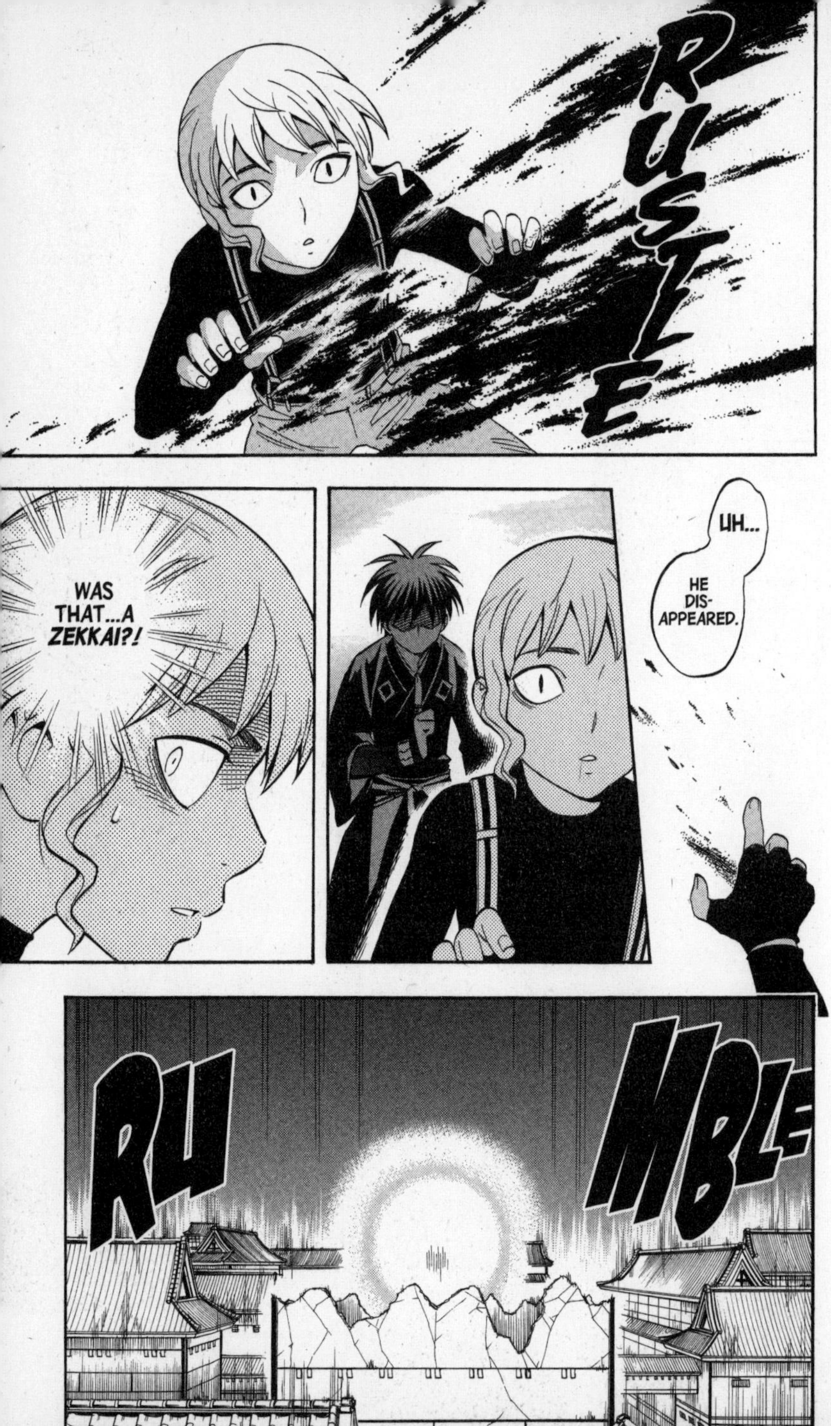
RUSTLE
UH...
HE DIS-APPEARED.
WAS THAT...A ZEKKAI?!
RUMBLE

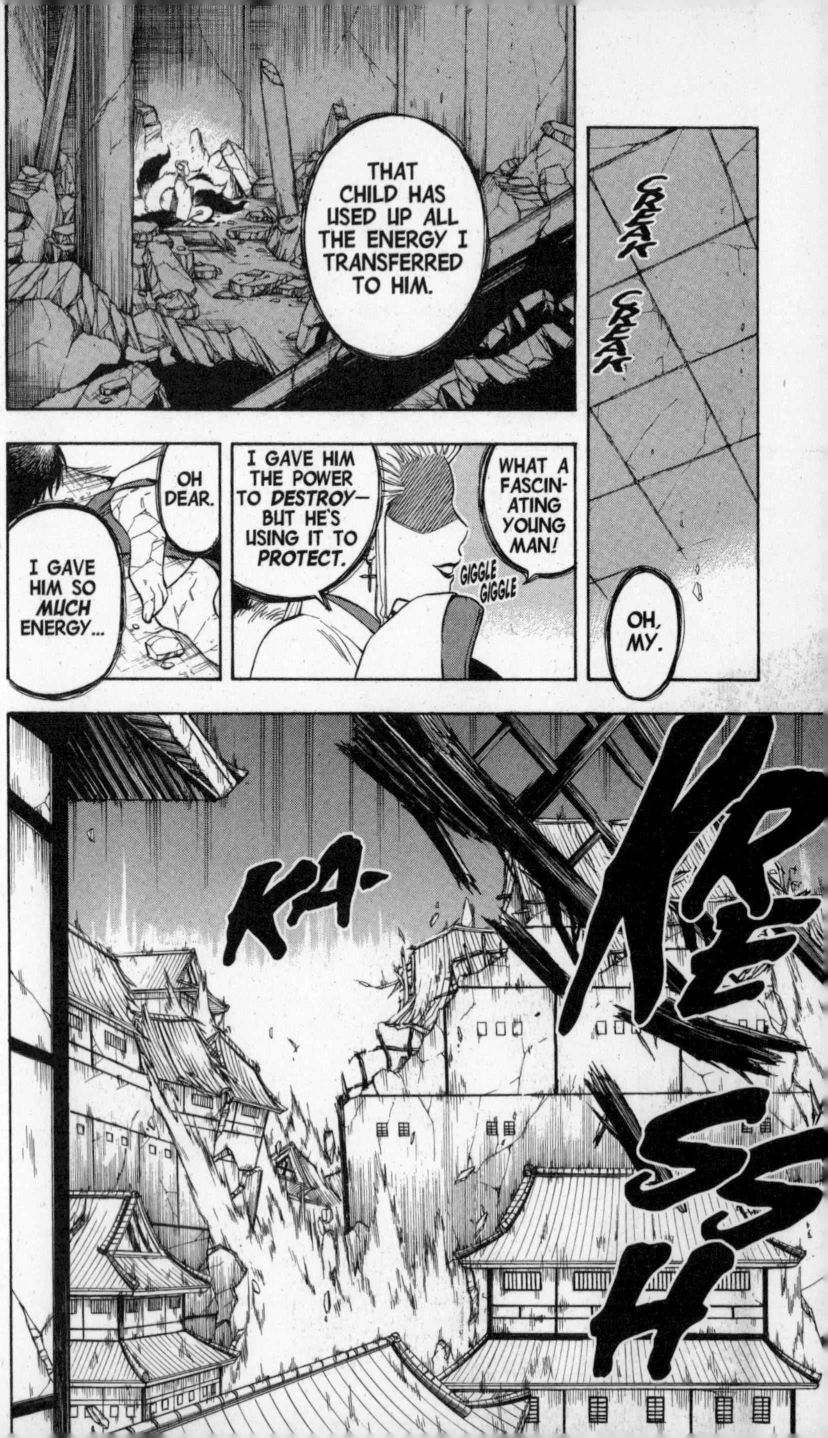
CREAK
CREAK
OH, MY.
THAT CHILD HAS USED UP ALL THE ENERGY I TRANSFERRED TO HIM.
WHAT A FASCINATING YOUNG MAN!
GIGGLE GIGGLE
I GAVE HIM THE POWER TO DESTROY—BUT HE'S USING IT TO PROTECT.
OH DEAR.
I GAVE HIM SO MUCH ENERGY...
KA-
KRESSH

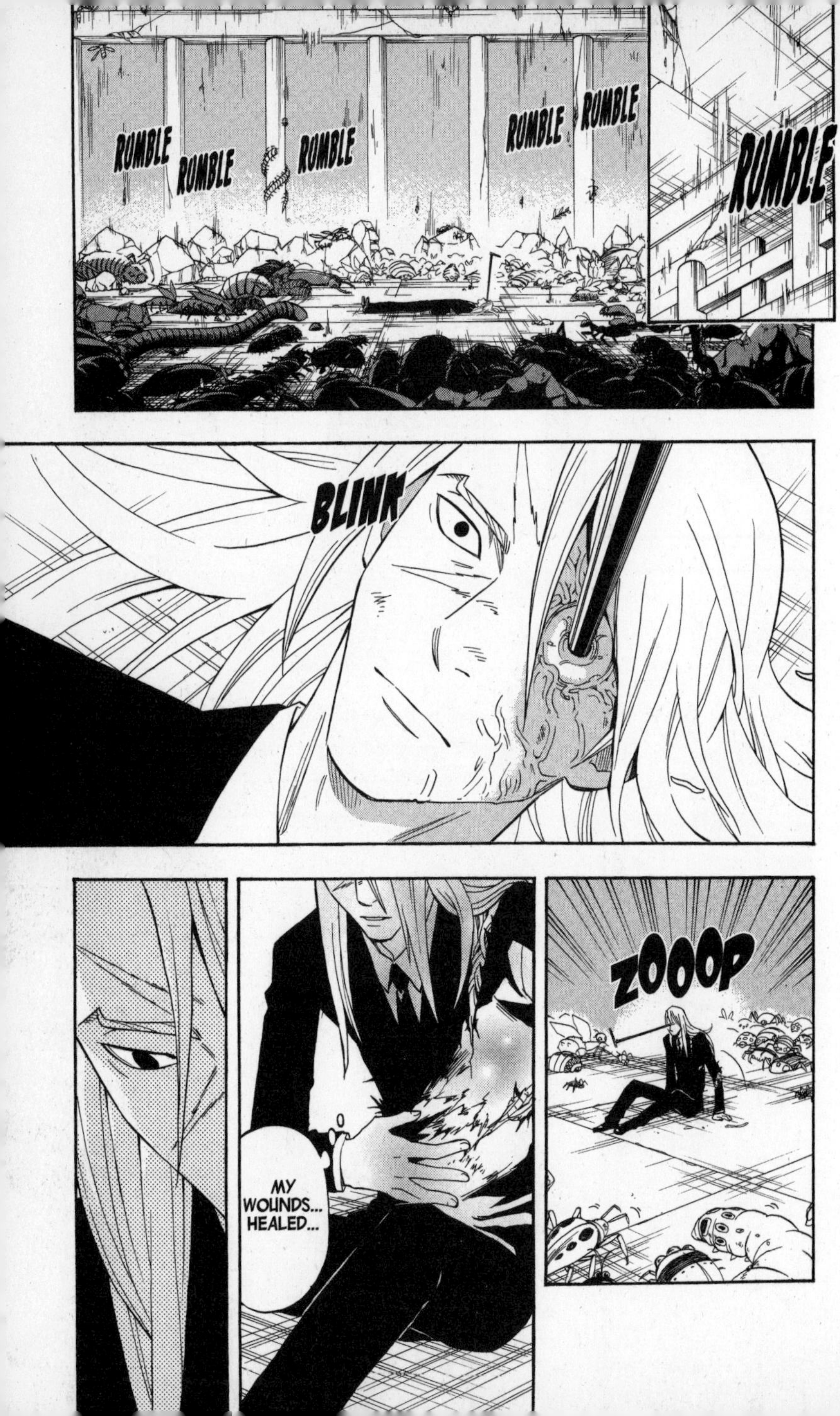
RUMBLE
RUMBLE
RUMBLE
RUMBLE
RUMBLE
RUMBLE
BLINK
ZOOOP
MY WOUNDS... HEALED...

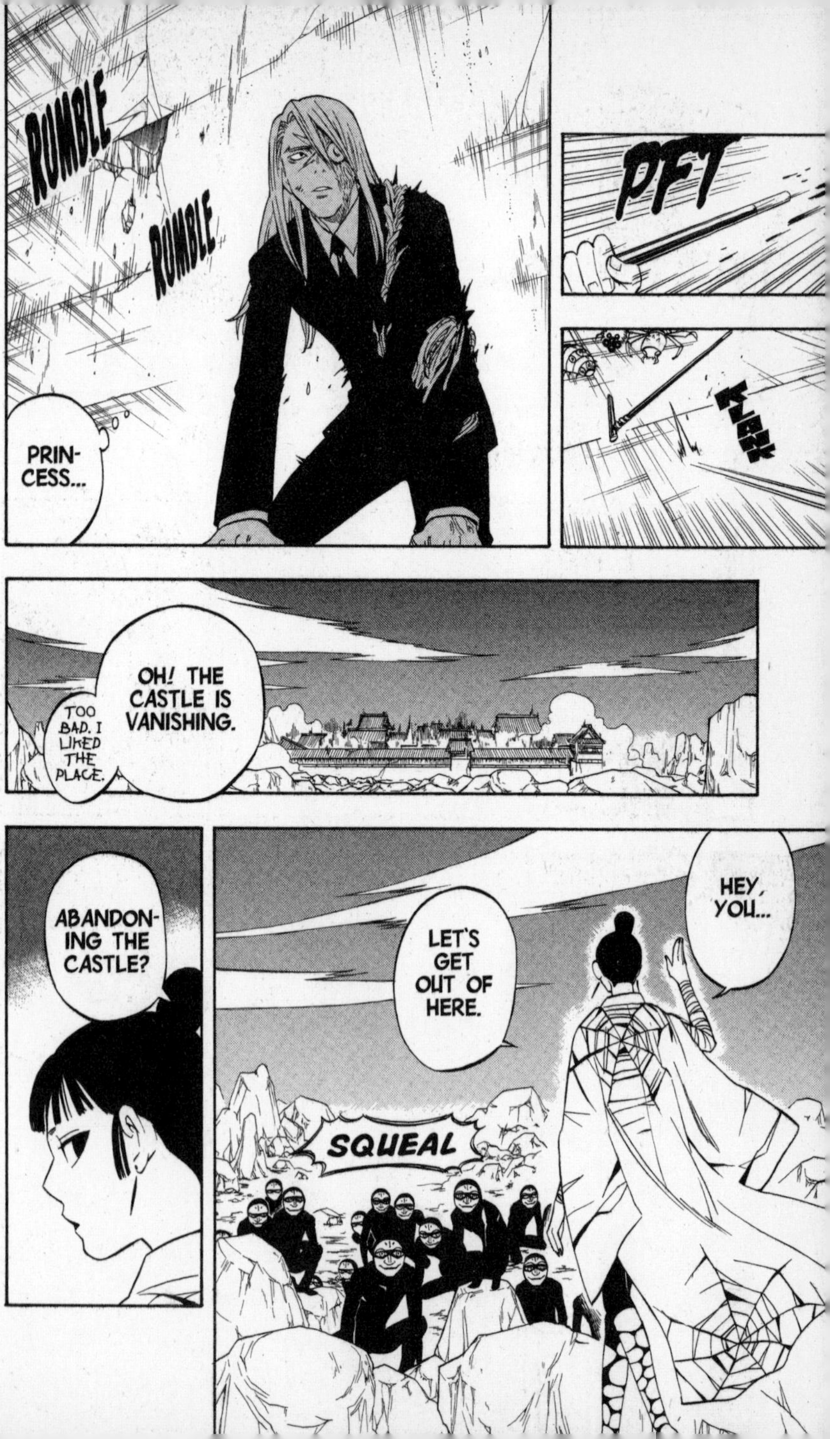
PFT
KLANK
RUMBLE
RUMBLE
PRIN-CESS...
OH! THE CASTLE IS VANISHING.
TOO BAD. I LIKED THE PLACE.
HEY, YOU...
LET'S GET OUT OF HERE.
SQUEAL
ABANDON-ING THE CASTLE?

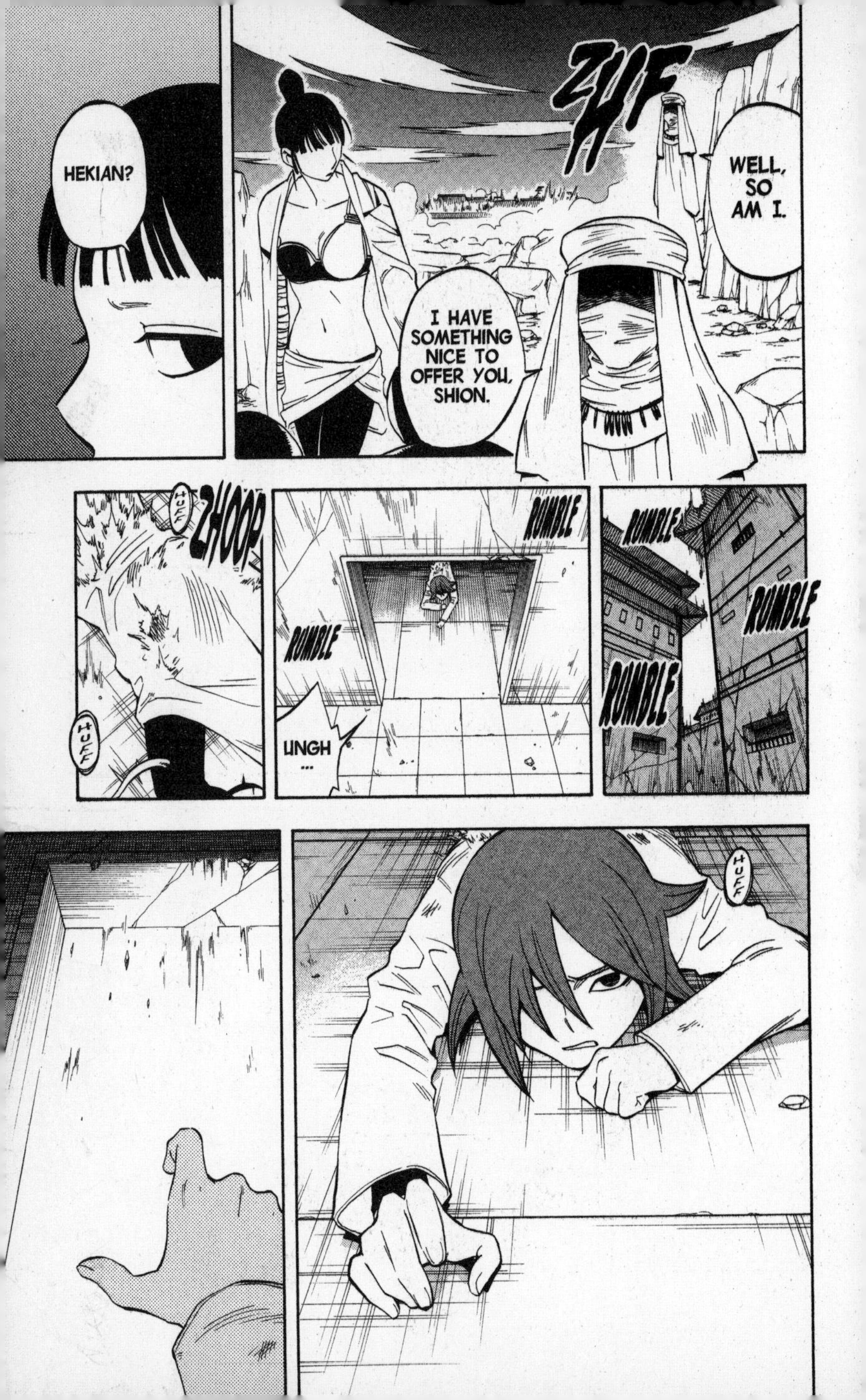
ZHF
WELL, SO AM I.
I HAVE SOMETHING NICE TO OFFER YOU, SHION.
HEKIAN?
RUMBLE
RUMBLE
RUMBLE
RUMBLE
RUMBLE
UNGH...
ZHOOP
HUFF
HUFF
HUFF

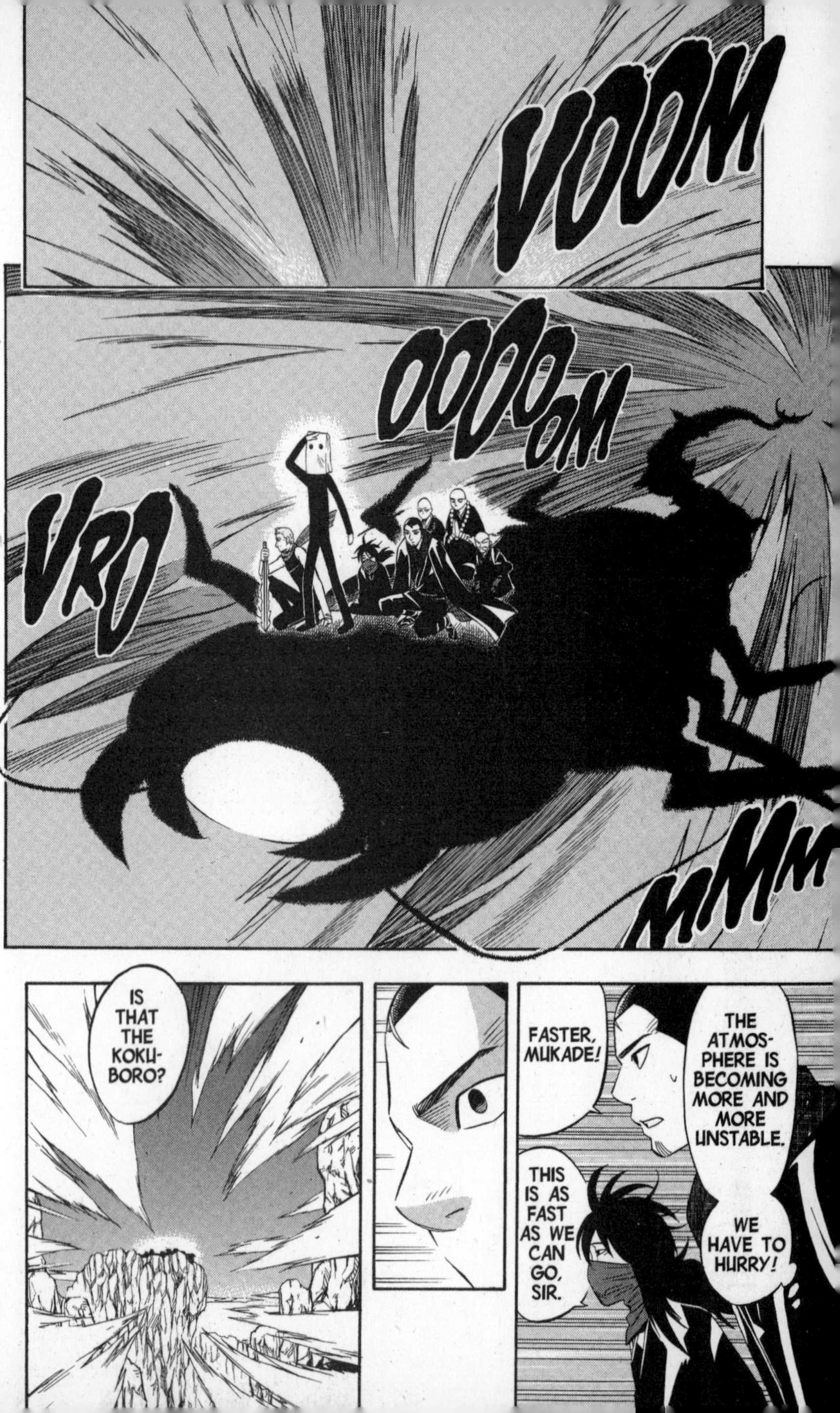
VOOM
VRO
OOOOOM
MMM
THE ATMOS-PHERE IS BECOMING MORE AND MORE UNSTABLE.
FASTER, MUKADE!
WE HAVE TO HURRY!
THIS IS AS FAST AS WE CAN GO, SIR.
IS THAT THE KOKU-BORO?

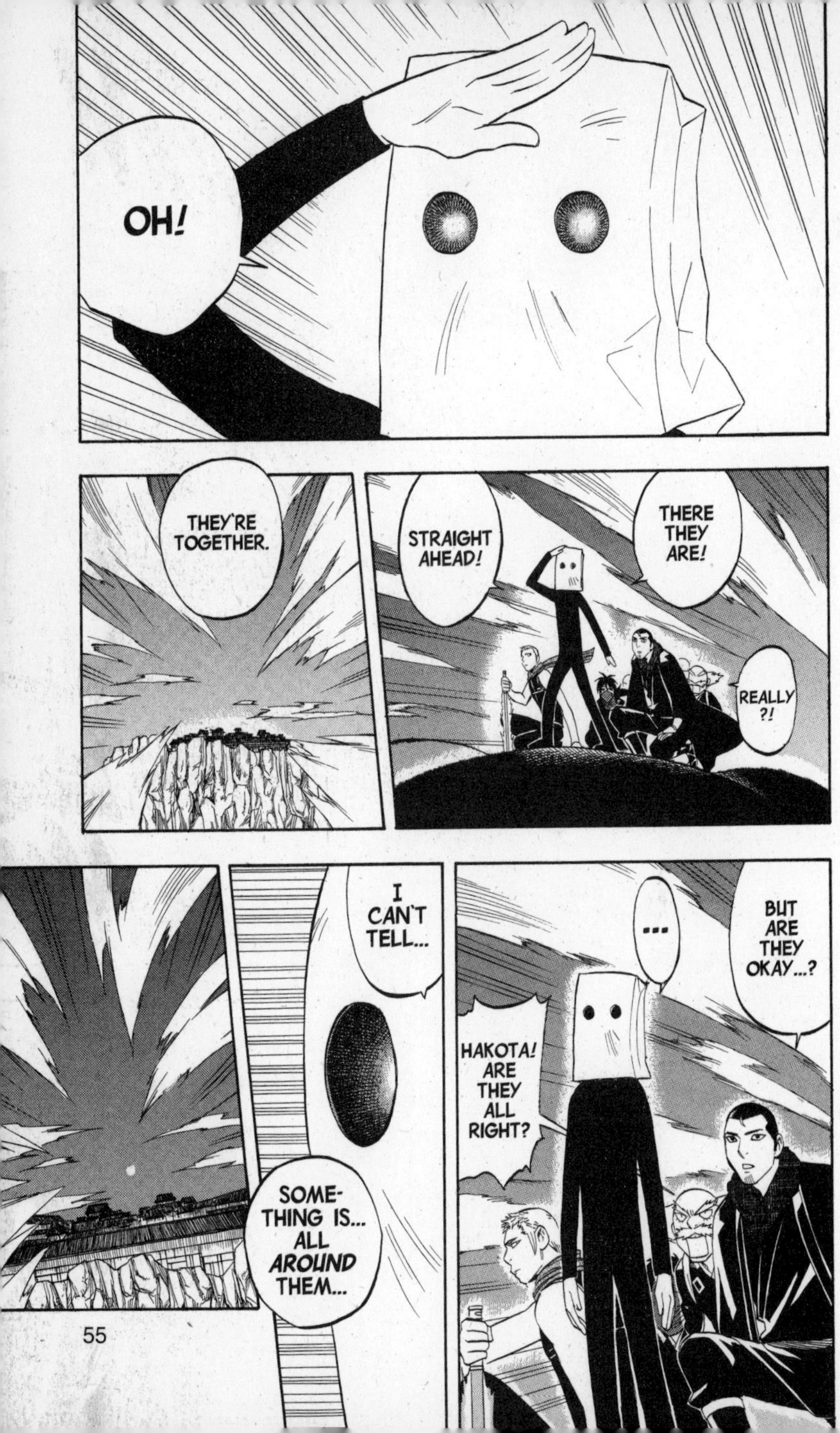
OH!
THERE THEY ARE!
STRAIGHT AHEAD!
REALLY ?!
THEY'RE TOGETHER.
BUT ARE THEY OKAY...?
...
HAKOTA! ARE THEY ALL RIGHT?
I CAN'T TELL...
SOME-THING IS... ALL *AROUND* THEM...

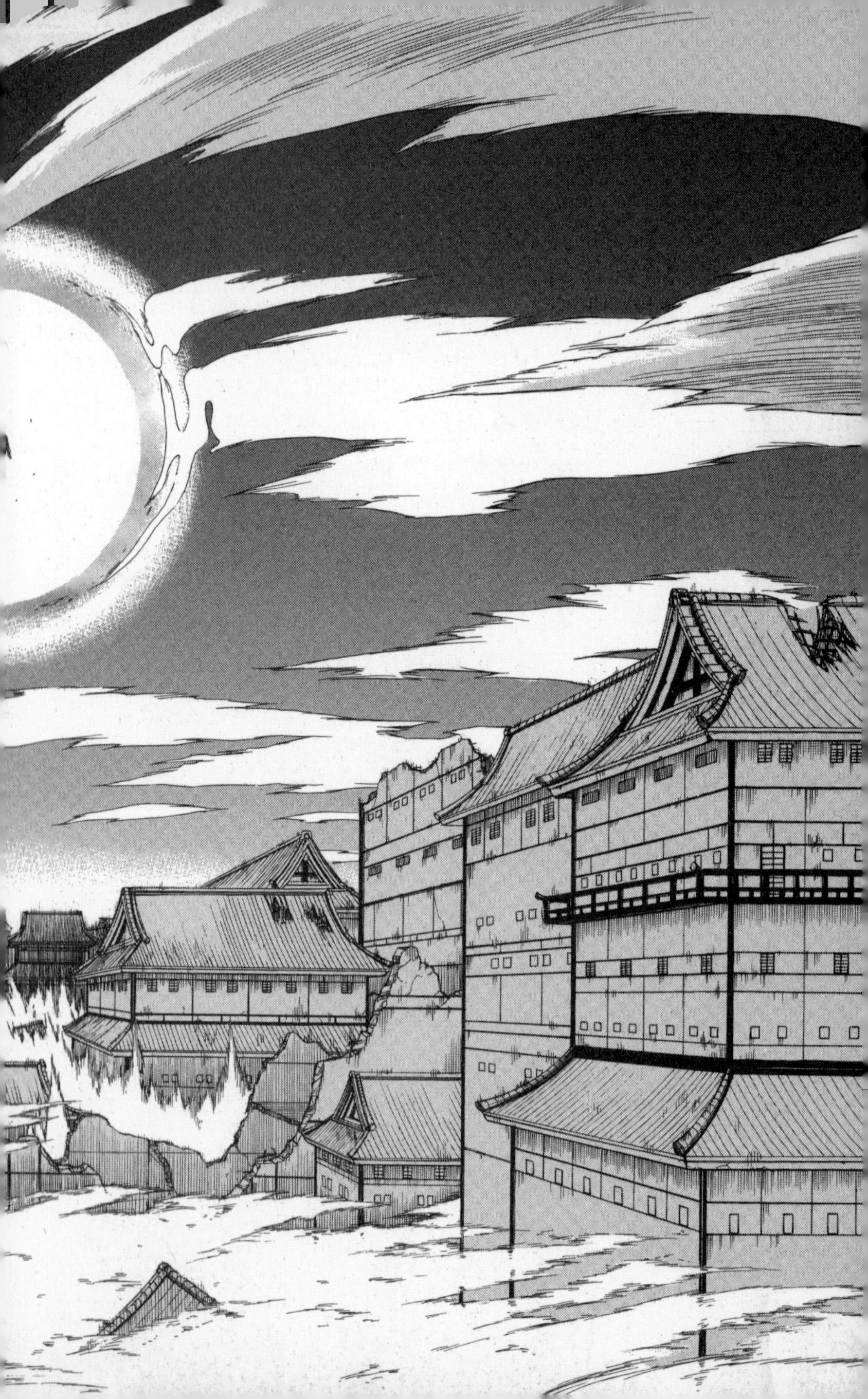

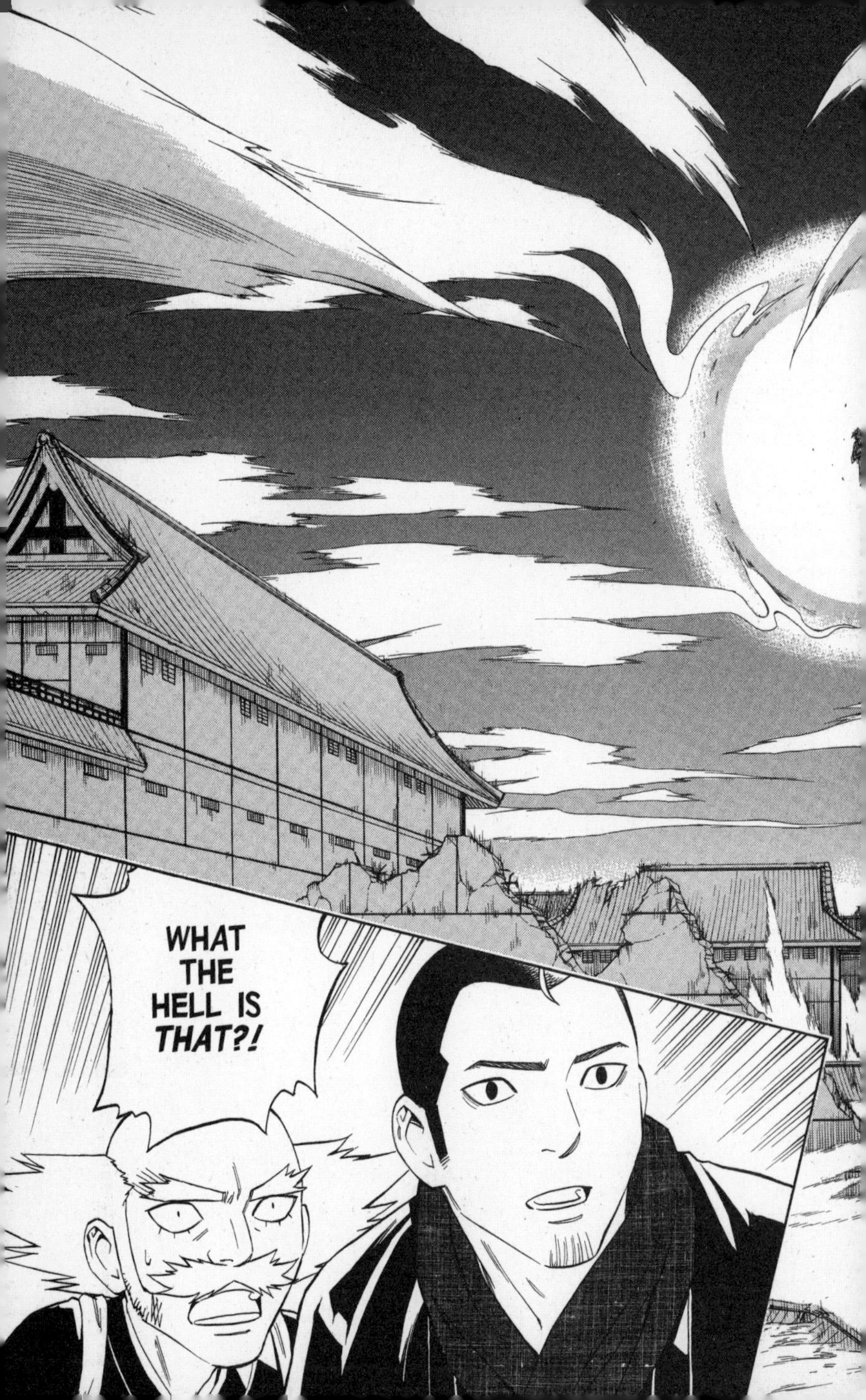
WHAT THE HELL IS THAT?!

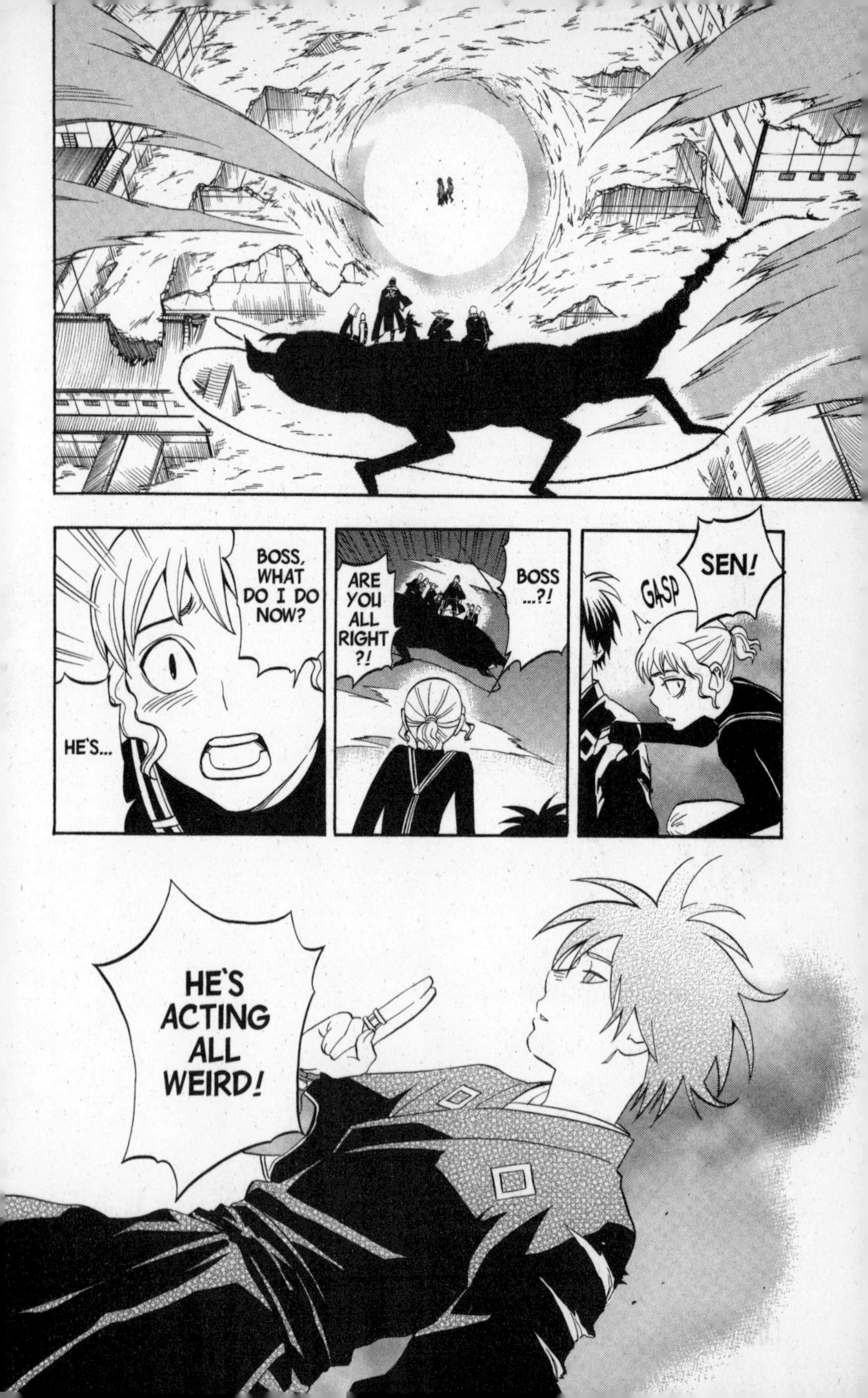
SEN!
GASP
BOSS ...?!
ARE YOU ALL RIGHT?!
BOSS, WHAT DO I DO NOW?
HE'S...
HE'S ACTING ALL WEIRD!

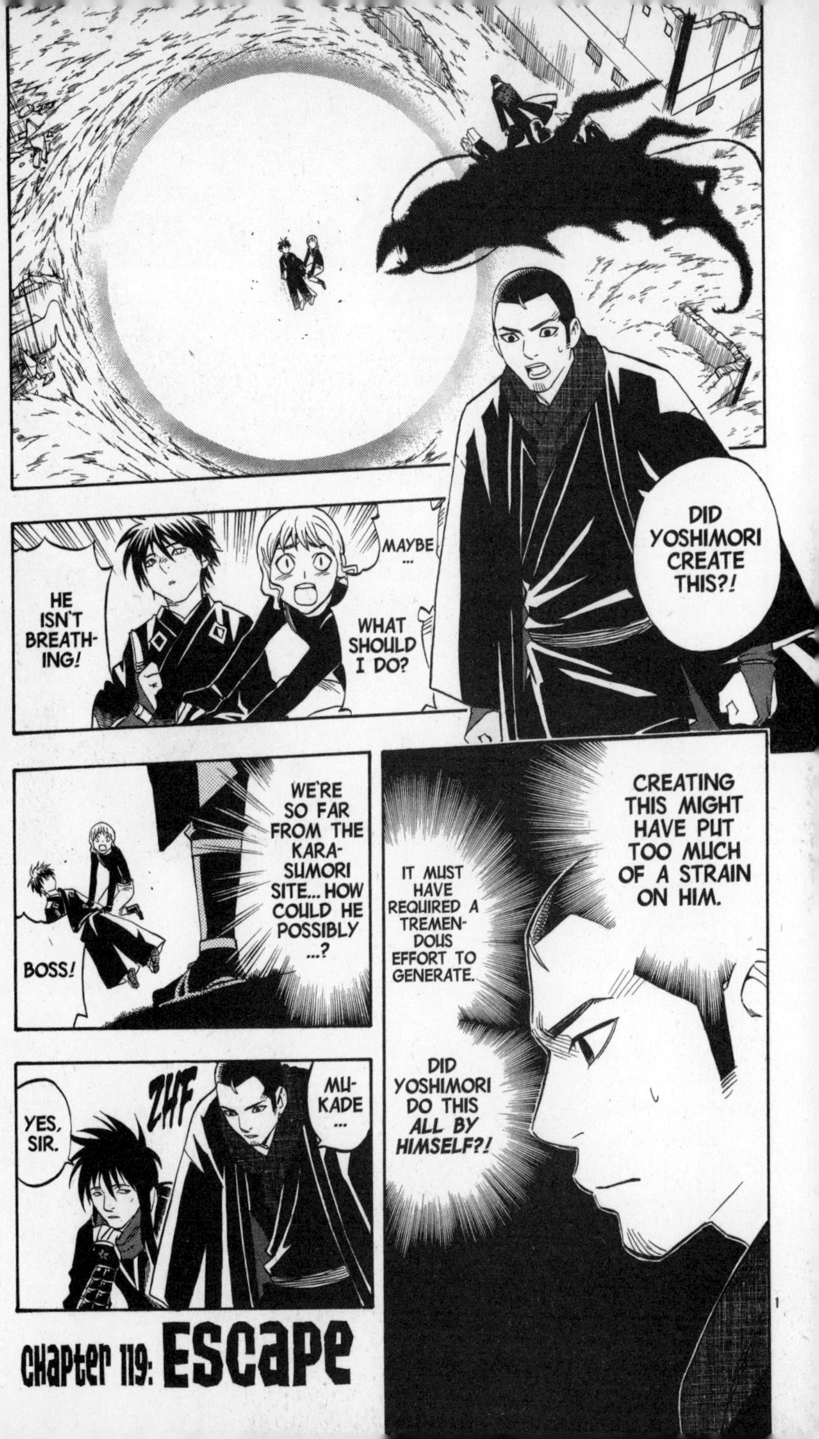
DID YOSHIMORI CREATE THIS?!
MAYBE ...
WHAT SHOULD I DO?
HE ISN'T BREATHING!
CREATING THIS MIGHT HAVE PUT TOO MUCH OF A STRAIN ON HIM.
IT MUST HAVE REQUIRED A TREMENDOUS EFFORT TO GENERATE.
DID YOSHIMORI DO THIS *ALL BY HIMSELF?!*
WE'RE SO FAR FROM THE KARASUMORI SITE... HOW COULD HE POSSIBLY ...?
BOSS!
MUKADE ...
ZHF
YES, SIR.

Chapter 119: Escape

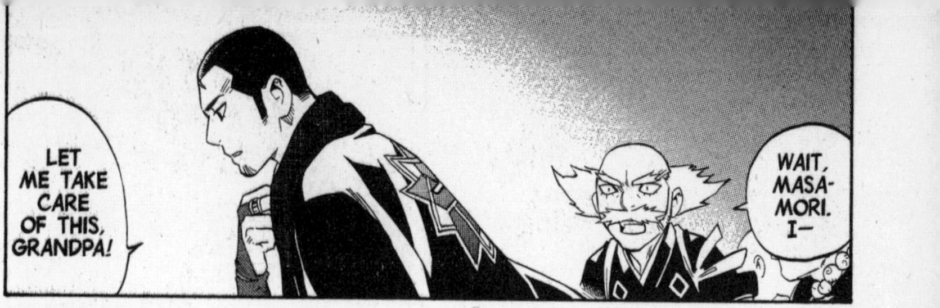
WAIT, MASAMORI. I—
LET ME TAKE CARE OF THIS, GRANDPA!

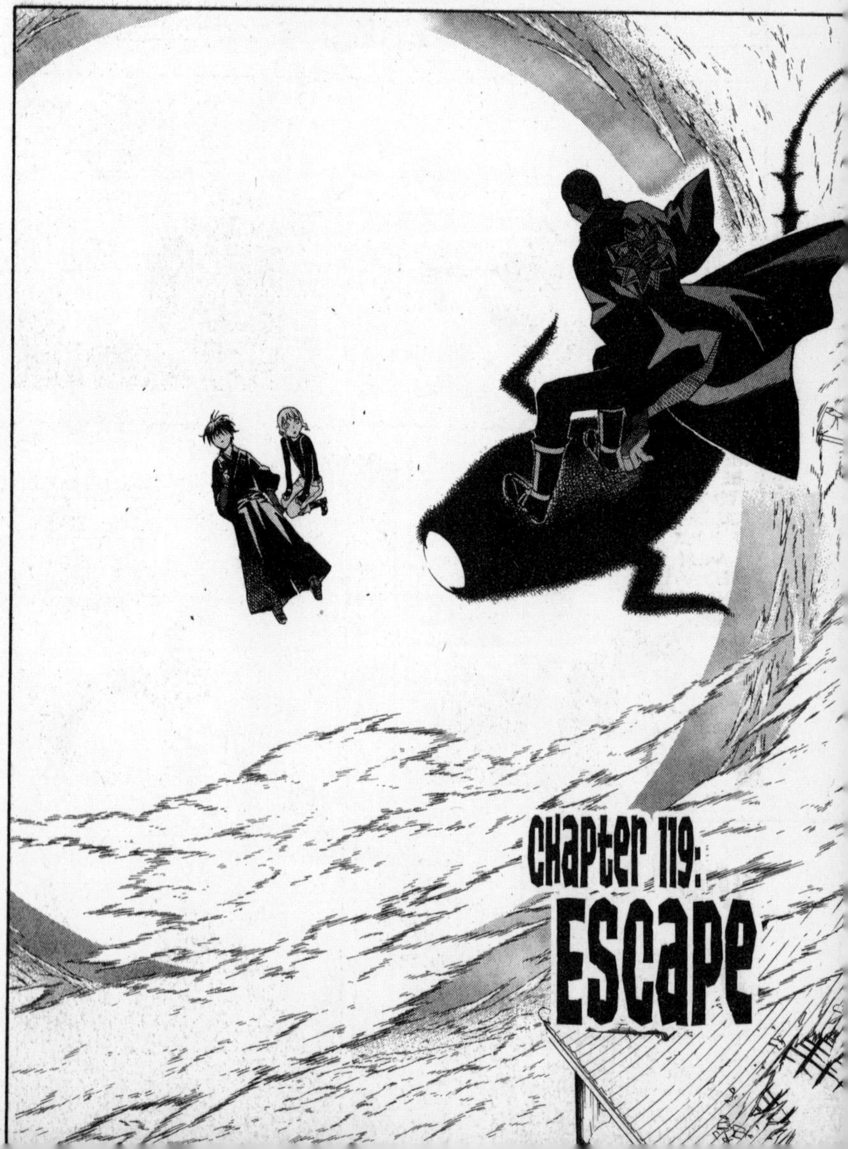
CHAPTER 119:
ESCAPE

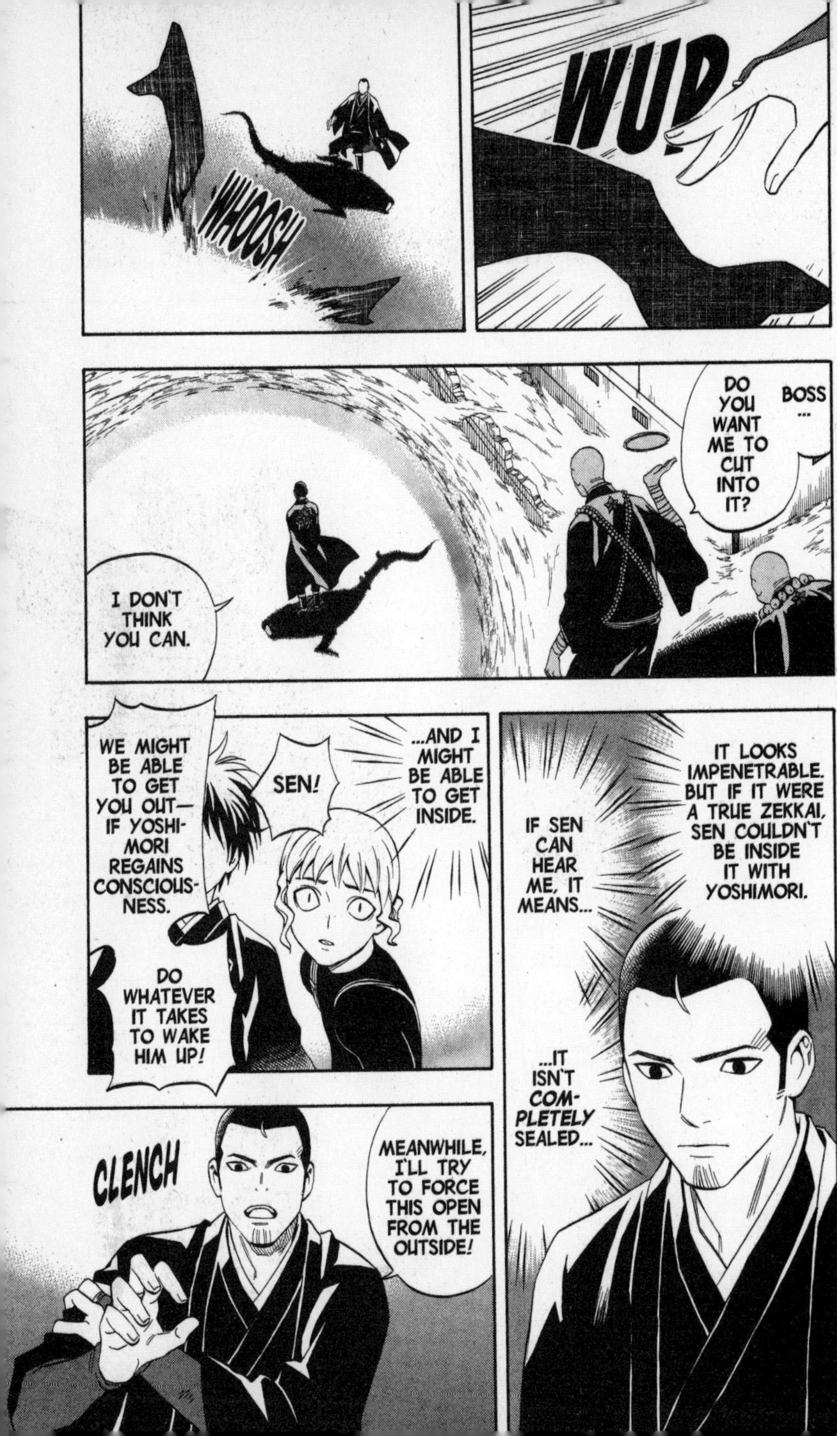
WUD
WHOOSH
BOSS...
DO YOU WANT ME TO CUT INTO IT?
I DON'T THINK YOU CAN.
IT LOOKS IMPENETRABLE. BUT IF IT WERE A TRUE ZEKKAI, SEN COULDN'T BE INSIDE IT WITH YOSHIMORI.
IF SEN CAN HEAR ME, IT MEANS...
...IT ISN'T COMPLETELY SEALED...
...AND I MIGHT BE ABLE TO GET INSIDE.
SEN!
WE MIGHT BE ABLE TO GET YOU OUT—IF YOSHIMORI REGAINS CONSCIOUSNESS.
DO WHATEVER IT TAKES TO WAKE HIM UP!
MEANWHILE, I'LL TRY TO FORCE THIS OPEN FROM THE OUTSIDE!
CLENCH

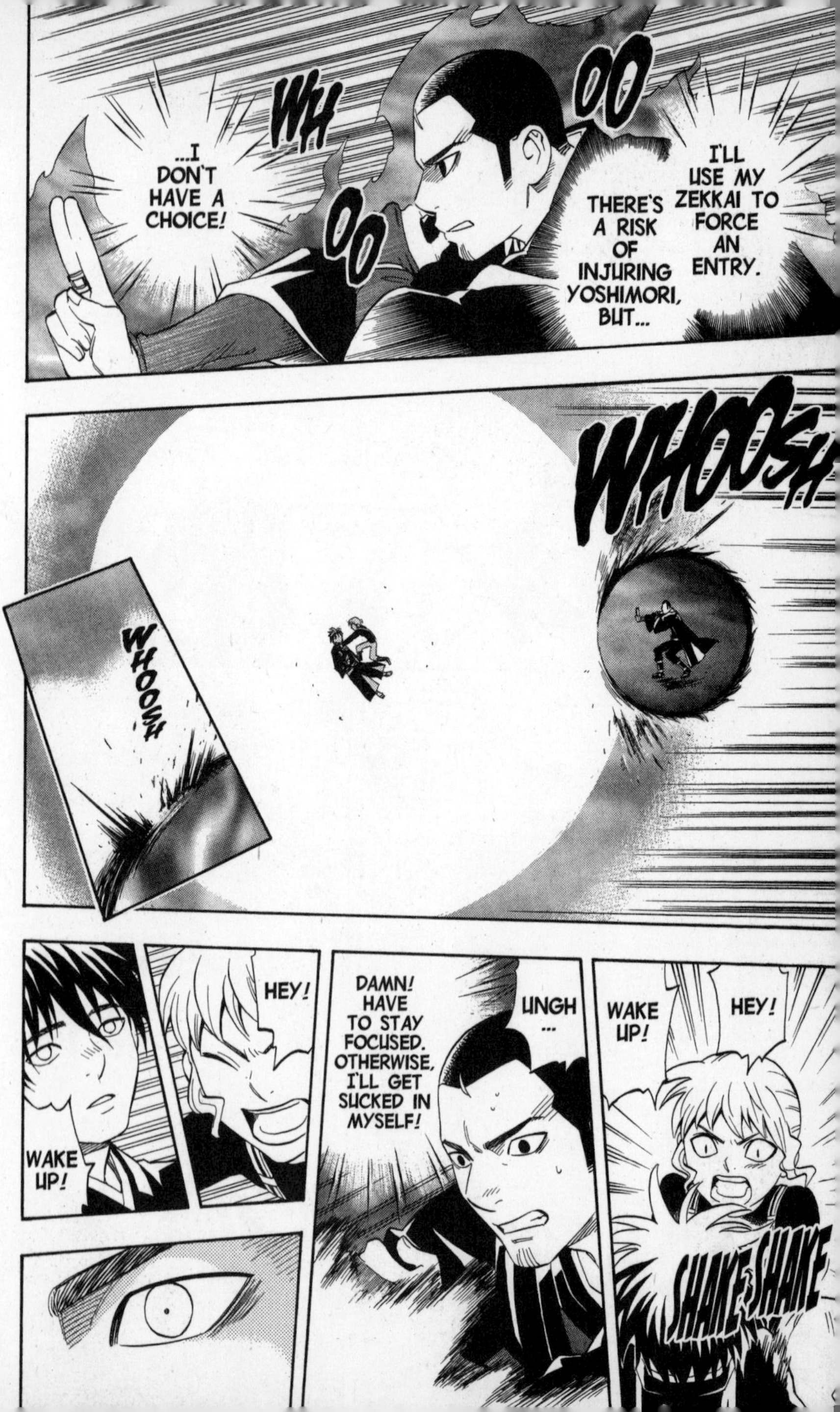

I'LL USE MY ZEKKAI TO FORCE AN ENTRY.
THERE'S A RISK OF INJURING YOSHIMORI, BUT...
OO
WH
OO
...I DON'T HAVE A CHOICE!
WHOOSH
WHOOSH
HEY!
WAKE UP!
SHAKE SHAKE
UNGH ...
DAMN! HAVE TO STAY FOCUSED. OTHERWISE, I'LL GET SUCKED IN MYSELF!
HEY!
WAKE UP!

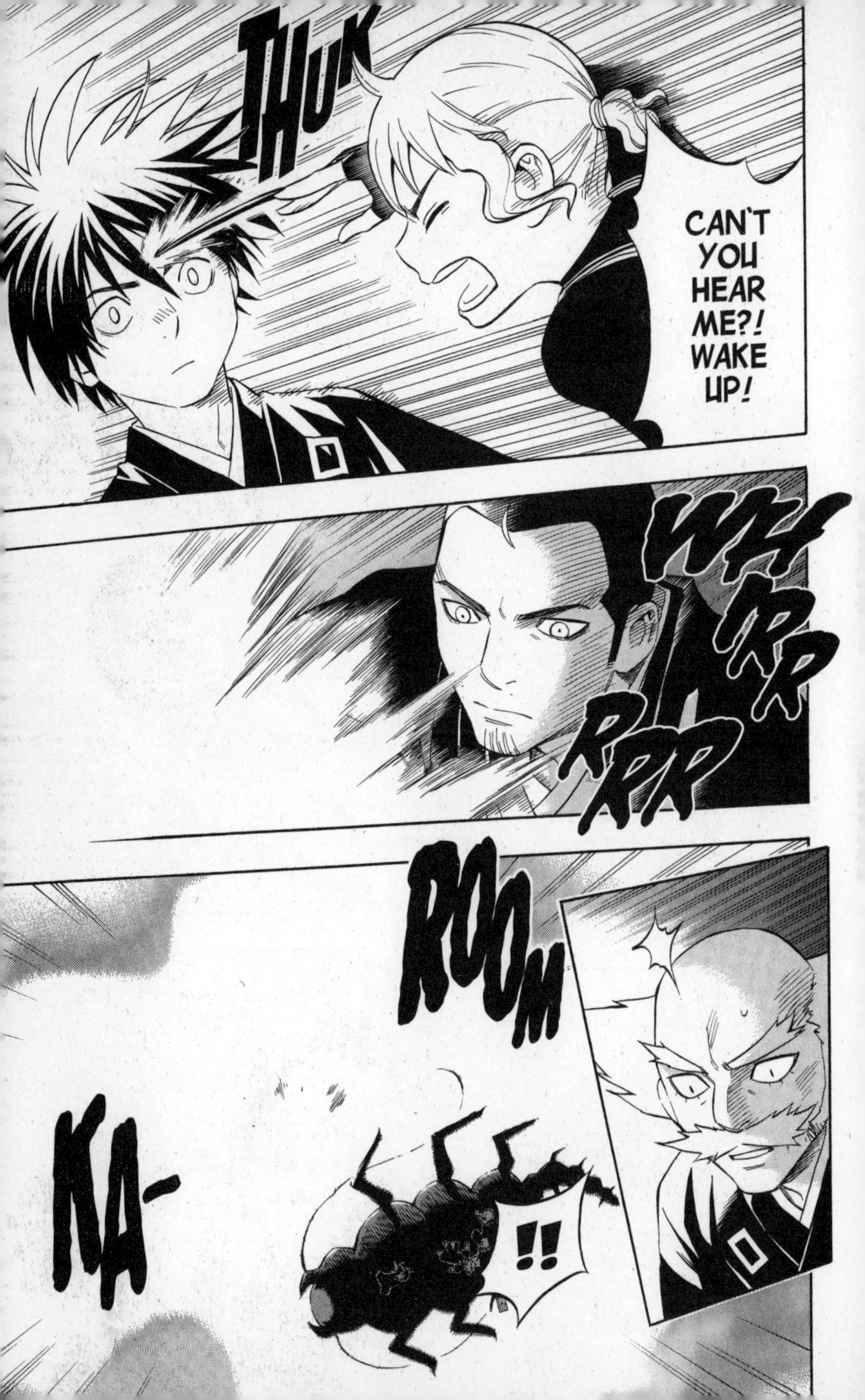
THUK
CAN'T YOU HEAR ME?! WAKE UP!
WHIRRRRR
!!
KA-
ROOM

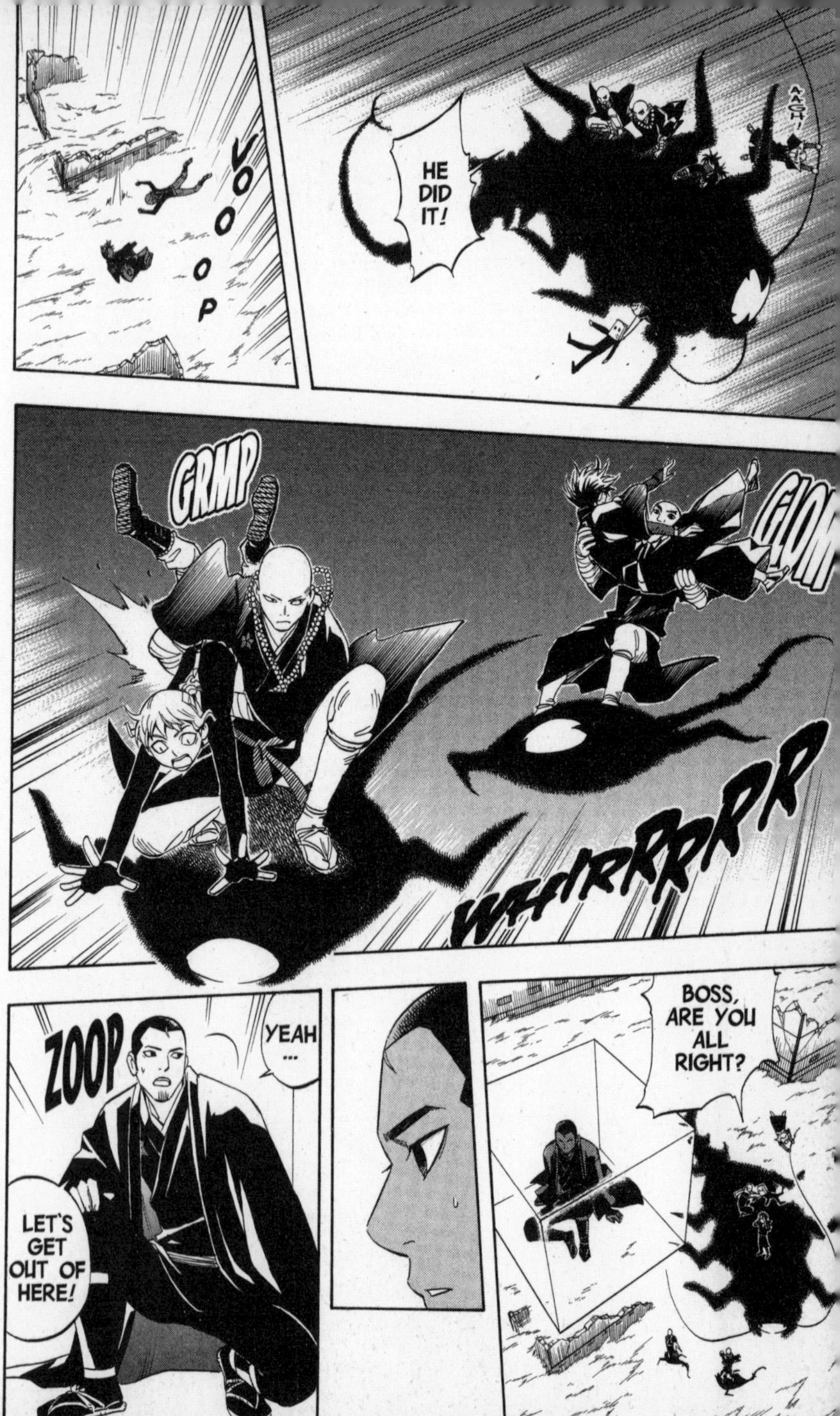
AACH!
HE DID IT!
VOOOOP
GLOM
GRMP
WHIRRRRRR
BOSS, ARE YOU ALL RIGHT?
YEAH ...
ZOOP
LET'S GET OUT OF HERE!

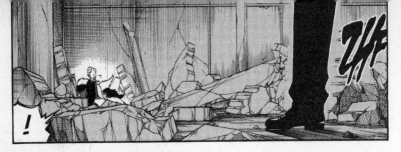

!

GO AWAY! YOU'RE USELESS TO ME. I DON'T NEED YOU ANYMORE!

SHOO SHOO

HMPH. THIS CASTLE IS ABOUT TO COLLAPSE.

BYAKU!

STAY AWAY FROM ME!

TAK

DON'T LOOK AT ME!

TAK TAK

WUP

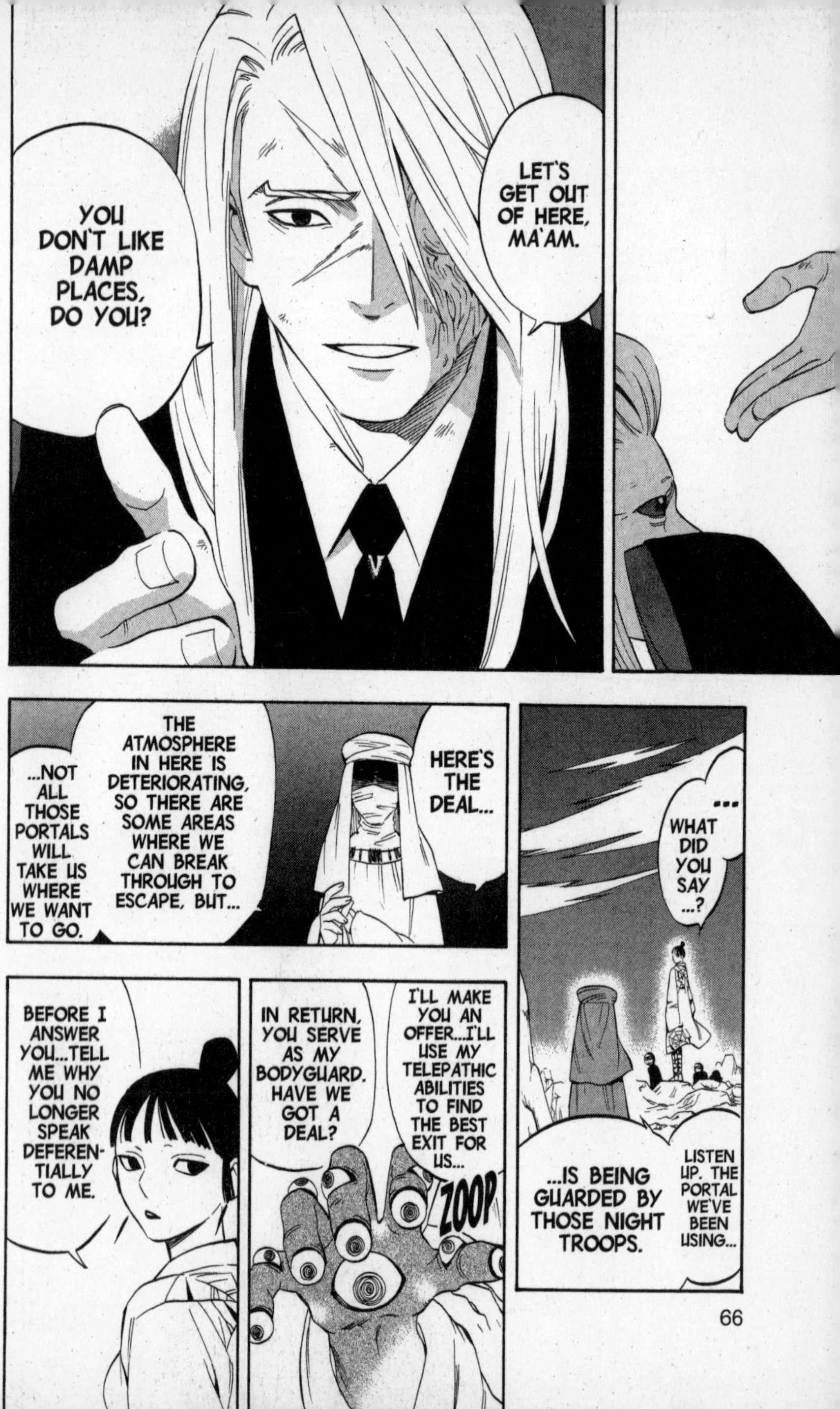
LET'S GET OUT OF HERE, MA'AM.
YOU DON'T LIKE DAMP PLACES, DO YOU?
... WHAT DID YOU SAY ...?
LISTEN UP. THE PORTAL WE'VE BEEN USING...
...IS BEING GUARDED BY THOSE NIGHT TROOPS.
HERE'S THE DEAL...
THE ATMOSPHERE IN HERE IS DETERIORATING, SO THERE ARE SOME AREAS WHERE WE CAN BREAK THROUGH TO ESCAPE, BUT...
...NOT ALL THOSE PORTALS WILL TAKE US WHERE WE WANT TO GO.
I'LL MAKE YOU AN OFFER...I'LL USE MY TELEPATHIC ABILITIES TO FIND THE BEST EXIT FOR US...
IN RETURN, YOU SERVE AS MY BODYGUARD. HAVE WE GOT A DEAL?
ZOOP
BEFORE I ANSWER YOU...TELL ME WHY YOU NO LONGER SPEAK DEFEREN-TIALLY TO ME.

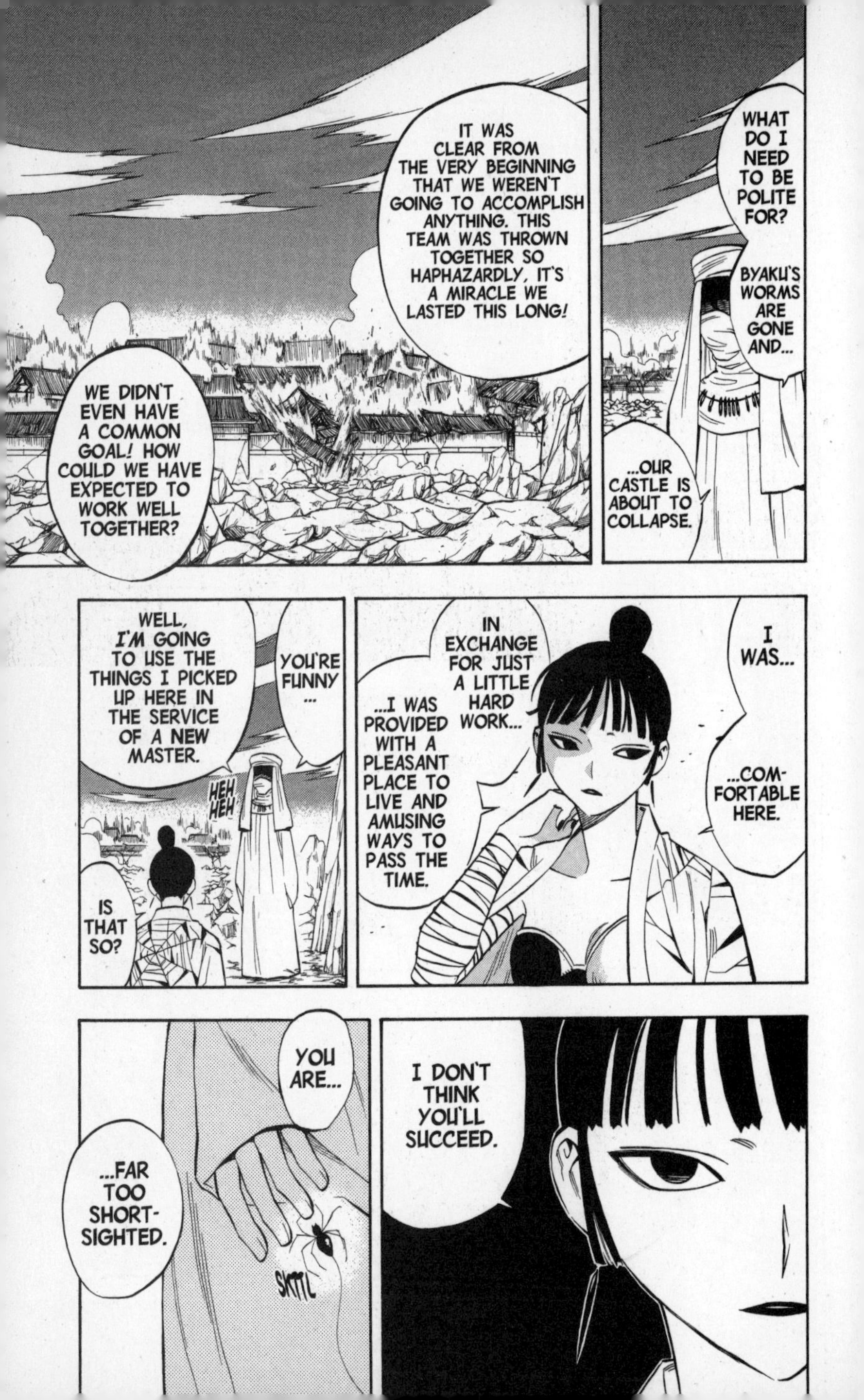
WHAT DO I NEED TO BE POLITE FOR?
BYAKU'S WORMS ARE GONE AND...
...OUR CASTLE IS ABOUT TO COLLAPSE.
IT WAS CLEAR FROM THE VERY BEGINNING THAT WE WEREN'T GOING TO ACCOMPLISH ANYTHING. THIS TEAM WAS THROWN TOGETHER SO HAPHAZARDLY, IT'S A MIRACLE WE LASTED THIS LONG!
WE DIDN'T EVEN HAVE A COMMON GOAL! HOW COULD WE HAVE EXPECTED TO WORK WELL TOGETHER?
I WAS...
...COM-FORTABLE HERE.
IN EXCHANGE FOR JUST A LITTLE HARD WORK...
...I WAS PROVIDED WITH A PLEASANT PLACE TO LIVE AND AMUSING WAYS TO PASS THE TIME.
YOU'RE FUNNY...
WELL, *I'M* GOING TO USE THE THINGS I PICKED UP HERE IN THE SERVICE OF A NEW MASTER.
HEH HEH
IS THAT SO?
I DON'T THINK YOU'LL SUCCEED.
YOU ARE...
...FAR TOO SHORT-SIGHTED.
SKTTL

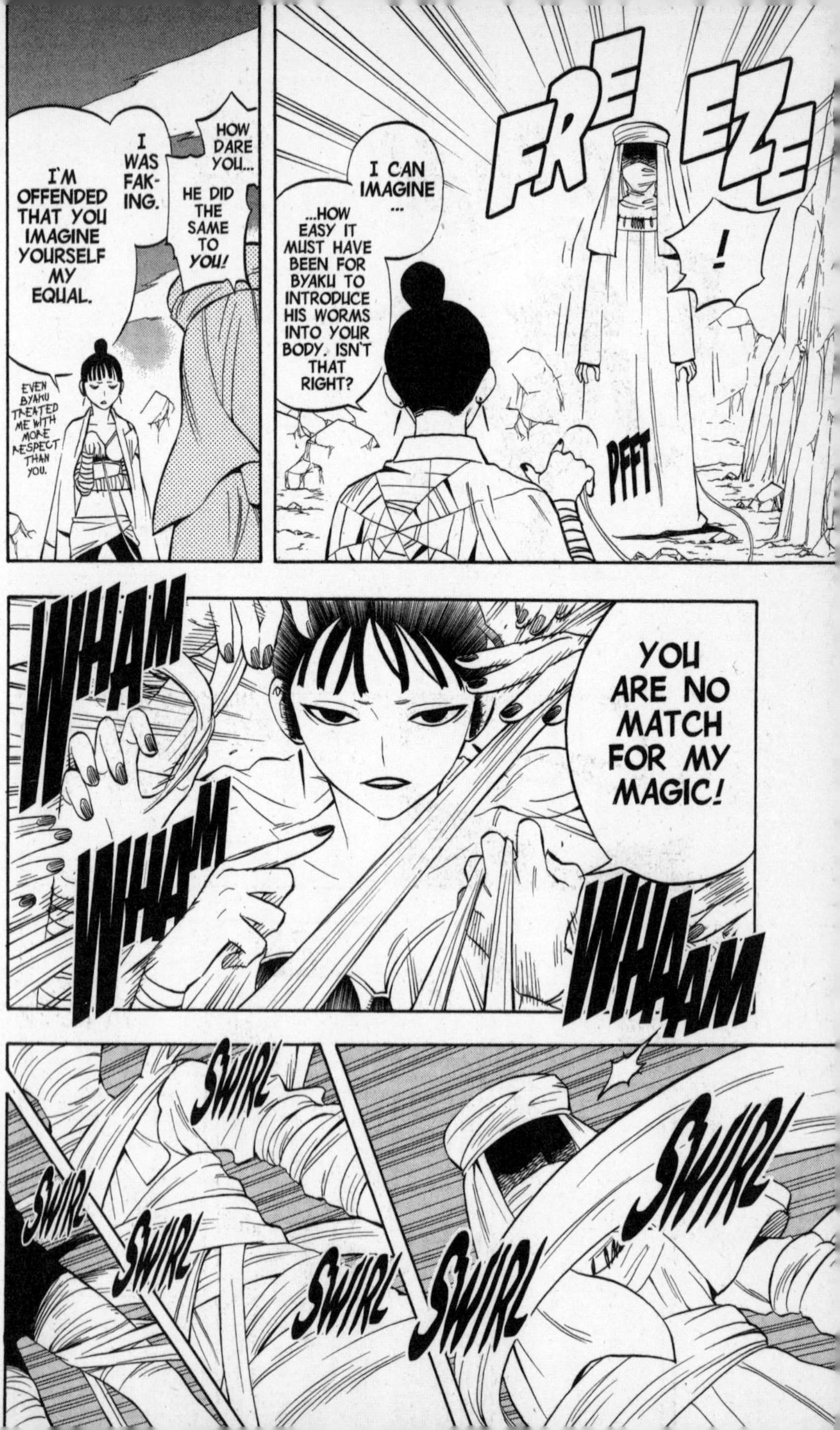
FREEZE
!
I CAN IMAGINE ...
...HOW EASY IT MUST HAVE BEEN FOR BYAKU TO INTRODUCE HIS WORMS INTO YOUR BODY. ISN'T THAT RIGHT?
PFFT
HOW DARE YOU...
HE DID THE SAME TO YOU!
I WAS FAKING.
I'M OFFENDED THAT YOU IMAGINE YOURSELF MY EQUAL.
EVEN BYAKU TREATED ME WITH MORE RESPECT THAN YOU.
YOU ARE NO MATCH FOR MY MAGIC!
WHAM
WHAM
WHAM
SWIRL
SWIRL
SWIRL
SWIRL
SWIRL
SWIRL
SWIRL
SWIRL

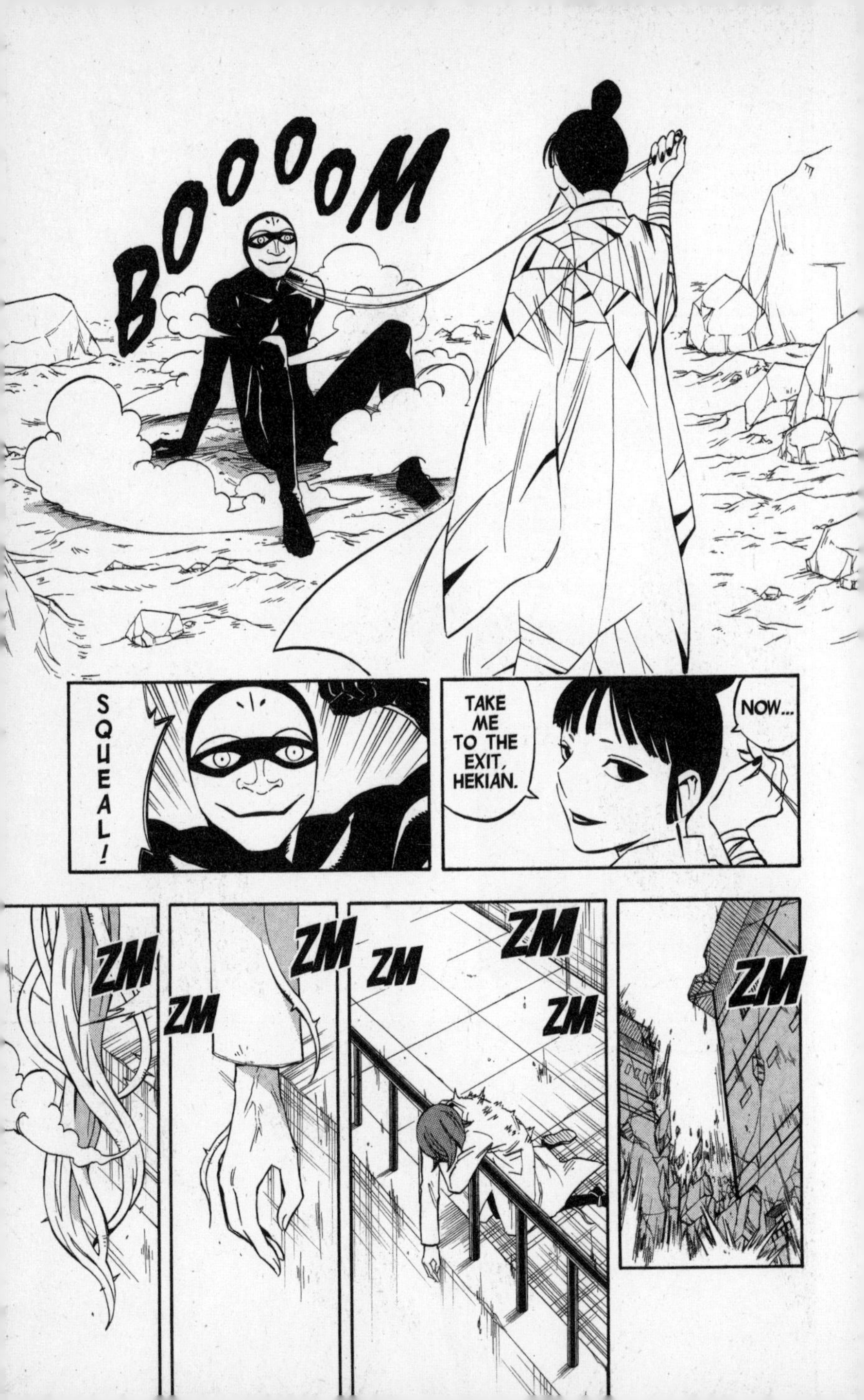
BOOOOM
NOW...
TAKE ME TO THE EXIT, HEKIAN.
SQUEAL!
ZM
ZM
ZM
ZM
ZM
ZM
ZM

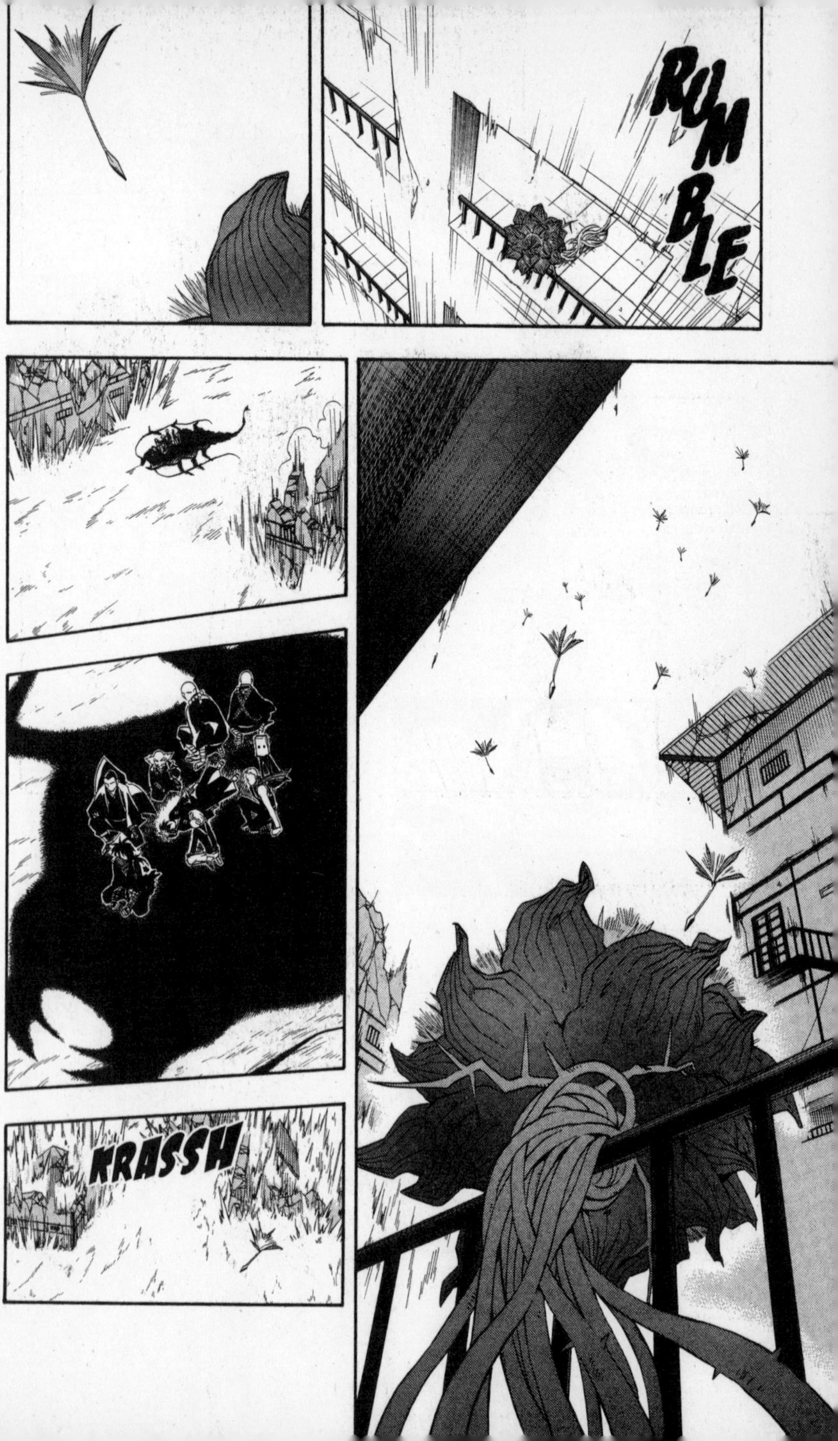
RUMBLE
KRASSH

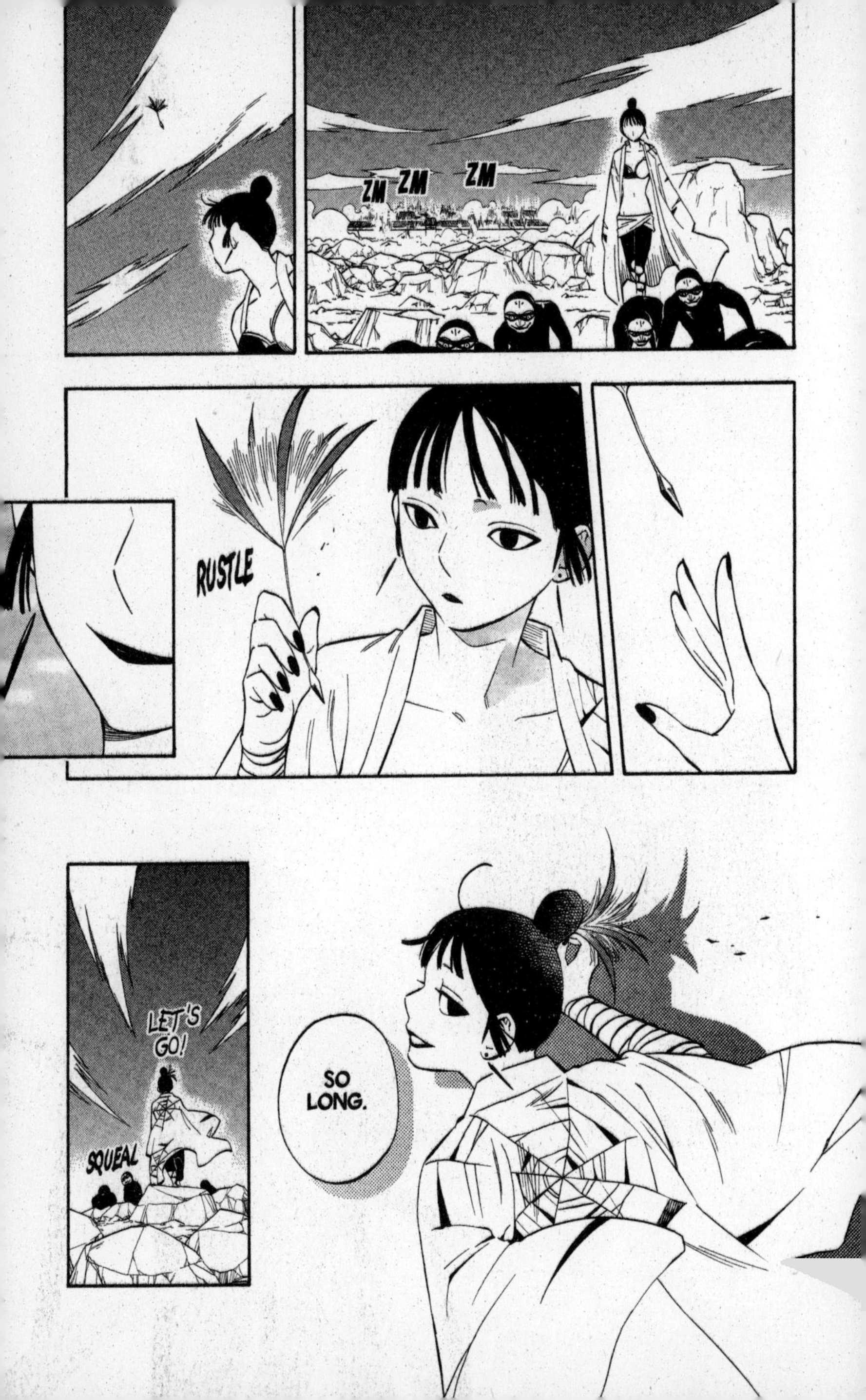
ZM
ZM
ZM
RUSTLE
SO LONG.
LET'S GO!
SQUEAL

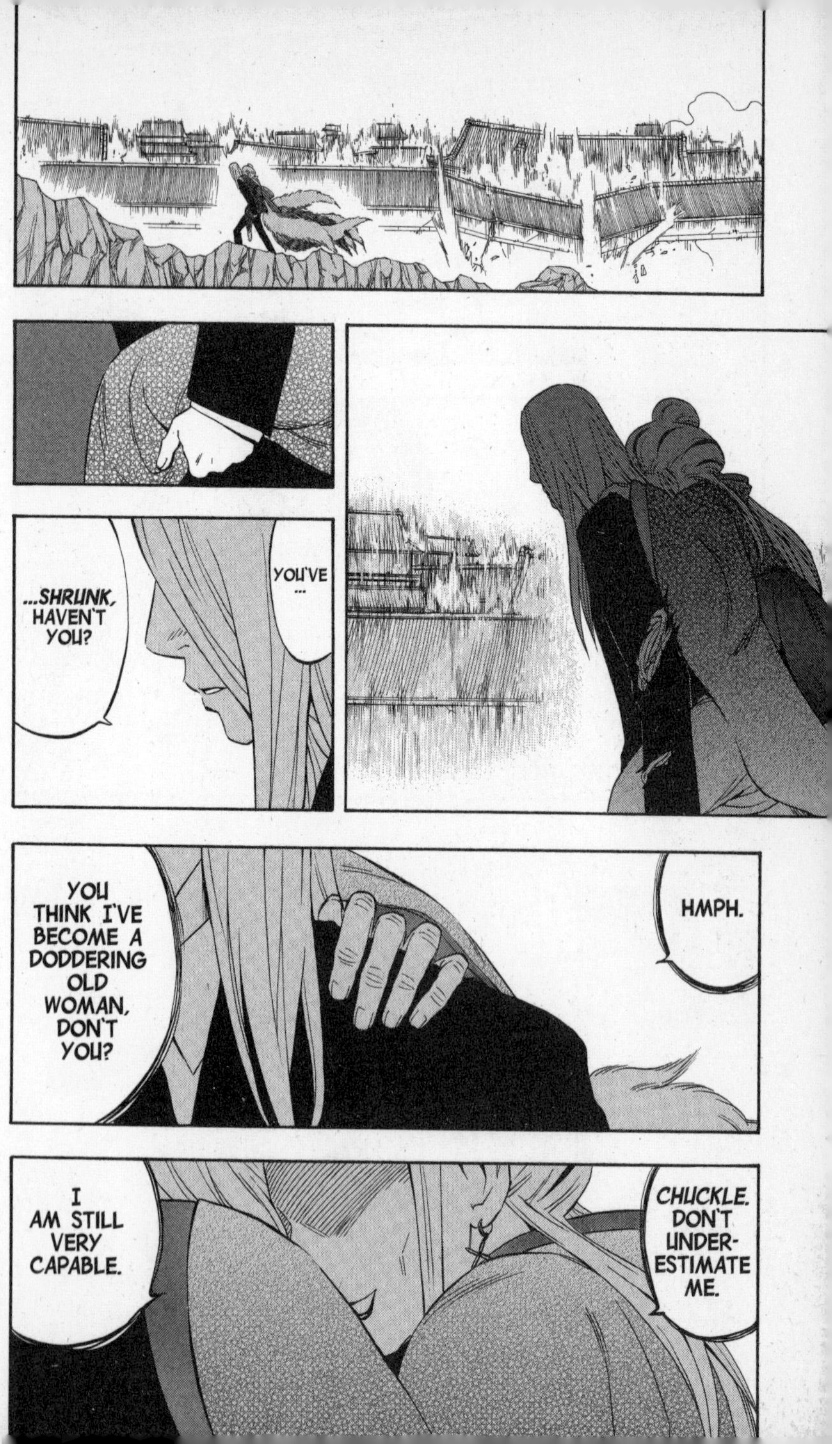

YOU'VE ...
...SHRUNK, HAVEN'T YOU?
HMPH.
YOU THINK I'VE BECOME A DODDERING OLD WOMAN, DON'T YOU?
CHUCKLE. DON'T UNDER-ESTIMATE ME.
I AM STILL VERY CAPABLE.

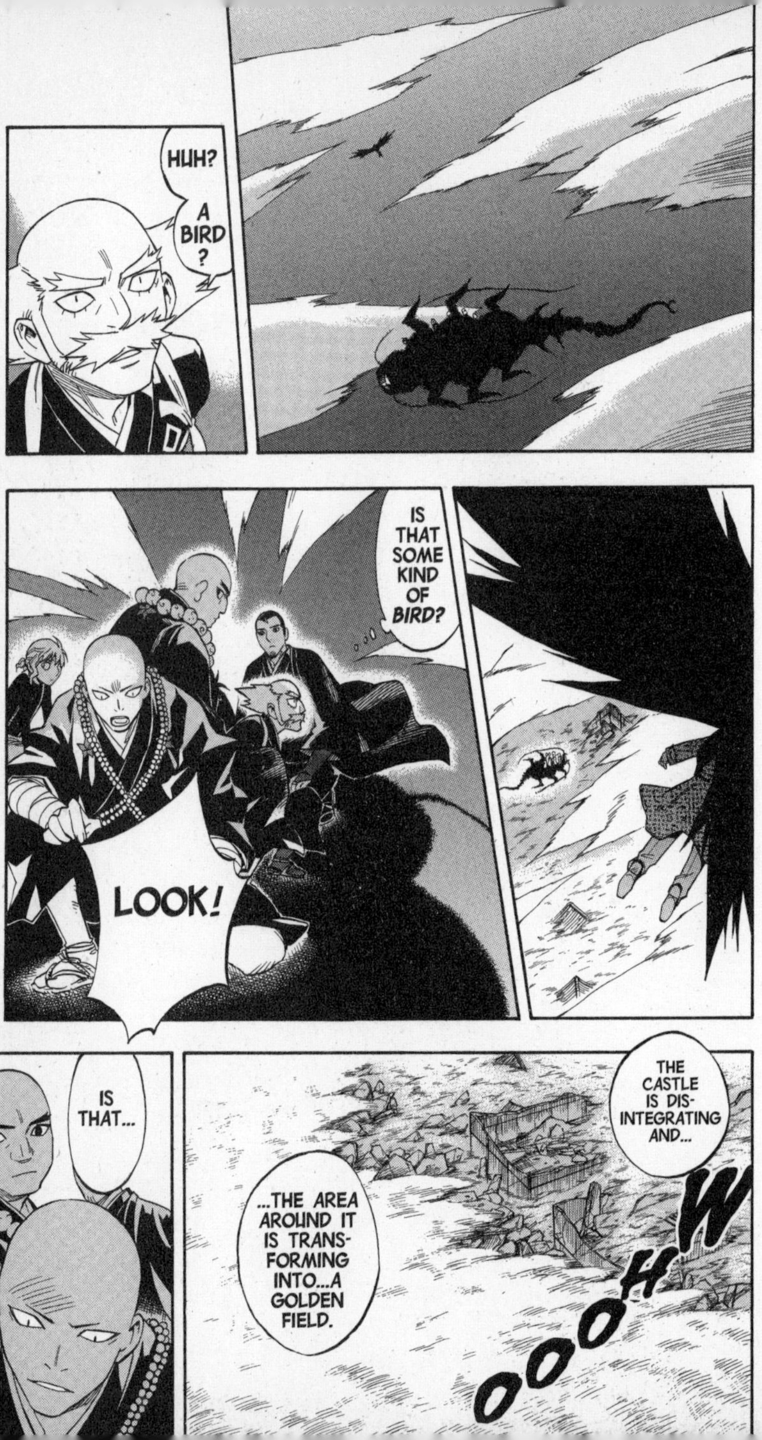

HUH?
A BIRD?
IS THAT SOME KIND OF BIRD?
LOOK!
THE CASTLE IS DIS-INTEGRATING AND...
...THE AREA AROUND IT IS TRANS-FORMING INTO...A GOLDEN FIELD.
OOOOHW
IS THAT...

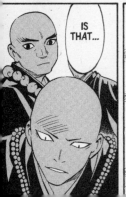

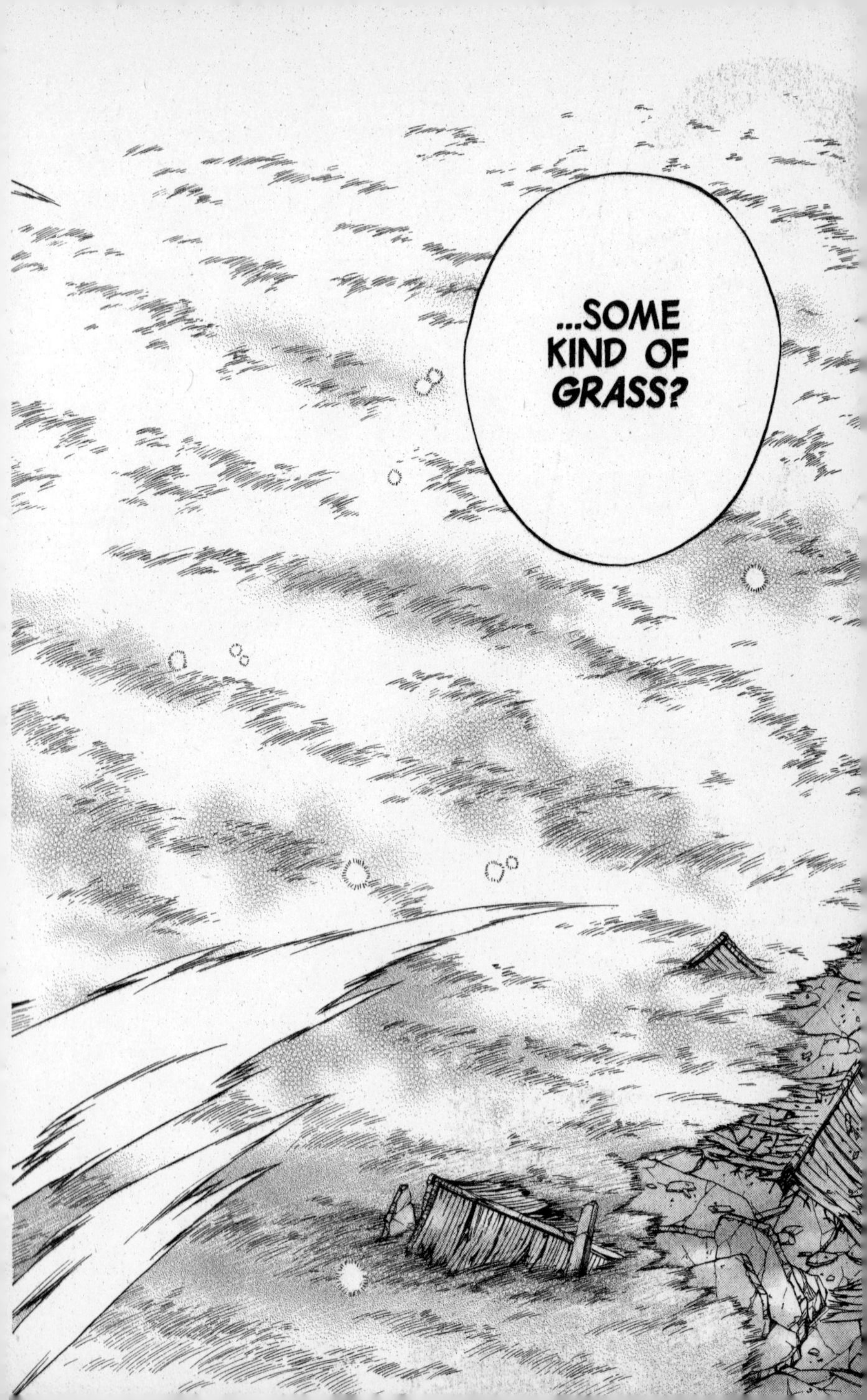
...SOME KIND OF GRASS?

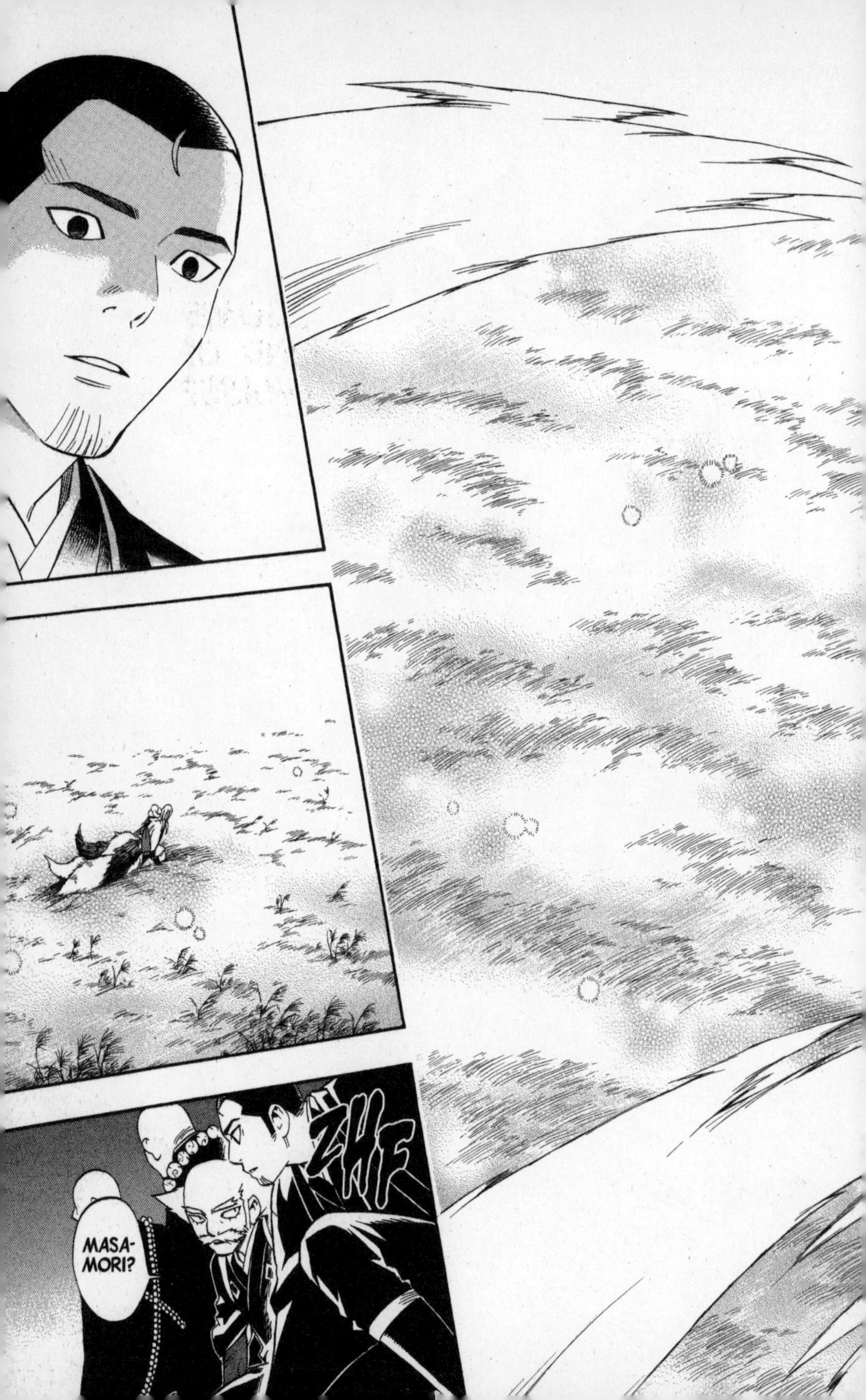
ZHF
MASA-
MORI?

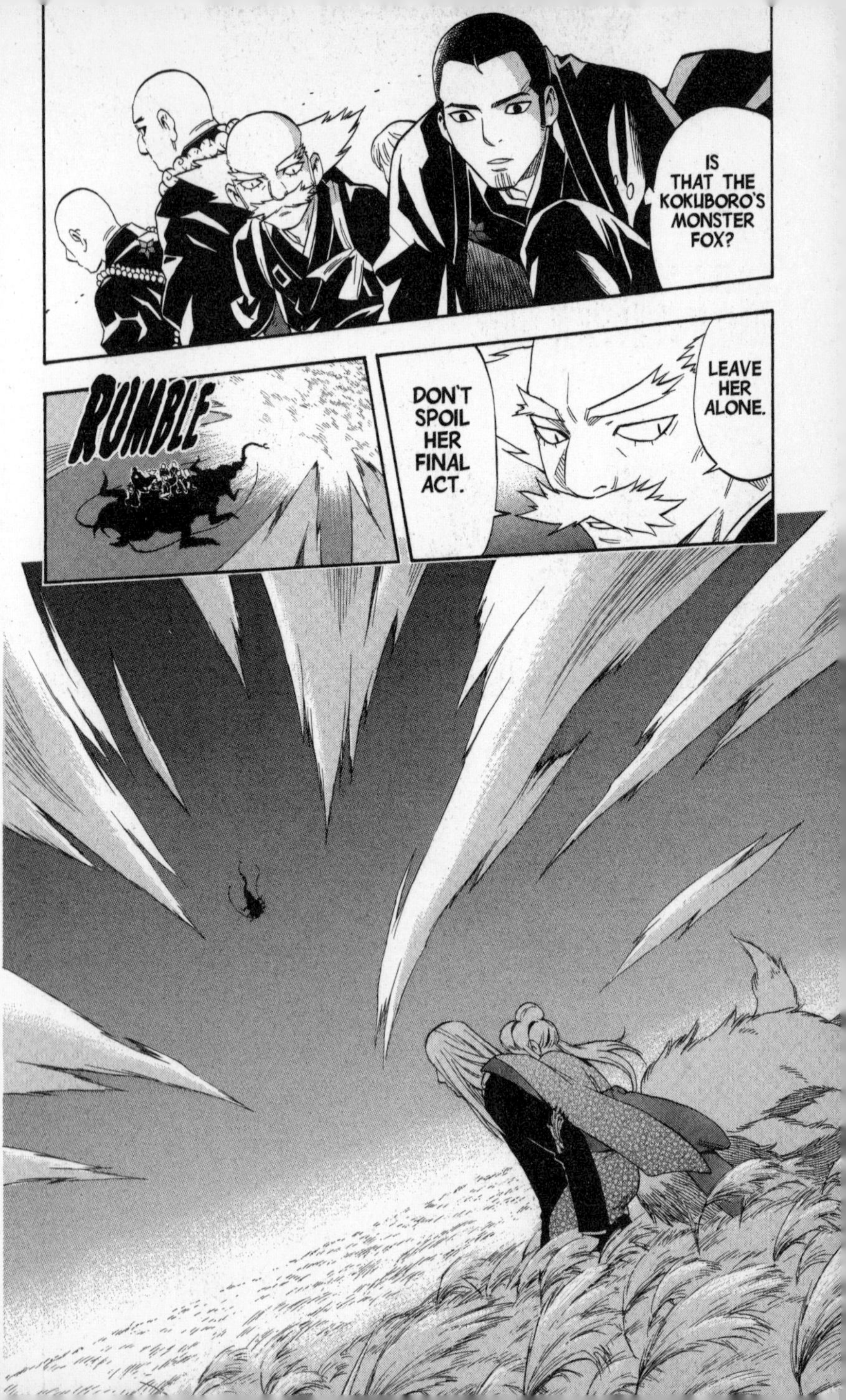
IS THAT THE KOKUBORO'S MONSTER FOX?
LEAVE HER ALONE.
DON'T SPOIL HER FINAL ACT.
RUMBLE

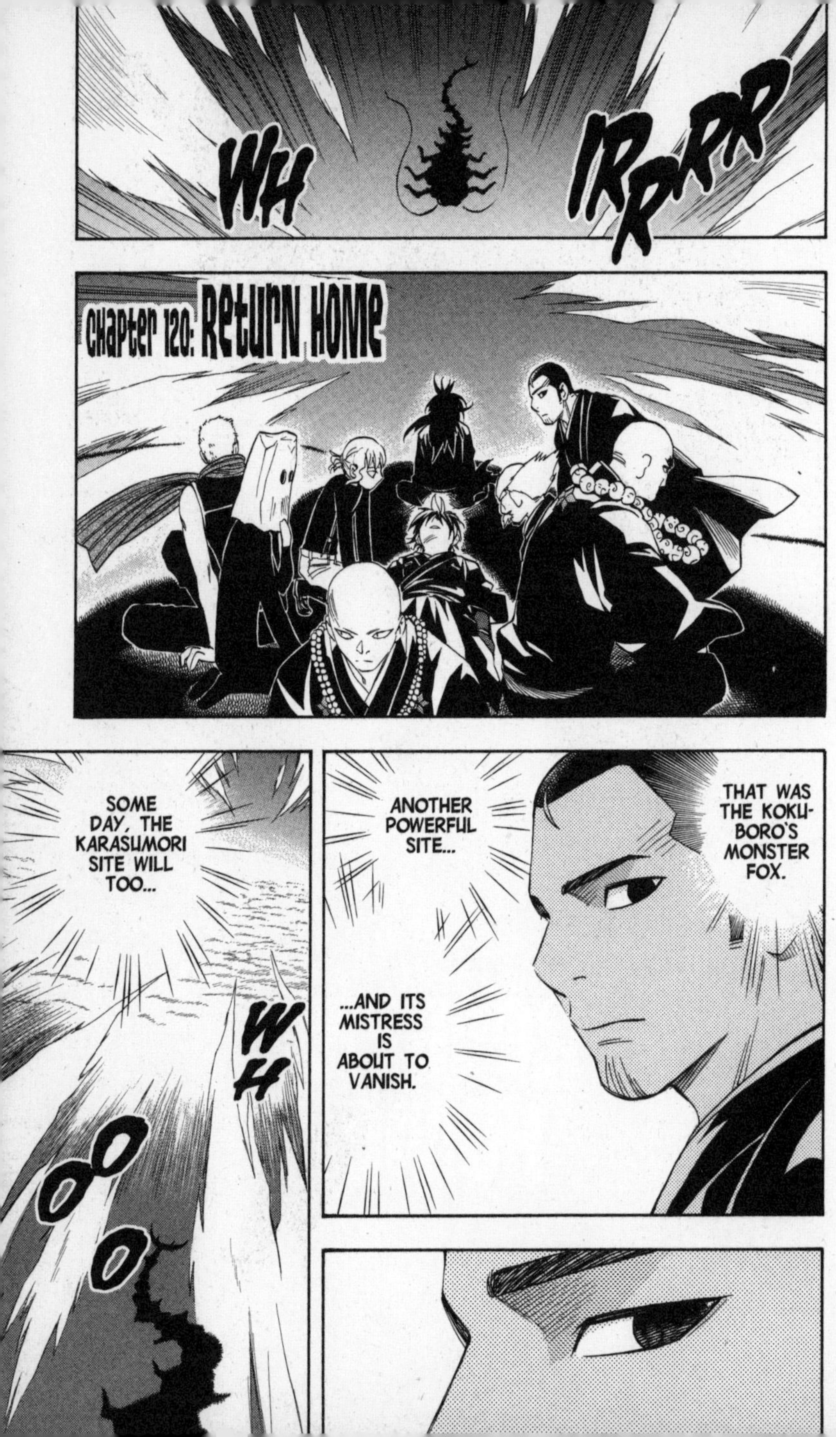
WH
IRRRRR
Chapter 120: Return Home
THAT WAS THE KOKU-BORO'S MONSTER FOX.
ANOTHER POWERFUL SITE...
...AND ITS MISTRESS IS ABOUT TO VANISH.
SOME DAY, THE KARASUMORI SITE WILL TOO...
WH
OOO

RETURN
HOME

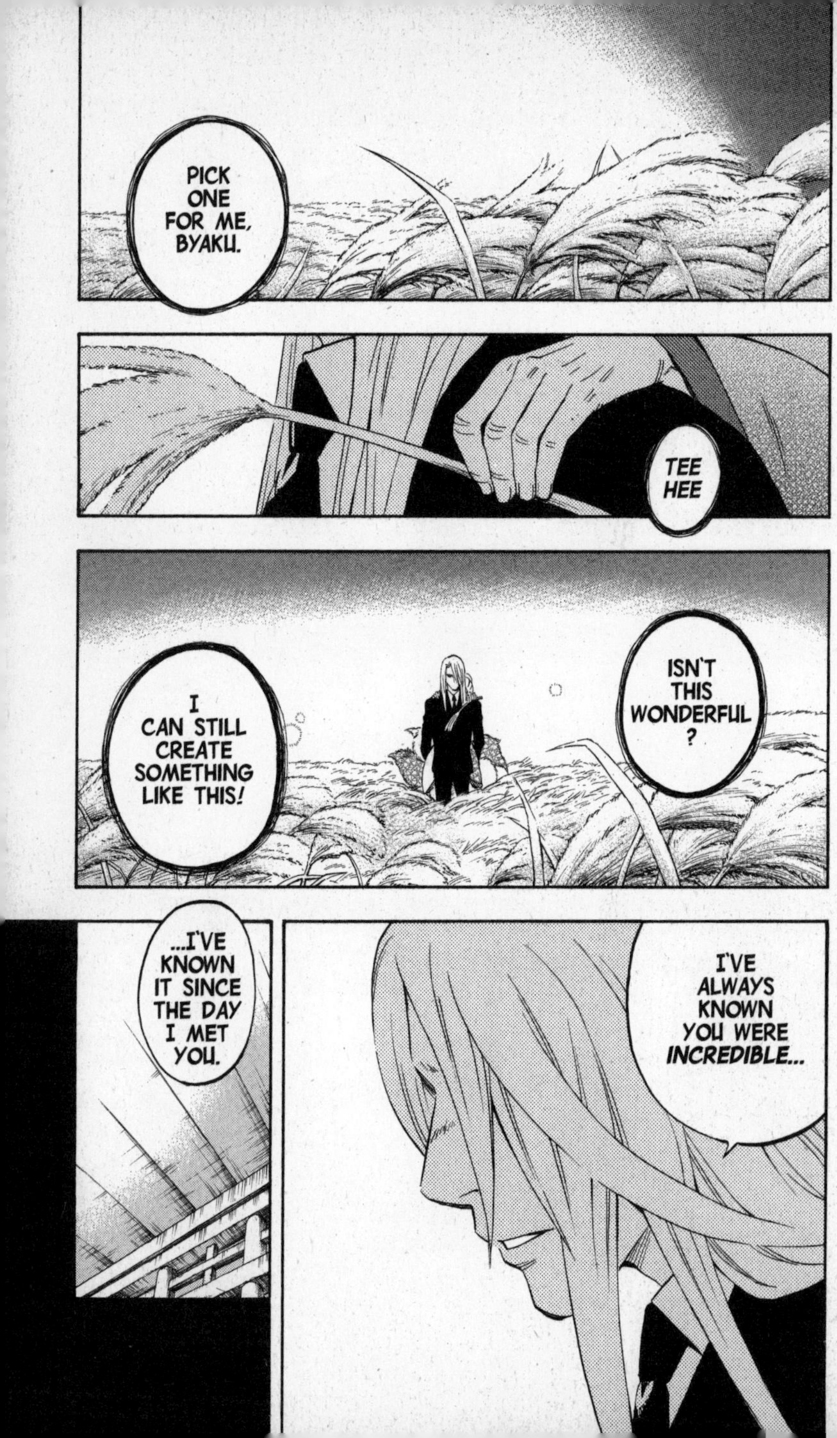
PICK ONE FOR ME, BYAKU.
TEE HEE
ISN'T THIS WONDERFUL?
I CAN STILL CREATE SOMETHING LIKE THIS!
I'VE ALWAYS KNOWN YOU WERE *INCREDIBLE...*
...I'VE KNOWN IT SINCE THE DAY I MET YOU.

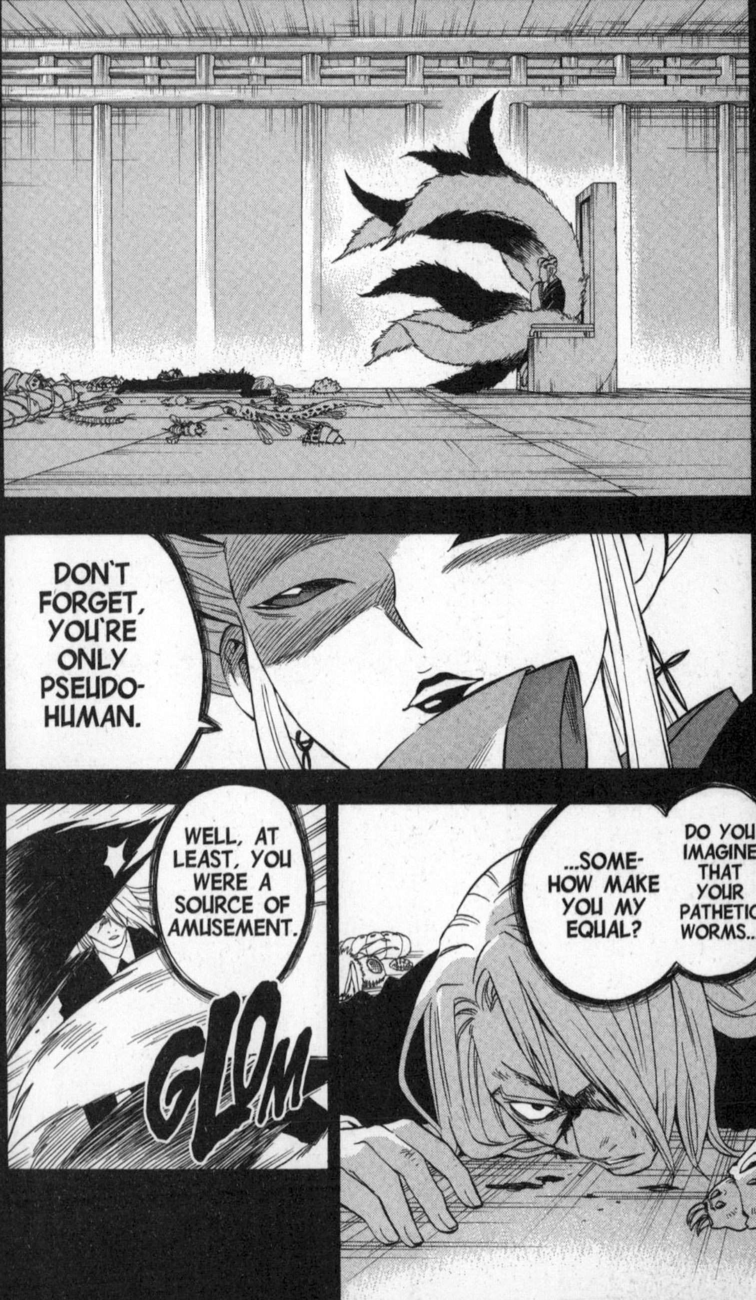
DON'T FORGET, YOU'RE ONLY PSEUDO-HUMAN.
DO YOU IMAGINE THAT YOUR PATHETIC WORMS...
...SOME-HOW MAKE YOU MY EQUAL?
WELL, AT LEAST, YOU WERE A SOURCE OF AMUSEMENT.
GLOM

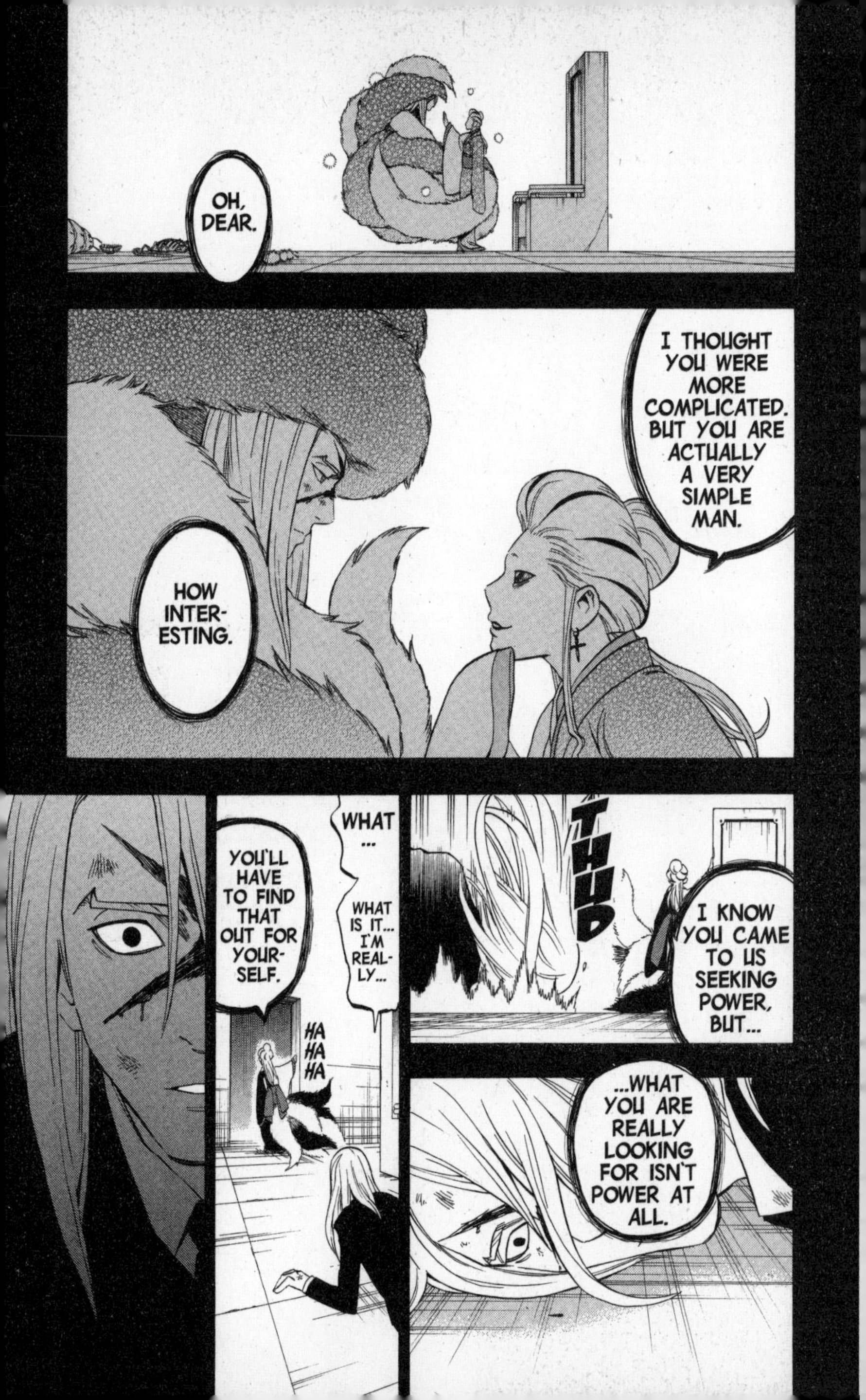
OH, DEAR.
I THOUGHT YOU WERE MORE COMPLICATED. BUT YOU ARE ACTUALLY A VERY SIMPLE MAN.
HOW INTER-ESTING.
THUD
I KNOW YOU CAME TO US SEEKING POWER, BUT...
...WHAT YOU ARE REALLY LOOKING FOR ISN'T POWER AT ALL.
WHAT ...
WHAT IS IT... I'M REAL-LY...
YOU'LL HAVE TO FIND THAT OUT FOR YOUR-SELF.
HA HA HA HA

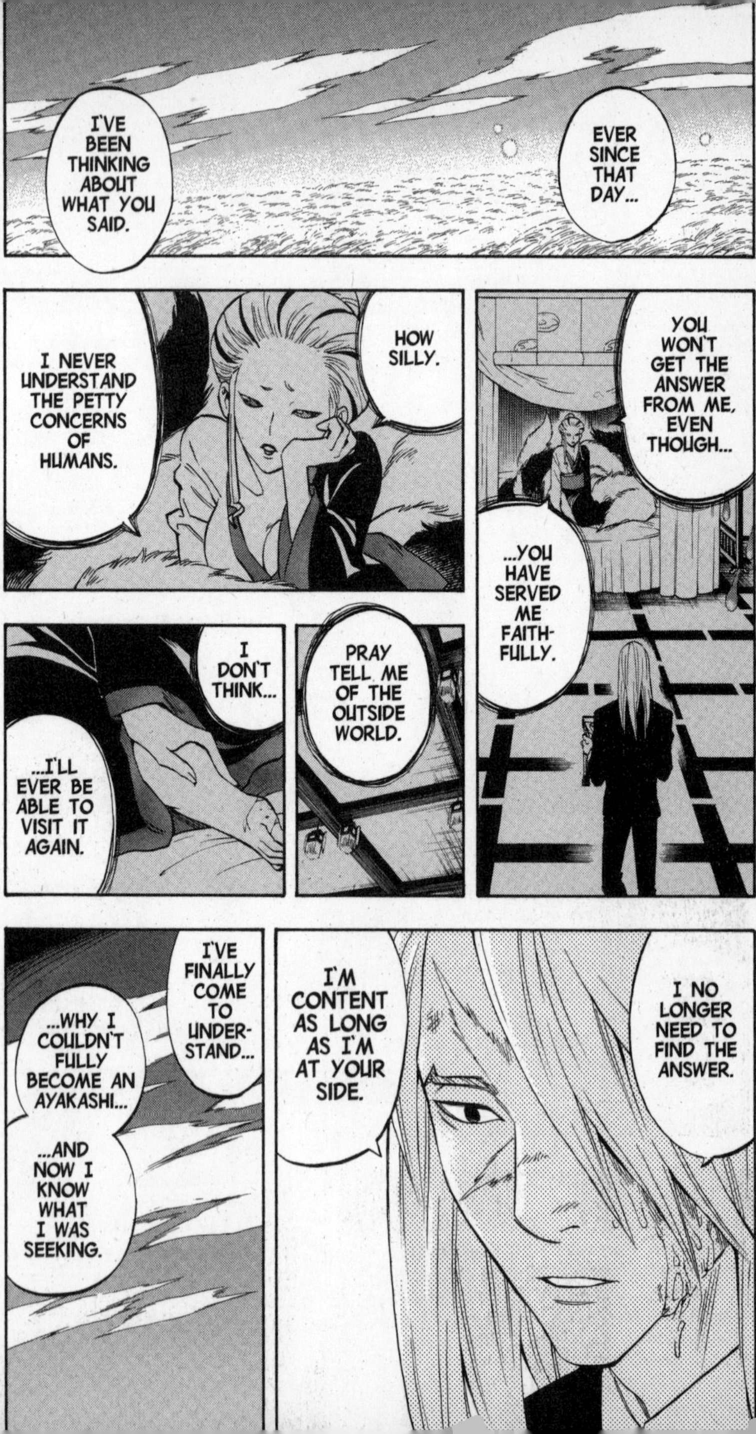
EVER SINCE THAT DAY...
I'VE BEEN THINKING ABOUT WHAT YOU SAID.
YOU WON'T GET THE ANSWER FROM ME, EVEN THOUGH...
...YOU HAVE SERVED ME FAITH-FULLY.
HOW SILLY.
I NEVER UNDERSTAND THE PETTY CONCERNS OF HUMANS.
PRAY TELL ME OF THE OUTSIDE WORLD.
I DON'T THINK...
...I'LL EVER BE ABLE TO VISIT IT AGAIN.
I NO LONGER NEED TO FIND THE ANSWER.
I'M CONTENT AS LONG AS I'M AT YOUR SIDE.
I'VE FINALLY COME TO UNDER-STAND...
...WHY I COULDN'T FULLY BECOME AN AYAKASHI...
...AND NOW I KNOW WHAT I WAS SEEKING.

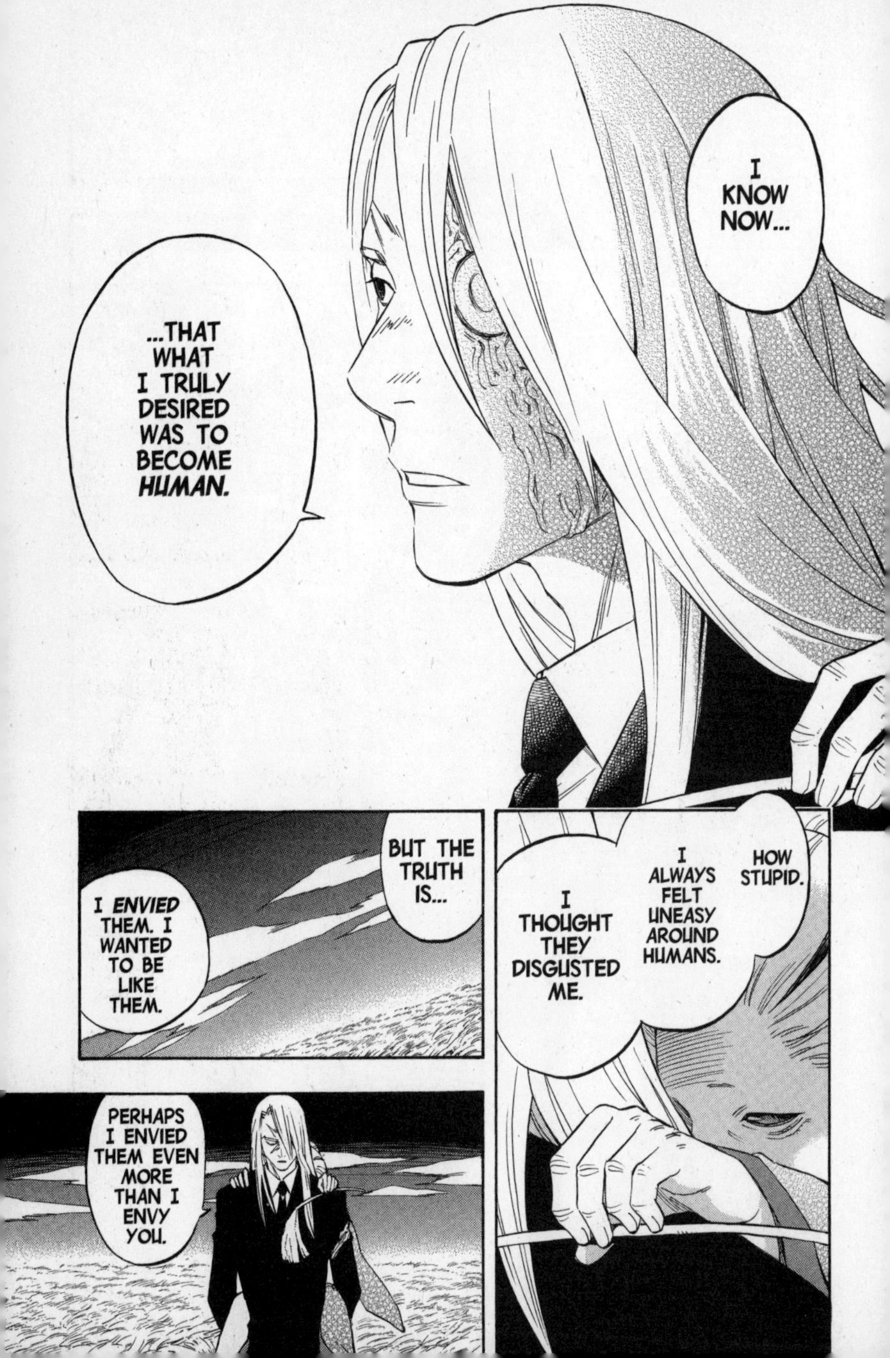
I KNOW NOW...
...THAT WHAT I TRULY DESIRED WAS TO BECOME *HUMAN*.
HOW STUPID.
I ALWAYS FELT UNEASY AROUND HUMANS.
I THOUGHT THEY DISGUSTED ME.
BUT THE TRUTH IS...
I *ENVIED* THEM. I WANTED TO BE LIKE THEM.
PERHAPS I ENVIED THEM EVEN MORE THAN I ENVY YOU.

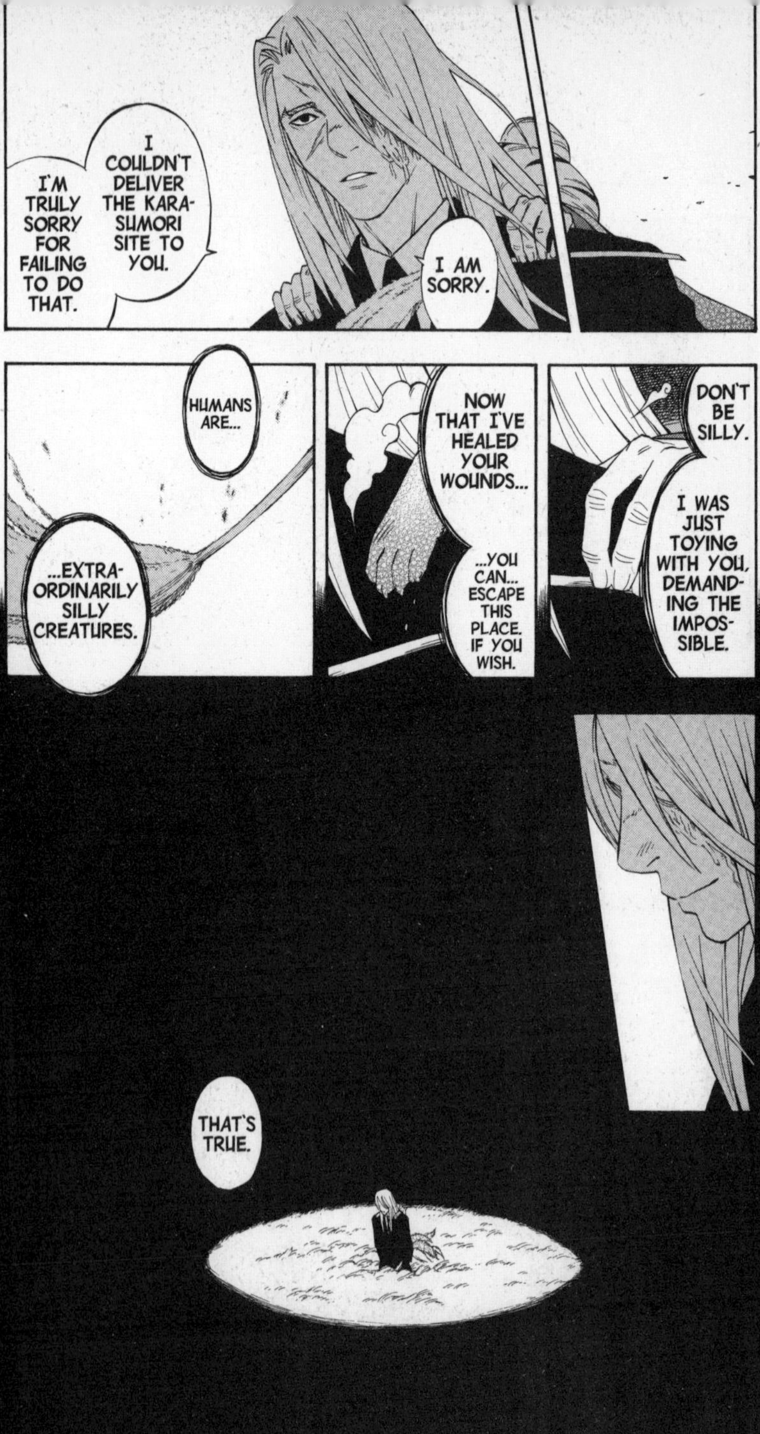
I AM SORRY.
I COULDN'T DELIVER THE KARA-SUMORI SITE TO YOU.
I'M TRULY SORRY FOR FAILING TO DO THAT.
DON'T BE SILLY.
I WAS JUST TOYING WITH YOU, DEMAND-ING THE IMPOS-SIBLE.
NOW THAT I'VE HEALED YOUR WOUNDS...
...YOU CAN... ESCAPE THIS PLACE. IF YOU WISH.
HUMANS ARE...
...EXTRA-ORDINARILY SILLY CREATURES.
THAT'S TRUE.

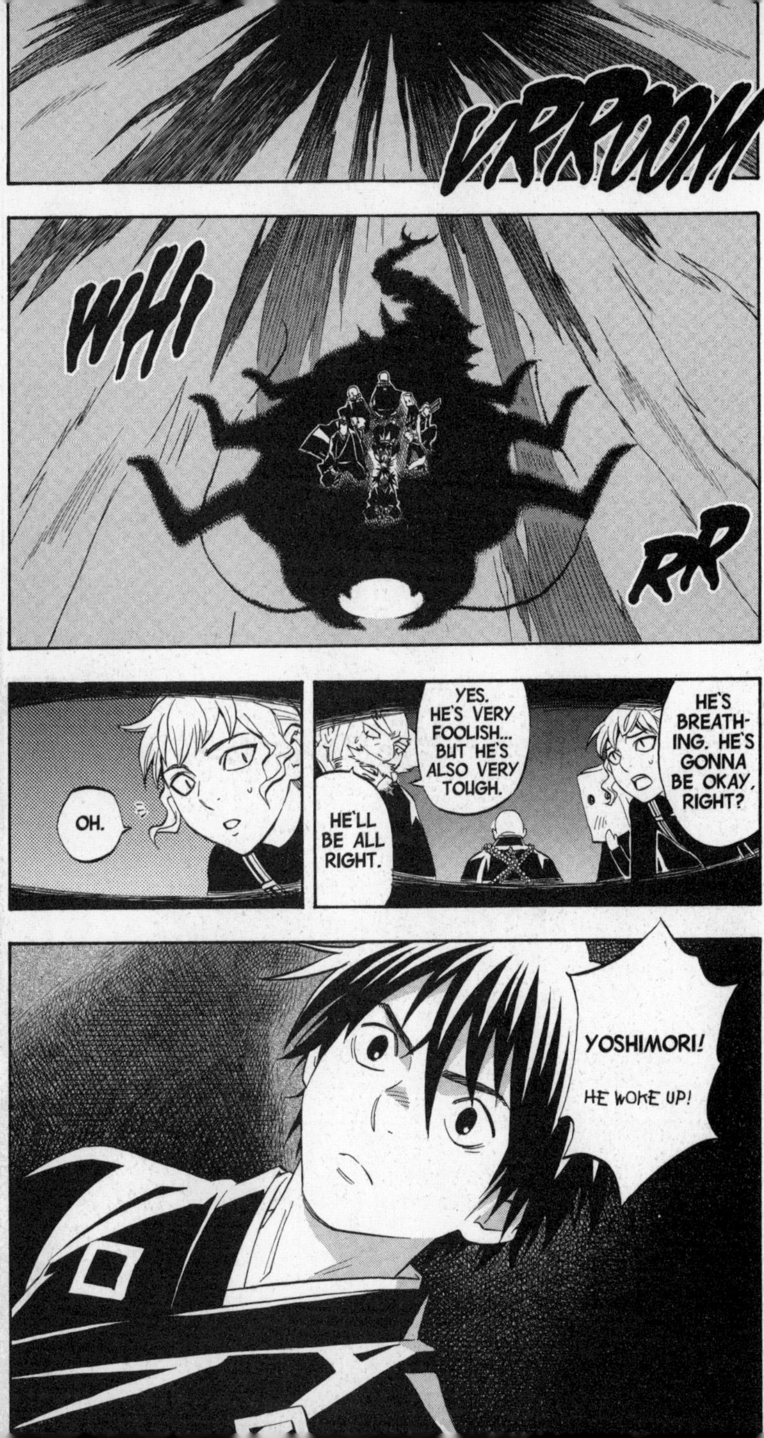
VRRROOM
WHI
RR
HE'S BREATHING. HE'S GONNA BE OKAY, RIGHT?
YES. HE'S VERY FOOLISH... BUT HE'S ALSO VERY TOUGH.
HE'LL BE ALL RIGHT.
OH.
YOSHIMORI!
HE WOKE UP!

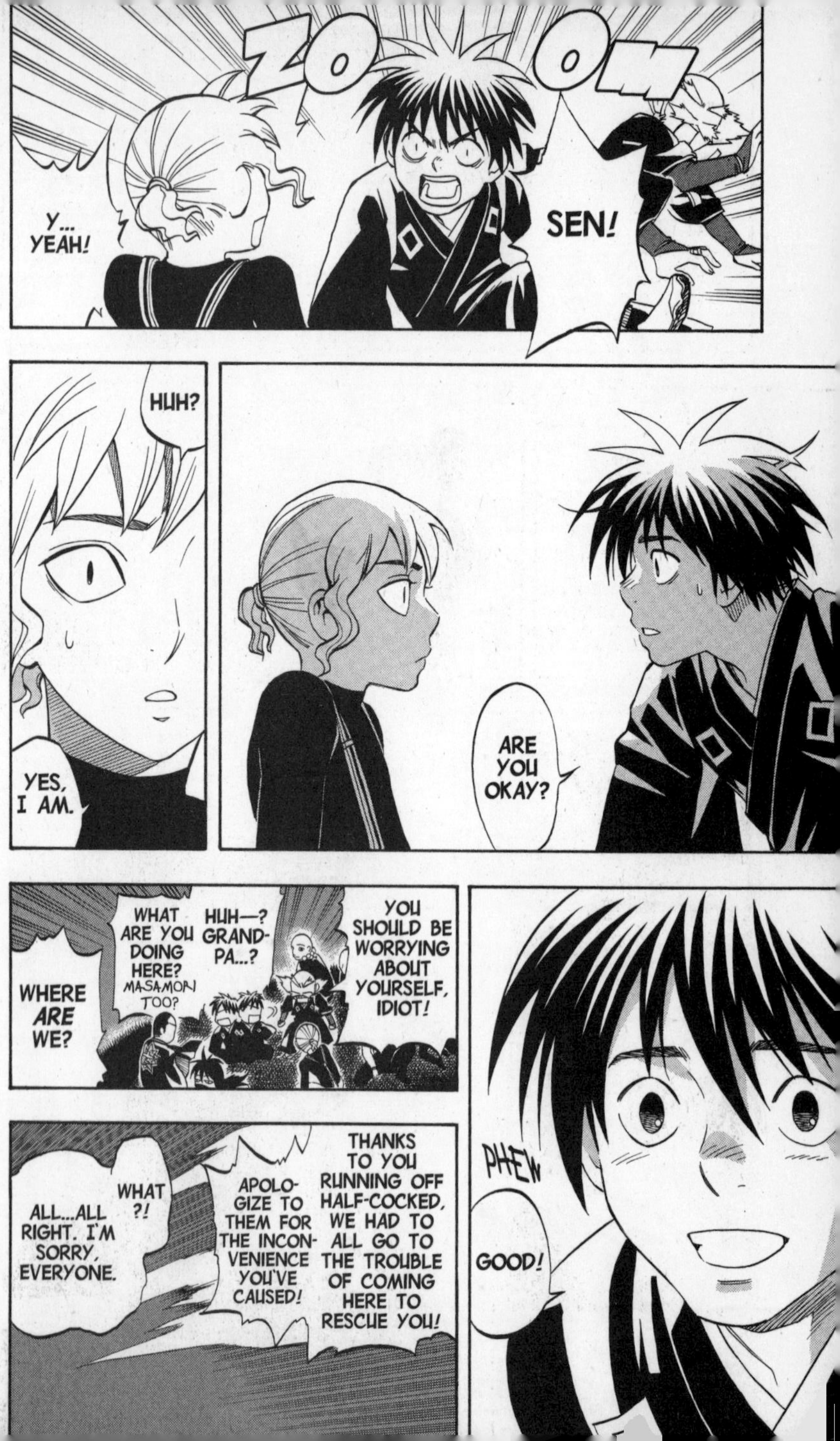
ZOOM
SEN!
Y... YEAH!
ARE YOU OKAY?
HUH?
YES, I AM.
PHEW
GOOD!
YOU SHOULD BE WORRYING ABOUT YOURSELF, IDIOT!
HUH—? GRANDPA...?
WHAT ARE YOU DOING HERE?
MASAMORI TOO?
WHERE *ARE* WE?
THANKS TO YOU RUNNING OFF HALF-COCKED, WE HAD TO ALL GO TO THE TROUBLE OF COMING HERE TO RESCUE YOU!
APOLOGIZE TO THEM FOR THE INCONVENIENCE YOU'VE CAUSED!
WHAT?!
ALL...ALL RIGHT. I'M SORRY, EVERYONE.

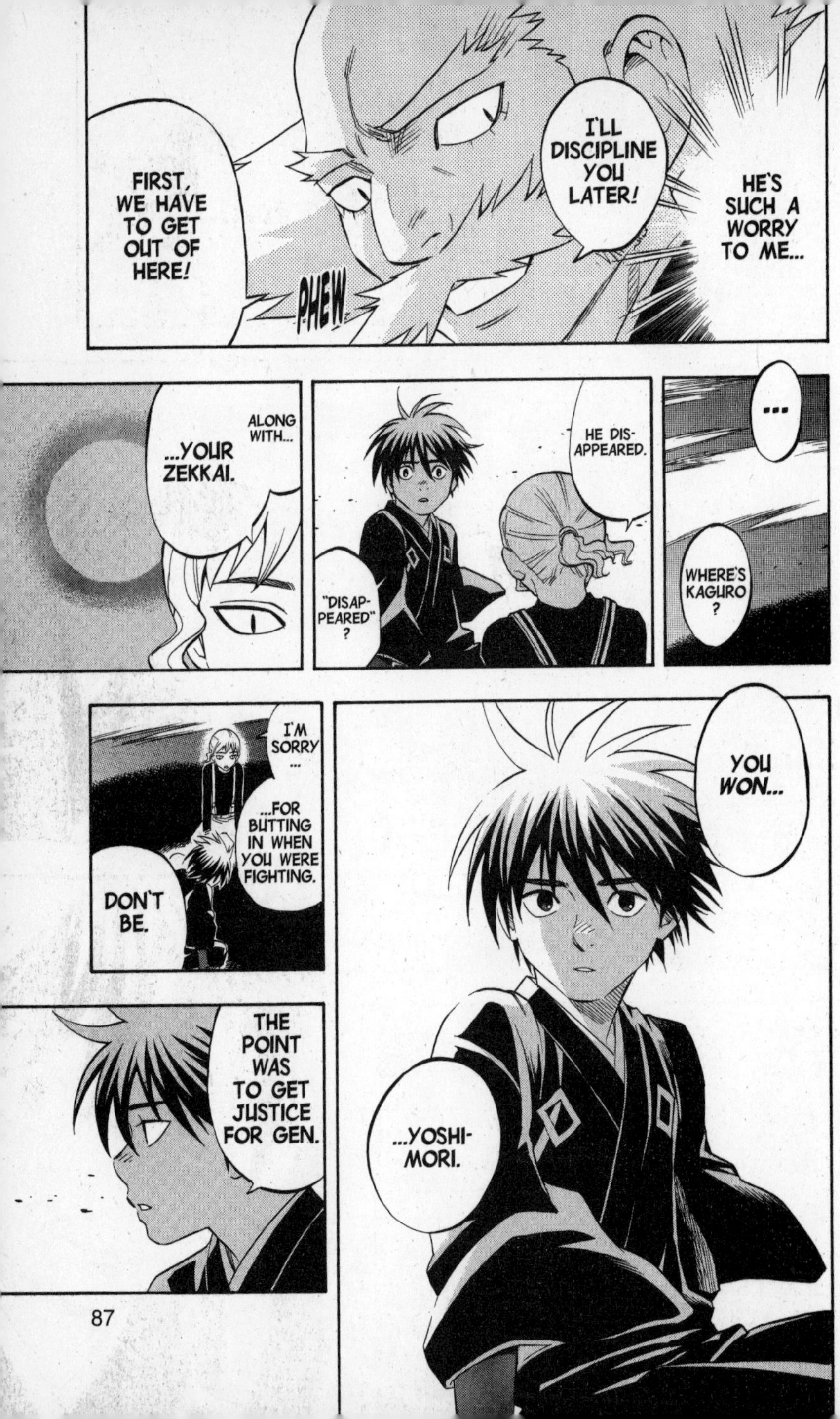
HE'S SUCH A WORRY TO ME...
I'LL DISCIPLINE YOU LATER!
PHEW
FIRST, WE HAVE TO GET OUT OF HERE!
...
WHERE'S KAGURO?
HE DIS-APPEARED.
"DISAP-PEARED"?
ALONG WITH...
...YOUR ZEKKAI.
YOU WON...
...YOSHI-MORI.
I'M SORRY...
...FOR BUTTING IN WHEN YOU WERE FIGHTING.
DON'T BE.
THE POINT WAS TO GET JUSTICE FOR GEN.

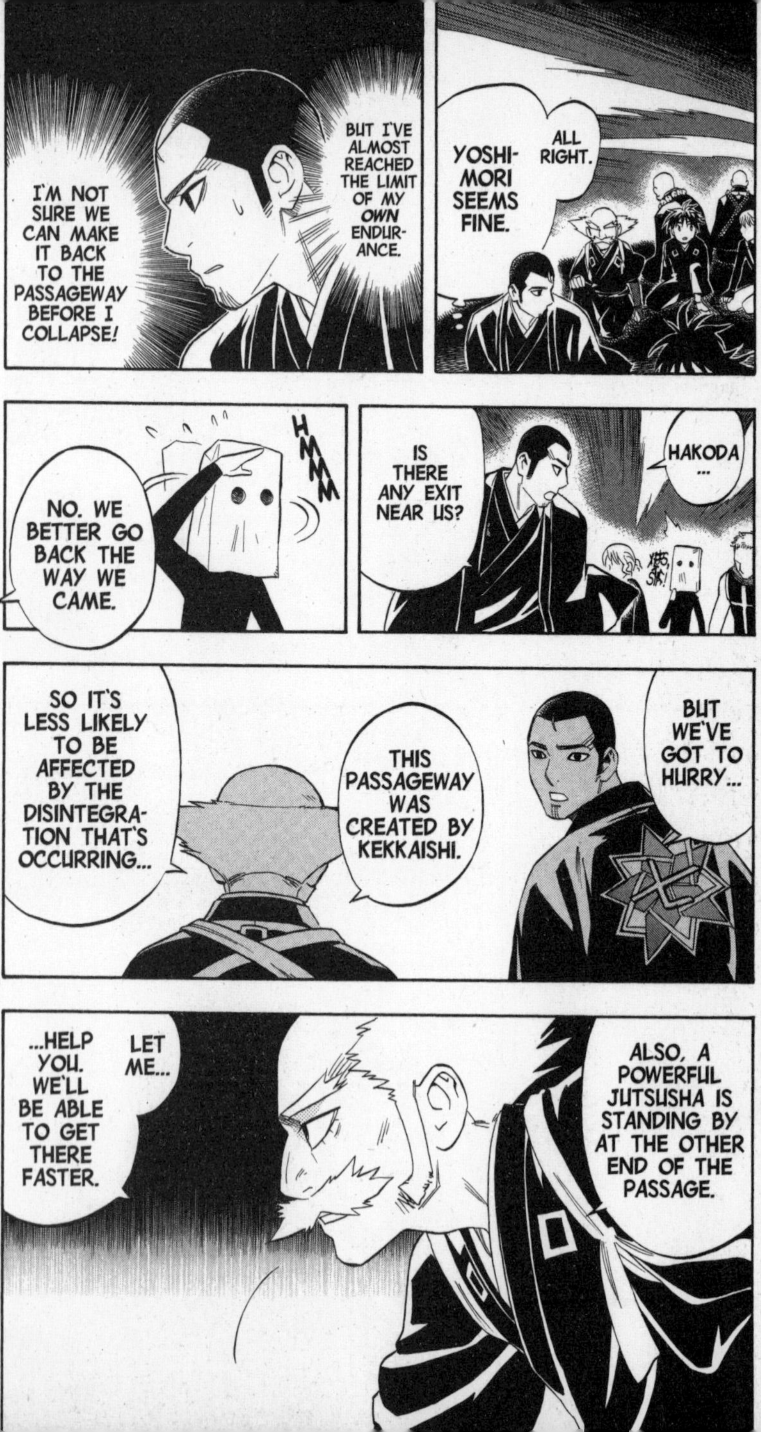
ALL RIGHT.
YOSHIMORI SEEMS FINE.
BUT I'VE ALMOST REACHED THE LIMIT OF MY *OWN* ENDURANCE.
I'M NOT SURE WE CAN MAKE IT BACK TO THE PASSAGEWAY BEFORE I COLLAPSE!
HAKODA ...
IS THERE ANY EXIT NEAR US?
HMMM
NO. WE BETTER GO BACK THE WAY WE CAME.
BUT WE'VE GOT TO HURRY...
THIS PASSAGEWAY WAS CREATED BY KEKKAISHI.
SO IT'S LESS LIKELY TO BE AFFECTED BY THE DISINTEGRATION THAT'S OCCURRING...
ALSO, A POWERFUL JUTSUSHA IS STANDING BY AT THE OTHER END OF THE PASSAGE.
LET ME...
...HELP YOU. WE'LL BE ABLE TO GET THERE FASTER.

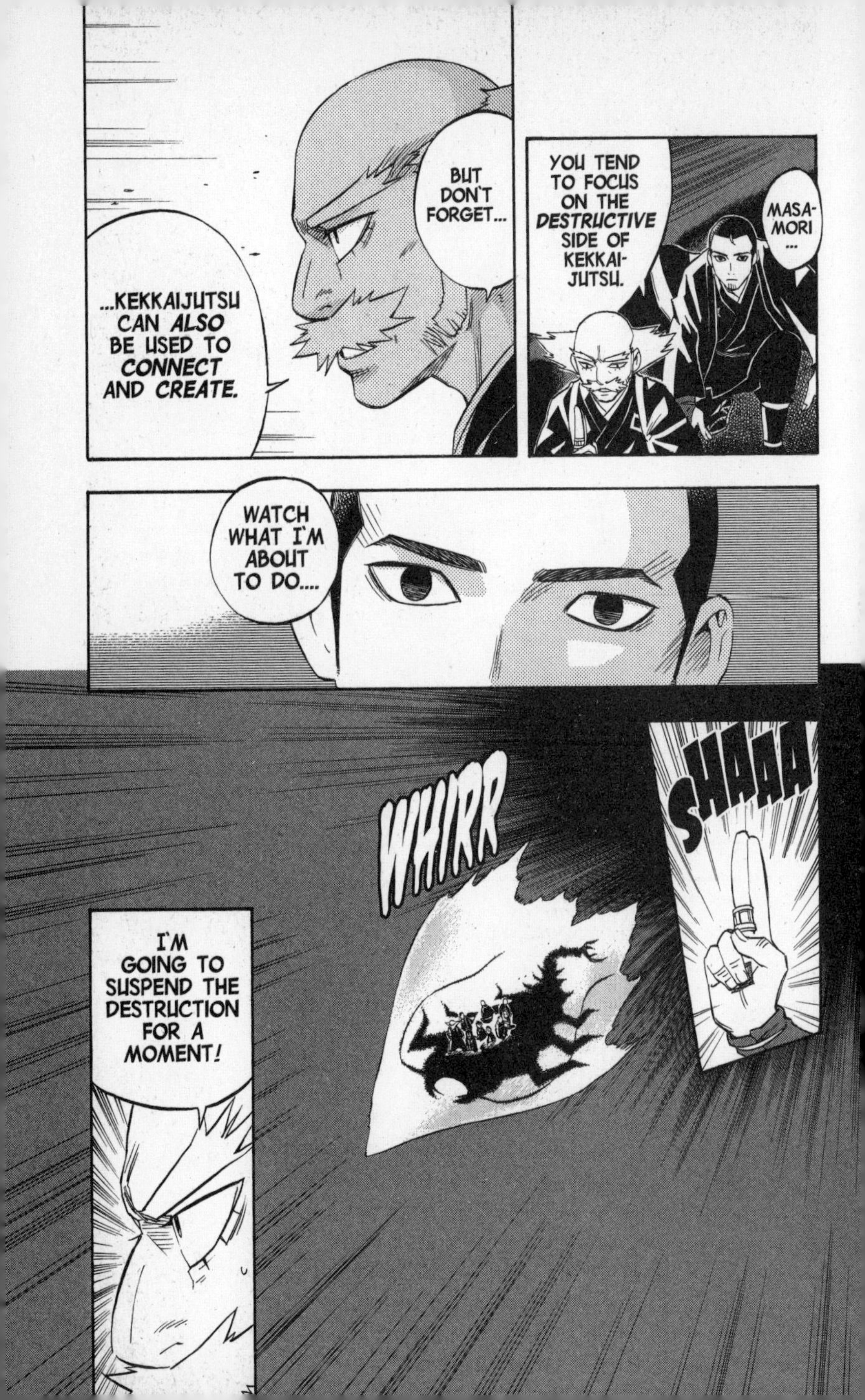
MASAMORI...
YOU TEND TO FOCUS ON THE DESTRUCTIVE SIDE OF KEKKAIJUTSU.
BUT DON'T FORGET...
...KEKKAIJUTSU CAN ALSO BE USED TO CONNECT AND CREATE.
WATCH WHAT I'M ABOUT TO DO....
SHAAA
WHIRR
I'M GOING TO SUSPEND THE DESTRUCTION FOR A MOMENT!

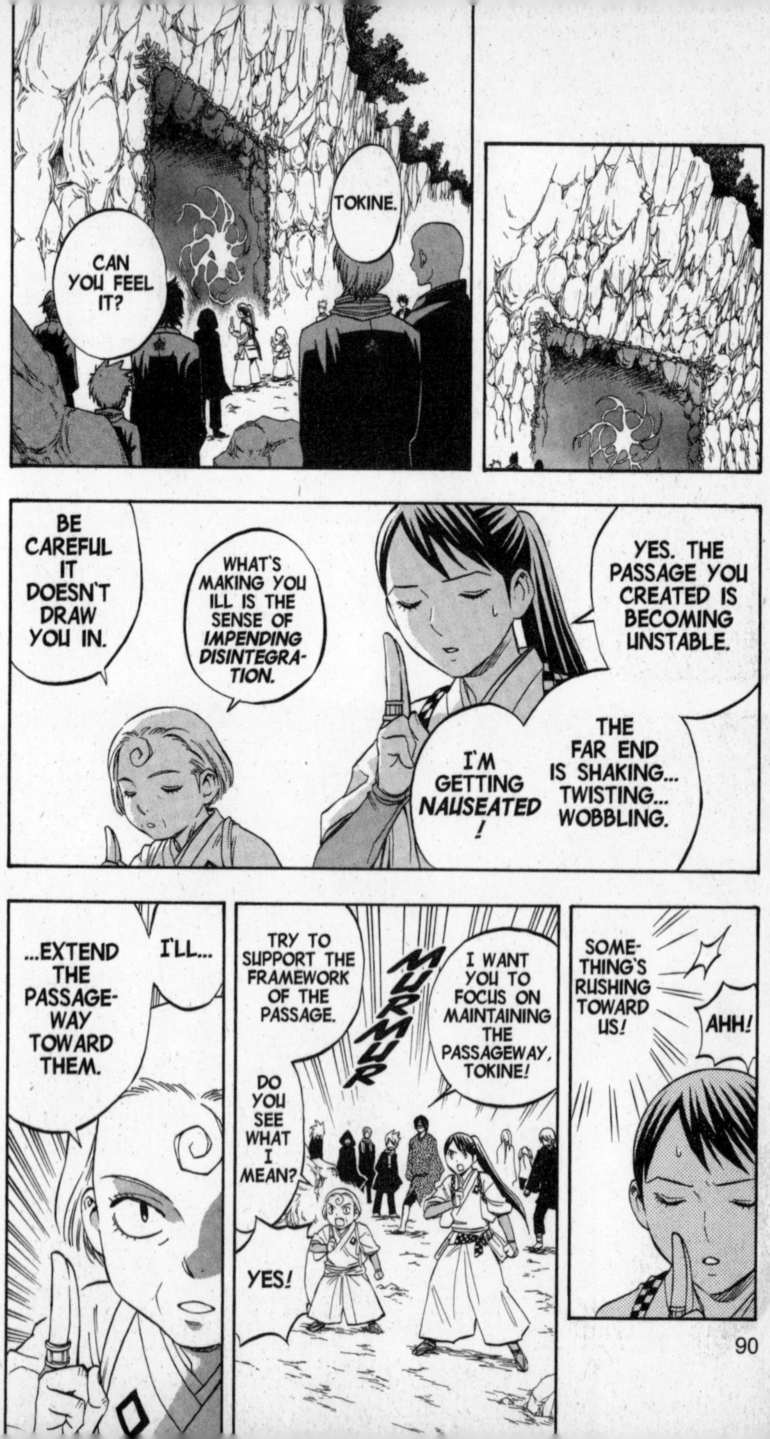
TOKINE.
CAN YOU FEEL IT?
YES. THE PASSAGE YOU CREATED IS BECOMING UNSTABLE.
THE FAR END IS SHAKING... TWISTING... WOBBLING.
I'M GETTING NAUSEATED!
WHAT'S MAKING YOU ILL IS THE SENSE OF IMPENDING DISINTEGRATION.
BE CAREFUL IT DOESN'T DRAW YOU IN.
AHH!
SOMETHING'S RUSHING TOWARD US!
I WANT YOU TO FOCUS ON MAINTAINING THE PASSAGEWAY, TOKINE!
MURMUR
TRY TO SUPPORT THE FRAMEWORK OF THE PASSAGE.
DO YOU SEE WHAT I MEAN?
YES!
I'LL...
...EXTEND THE PASSAGEWAY TOWARD THEM.

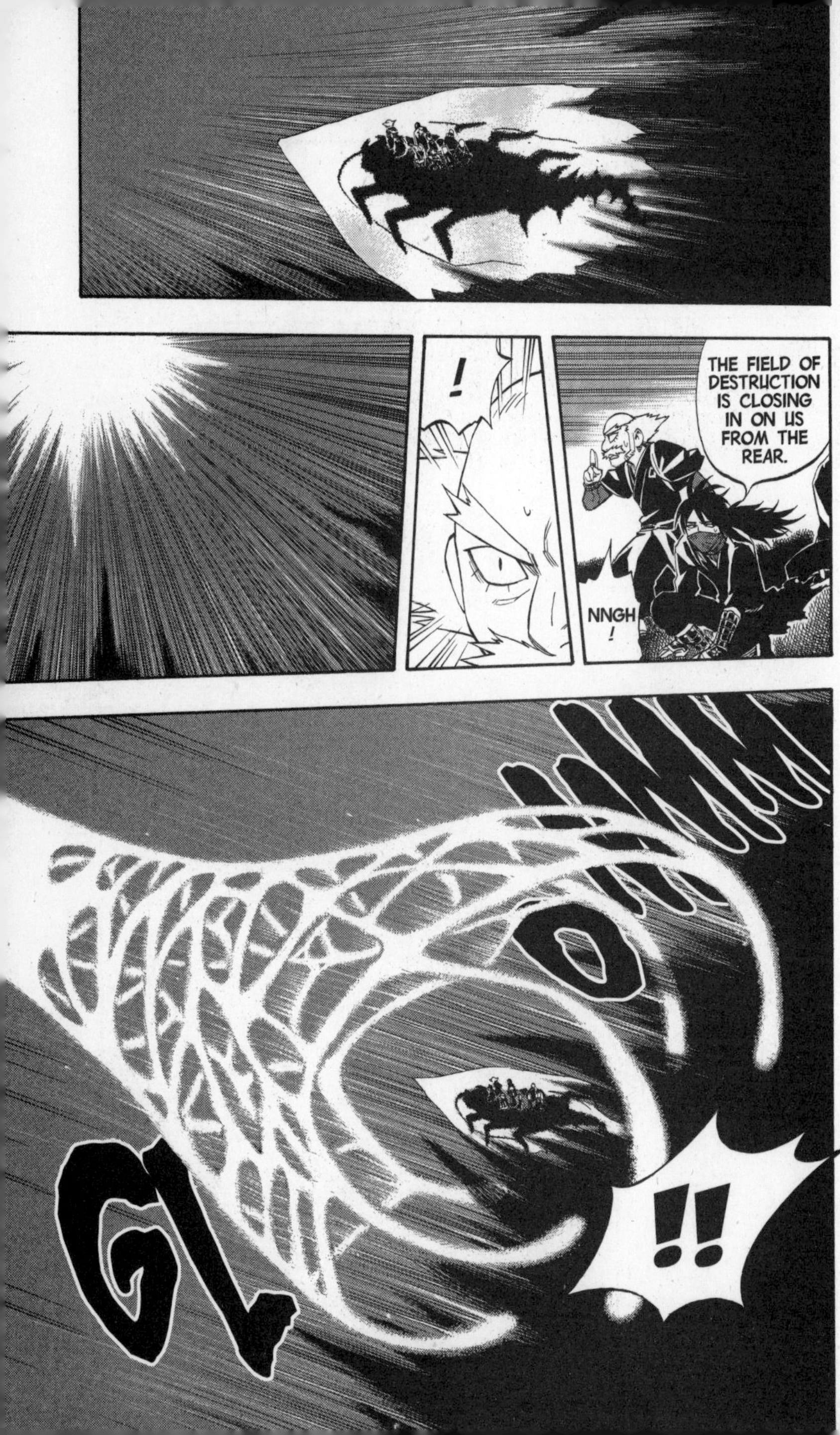
THE FIELD OF DESTRUCTION IS CLOSING IN ON US FROM THE REAR.
NNGH!
!
!!

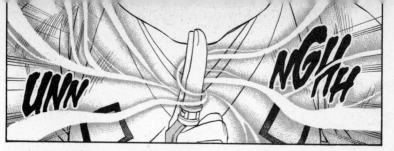

NGHHH
UNN
GRANDMA IS AMAZINGLY POWERFUL!
HER ENERGY IS ALMOST OVER-WHELMING!
SHA
STAY BACK, EVERYONE!

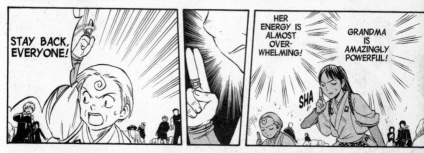

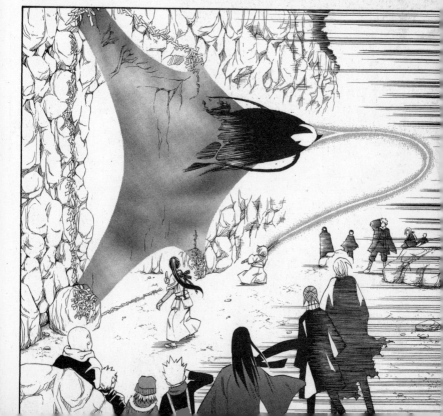

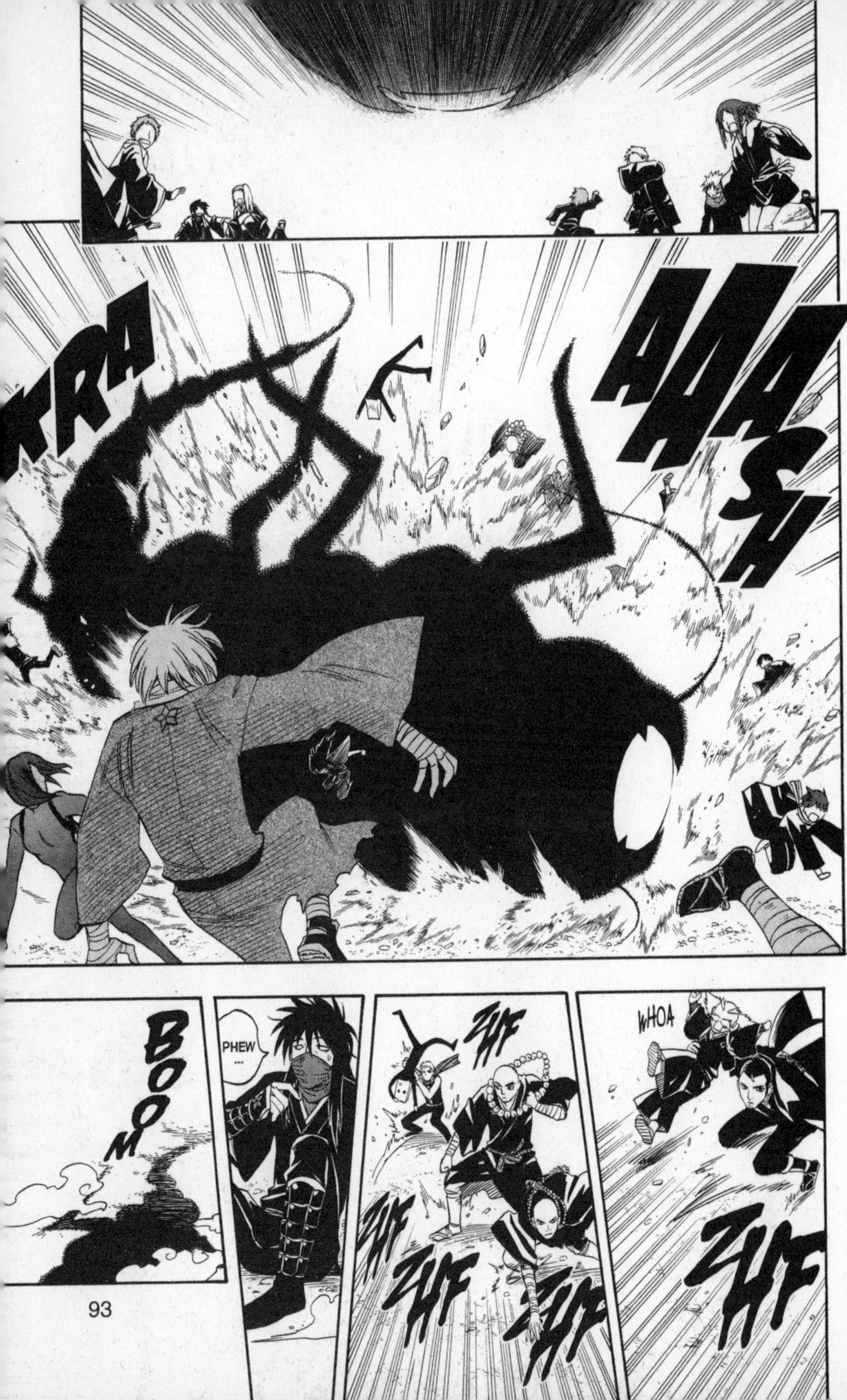
KRA
AAASH
WHOA
ZHF
ZHF
ZHF
ZHF
ZHF
PHEW ...
BOOM

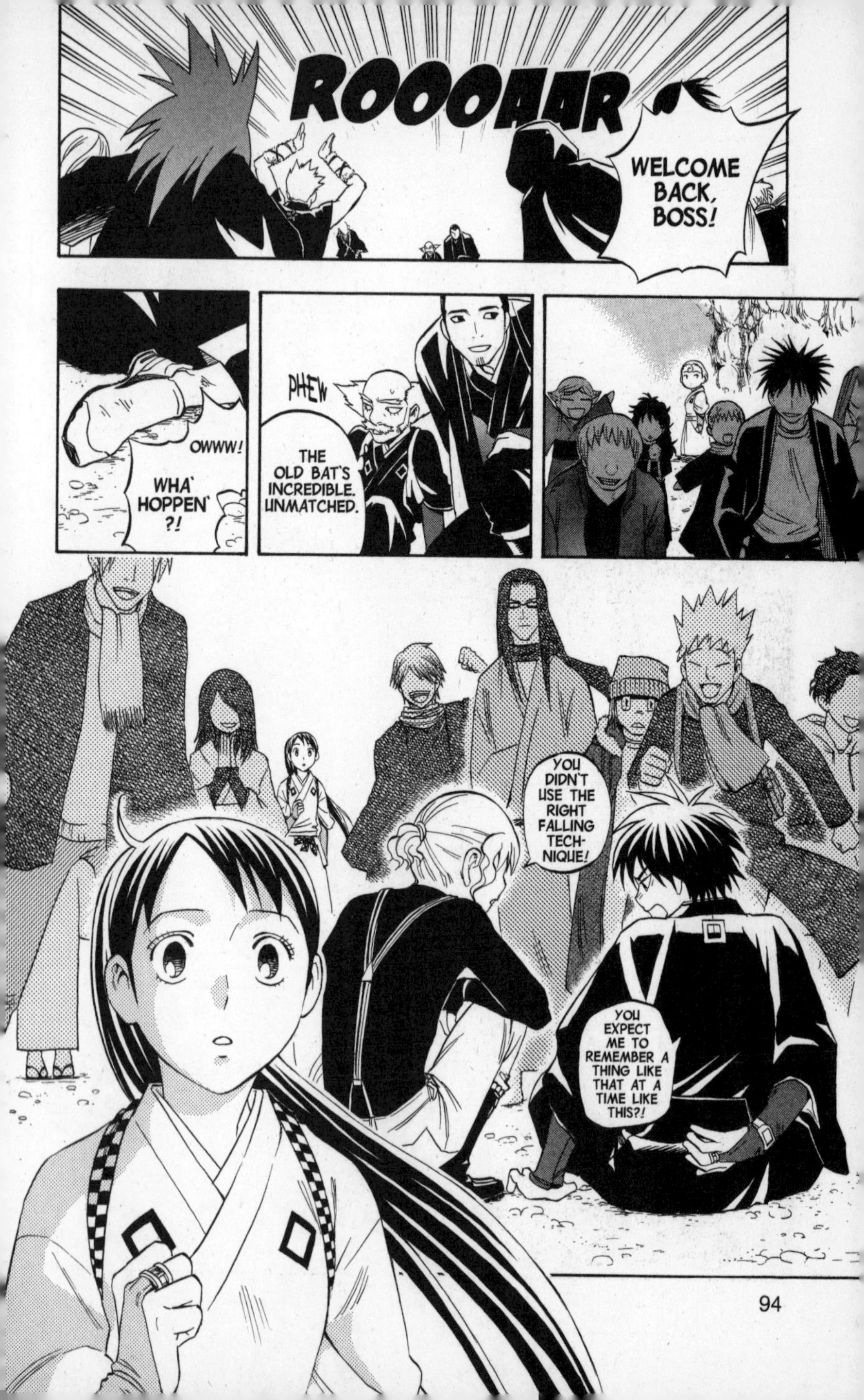
ROOOAAR
WELCOME BACK, BOSS!
PHEW
THE OLD BAT'S INCREDIBLE. UNMATCHED.
OWWW!
WHA' HOPPEN' ?!
YOU DIDN'T USE THE RIGHT FALLING TECH-NIQUE!
YOU EXPECT ME TO REMEMBER A THING LIKE THAT AT A TIME LIKE THIS?!

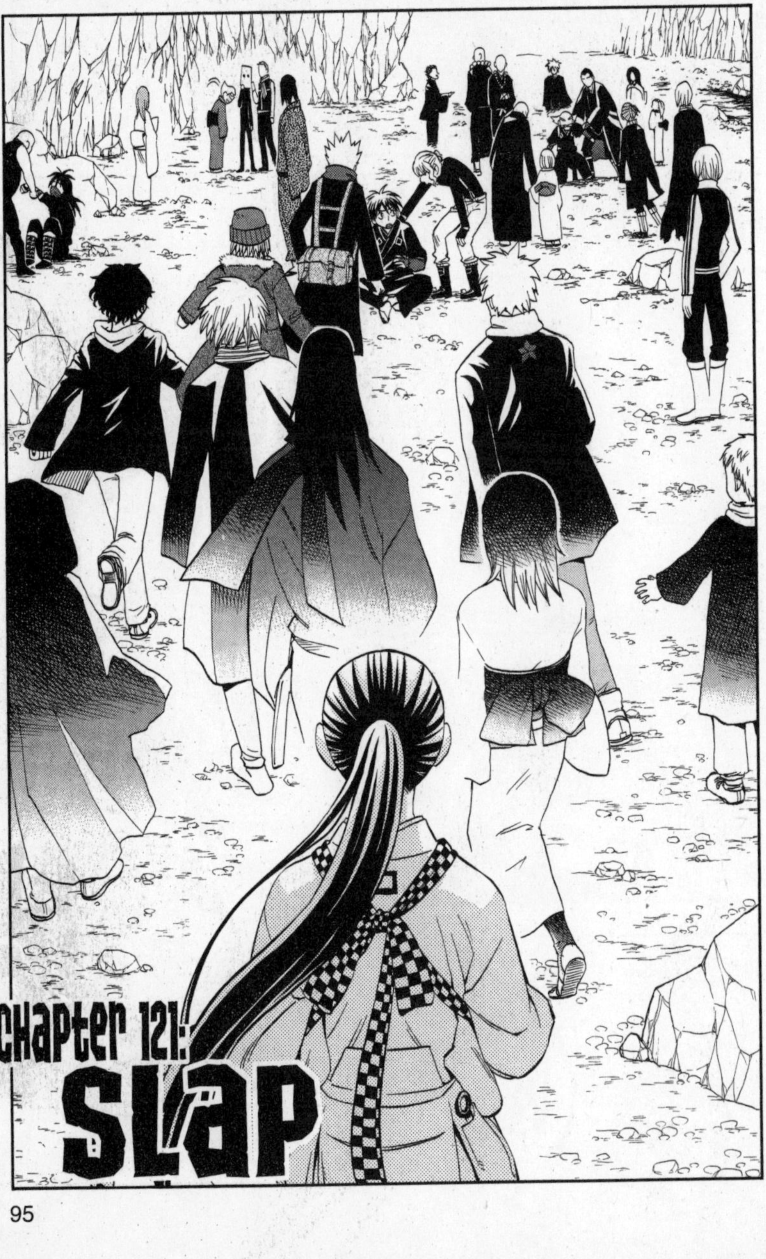
Chapter 121:
Slap

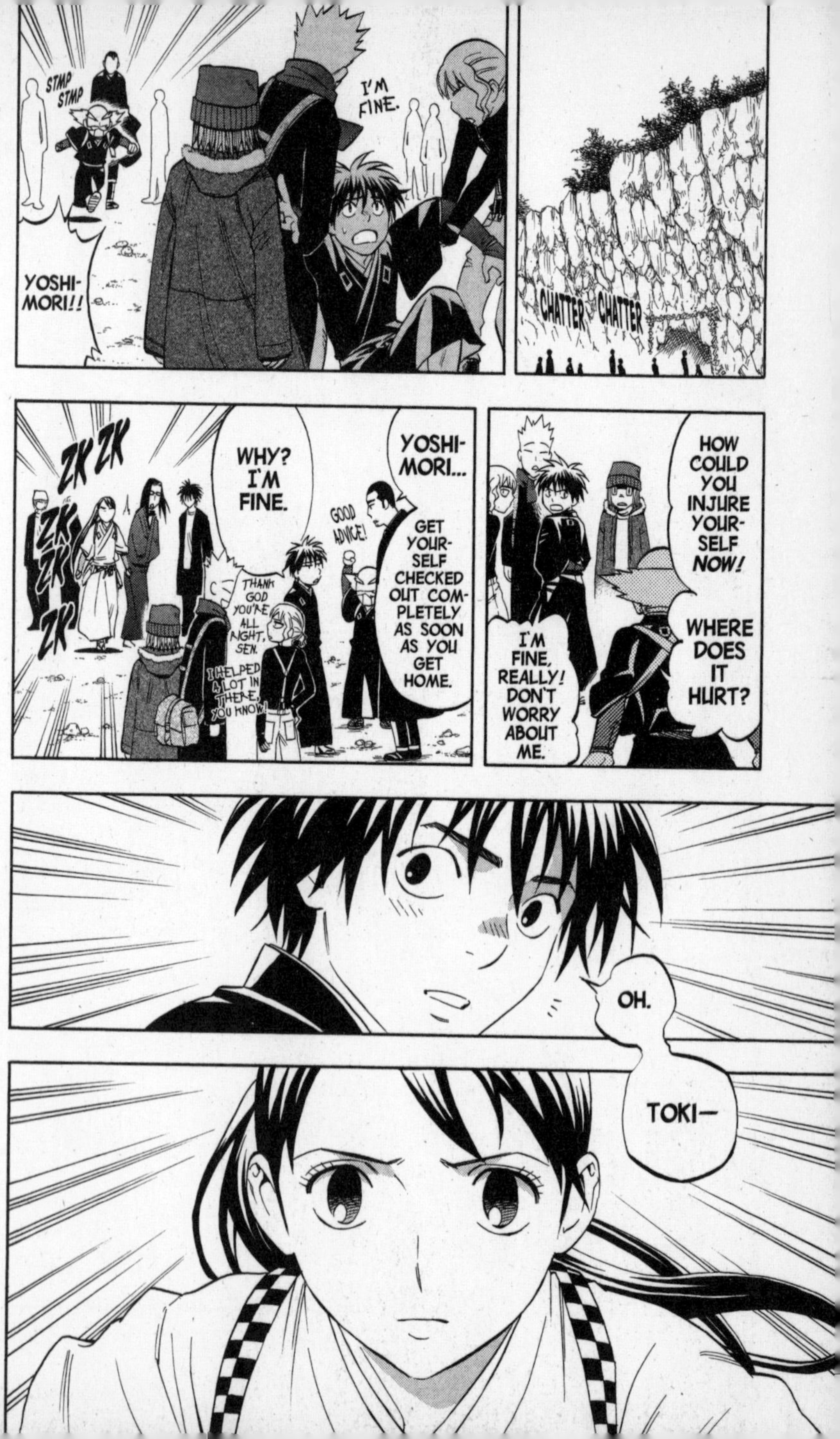
CHATTER CHATTER
I'M FINE.
STMP STMP
YOSHI-MORI!!
HOW COULD YOU INJURE YOURSELF NOW!
WHERE DOES IT HURT?
I'M FINE, REALLY! DON'T WORRY ABOUT ME.
YOSHI-MORI...
GET YOURSELF CHECKED OUT COMPLETELY AS SOON AS YOU GET HOME.
GOOD ADVICE!
WHY? I'M FINE.
ZK ZK ZK ZK ZK
THANK GOD YOU'RE ALL RIGHT, SEN.
I HELPED A LOT IN THERE, YOU KNOW!
OH.
TOKI—

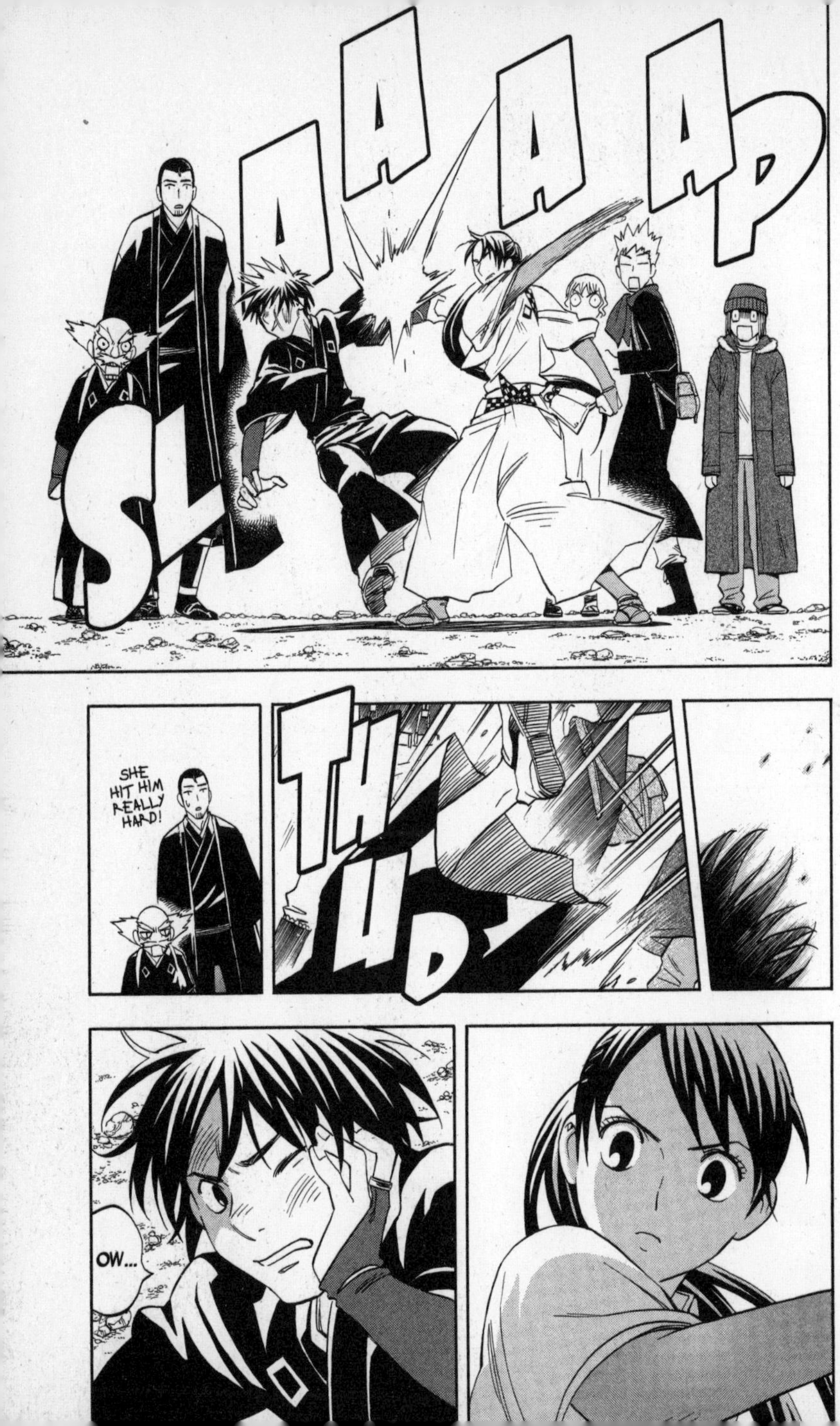
SLAAAAP
THUD
SHE HIT HIM REALLY HARD!
OW...

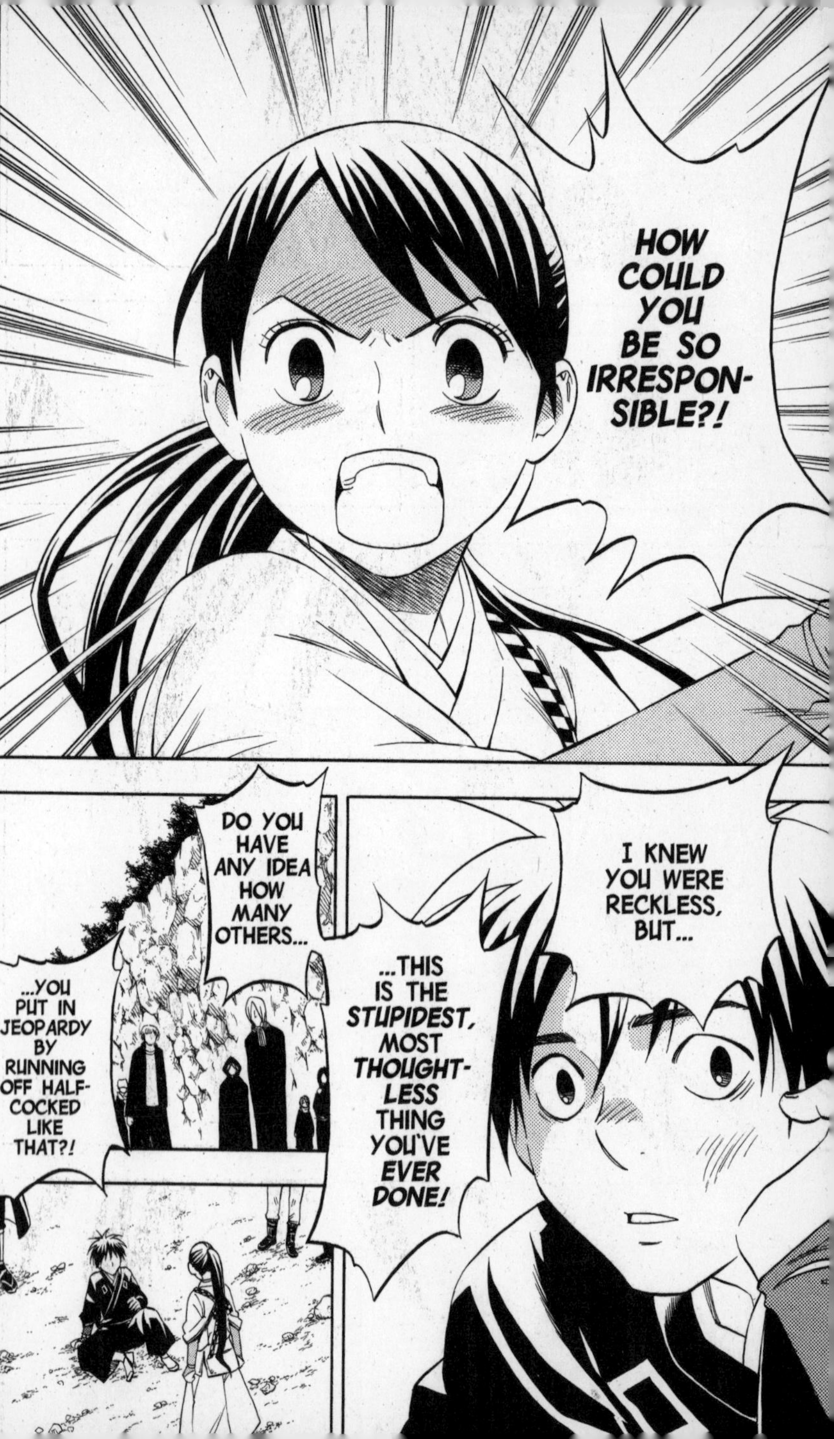
HOW COULD YOU BE SO IRRESPONSIBLE?!
I KNEW YOU WERE RECKLESS, BUT...
...THIS IS THE STUPIDEST, MOST THOUGHTLESS THING YOU'VE EVER DONE!
DO YOU HAVE ANY IDEA HOW MANY OTHERS...
...YOU PUT IN JEOPARDY BY RUNNING OFF HALF-COCKED LIKE THAT?!

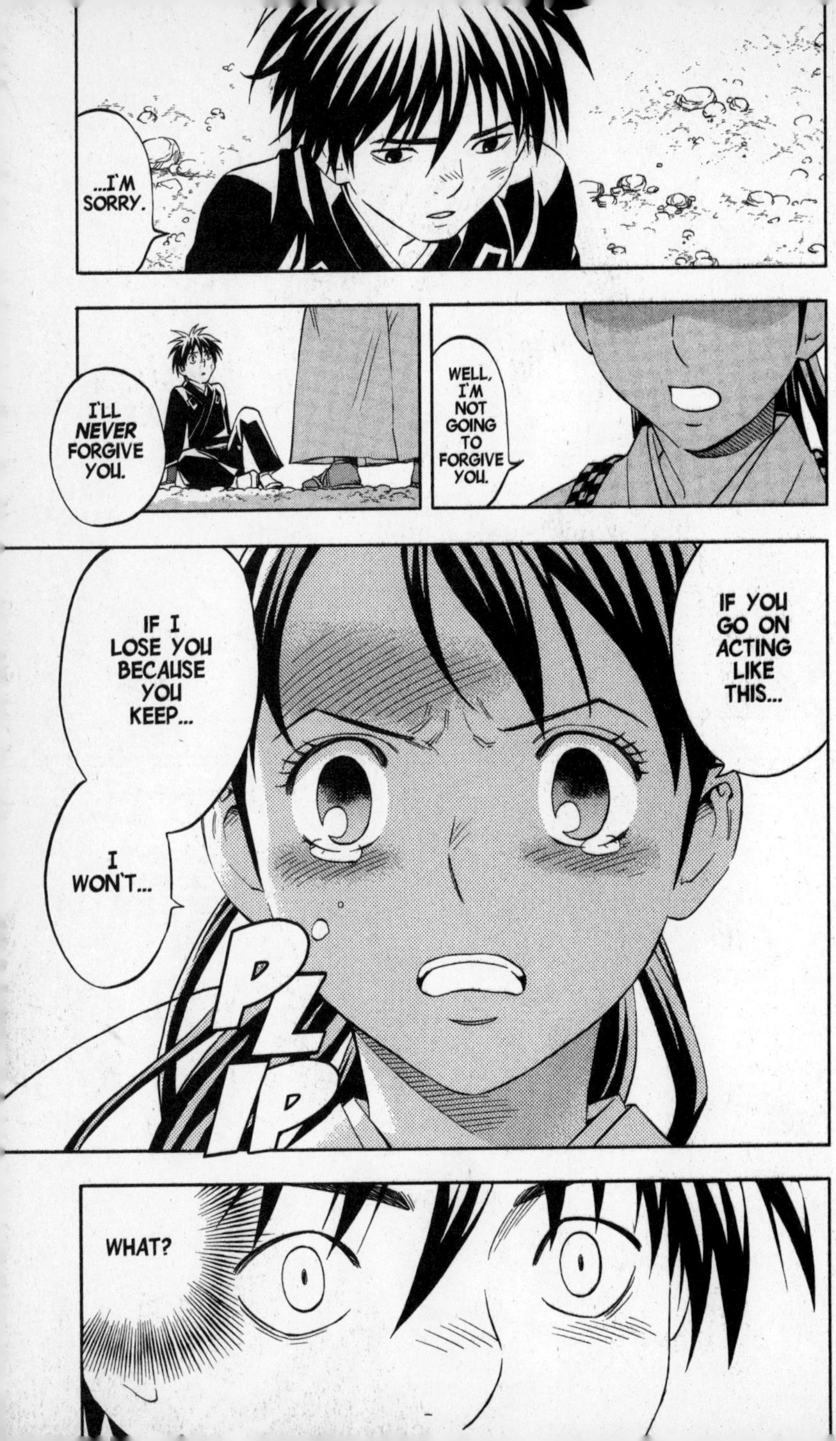
...I'M SORRY.
WELL, I'M NOT GOING TO FORGIVE YOU.
I'LL *NEVER* FORGIVE YOU.
IF YOU GO ON ACTING LIKE THIS...
IF I LOSE YOU BECAUSE YOU KEEP...
I WON'T...
PLIP
WHAT?

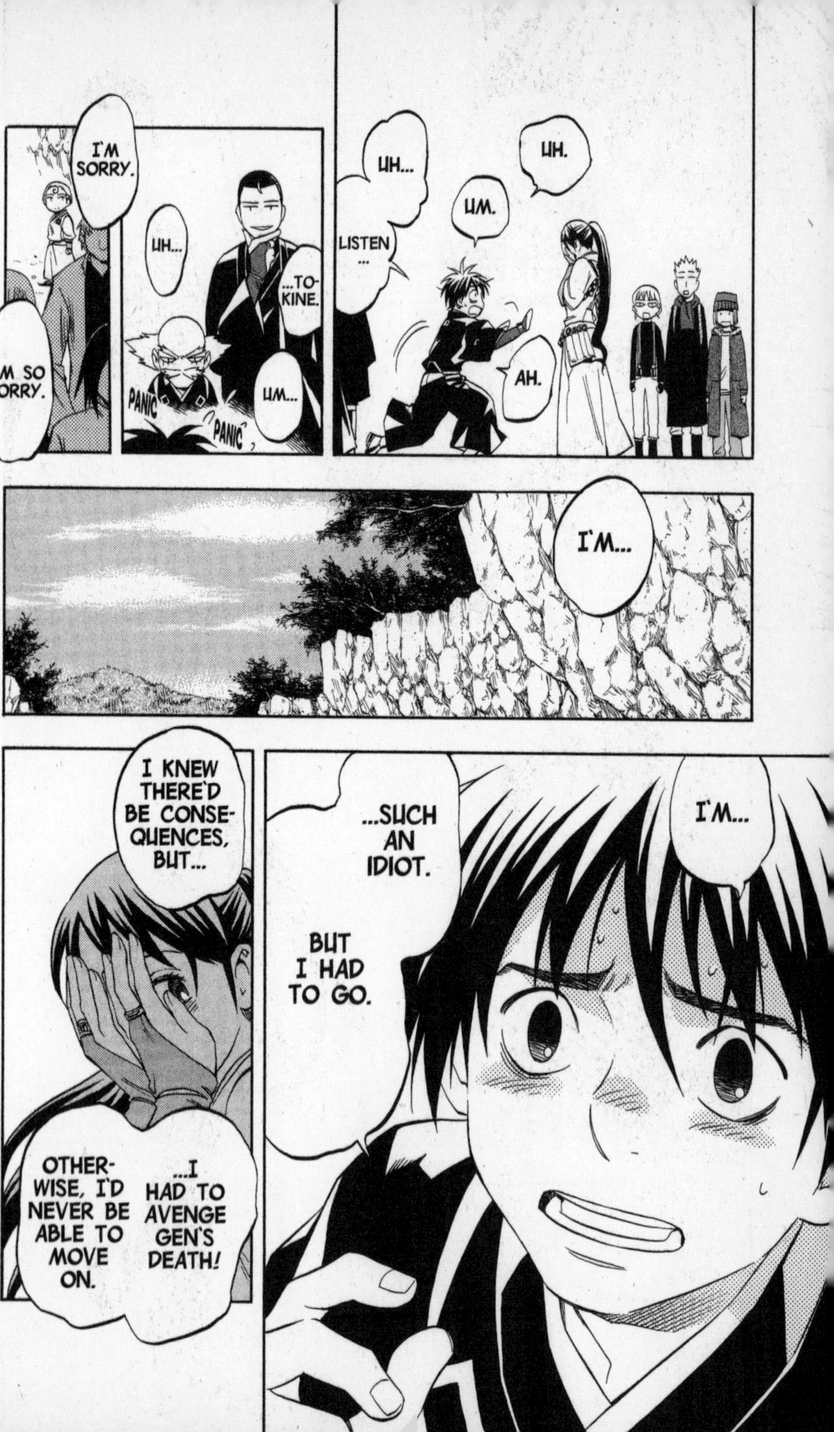
UH.
UH...
UM.
LISTEN ...
AH.
UH...
...TO-KINE.
UM...
PANIC PANIC
I'M SORRY.
I'M SO SORRY.
I'M...
I'M...
...SUCH AN IDIOT.
BUT I HAD TO GO.
I KNEW THERE'D BE CONSEQUENCES, BUT...
...I HAD TO AVENGE GEN'S DEATH!
OTHERWISE, I'D NEVER BE ABLE TO MOVE ON.

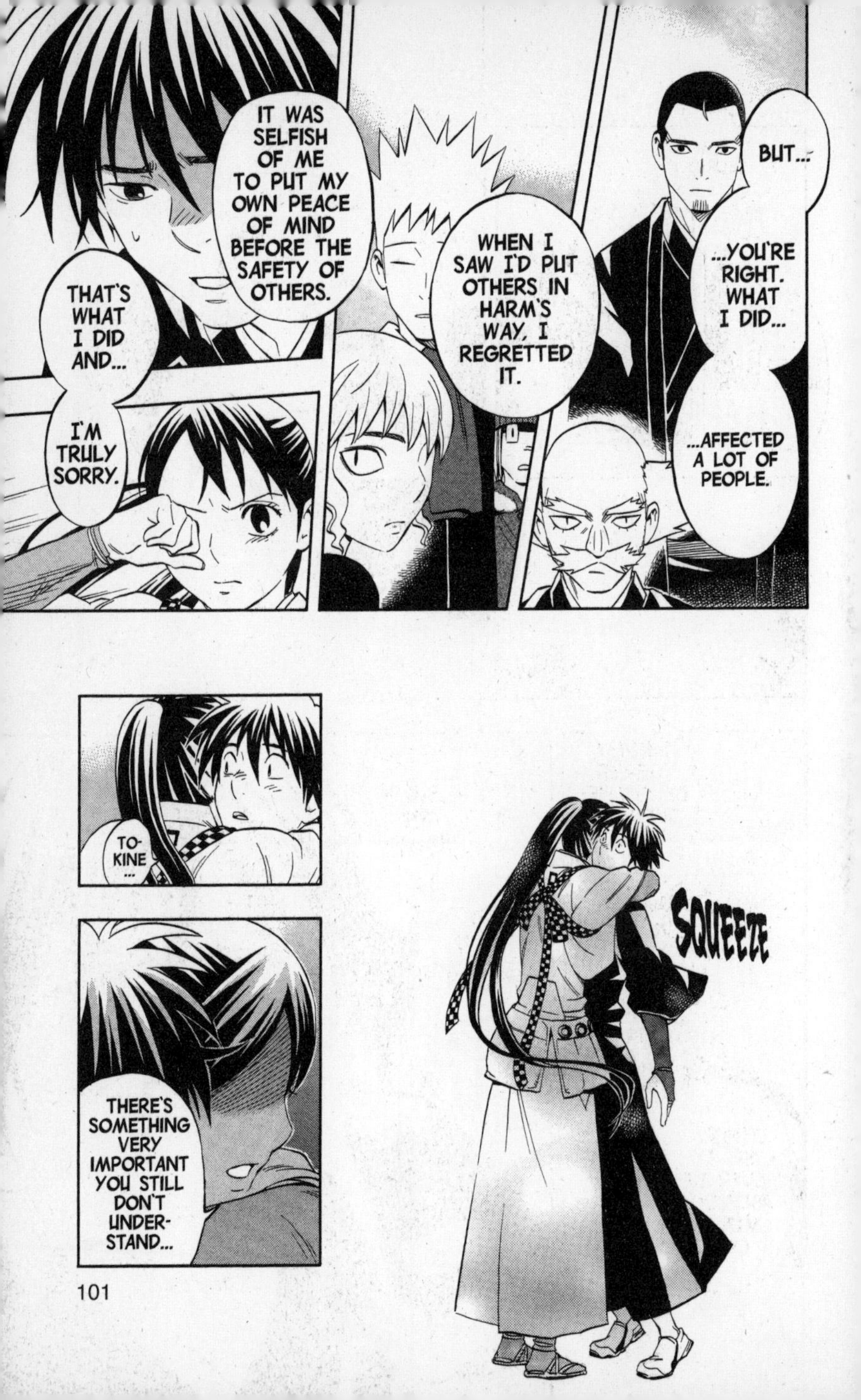
BUT...
...YOU'RE RIGHT. WHAT I DID...
...AFFECTED A LOT OF PEOPLE.
WHEN I SAW I'D PUT OTHERS IN HARM'S WAY, I REGRETTED IT.
IT WAS SELFISH OF ME TO PUT MY OWN PEACE OF MIND BEFORE THE SAFETY OF OTHERS.
THAT'S WHAT I DID AND...
I'M TRULY SORRY.
SQUEEZE
TO-KINE...
THERE'S SOMETHING VERY IMPORTANT YOU STILL DON'T UNDER-STAND...

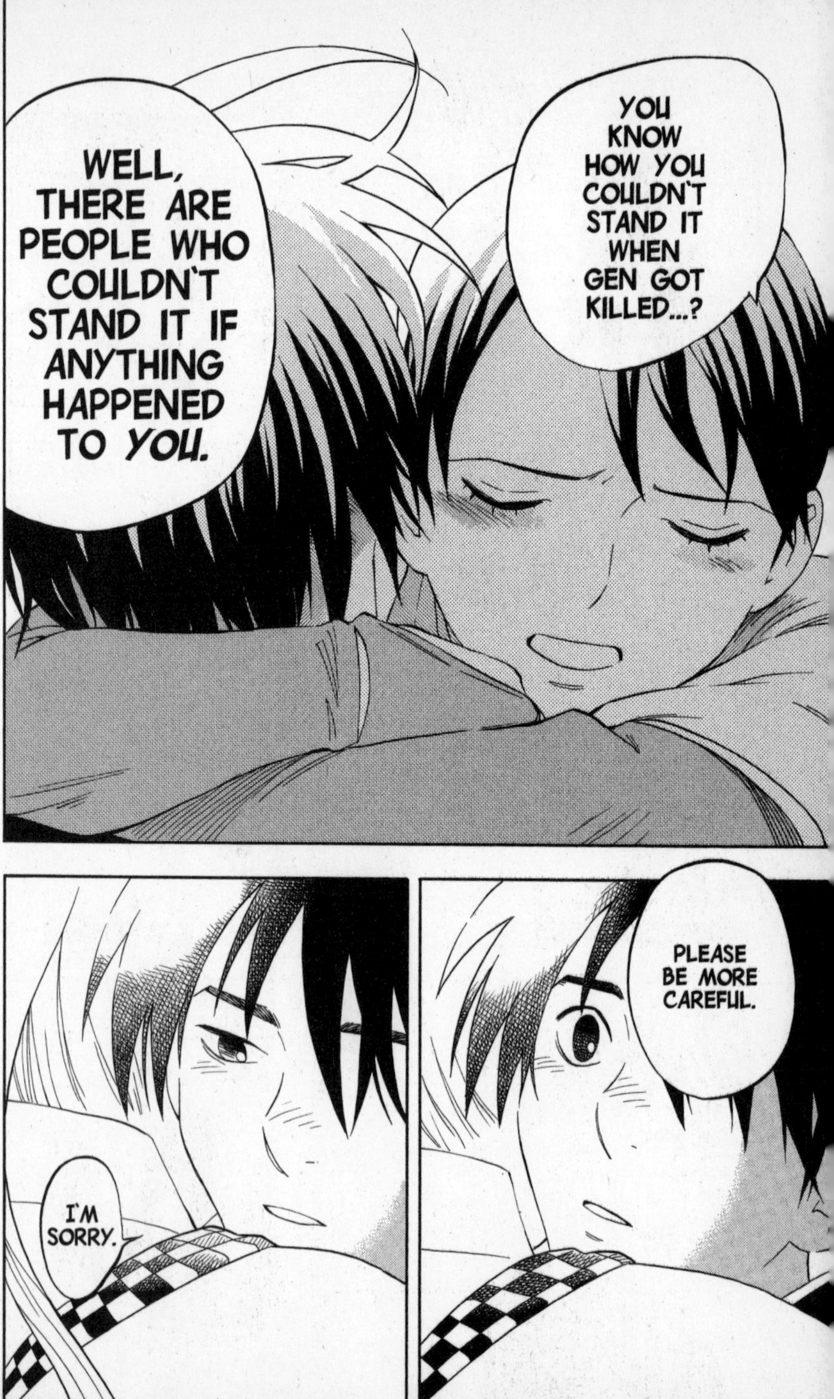
YOU KNOW HOW YOU COULDN'T STAND IT WHEN GEN GOT KILLED...?
WELL, THERE ARE PEOPLE WHO COULDN'T STAND IT IF ANYTHING HAPPENED TO *YOU.*
PLEASE BE MORE CAREFUL.
I'M SORRY.

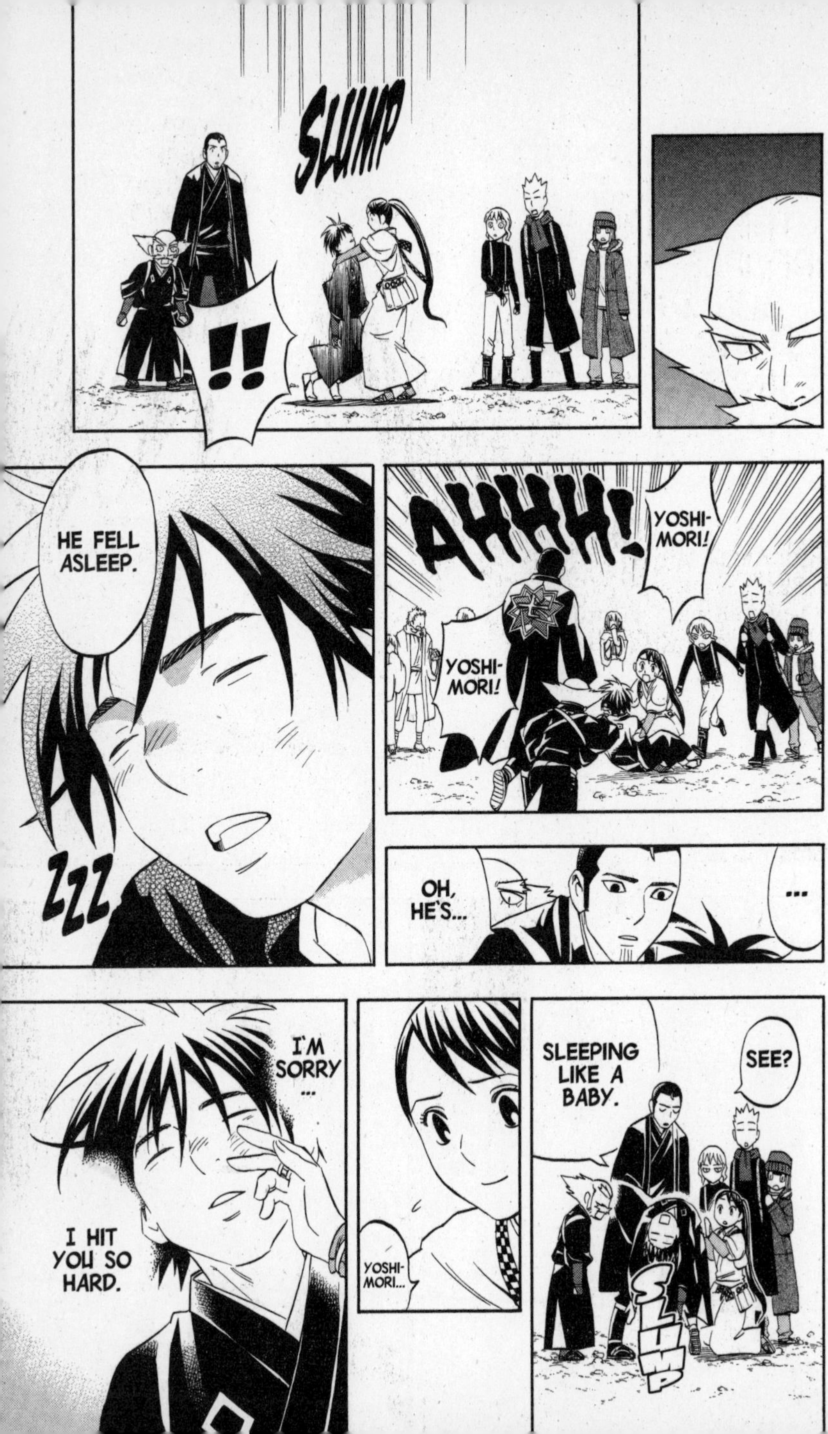
SLUMP
!!
YOSHI-MORI!
AHHH!
YOSHI-MORI!
...
OH, HE'S...
HE FELL ASLEEP.
ZZZ
SEE?
SLEEPING LIKE A BABY.
SLUMP
YOSHI-MORI...
I'M SORRY...
I HIT YOU SO HARD.

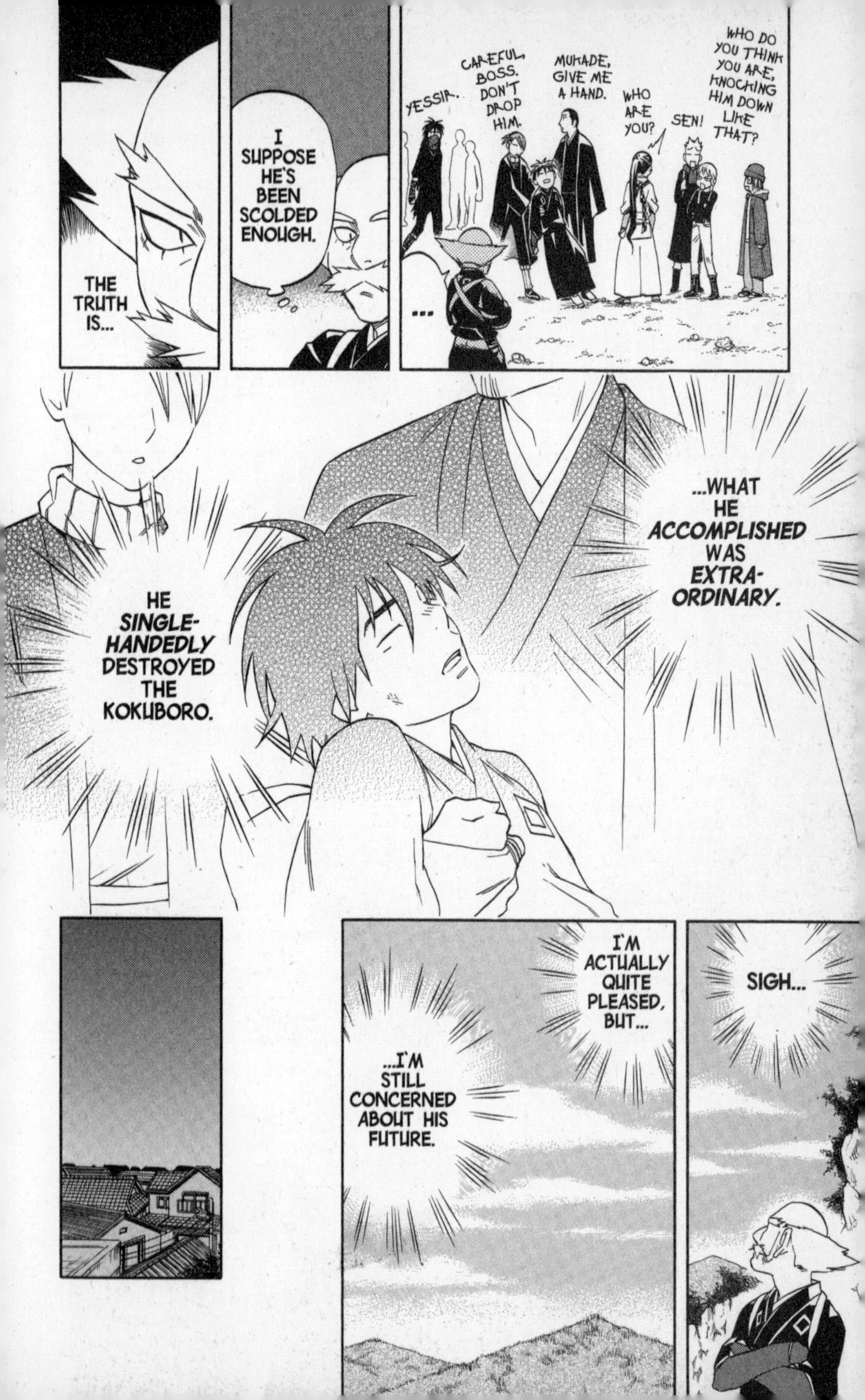
WHO DO YOU THINK YOU ARE, KNOCKING HIM DOWN LIKE THAT?
SEN!
WHO ARE YOU?
MUKADE, GIVE ME A HAND.
CAREFUL, BOSS. DON'T DROP HIM.
YESSIR.
...
I SUPPOSE HE'S BEEN SCOLDED ENOUGH.
THE TRUTH IS...
...WHAT HE *ACCOMPLISHED* WAS *EXTRA-ORDINARY*.
HE *SINGLE-HANDEDLY* DESTROYED THE KOKUBORO.
SIGH...
I'M ACTUALLY QUITE PLEASED, BUT...
...I'M STILL CONCERNED ABOUT HIS FUTURE.

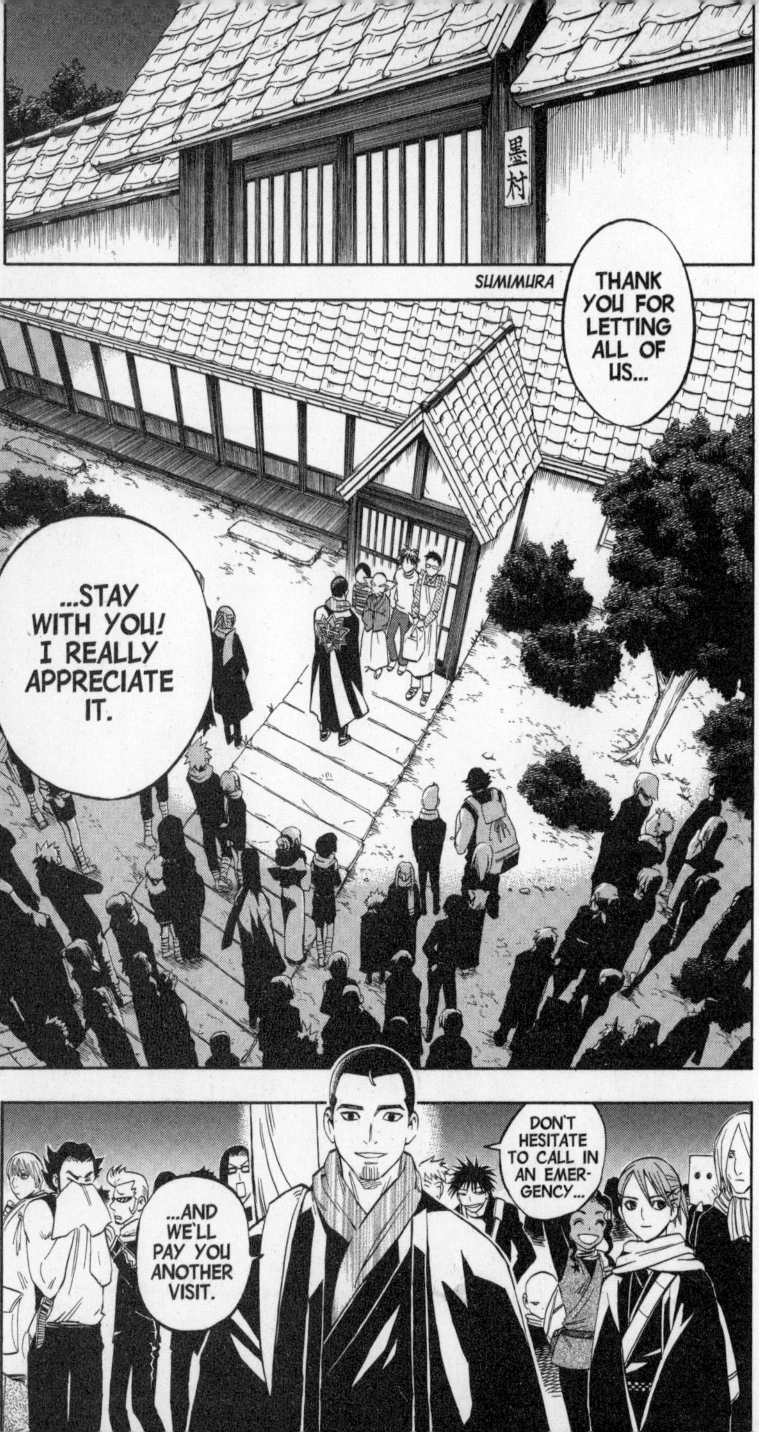
墨村
SUMIMURA
THANK YOU FOR LETTING ALL OF US...
...STAY WITH YOU! I REALLY APPRECIATE IT.
DON'T HESITATE TO CALL IN AN EMERGENCY...
...AND WE'LL PAY YOU ANOTHER VISIT.

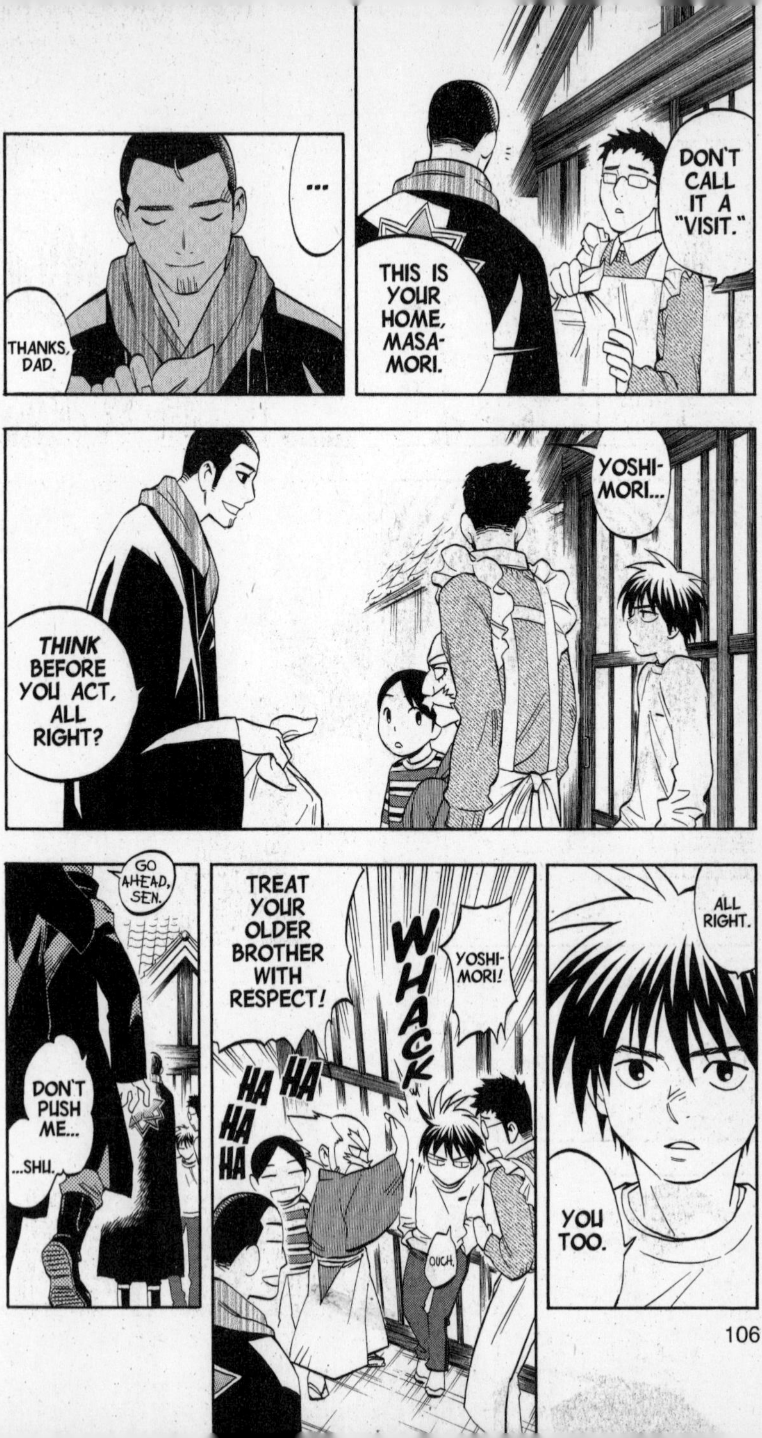
DON'T CALL IT A "VISIT."
THIS IS YOUR HOME, MASAMORI.
...
THANKS, DAD.
YOSHIMORI...
THINK BEFORE YOU ACT, ALL RIGHT?
ALL RIGHT.
YOU TOO.
YOSHIMORI!
WHACK
TREAT YOUR OLDER BROTHER WITH RESPECT!
HA HA HA HA HA
OUCH.
GO AHEAD, SEN.
DON'T PUSH ME...
...SHU.

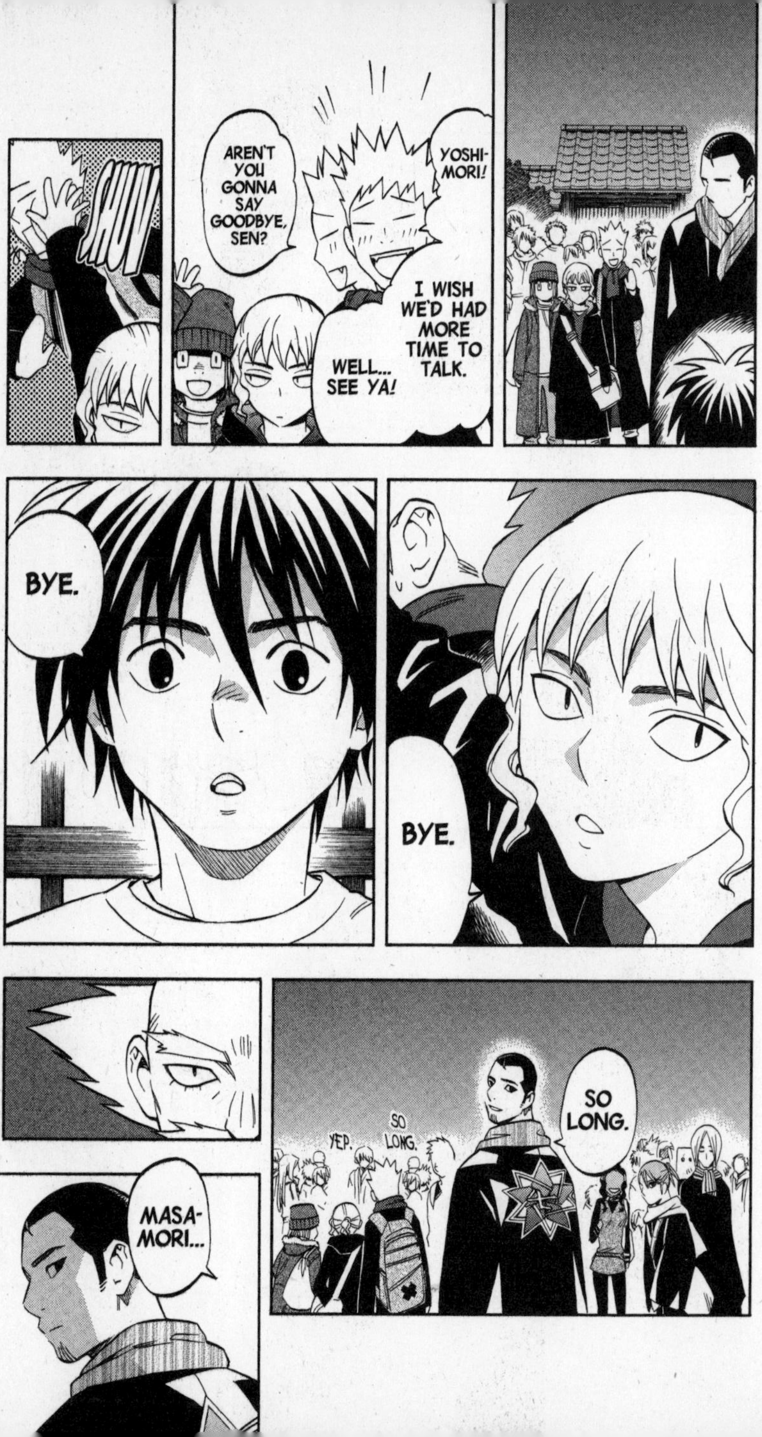

YOSHI-MORI!
I WISH WE'D HAD MORE TIME TO TALK.
WELL... SEE YA!
AREN'T YOU GONNA SAY GOODBYE, SEN?
BYE.
BYE.
SO LONG.
SO LONG.
YEP.
MASA-MORI...

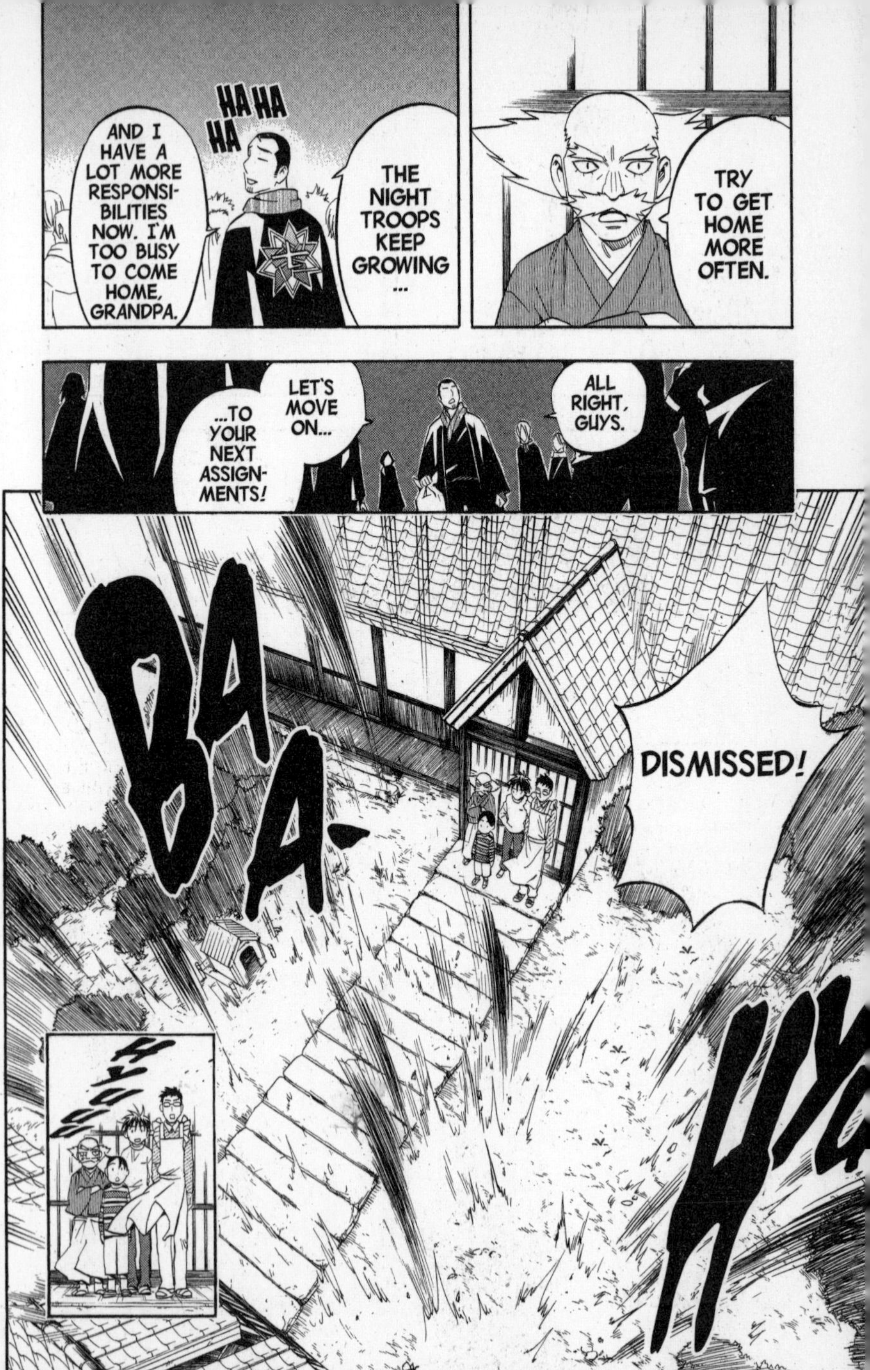
TRY TO GET HOME MORE OFTEN.
THE NIGHT TROOPS KEEP GROWING...
HA HA HA
AND I HAVE A LOT MORE RESPONSIBILITIES NOW. I'M TOO BUSY TO COME HOME, GRANDPA.
ALL RIGHT, GUYS.
LET'S MOVE ON...
...TO YOUR NEXT ASSIGNMENTS!
DISMISSED!
BAA-

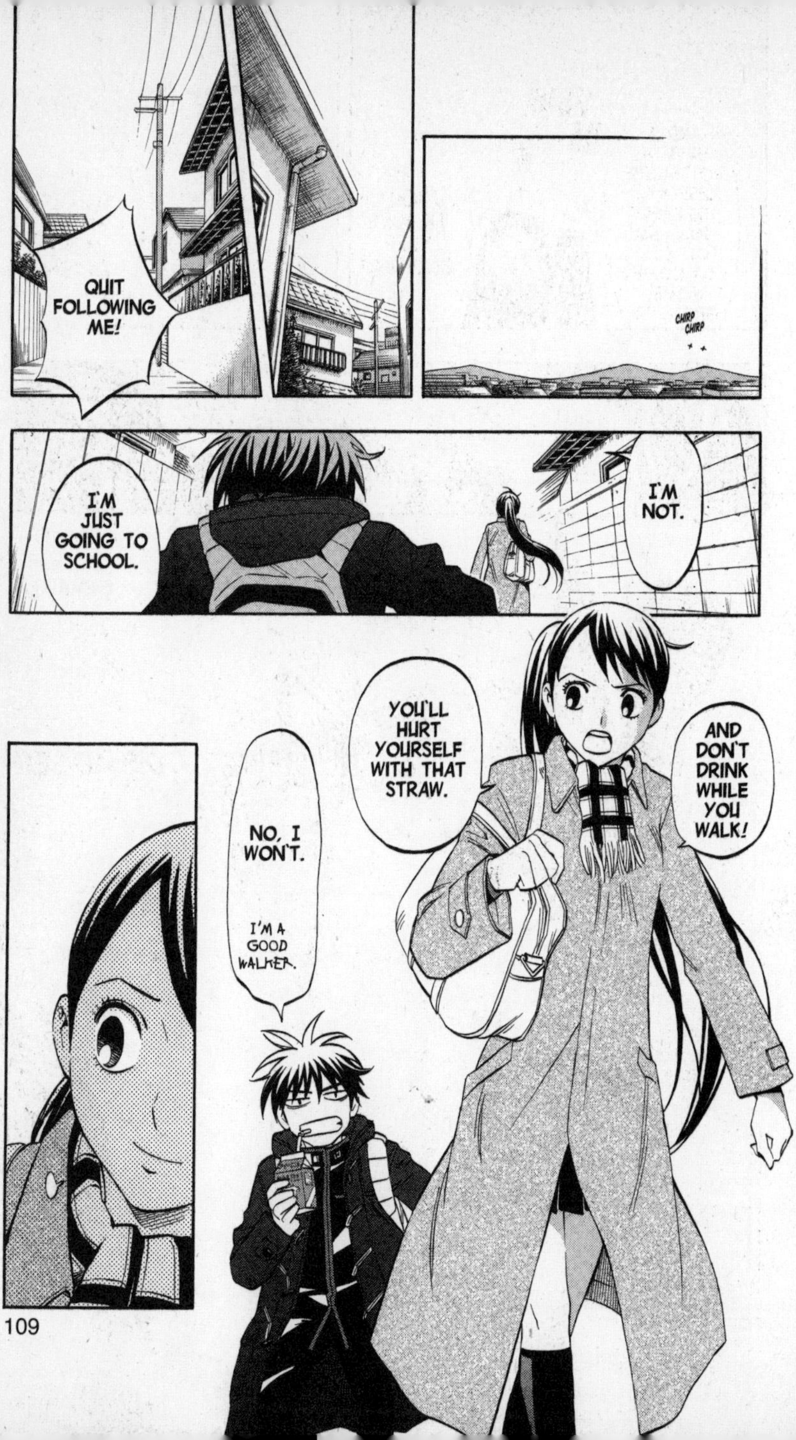
CHIRP CHIRP
QUIT FOLLOWING ME!
I'M NOT.
I'M JUST GOING TO SCHOOL.
AND DON'T DRINK WHILE YOU WALK!
YOU'LL HURT YOURSELF WITH THAT STRAW.
NO, I WON'T.
I'M A GOOD WALKER.

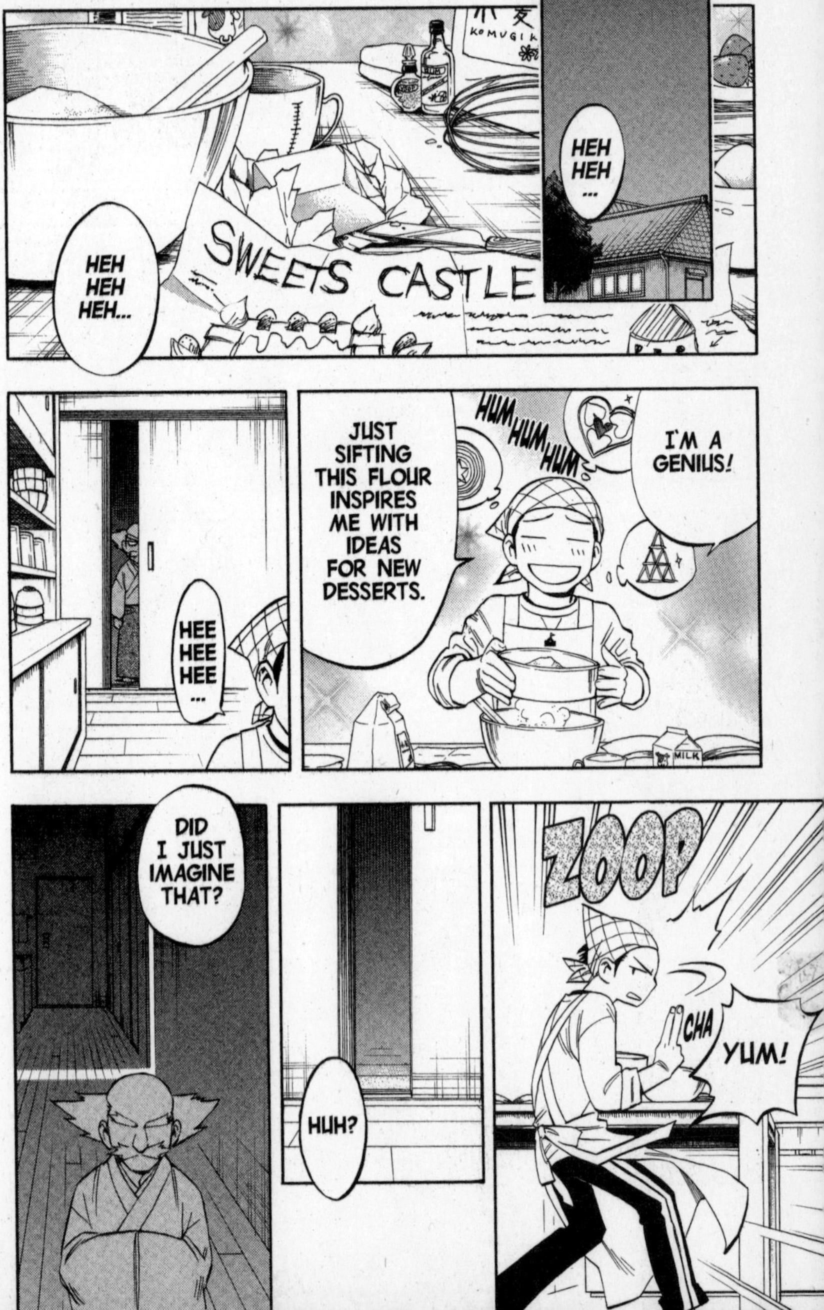
HEH HEH ...
KOMUGIKO
SWEETS CASTLE
HEH HEH HEH...
HUM HUM HUM
I'M A GENIUS!
JUST SIFTING THIS FLOUR INSPIRES ME WITH IDEAS FOR NEW DESSERTS.
MILK
HEE HEE HEE ...
ZOOP
CHA
YUM!
HUH?
DID I JUST IMAGINE THAT?

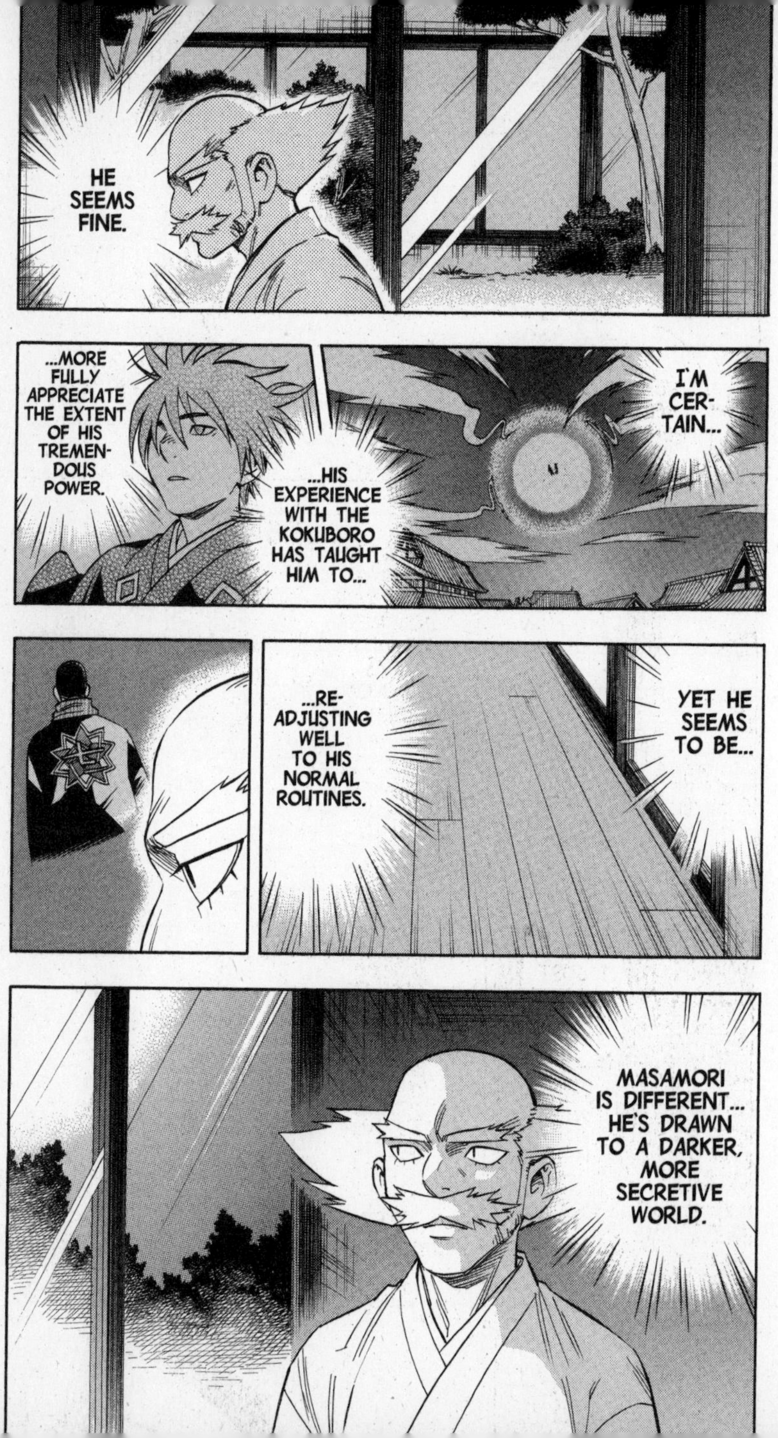
HE SEEMS FINE.
I'M CERTAIN...
...HIS EXPERIENCE WITH THE KOKUBORO HAS TAUGHT HIM TO...
...MORE FULLY APPRECIATE THE EXTENT OF HIS TREMENDOUS POWER.
YET HE SEEMS TO BE...
...RE-ADJUSTING WELL TO HIS NORMAL ROUTINES.
MASAMORI IS DIFFERENT... HE'S DRAWN TO A DARKER, MORE SECRETIVE WORLD.

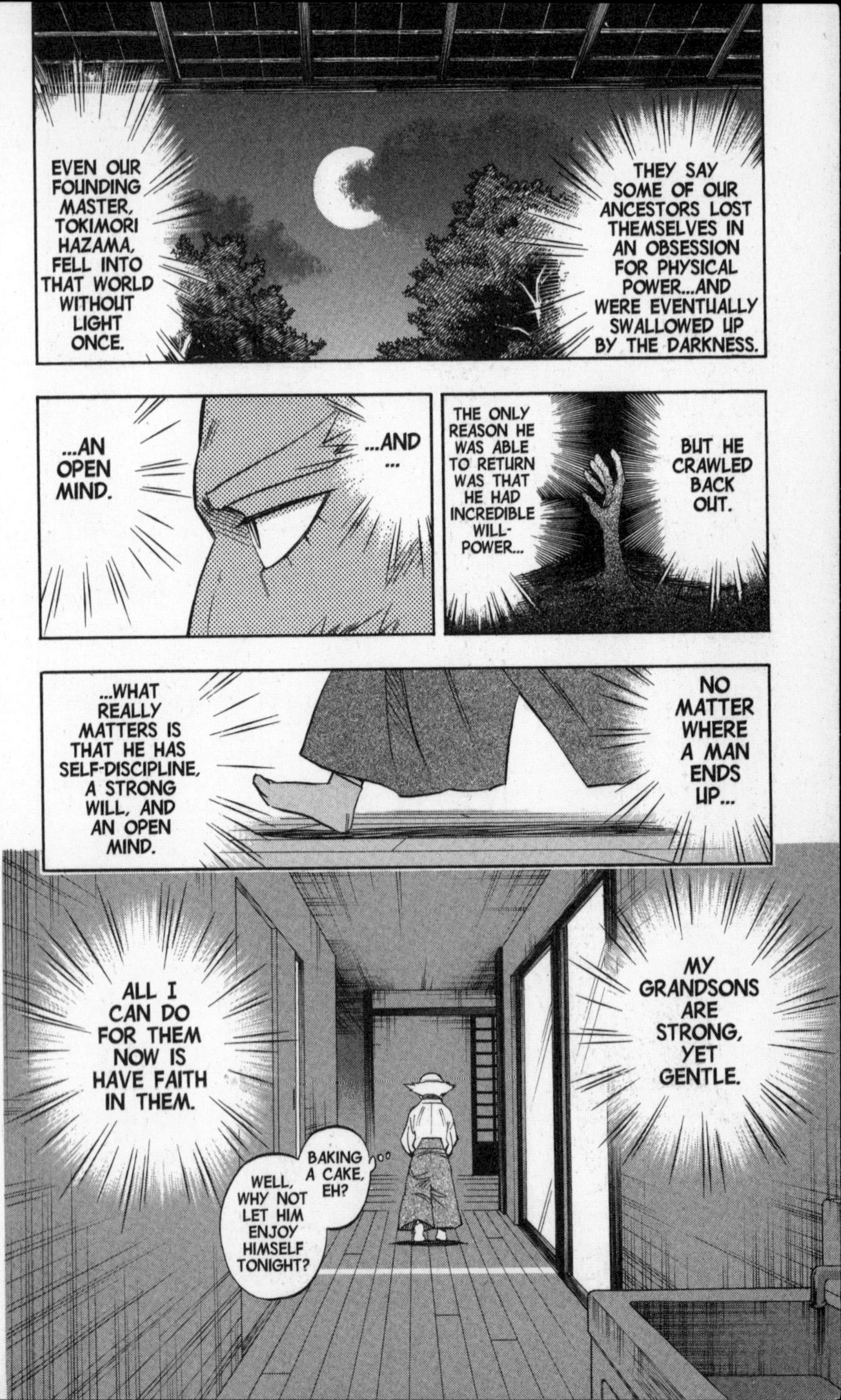
THEY SAY SOME OF OUR ANCESTORS LOST THEMSELVES IN AN OBSESSION FOR PHYSICAL POWER...AND WERE EVENTUALLY SWALLOWED UP BY THE DARKNESS.
EVEN OUR FOUNDING MASTER, TOKIMORI HAZAMA, FELL INTO THAT WORLD WITHOUT LIGHT ONCE.
BUT HE CRAWLED BACK OUT.
THE ONLY REASON HE WAS ABLE TO RETURN WAS THAT HE HAD INCREDIBLE WILL-POWER...
...AND ...
...AN OPEN MIND.
NO MATTER WHERE A MAN ENDS UP...
...WHAT REALLY MATTERS IS THAT HE HAS SELF-DISCIPLINE, A STRONG WILL, AND AN OPEN MIND.
MY GRANDSONS ARE STRONG, YET GENTLE.
ALL I CAN DO FOR THEM NOW IS HAVE FAITH IN THEM.
BAKING A CAKE, EH?
WELL, WHY NOT LET HIM ENJOY HIMSELF TONIGHT?

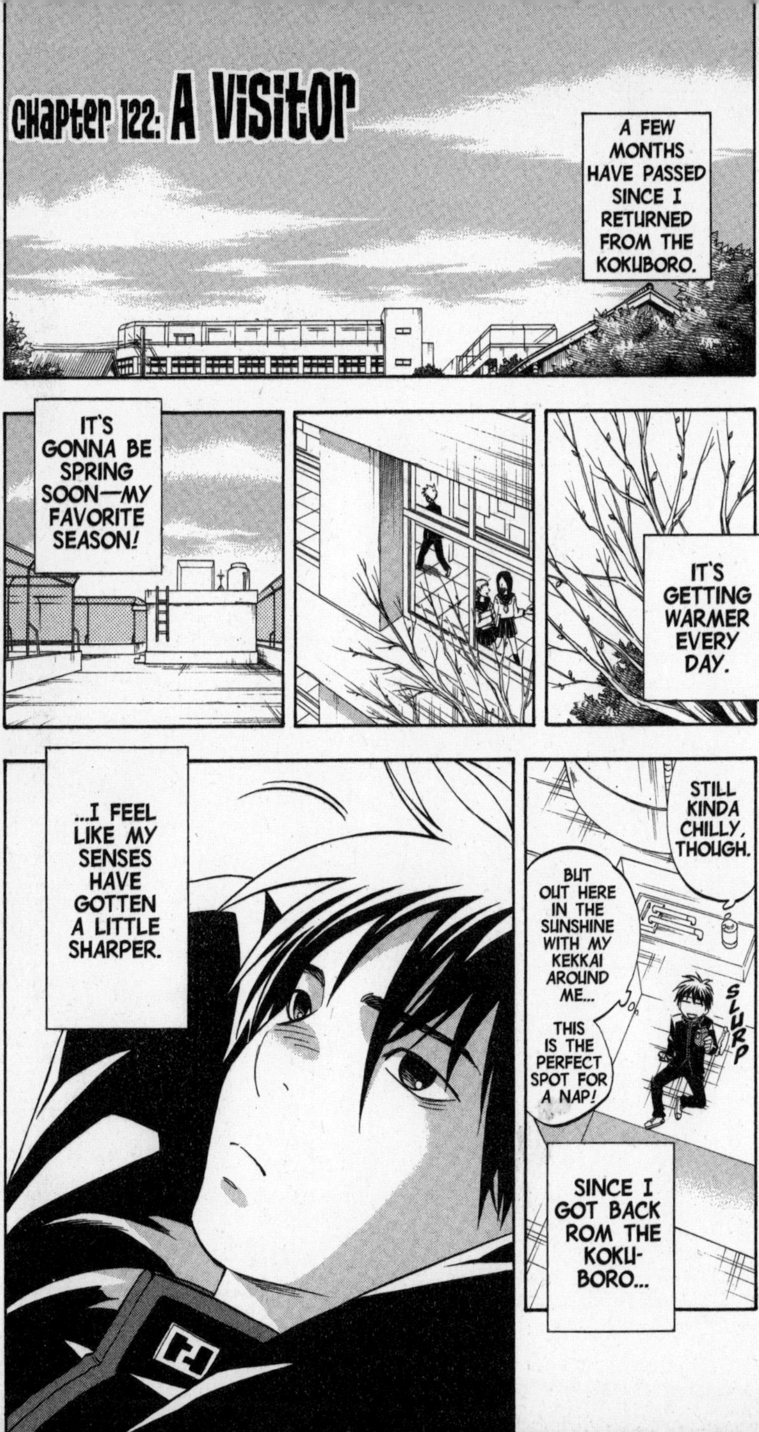
Chapter 122: A Visitor
A FEW MONTHS HAVE PASSED SINCE I RETURNED FROM THE KOKUBORO.
IT'S GETTING WARMER EVERY DAY.
IT'S GONNA BE SPRING SOON—MY FAVORITE SEASON!
STILL KINDA CHILLY, THOUGH.
BUT OUT HERE IN THE SUNSHINE WITH MY KEKKAI AROUND ME...
THIS IS THE PERFECT SPOT FOR A NAP!
SLURP
SINCE I GOT BACK ROM THE KOKU-BORO...
...I FEEL LIKE MY SENSES HAVE GOTTEN A LITTLE SHARPER.

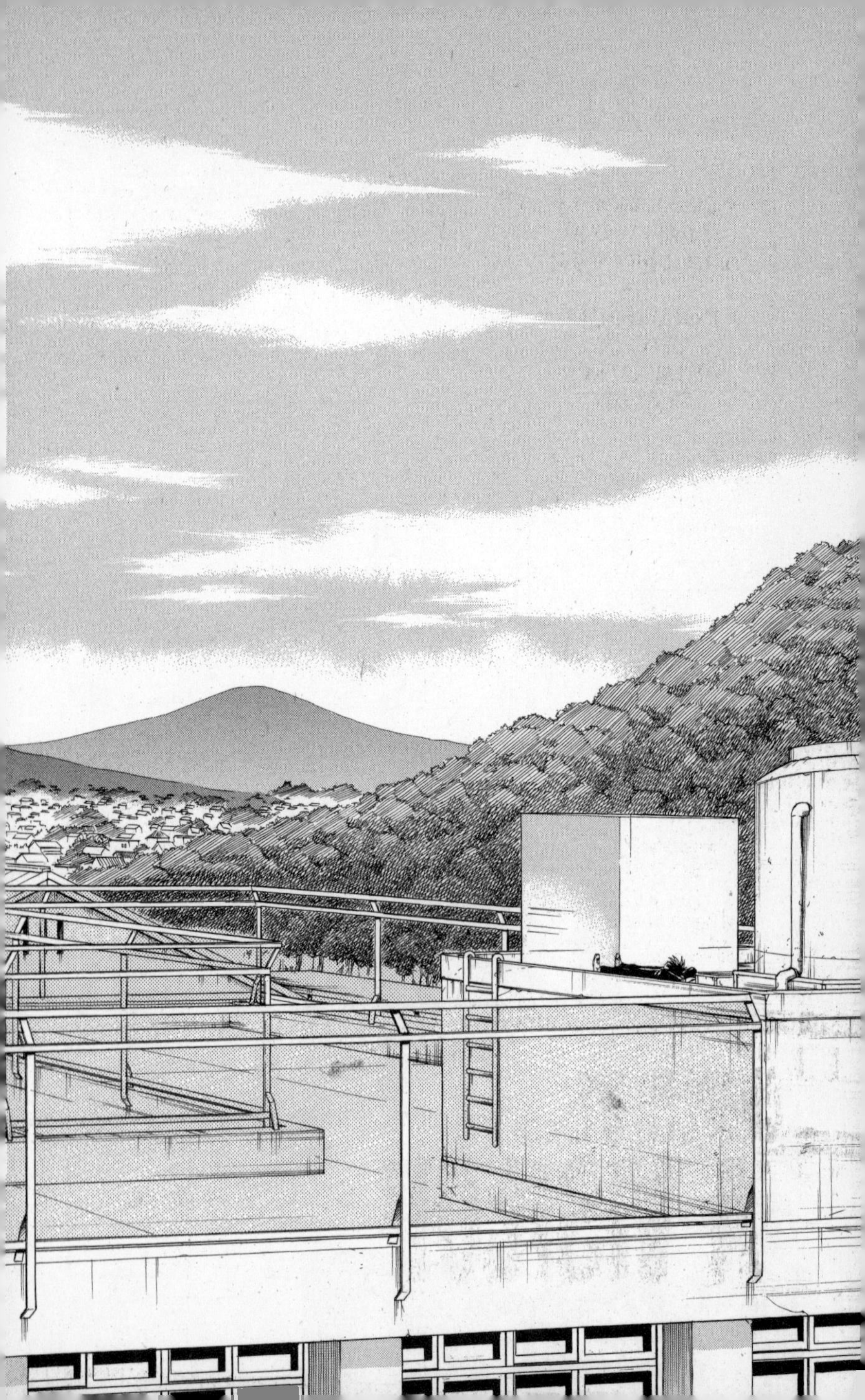

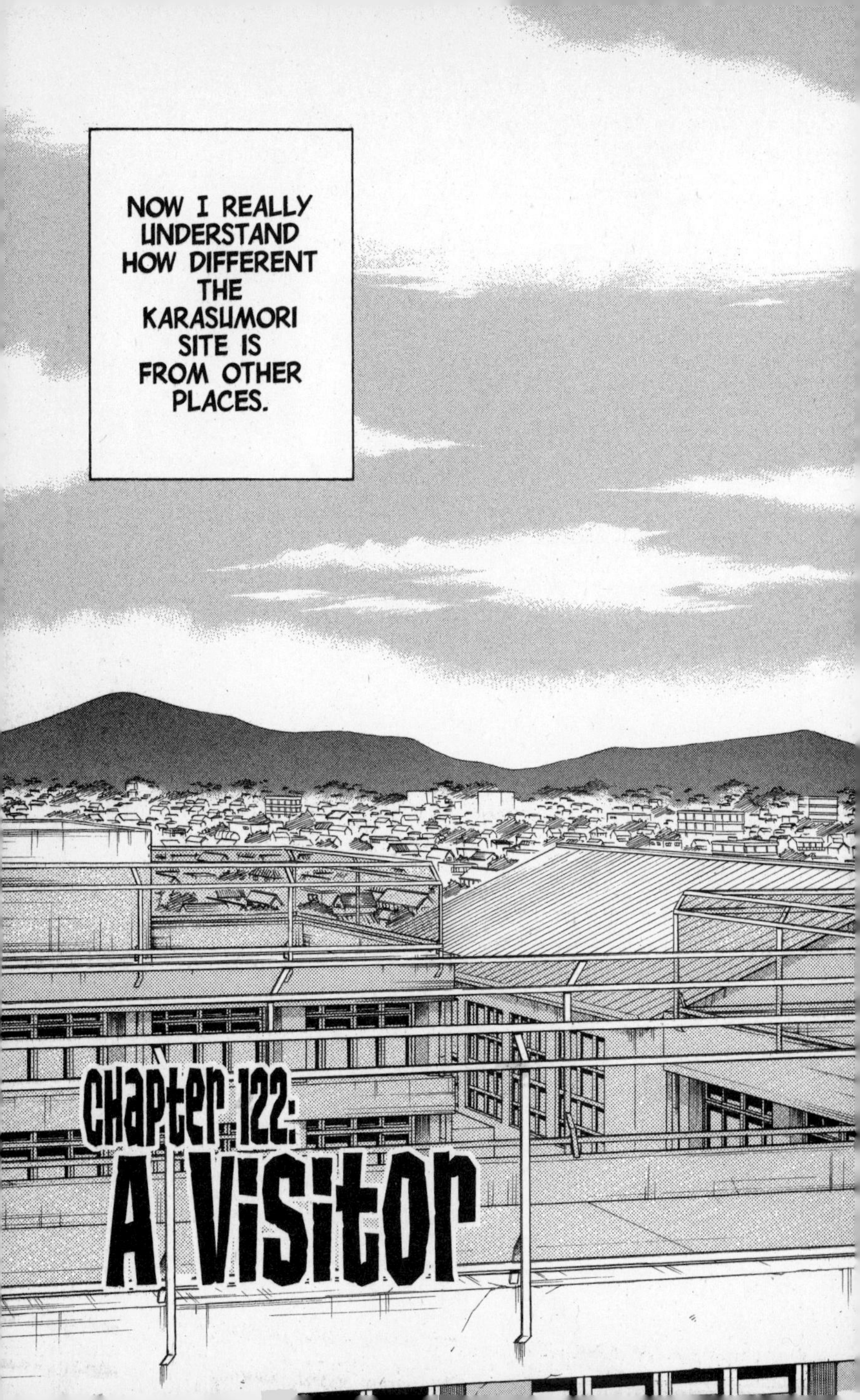
NOW I REALLY UNDERSTAND HOW DIFFERENT THE KARASUMORI SITE IS FROM OTHER PLACES.
Chapter 122:
A Visitor

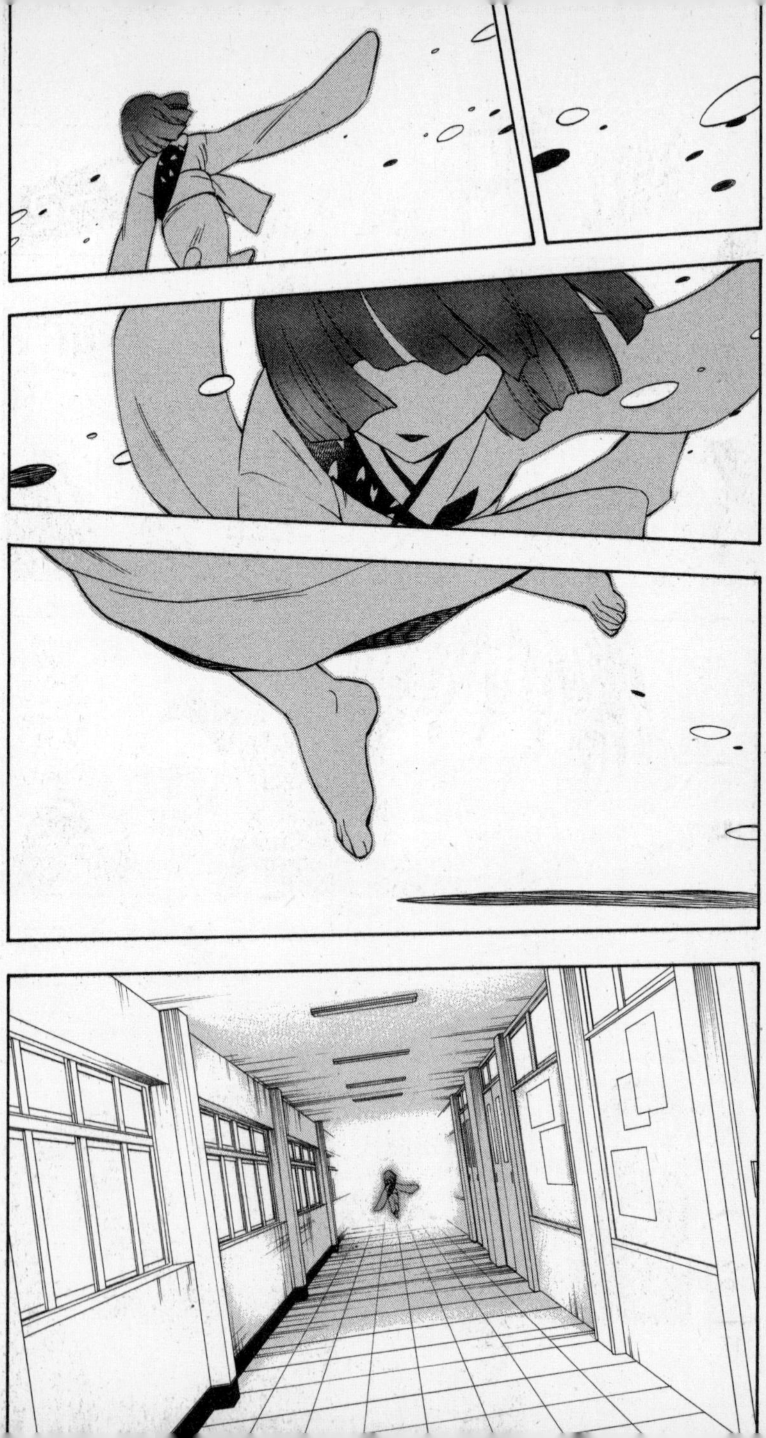

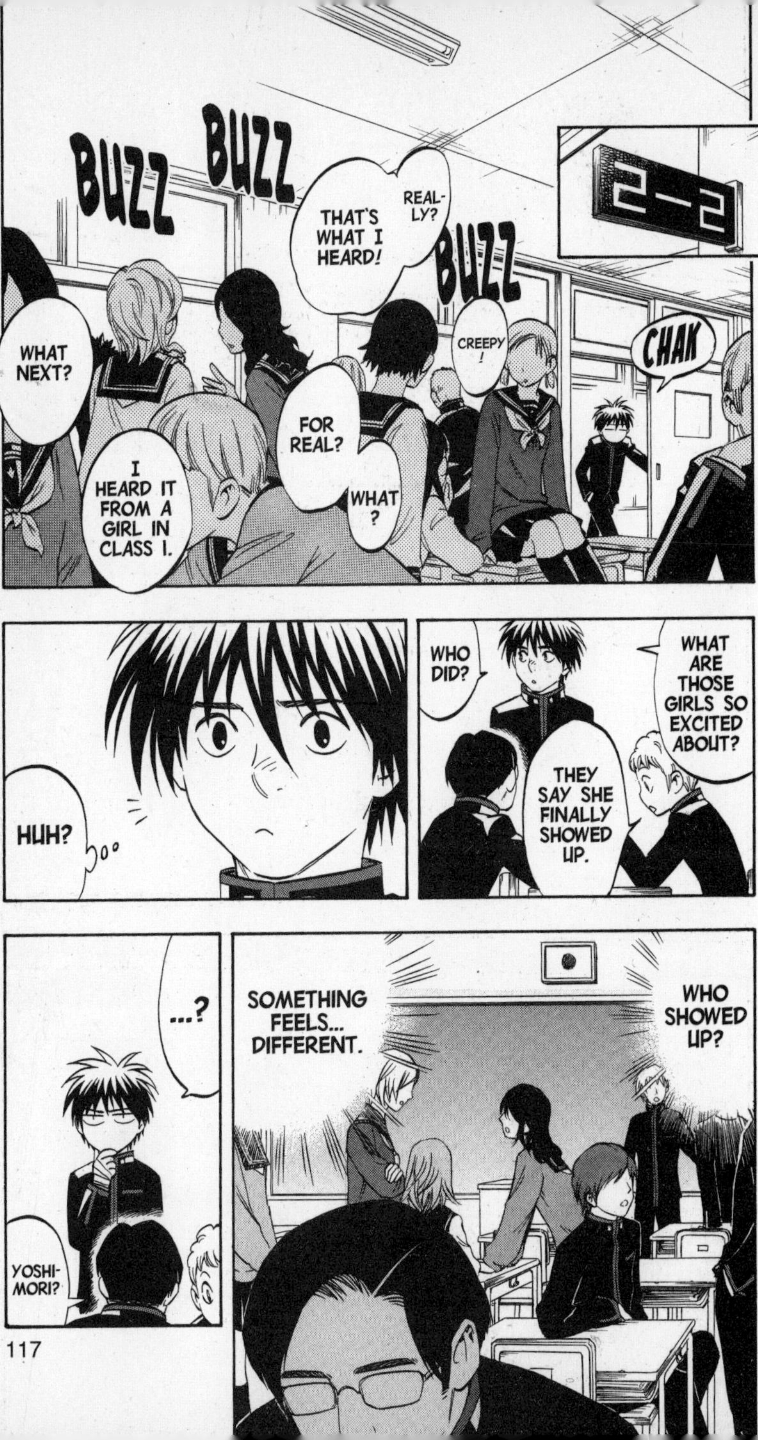
2-2
BUZZ
REAL-LY?
THAT'S WHAT I HEARD!
BUZZ
BUZZ
CHAK
CREEPY!
WHAT NEXT?
FOR REAL?
WHAT?
I HEARD IT FROM A GIRL IN CLASS 1.
WHAT ARE THOSE GIRLS SO EXCITED ABOUT?
WHO DID?
THEY SAY SHE FINALLY SHOWED UP.
HUH?
WHO SHOWED UP?
SOMETHING FEELS... DIFFERENT.
...?
YOSHI-MORI?

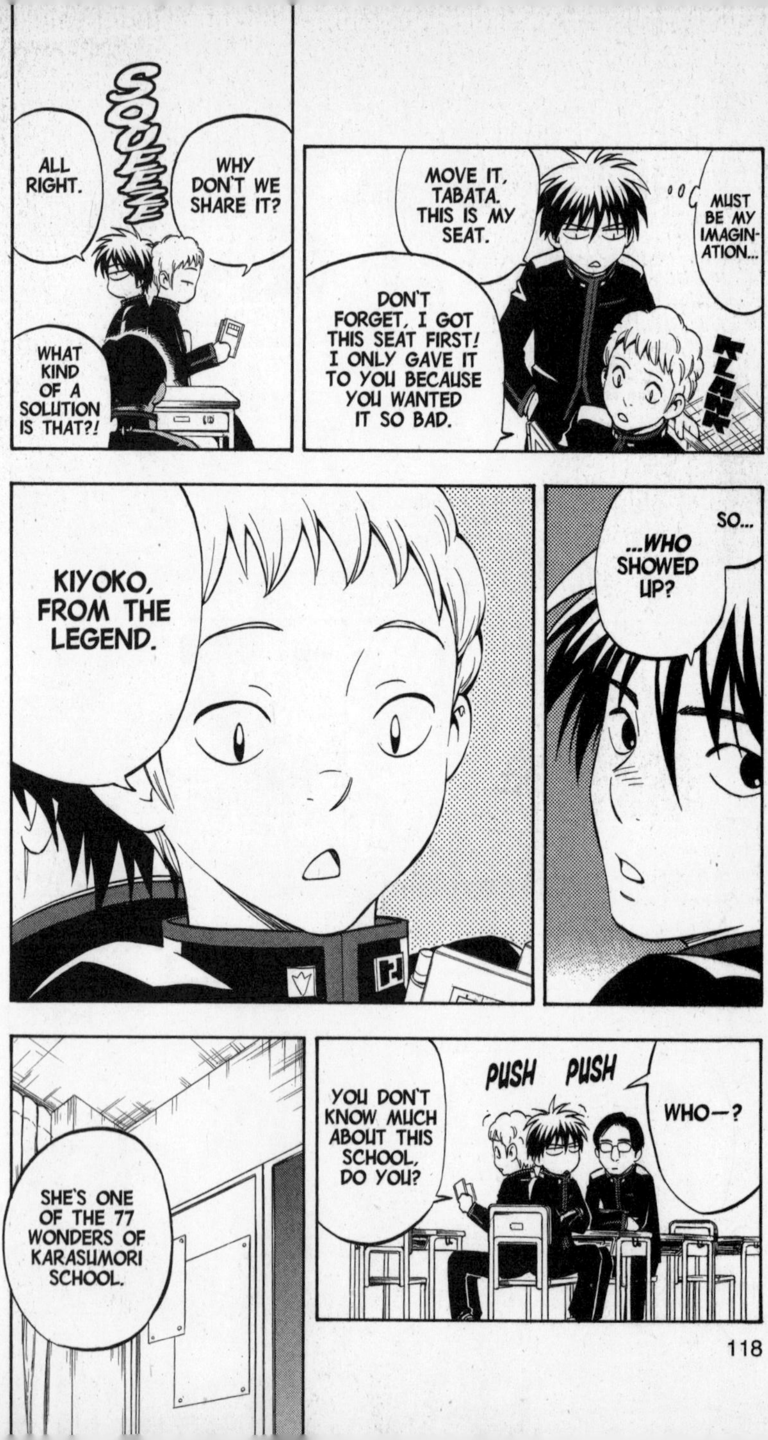
MUST BE MY IMAGINATION...
KLANK
MOVE IT, TABATA. THIS IS MY SEAT.
DON'T FORGET, I GOT THIS SEAT FIRST! I ONLY GAVE IT TO YOU BECAUSE YOU WANTED IT SO BAD.
WHY DON'T WE SHARE IT?
SQUEEZE
ALL RIGHT.
WHAT KIND OF A SOLUTION IS THAT?!
SO...
...WHO SHOWED UP?
KIYOKO, FROM THE LEGEND.
WHO—?
PUSH PUSH
YOU DON'T KNOW MUCH ABOUT THIS SCHOOL, DO YOU?
SHE'S ONE OF THE 77 WONDERS OF KARASUMORI SCHOOL.

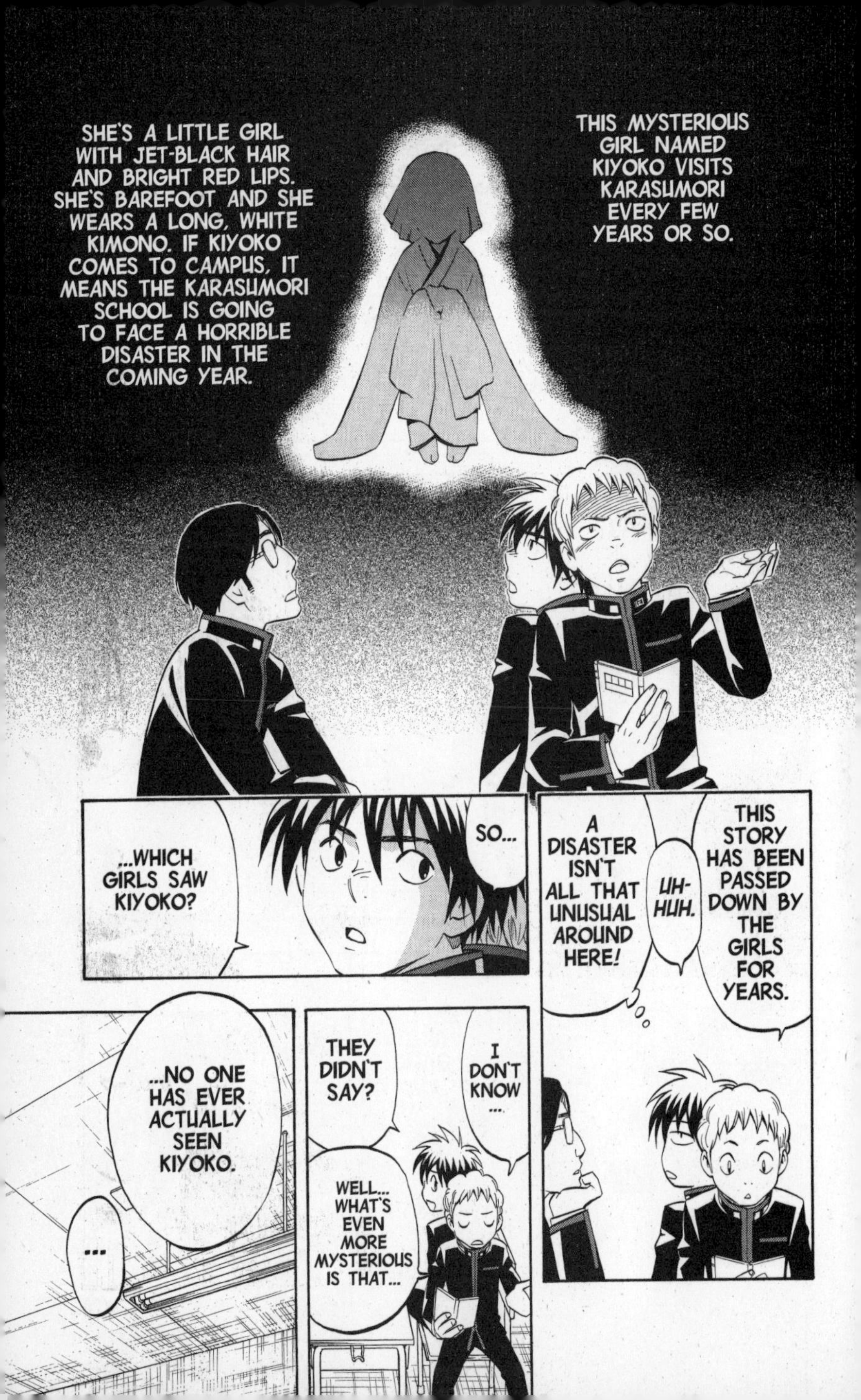
THIS MYSTERIOUS GIRL NAMED KIYOKO VISITS KARASUMORI EVERY FEW YEARS OR SO.
SHE'S A LITTLE GIRL WITH JET-BLACK HAIR AND BRIGHT RED LIPS. SHE'S BAREFOOT AND SHE WEARS A LONG, WHITE KIMONO. IF KIYOKO COMES TO CAMPUS, IT MEANS THE KARASUMORI SCHOOL IS GOING TO FACE A HORRIBLE DISASTER IN THE COMING YEAR.
THIS STORY HAS BEEN PASSED DOWN BY THE GIRLS FOR YEARS.
UH-HUH.
A DISASTER ISN'T ALL THAT UNUSUAL AROUND HERE!
SO...
...WHICH GIRLS SAW KIYOKO?
I DON'T KNOW...
THEY DIDN'T SAY?
WELL... WHAT'S EVEN MORE MYSTERIOUS IS THAT...
...NO ONE HAS EVER ACTUALLY SEEN KIYOKO.
...

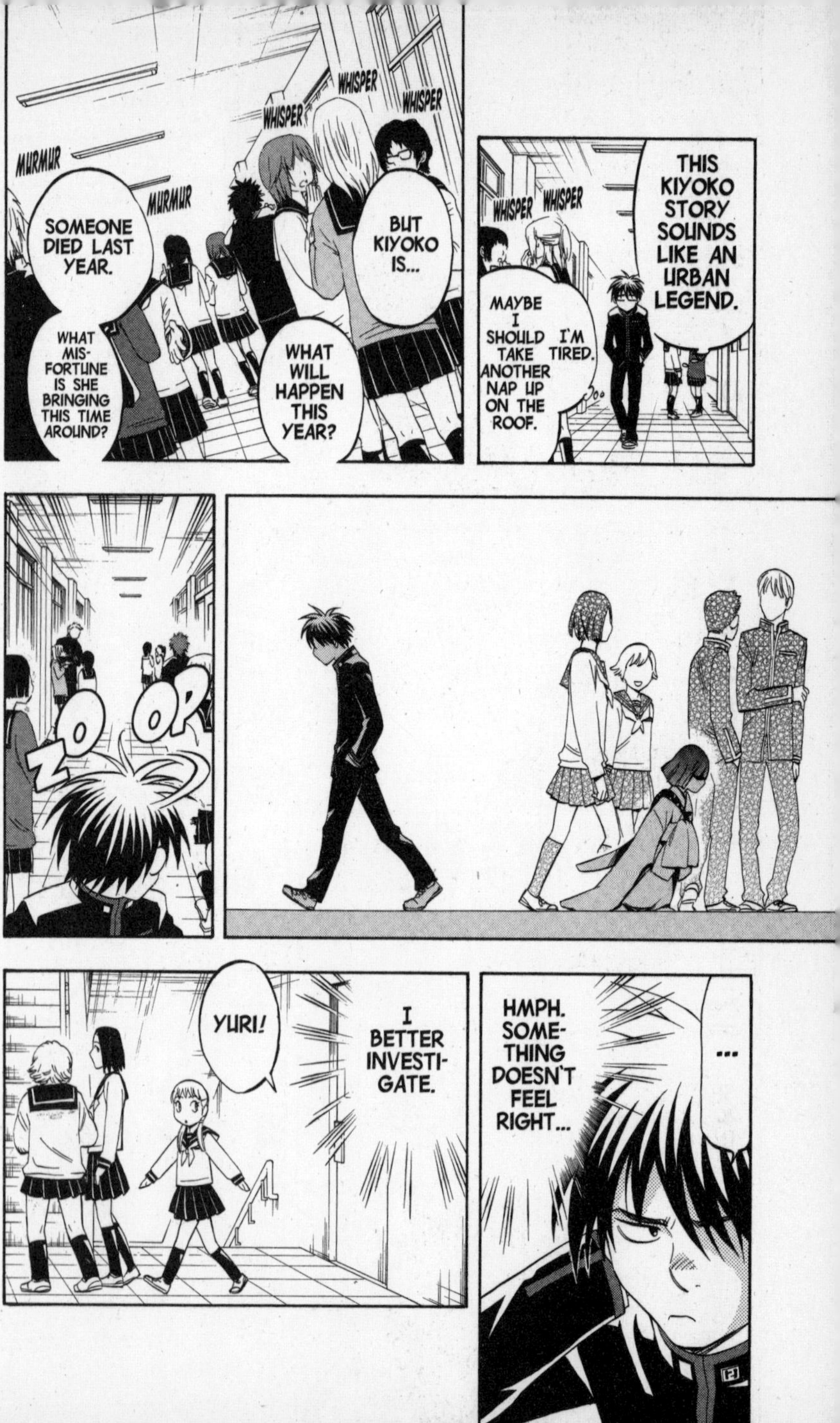
THIS KIYOKO STORY SOUNDS LIKE AN URBAN LEGEND.
WHISPER WHISPER
I'M TIRED.
MAYBE I SHOULD TAKE ANOTHER NAP UP ON THE ROOF.
WHISPER
WHISPER
WHISPER
BUT KIYOKO IS...
MURMUR
MURMUR
SOMEONE DIED LAST YEAR.
WHAT WILL HAPPEN THIS YEAR?
WHAT MIS-FORTUNE IS SHE BRINGING THIS TIME AROUND?
ZOOP
...
HMPH. SOME-THING DOESN'T FEEL RIGHT...
I BETTER INVESTI-GATE.
YURI!

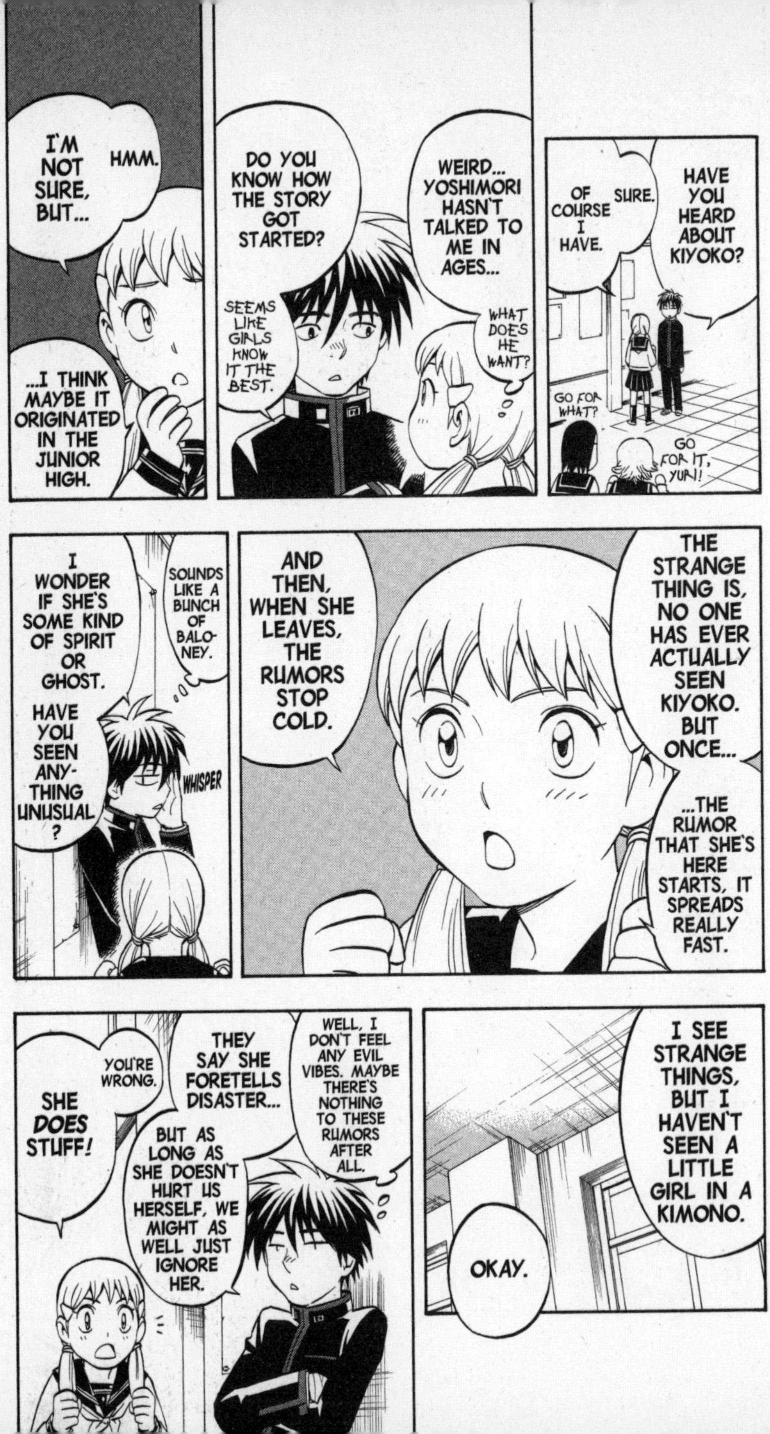
HAVE YOU HEARD ABOUT KIYOKO?
SURE.
OF COURSE I HAVE.
GO FOR IT, YURI!
GO FOR WHAT?
WEIRD... YOSHIMORI HASN'T TALKED TO ME IN AGES...
DO YOU KNOW HOW THE STORY GOT STARTED?
WHAT DOES HE WANT?
SEEMS LIKE GIRLS KNOW IT THE BEST.
HMM.
I'M NOT SURE, BUT...
...I THINK MAYBE IT ORIGINATED IN THE JUNIOR HIGH.
THE STRANGE THING IS, NO ONE HAS EVER ACTUALLY SEEN KIYOKO. BUT ONCE...
...THE RUMOR THAT SHE'S HERE STARTS, IT SPREADS REALLY FAST.
AND THEN, WHEN SHE LEAVES, THE RUMORS STOP COLD.
SOUNDS LIKE A BUNCH OF BALONEY.
I WONDER IF SHE'S SOME KIND OF SPIRIT OR GHOST.
HAVE YOU SEEN ANYTHING UNUSUAL?
WHISPER
I SEE STRANGE THINGS, BUT I HAVEN'T SEEN A LITTLE GIRL IN A KIMONO.
OKAY.
WELL, I DON'T FEEL ANY EVIL VIBES. MAYBE THERE'S NOTHING TO THESE RUMORS AFTER ALL.
THEY SAY SHE FORETELLS DISASTER...
BUT AS LONG AS SHE DOESN'T HURT US HERSELF, WE MIGHT AS WELL JUST IGNORE HER.
YOU'RE WRONG.
SHE DOES STUFF!

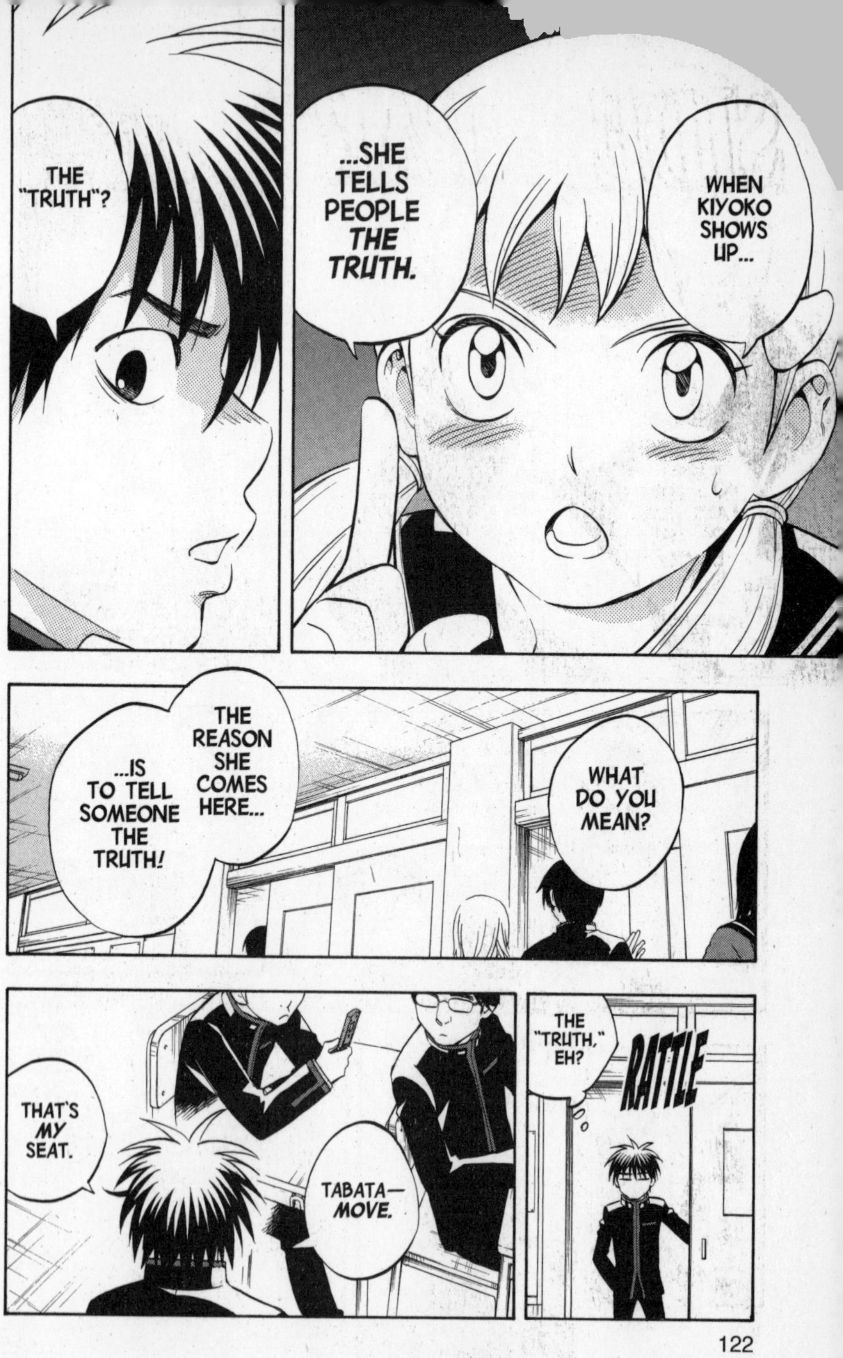
WHEN KIYOKO SHOWS UP...
...SHE TELLS PEOPLE *THE TRUTH.*
THE "TRUTH"?
WHAT DO YOU MEAN?
THE REASON SHE COMES HERE...
...IS TO TELL SOMEONE THE TRUTH!
THE "TRUTH," EH?
RATTLE
THAT'S *MY* SEAT.
TABATA—*MOVE.*

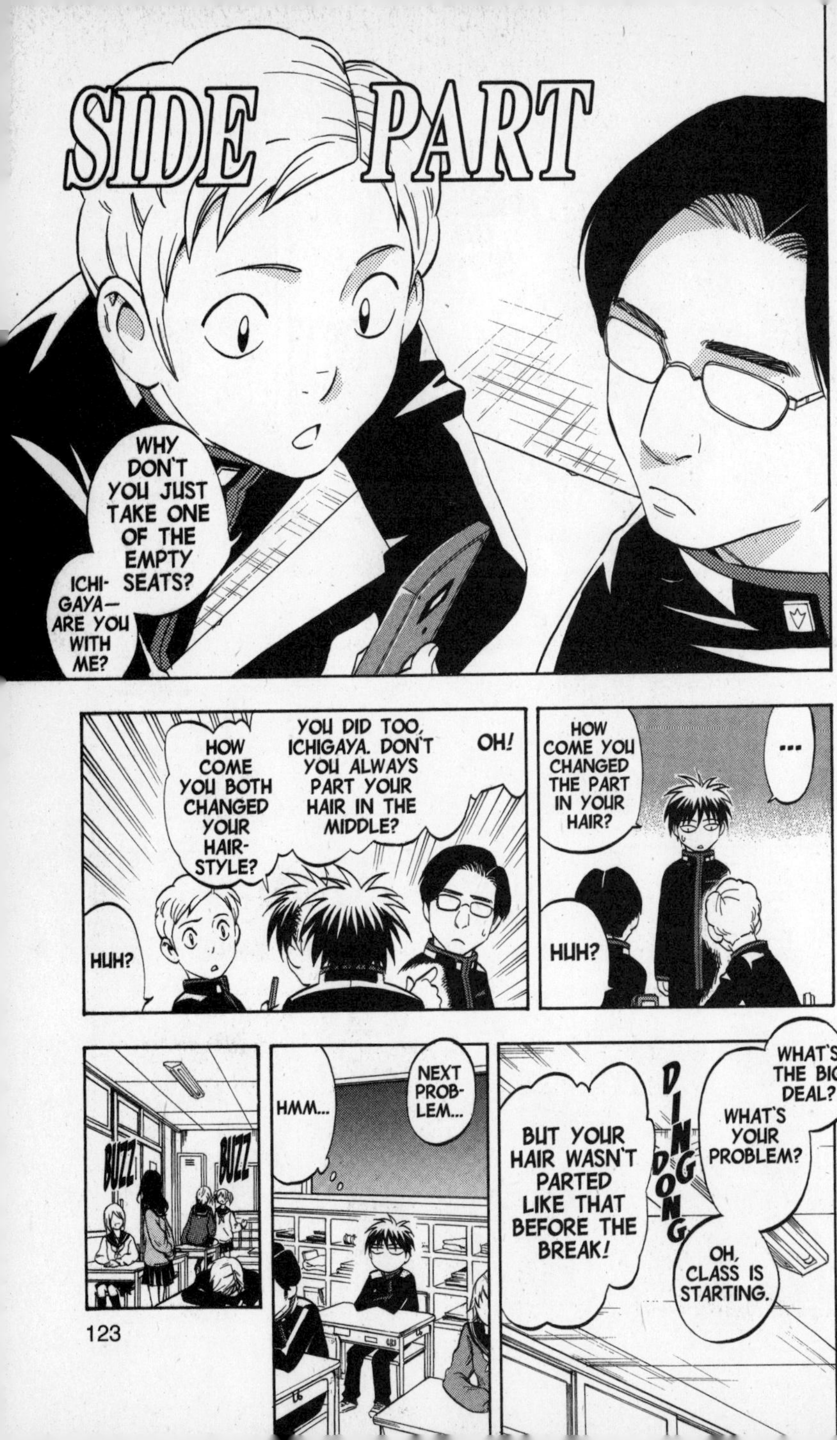
SIDE PART
WHY DON'T YOU JUST TAKE ONE OF THE EMPTY SEATS?
ICHI-GAYA—ARE YOU WITH ME?
...
HOW COME YOU CHANGED THE PART IN YOUR HAIR?
HUH?
OH!
YOU DID TOO, ICHIGAYA. DON'T YOU ALWAYS PART YOUR HAIR IN THE MIDDLE?
HOW COME YOU BOTH CHANGED YOUR HAIR-STYLE?
HUH?
WHAT'S THE BIG DEAL?
WHAT'S YOUR PROBLEM?
BUT YOUR HAIR WASN'T PARTED LIKE THAT BEFORE THE BREAK!
DING DONG
OH, CLASS IS STARTING.
NEXT PROB-LEM...
HMM...
BUZZ
BUZZ

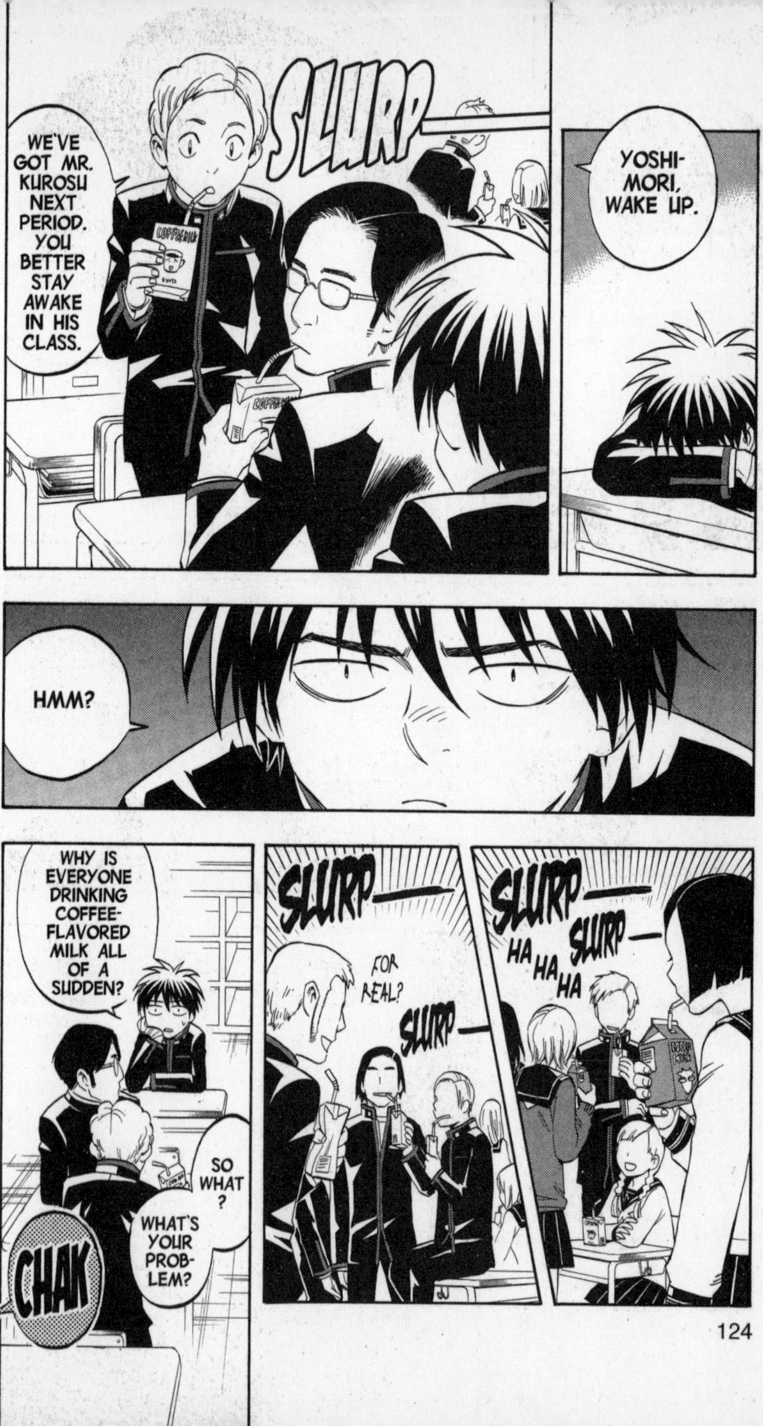
YOSHI-MORI, WAKE UP.
SLURP
WE'VE GOT MR. KUROSU NEXT PERIOD. YOU BETTER STAY AWAKE IN HIS CLASS.
HMM?
SLURP—
HA HA HA
SLURP—
SLURP—
FOR REAL?
SLURP—
WHY IS EVERYONE DRINKING COFFEE-FLAVORED MILK ALL OF A SUDDEN?
SO WHAT?
WHAT'S YOUR PROB-LEM?
CHAK

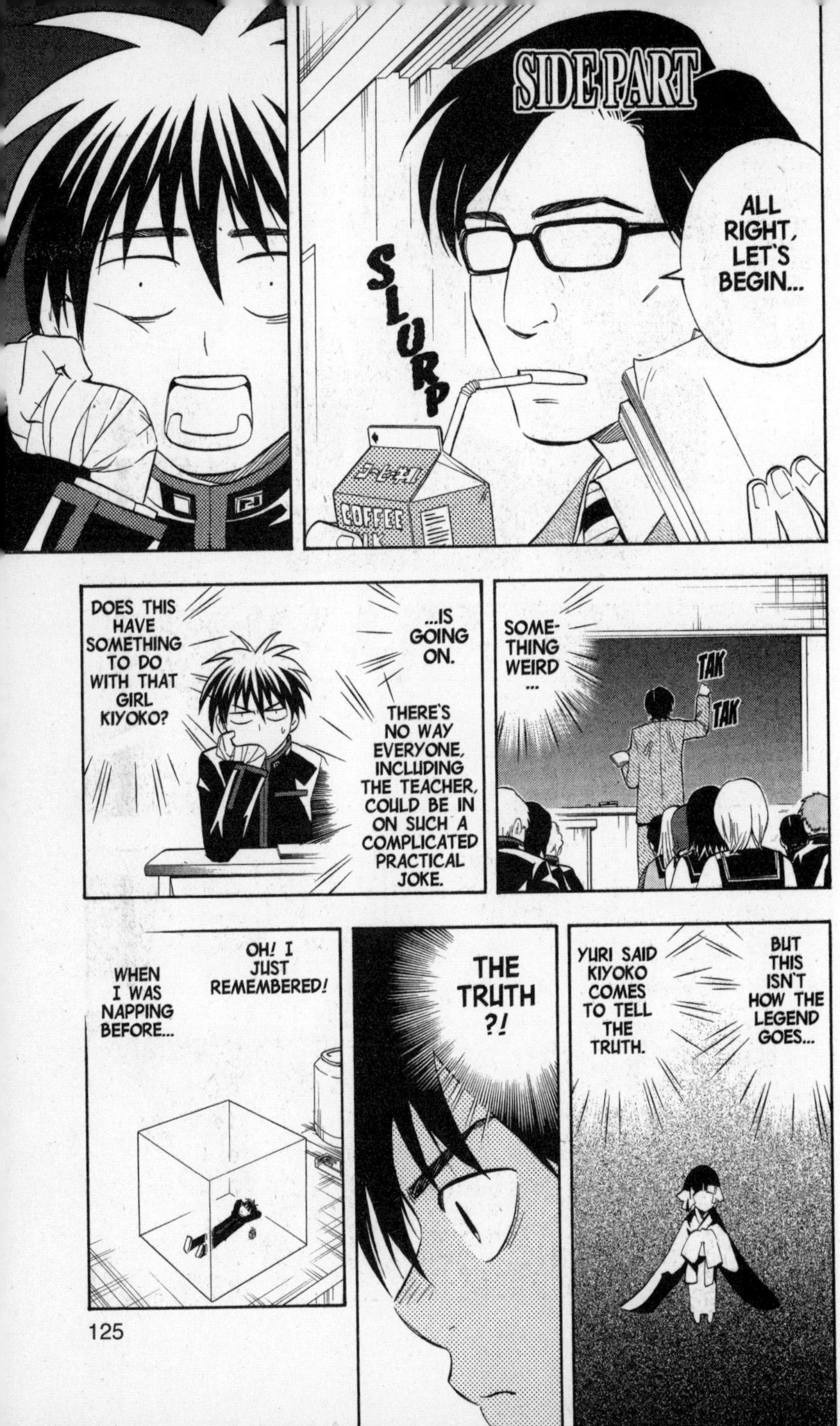
SIDE PART
ALL RIGHT, LET'S BEGIN...
SLURP
COFFEE
SOMETHING WEIRD ...
TAK
TAK
...IS GOING ON.
THERE'S NO WAY EVERYONE, INCLUDING THE TEACHER, COULD BE IN ON SUCH A COMPLICATED PRACTICAL JOKE.
DOES THIS HAVE SOMETHING TO DO WITH THAT GIRL KIYOKO?
BUT THIS ISN'T HOW THE LEGEND GOES...
YURI SAID KIYOKO COMES TO TELL THE TRUTH.
THE TRUTH ?!
OH! I JUST REMEMBERED!
WHEN I WAS NAPPING BEFORE...

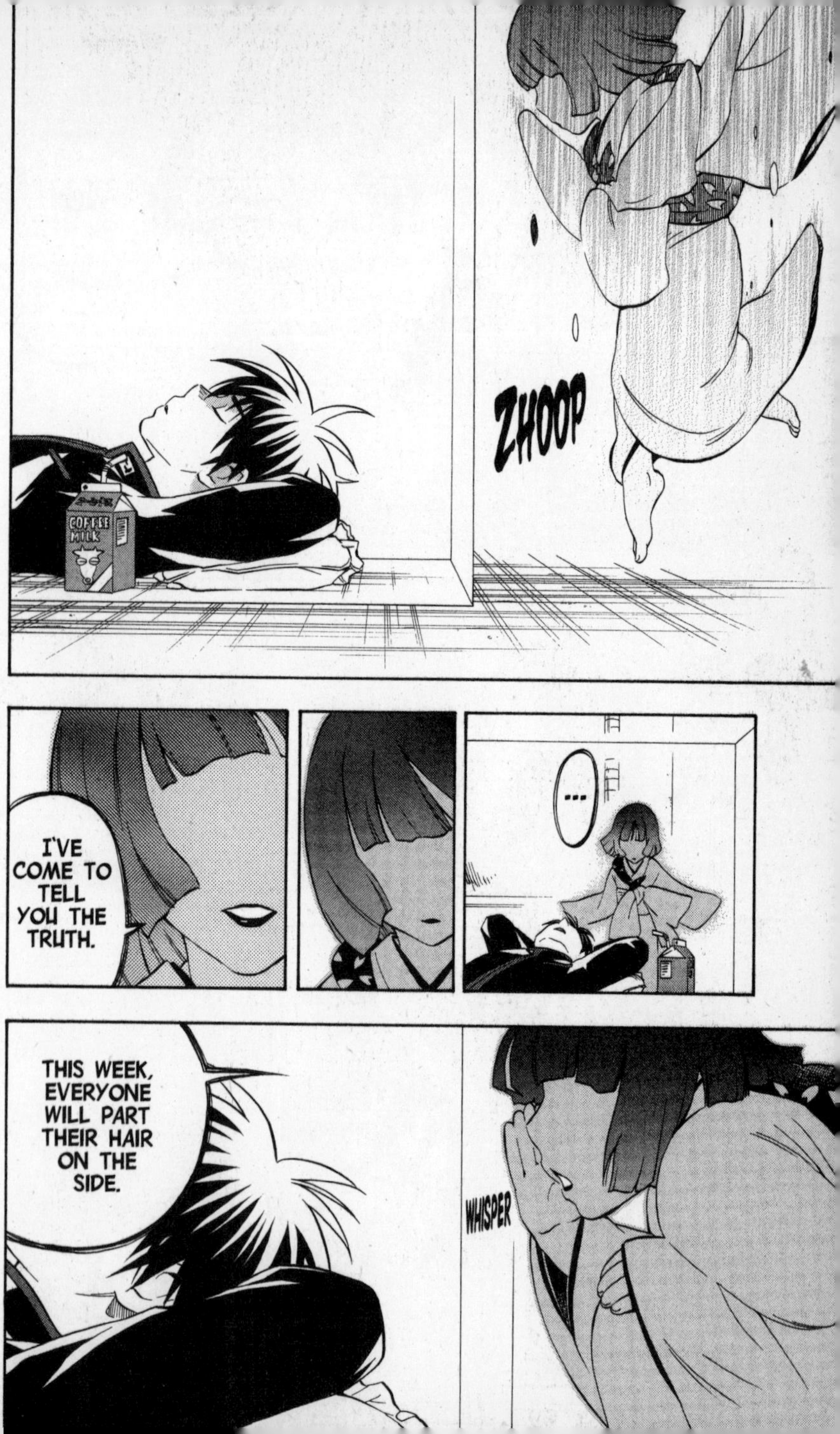
ZHOOP
COFFEE MILK
...
I'VE COME TO TELL YOU THE TRUTH.
WHISPER
THIS WEEK, EVERYONE WILL PART THEIR HAIR ON THE SIDE.

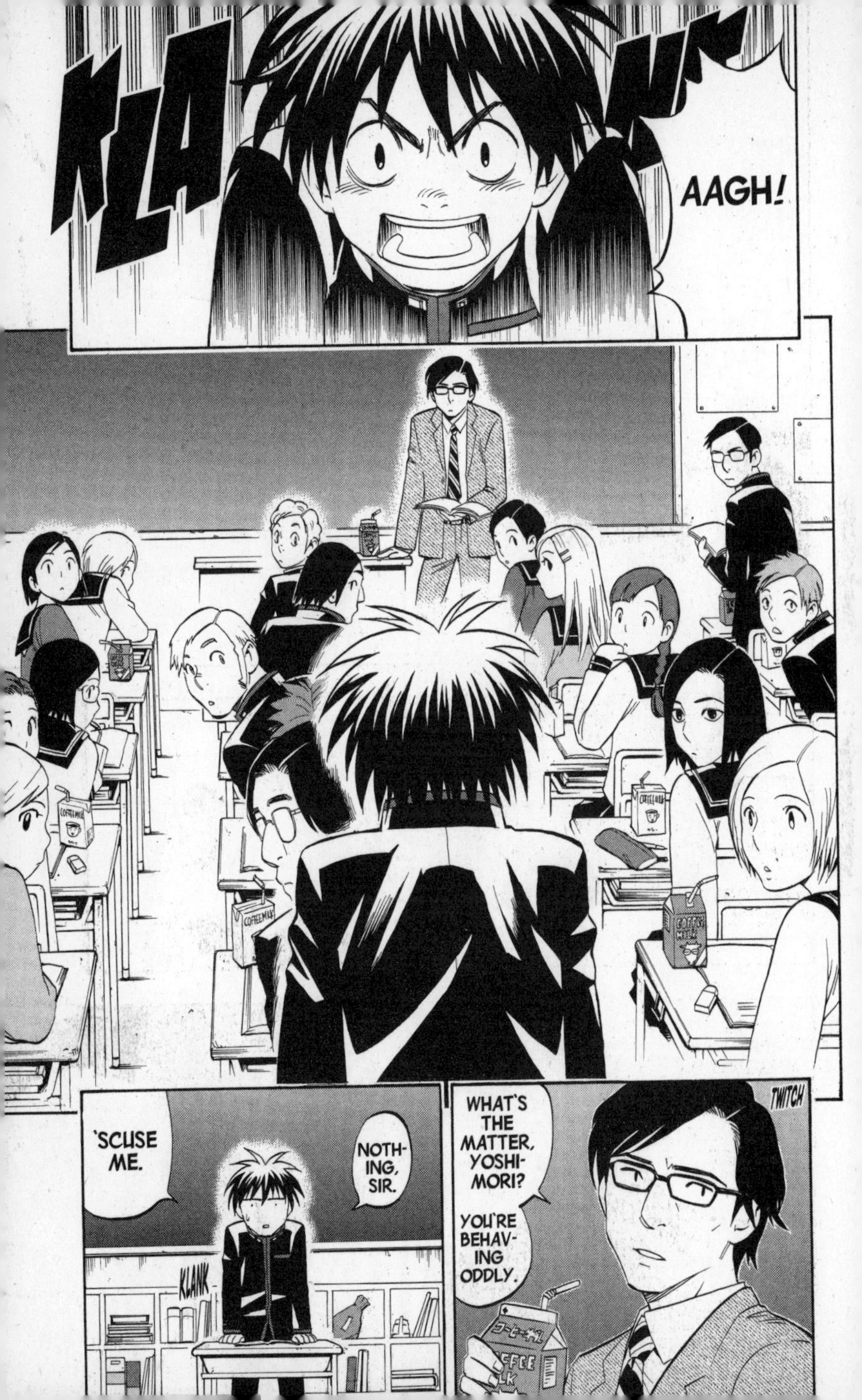
KLANK
AAGH!
TWITCH
WHAT'S THE MATTER, YOSHIMORI?
YOU'RE BEHAVING ODDLY.
NOTHING, SIR.
'SCUSE ME.
KLANK

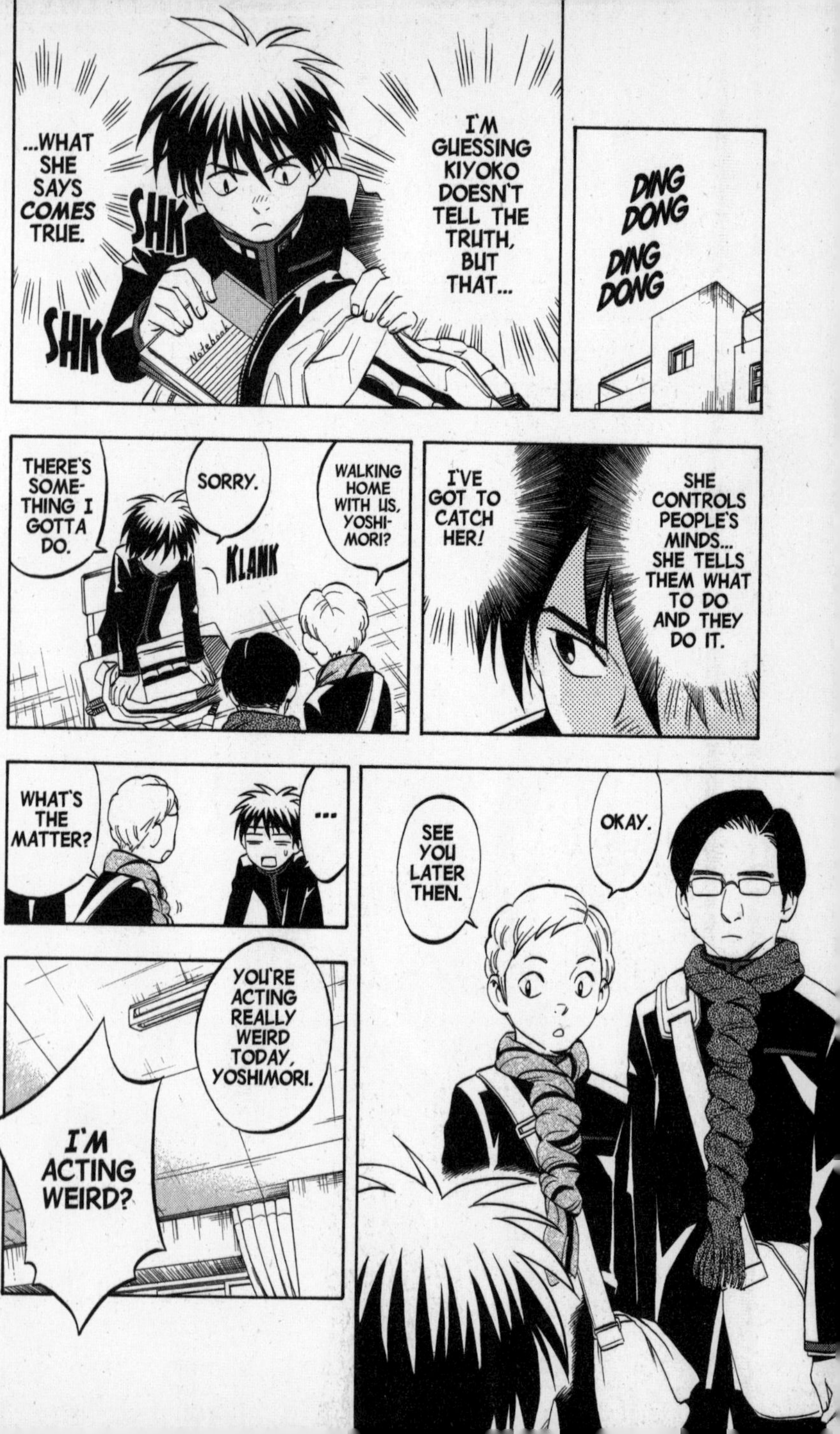
DING DONG
DING DONG
I'M GUESSING KIYOKO DOESN'T TELL THE TRUTH, BUT THAT...
...WHAT SHE SAYS COMES TRUE.
SHK
SHK
Notebook
SHE CONTROLS PEOPLE'S MINDS... SHE TELLS THEM WHAT TO DO AND THEY DO IT.
I'VE GOT TO CATCH HER!
WALKING HOME WITH US, YOSHIMORI?
SORRY.
KLANK
THERE'S SOMETHING I GOTTA DO.
OKAY.
SEE YOU LATER THEN.
...
WHAT'S THE MATTER?
YOU'RE ACTING REALLY WEIRD TODAY, YOSHIMORI.
I'M ACTING WEIRD?

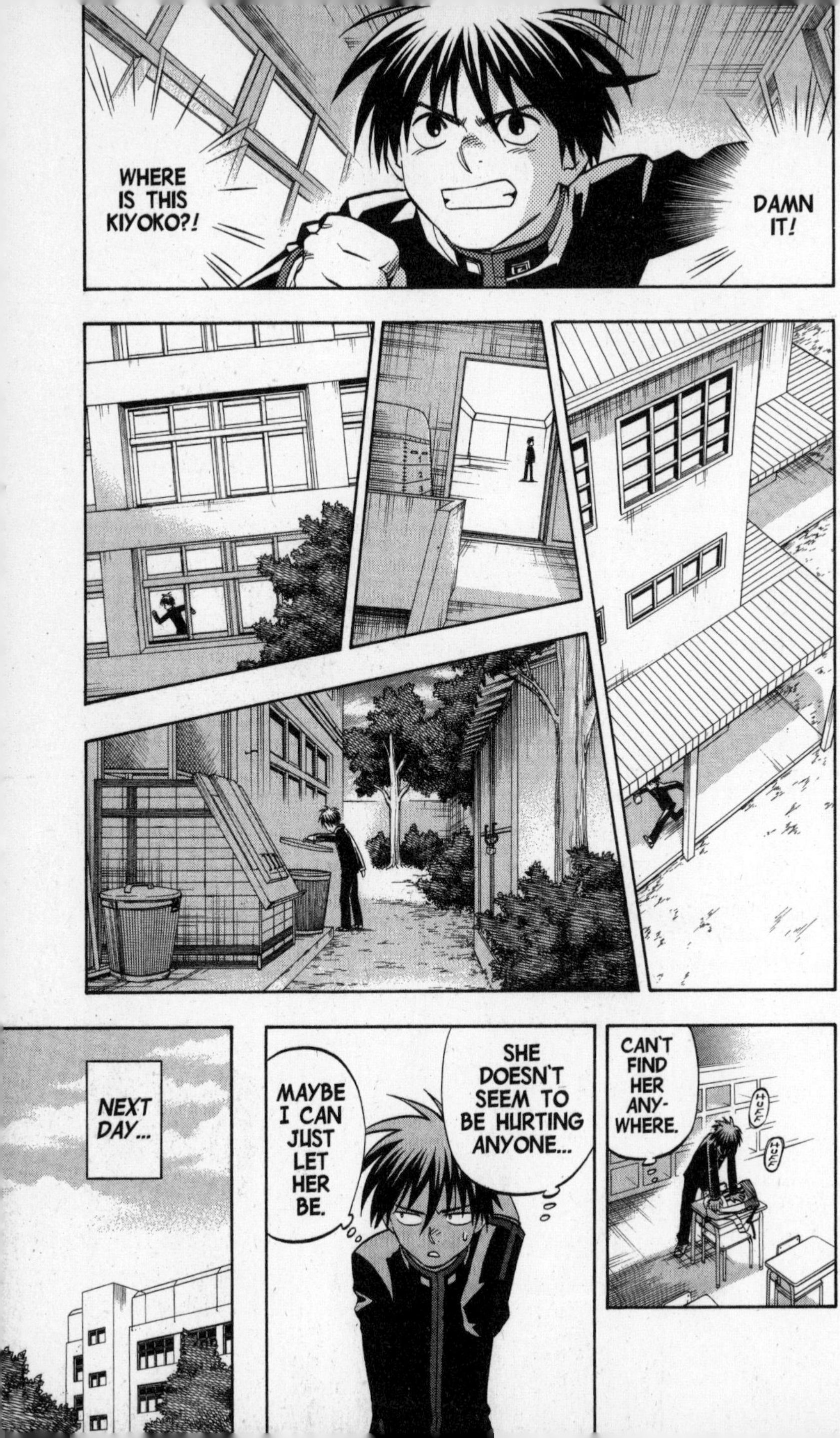
DAMN IT!
WHERE IS THIS KIYOKO?!
CAN'T FIND HER ANY-WHERE.
HUFF
HUFF
SHE DOESN'T SEEM TO BE HURTING ANYONE...
MAYBE I CAN JUST LET HER BE.
NEXT DAY...

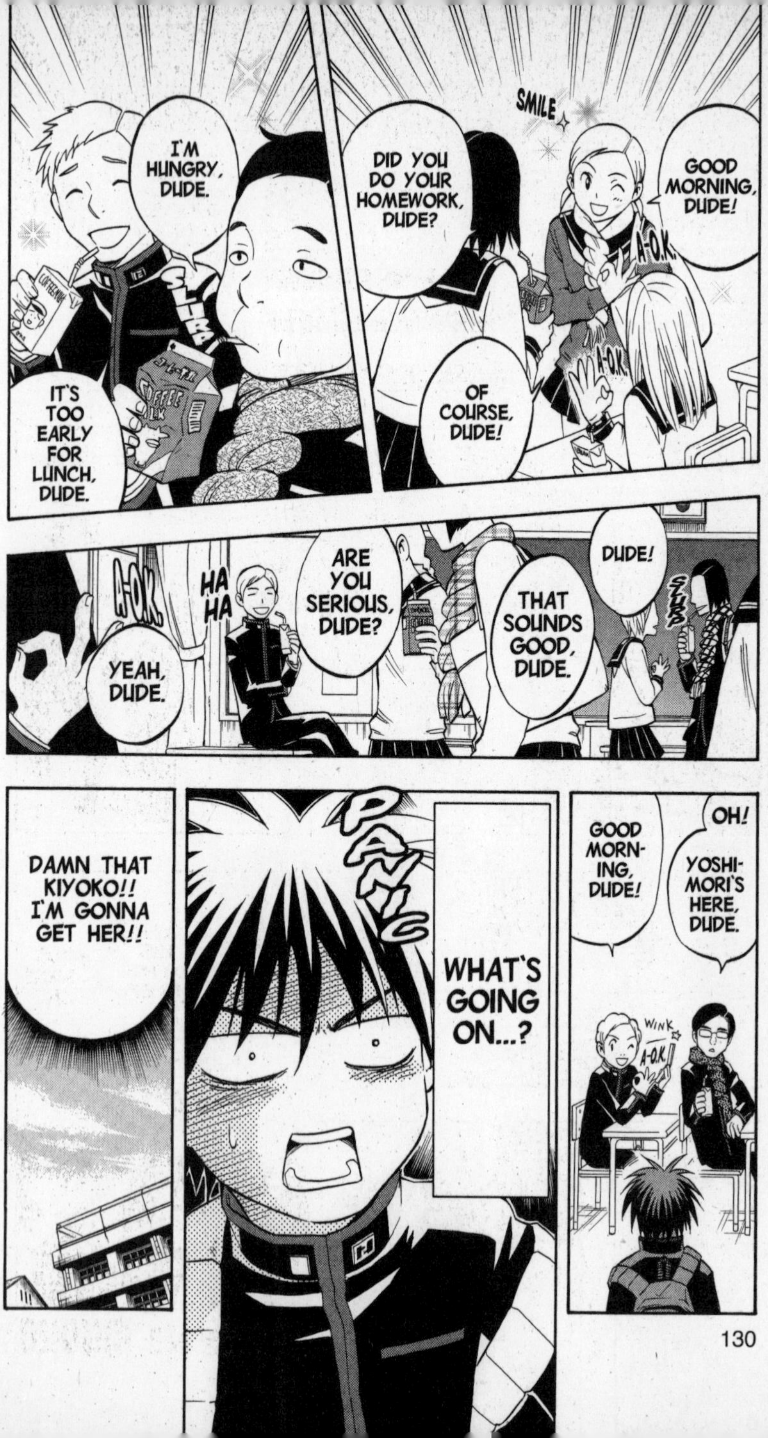
SMILE
GOOD MORNING, DUDE!
A-O.K.
DID YOU DO YOUR HOMEWORK, DUDE?
A-O.K.
OF COURSE, DUDE!
I'M HUNGRY, DUDE.
SLURP
IT'S TOO EARLY FOR LUNCH, DUDE.
DUDE!
SLURP
THAT SOUNDS GOOD, DUDE.
ARE YOU SERIOUS, DUDE?
HA HA
A-O.K.
YEAH, DUDE.
OH!
YOSHI-MORI'S HERE, DUDE.
GOOD MORN-ING, DUDE!
WINK
A-O.K.
PANG
WHAT'S GOING ON...?
DAMN THAT KIYOKO!! I'M GONNA GET HER!!

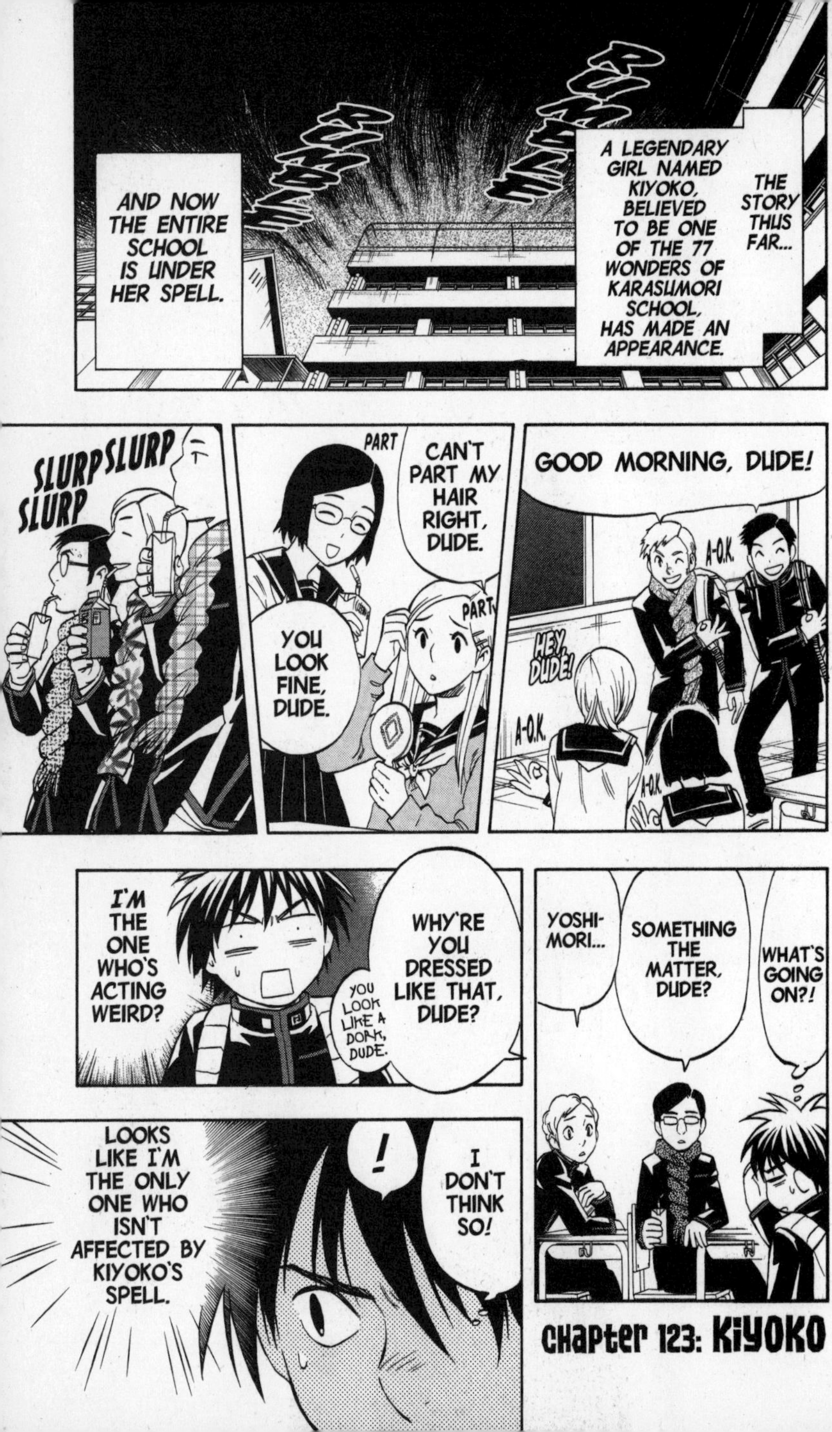
THE STORY THUS FAR...
A LEGENDARY GIRL NAMED KIYOKO, BELIEVED TO BE ONE OF THE 77 WONDERS OF KARASUMORI SCHOOL, HAS MADE AN APPEARANCE.
RUMBLE
RUMBLE
AND NOW THE ENTIRE SCHOOL IS UNDER HER SPELL.
GOOD MORNING, DUDE!
A-O.K.
HEY, DUDE!
A-O.K.
A-O.K.
PART
CAN'T PART MY HAIR RIGHT, DUDE.
PART
YOU LOOK FINE, DUDE.
SLURP SLURP
SLURP
WHAT'S GOING ON?!
SOMETHING THE MATTER, DUDE?
YOSHIMORI...
Chapter 123: Kiyoko
WHY'RE YOU DRESSED LIKE THAT, DUDE?
YOU LOOK LIKE A DORK, DUDE.
I'M THE ONE WHO'S ACTING WEIRD?
!
I DON'T THINK SO!
LOOKS LIKE I'M THE ONLY ONE WHO ISN'T AFFECTED BY KIYOKO'S SPELL.

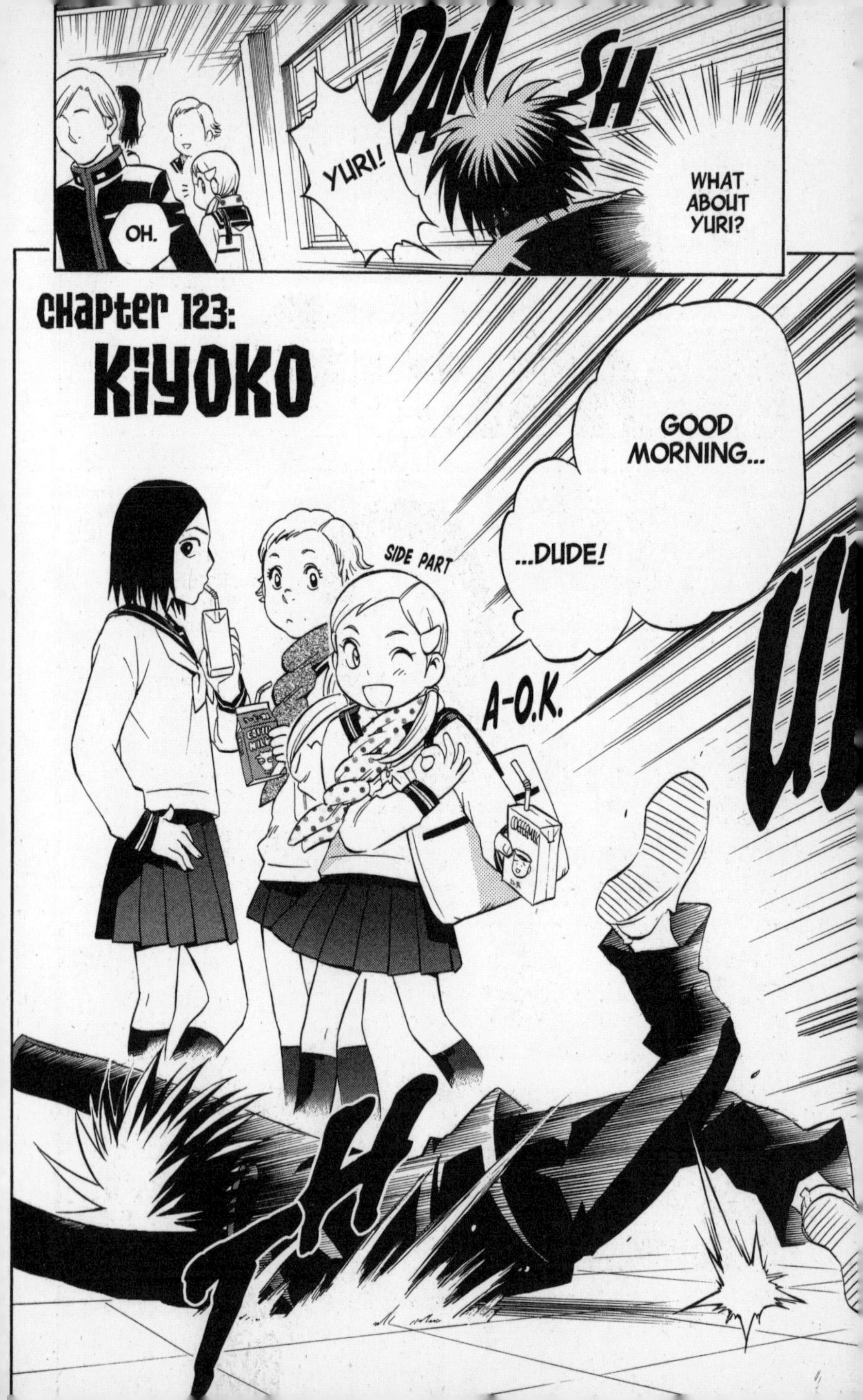
WHAT ABOUT YURI?
DA SH
YURI!
OH.
Chapter 123:
Kiyoko
GOOD MORNING...
...DUDE!
A-O.K.
SIDE PART

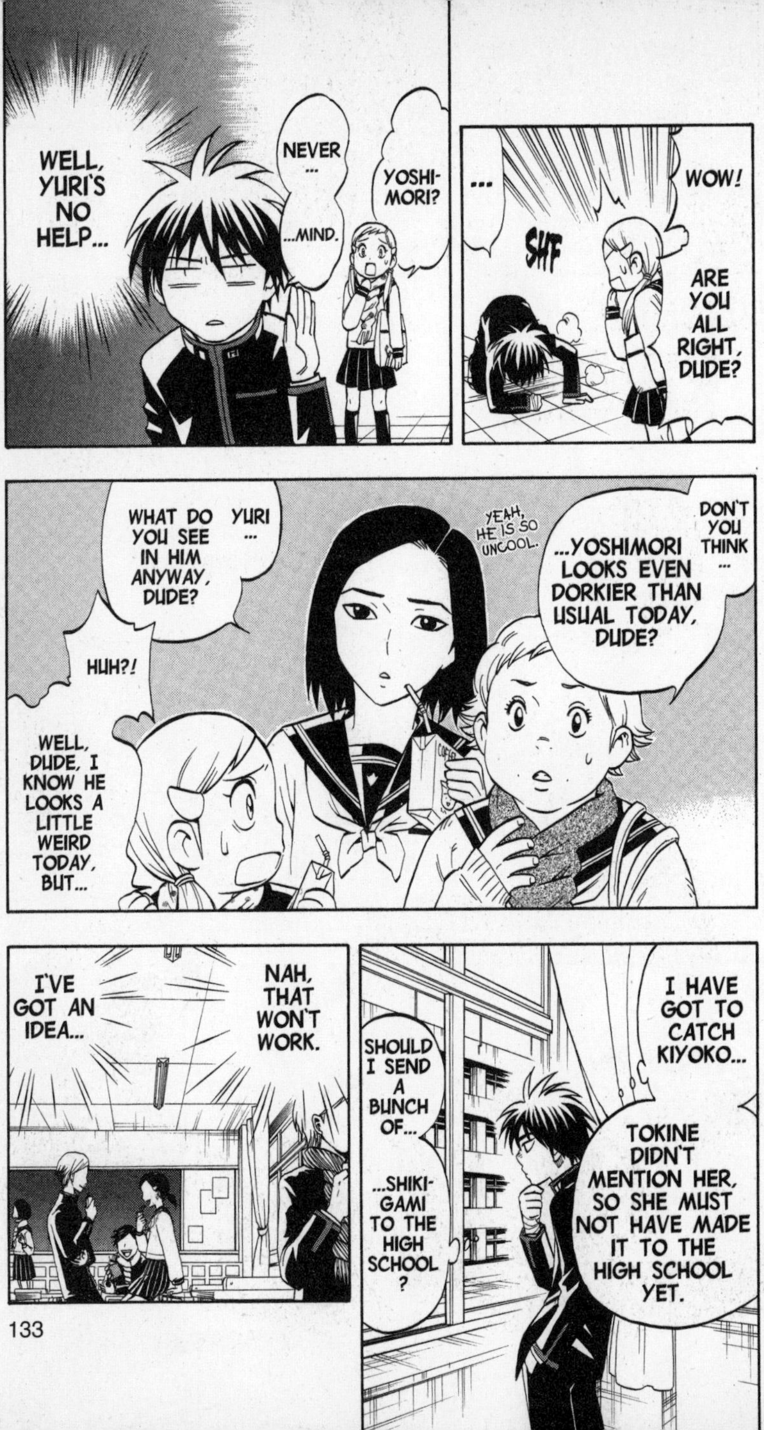
WOW!
...
SHF
ARE YOU ALL RIGHT, DUDE?
YOSHIMORI?
NEVER... ...MIND.
WELL, YURI'S NO HELP...
DON'T YOU THINK... ...YOSHIMORI LOOKS EVEN DORKIER THAN USUAL TODAY, DUDE?
YEAH, HE IS SO UNCOOL.
YURI... WHAT DO YOU SEE IN HIM ANYWAY, DUDE?
HUH?!
WELL, DUDE, I KNOW HE LOOKS A LITTLE WEIRD TODAY, BUT...
I HAVE GOT TO CATCH KIYOKO...
TOKINE DIDN'T MENTION HER, SO SHE MUST NOT HAVE MADE IT TO THE HIGH SCHOOL YET.
SHOULD I SEND A BUNCH OF...
...SHIKIGAMI TO THE HIGH SCHOOL?
I'VE GOT AN IDEA...
NAH, THAT WON'T WORK.

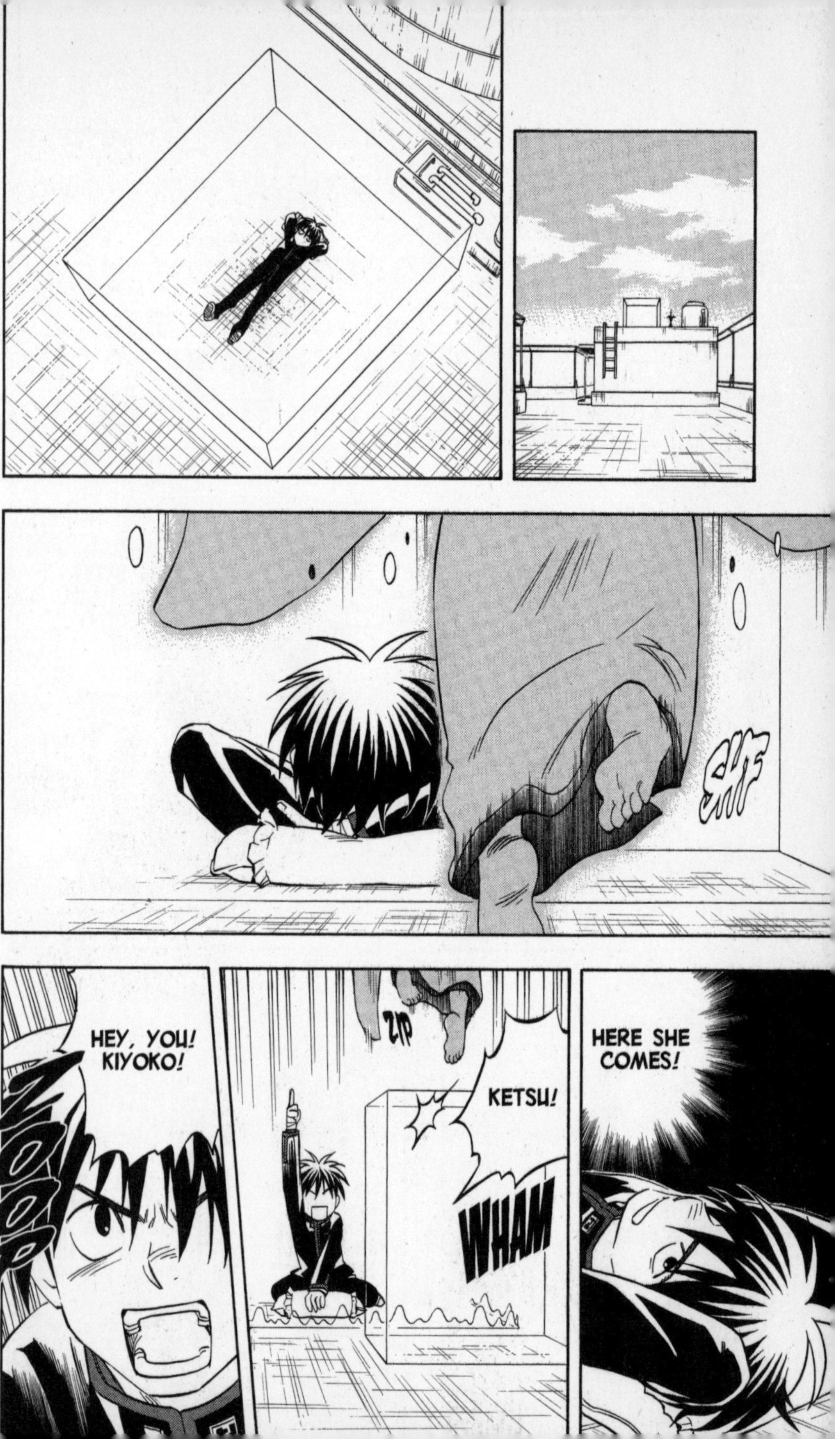
SHF
HERE SHE COMES!
ZIP
KETSU!
WHAM
HEY, YOU! KIYOKO!
WOOP

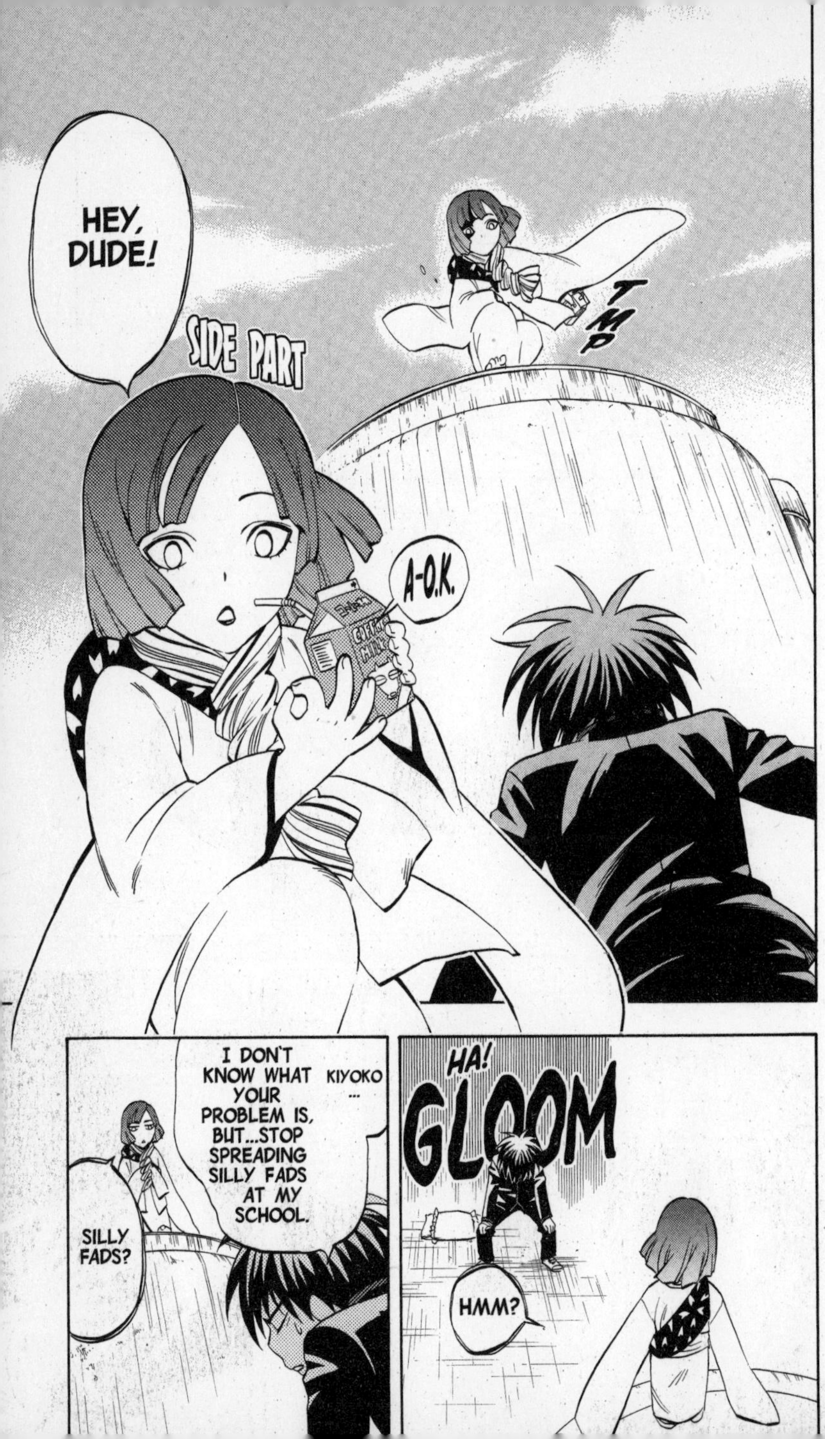
TMP
HEY, DUDE!
SIDE PART
A-O.K.
HA!
GLOOM
HMM?
KIYOKO...
I DON'T KNOW WHAT YOUR PROBLEM IS, BUT...STOP SPREADING SILLY FADS AT MY SCHOOL.
SILLY FADS?

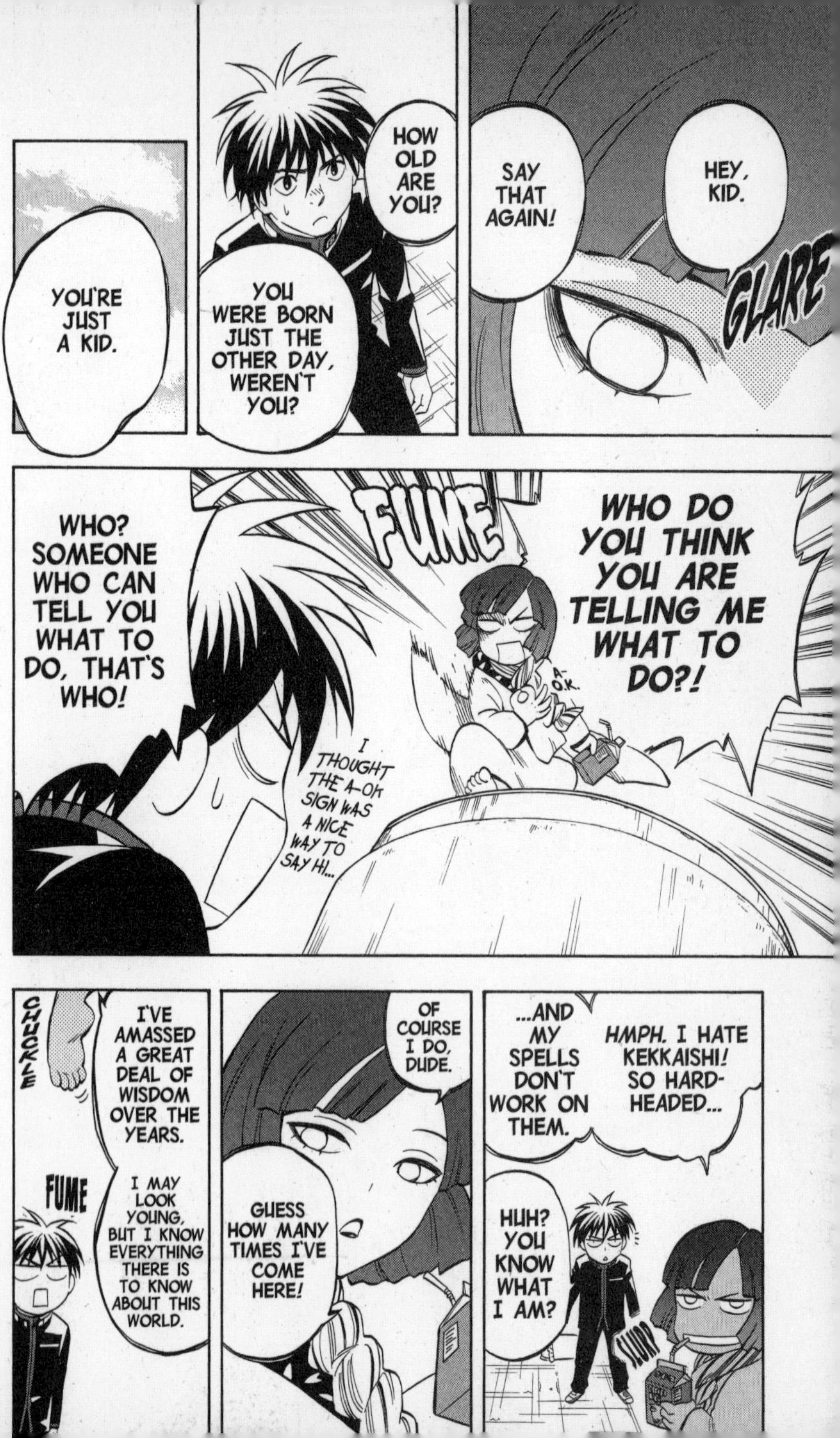
GLARE
HEY, KID.
SAY THAT AGAIN!
HOW OLD ARE YOU?
YOU WERE BORN JUST THE OTHER DAY, WEREN'T YOU?
YOU'RE JUST A KID.
WHO DO YOU THINK YOU ARE TELLING ME WHAT TO DO?!
A-O.K.
FUME
WHO? SOMEONE WHO CAN TELL YOU WHAT TO DO, THAT'S WHO!
I THOUGHT THE A-OK SIGN WAS A NICE WAY TO SAY HI...
HMPH. I HATE KEKKAISHI! SO HARD-HEADED...
...AND MY SPELLS DON'T WORK ON THEM.
HUH? YOU KNOW WHAT I AM?
SLURP
OF COURSE I DO, DUDE.
GUESS HOW MANY TIMES I'VE COME HERE!
CHUCKLE
I'VE AMASSED A GREAT DEAL OF WISDOM OVER THE YEARS.
I MAY LOOK YOUNG, BUT I KNOW EVERYTHING THERE IS TO KNOW ABOUT THIS WORLD.
FUME

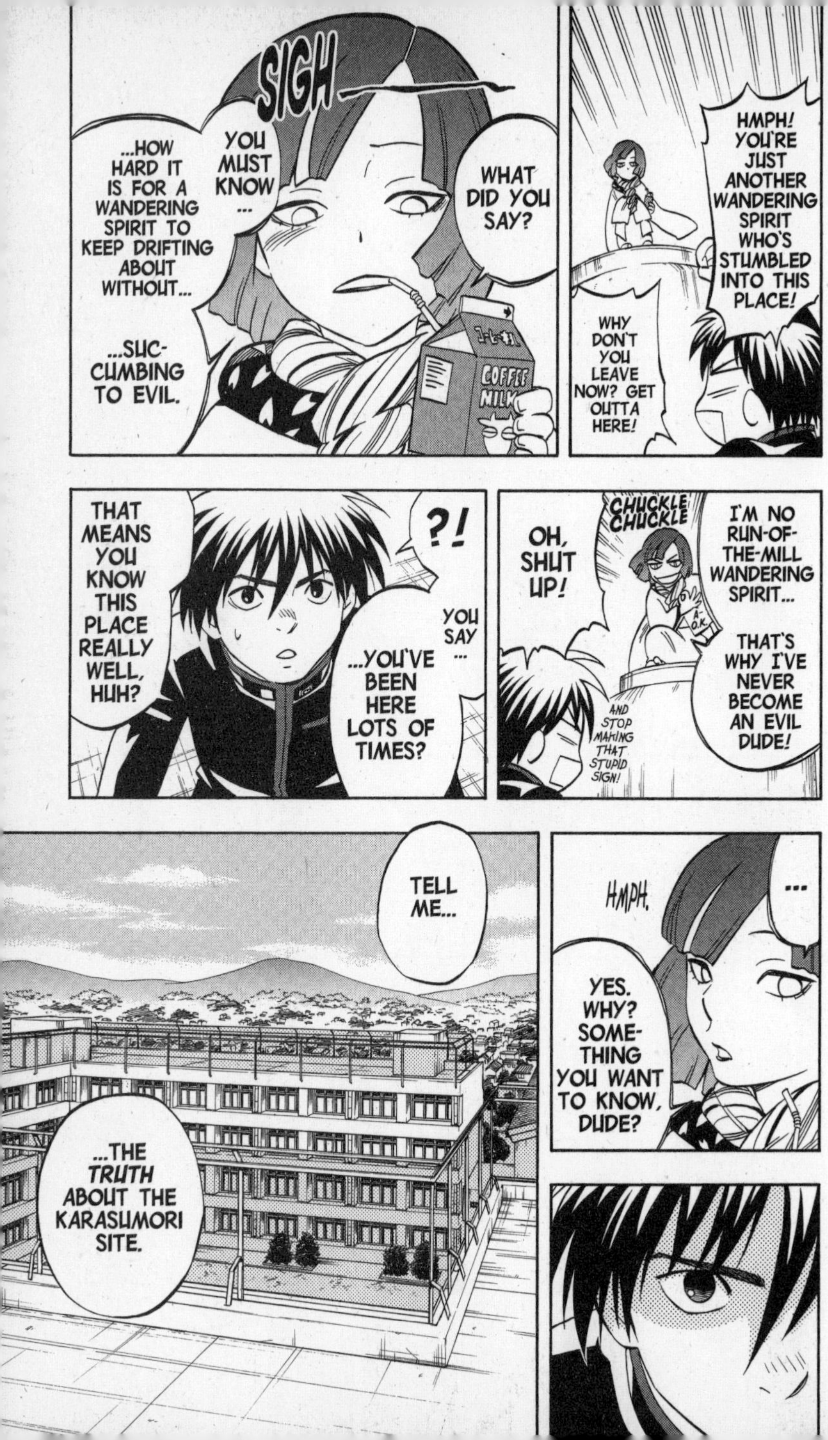
HMPH! YOU'RE JUST ANOTHER WANDERING SPIRIT WHO'S STUMBLED INTO THIS PLACE!
WHY DON'T YOU LEAVE NOW? GET OUTTA HERE!
WHAT DID YOU SAY?
SIGH
YOU MUST KNOW...
...HOW HARD IT IS FOR A WANDERING SPIRIT TO KEEP DRIFTING ABOUT WITHOUT...
...SUC-CUMBING TO EVIL.
COFFEE MILK
CHUCKLE CHUCKLE
I'M NO RUN-OF-THE-MILL WANDERING SPIRIT...
A-O.K.
THAT'S WHY I'VE NEVER BECOME AN EVIL DUDE!
OH, SHUT UP!
AND STOP MAKING THAT STUPID SIGN!
?!
YOU SAY...
...YOU'VE BEEN HERE LOTS OF TIMES?
THAT MEANS YOU KNOW THIS PLACE REALLY WELL, HUH?
...
HMPH.
YES. WHY? SOME-THING YOU WANT TO KNOW, DUDE?
TELL ME...
...THE TRUTH ABOUT THE KARASUMORI SITE.

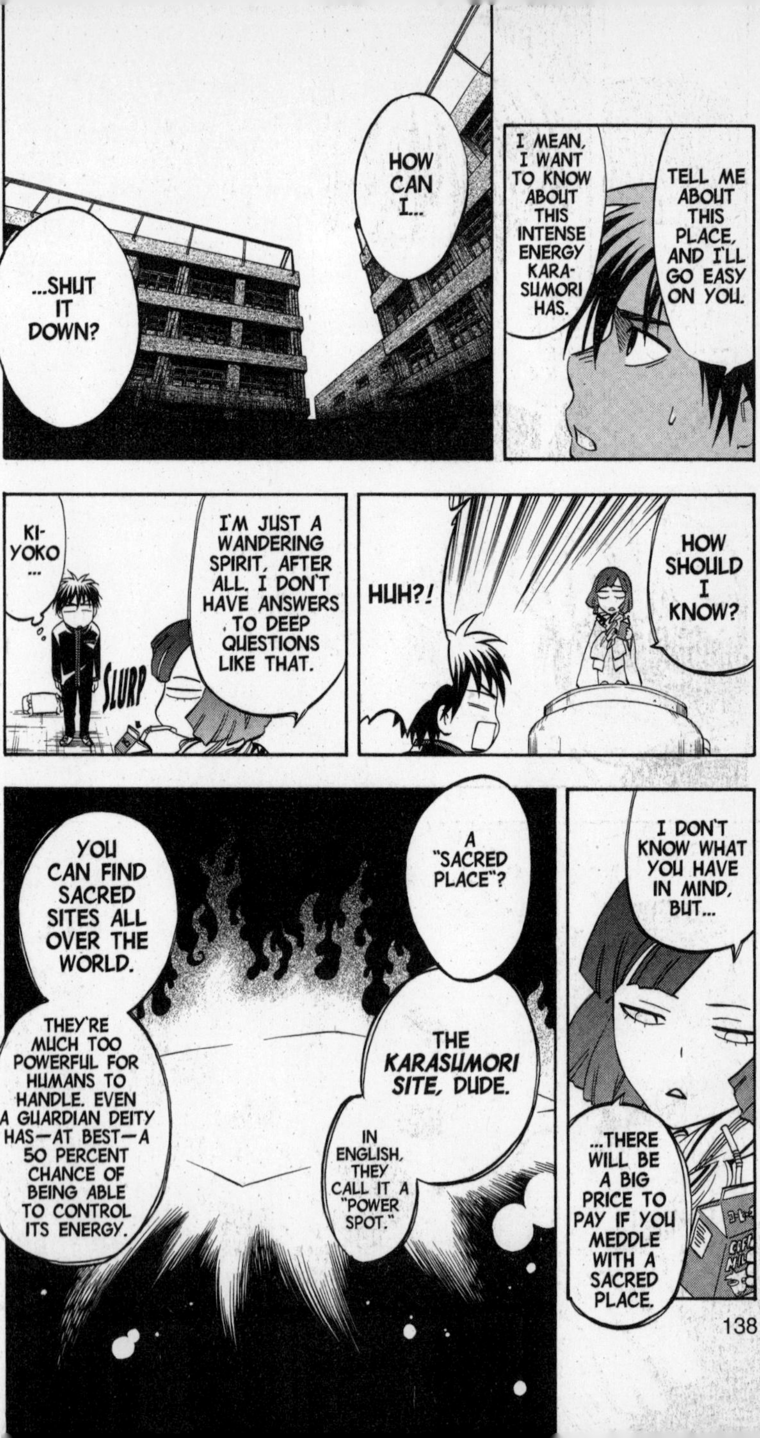
TELL ME ABOUT THIS PLACE, AND I'LL GO EASY ON YOU.
I MEAN, I WANT TO KNOW ABOUT THIS INTENSE ENERGY KARASUMORI HAS.
HOW CAN I...
...SHUT IT DOWN?
HOW SHOULD I KNOW?
HUH?!
I'M JUST A WANDERING SPIRIT, AFTER ALL. I DON'T HAVE ANSWERS TO DEEP QUESTIONS LIKE THAT.
KI-YOKO...
SLURP
I DON'T KNOW WHAT YOU HAVE IN MIND, BUT...
...THERE WILL BE A BIG PRICE TO PAY IF YOU MEDDLE WITH A SACRED PLACE.
A "SACRED PLACE"?
THE *KARASUMORI SITE*, DUDE.
IN ENGLISH, THEY CALL IT A "POWER SPOT."
YOU CAN FIND SACRED SITES ALL OVER THE WORLD.
THEY'RE MUCH TOO POWERFUL FOR HUMANS TO HANDLE. EVEN A GUARDIAN DEITY HAS—AT BEST—A 50 PERCENT CHANCE OF BEING ABLE TO CONTROL ITS ENERGY.

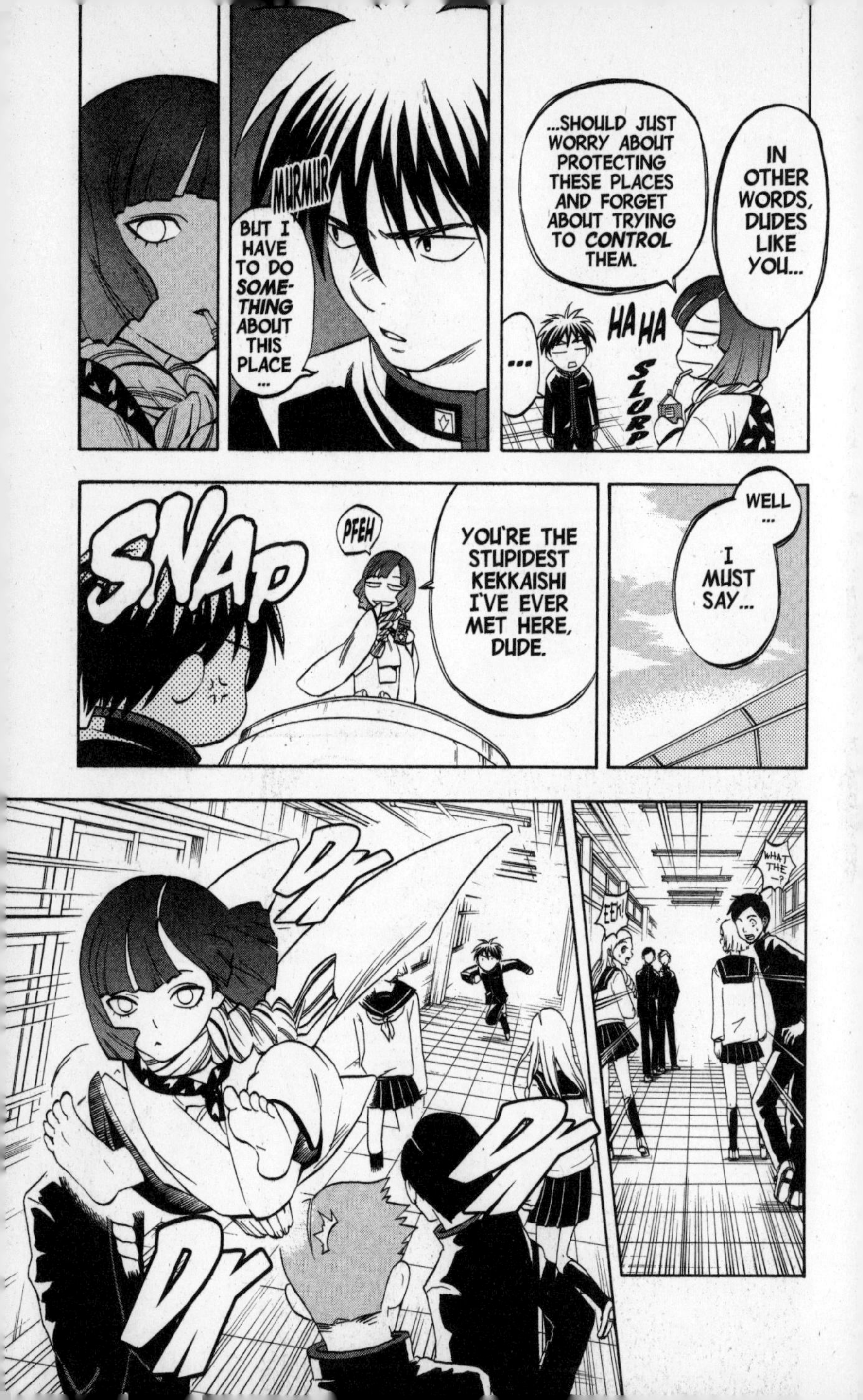
IN OTHER WORDS, DUDES LIKE YOU...
...SHOULD JUST WORRY ABOUT PROTECTING THESE PLACES AND FORGET ABOUT TRYING TO CONTROL THEM.
HA HA
SLURP
...
MURMUR
BUT I HAVE TO DO SOMETHING ABOUT THIS PLACE...
WELL...
I MUST SAY...
YOU'RE THE STUPIDEST KEKKAISHI I'VE EVER MET HERE, DUDE.
PFEH
SNAP
WHAT THE—?
EEK!
DV
DV

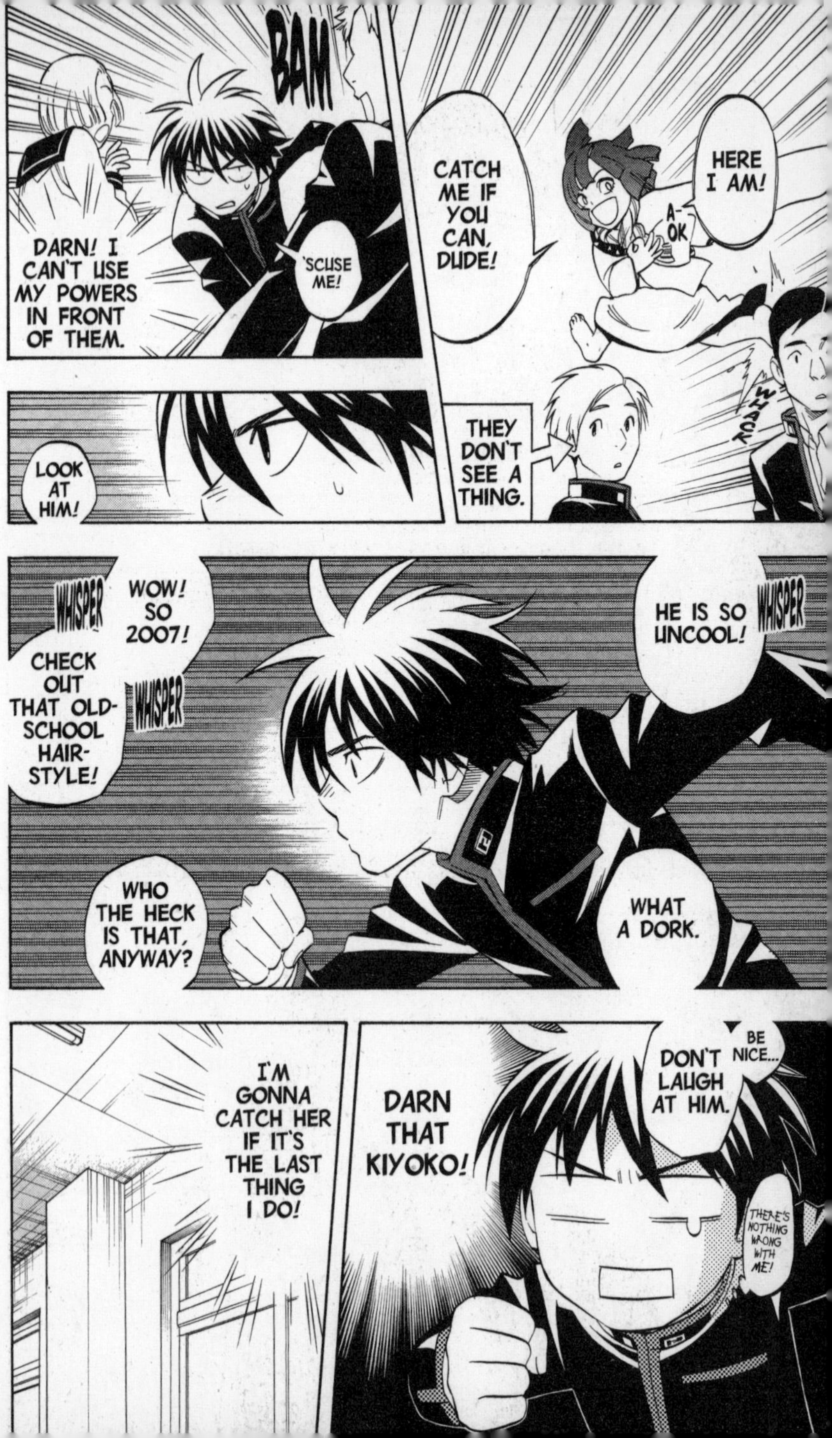
HERE I AM!
A-OK
CATCH ME IF YOU CAN, DUDE!
BAM
'SCUSE ME!
DARN! I CAN'T USE MY POWERS IN FRONT OF THEM.
WHACK
THEY DON'T SEE A THING.
LOOK AT HIM!
WHISPER
HE IS SO UNCOOL!
WHAT A DORK.
WHISPER
WOW! SO 2007!
WHISPER
CHECK OUT THAT OLD-SCHOOL HAIR-STYLE!
WHO THE HECK IS THAT, ANYWAY?
BE NICE...
DON'T LAUGH AT HIM.
THERE'S NOTHING WRONG WITH ME!
DARN THAT KIYOKO!
I'M GONNA CATCH HER IF IT'S THE LAST THING I DO!

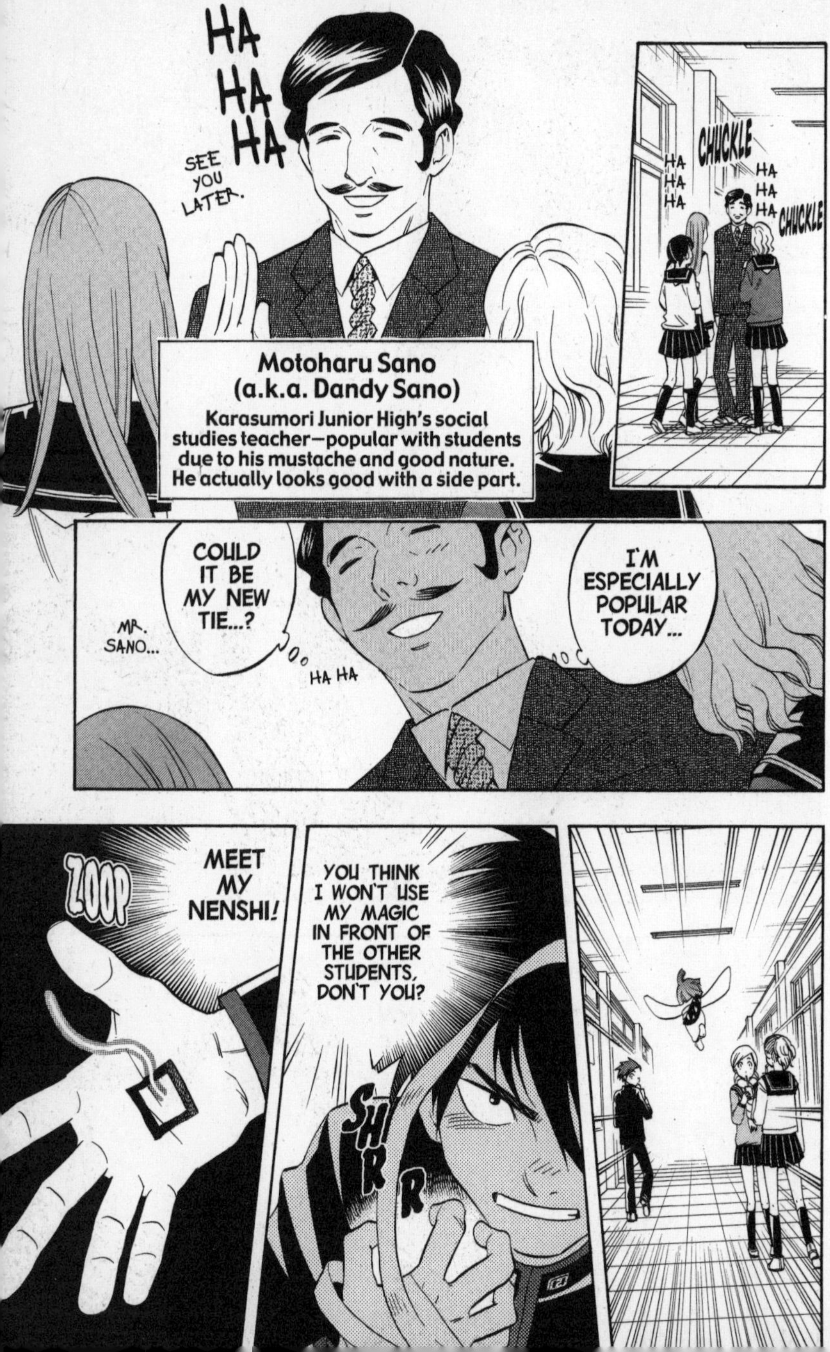
HA HA HA
CHUCKLE
HA HA HA
CHUCKLE
HA HA HA
SEE YOU LATER.
Motoharu Sano (a.k.a. Dandy Sano)
Karasumori Junior High's social studies teacher—popular with students due to his mustache and good nature. He actually looks good with a side part.
I'M ESPECIALLY POPULAR TODAY...
COULD IT BE MY NEW TIE...?
HA HA
MR. SANO...
YOU THINK I WON'T USE MY MAGIC IN FRONT OF THE OTHER STUDENTS, DON'T YOU?
SHRR
MEET MY NENSHI!
ZOOP

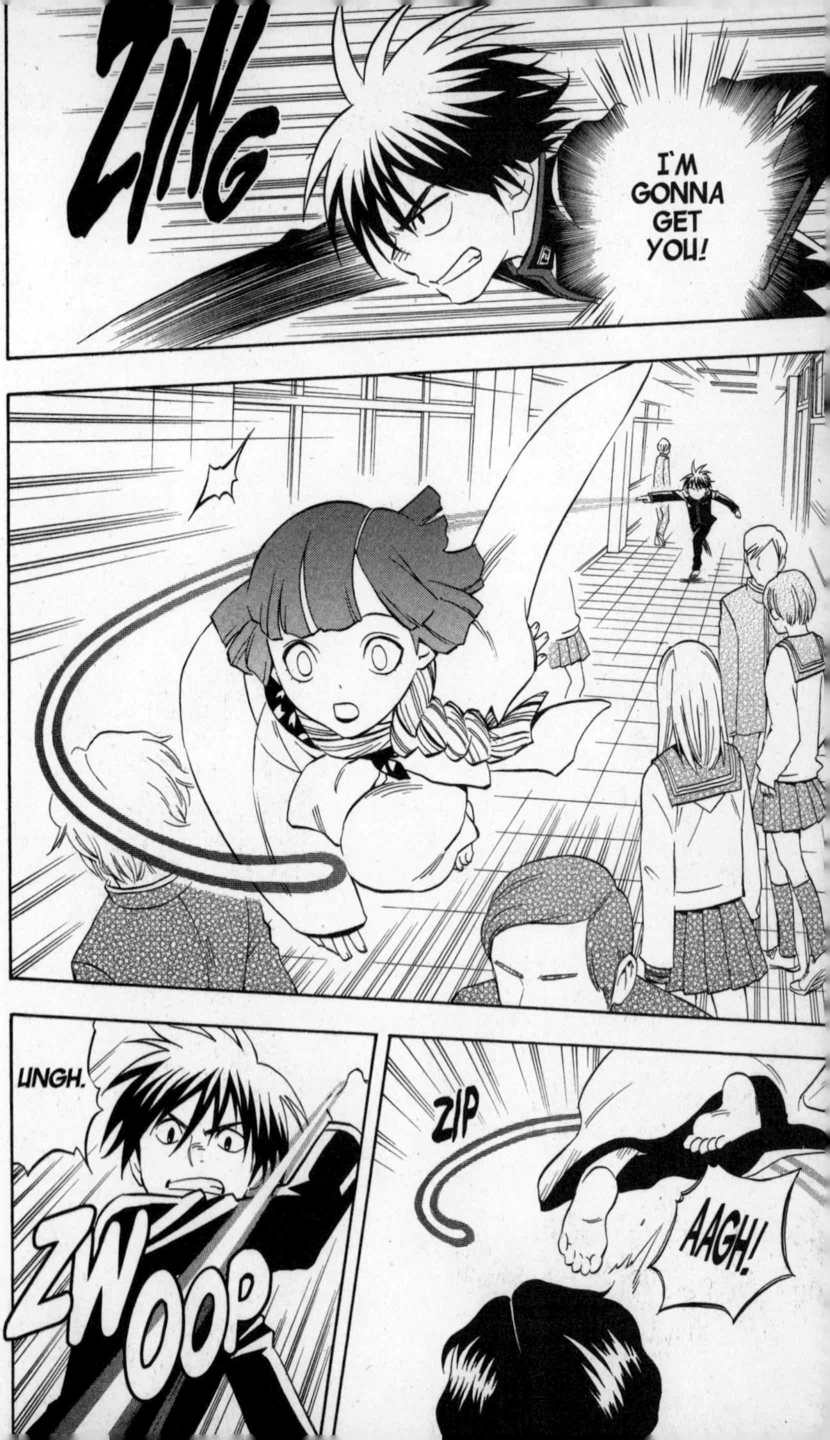
ZING
I'M GONNA GET YOU!
ZIP
AAGH!
UNGH.
ZWOOP

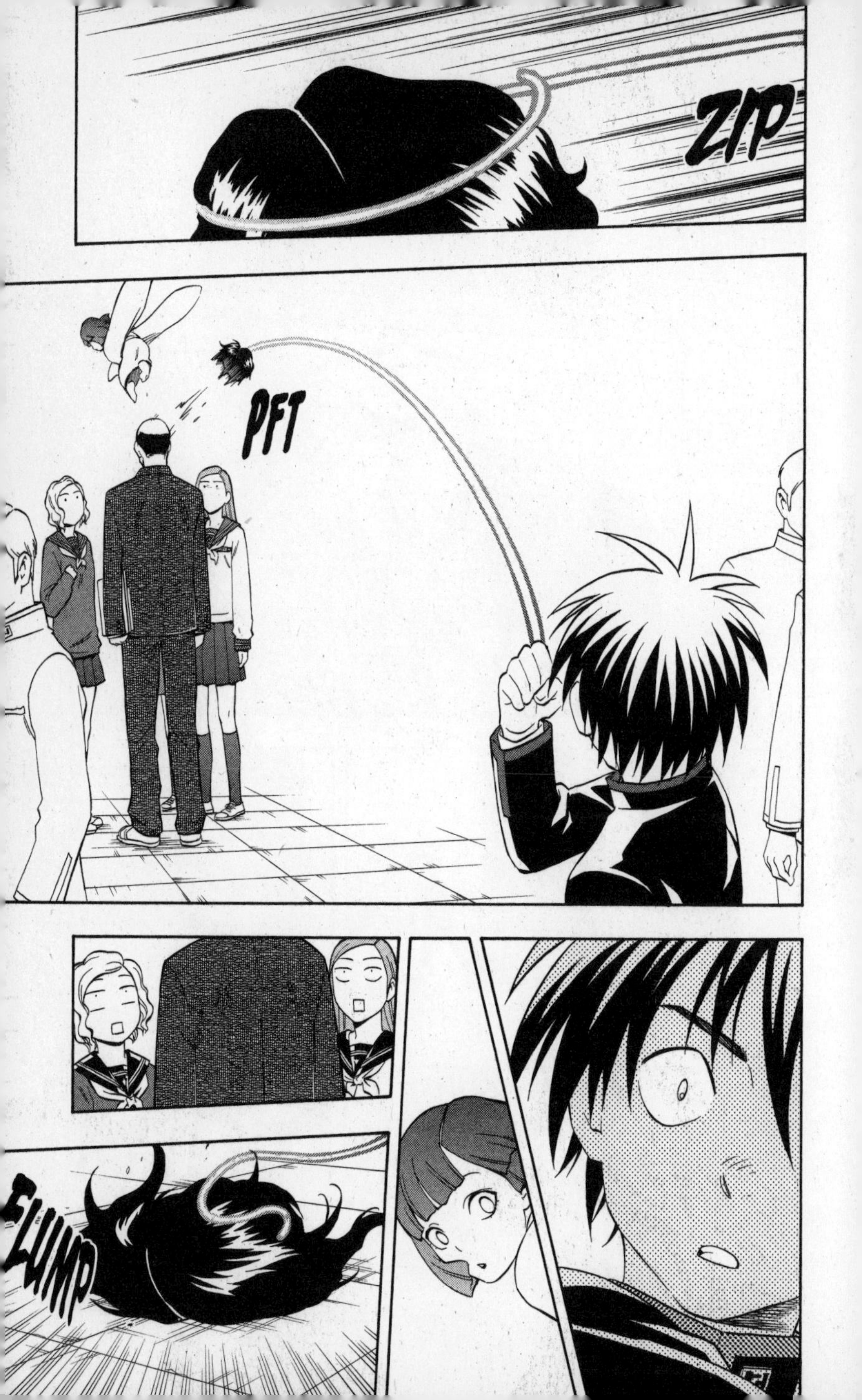
ZIP
PFT
FLUMP

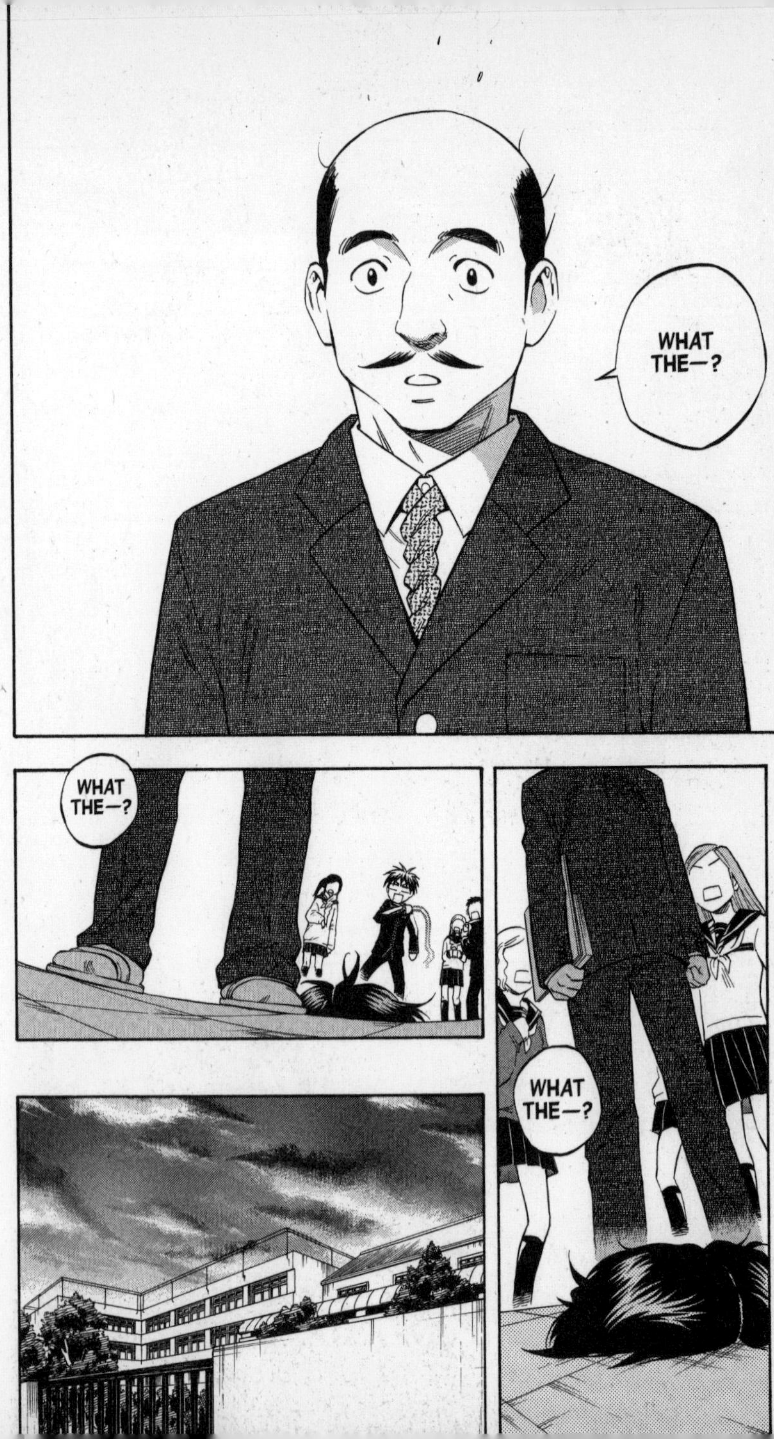
WHAT THE—?
WHAT THE—?
WHAT THE—?

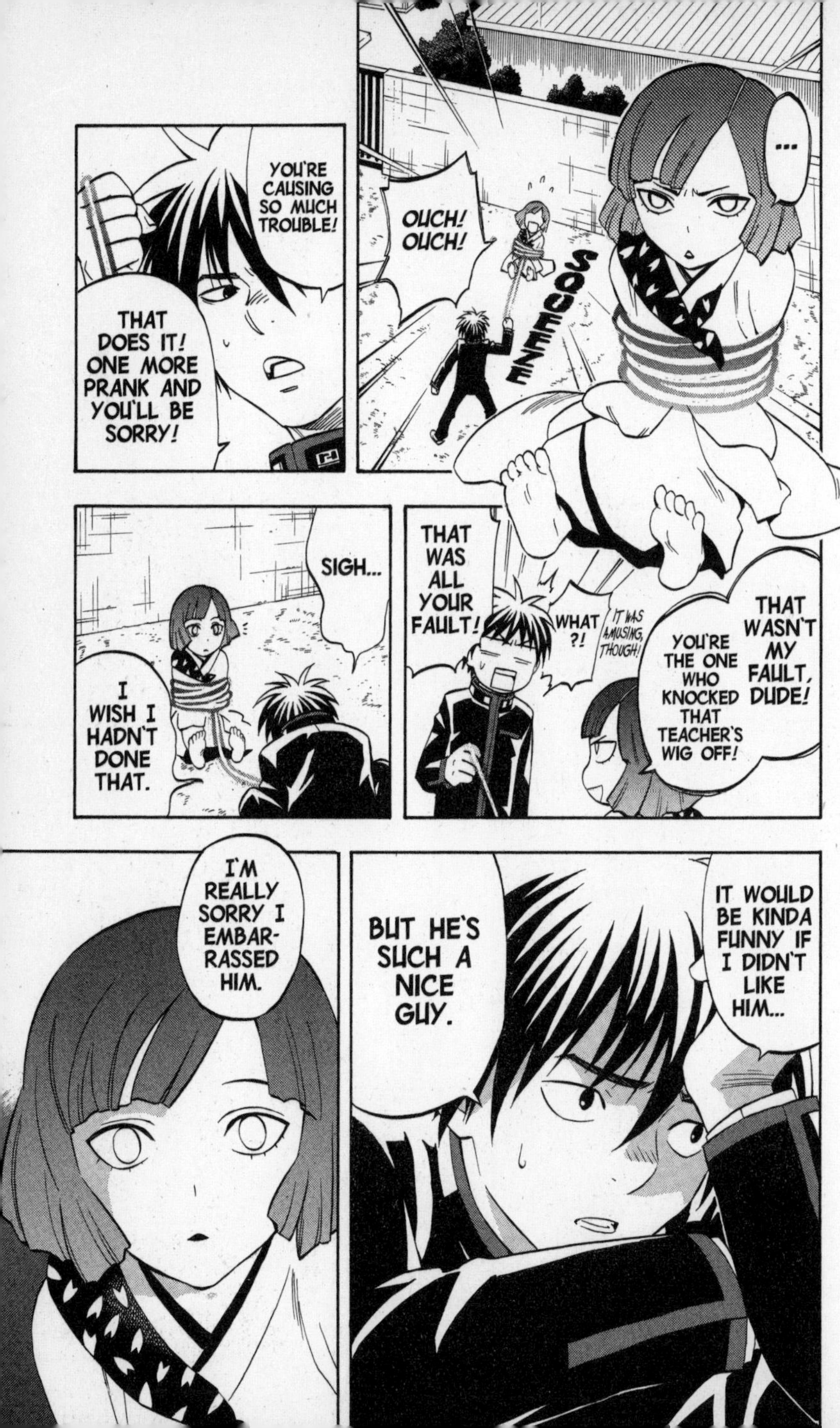
...
OUCH! OUCH!
SQUEEZE
YOU'RE CAUSING SO MUCH TROUBLE!
THAT DOES IT! ONE MORE PRANK AND YOU'LL BE SORRY!
THAT WAS ALL YOUR FAULT!
WHAT?!
IT WAS AMUSING, THOUGH!
THAT WASN'T MY FAULT, DUDE!
YOU'RE THE ONE WHO KNOCKED THAT TEACHER'S WIG OFF!
SIGH...
I WISH I HADN'T DONE THAT.
IT WOULD BE KINDA FUNNY IF I DIDN'T LIKE HIM...
BUT HE'S SUCH A NICE GUY.
I'M REALLY SORRY I EMBARRASSED HIM.

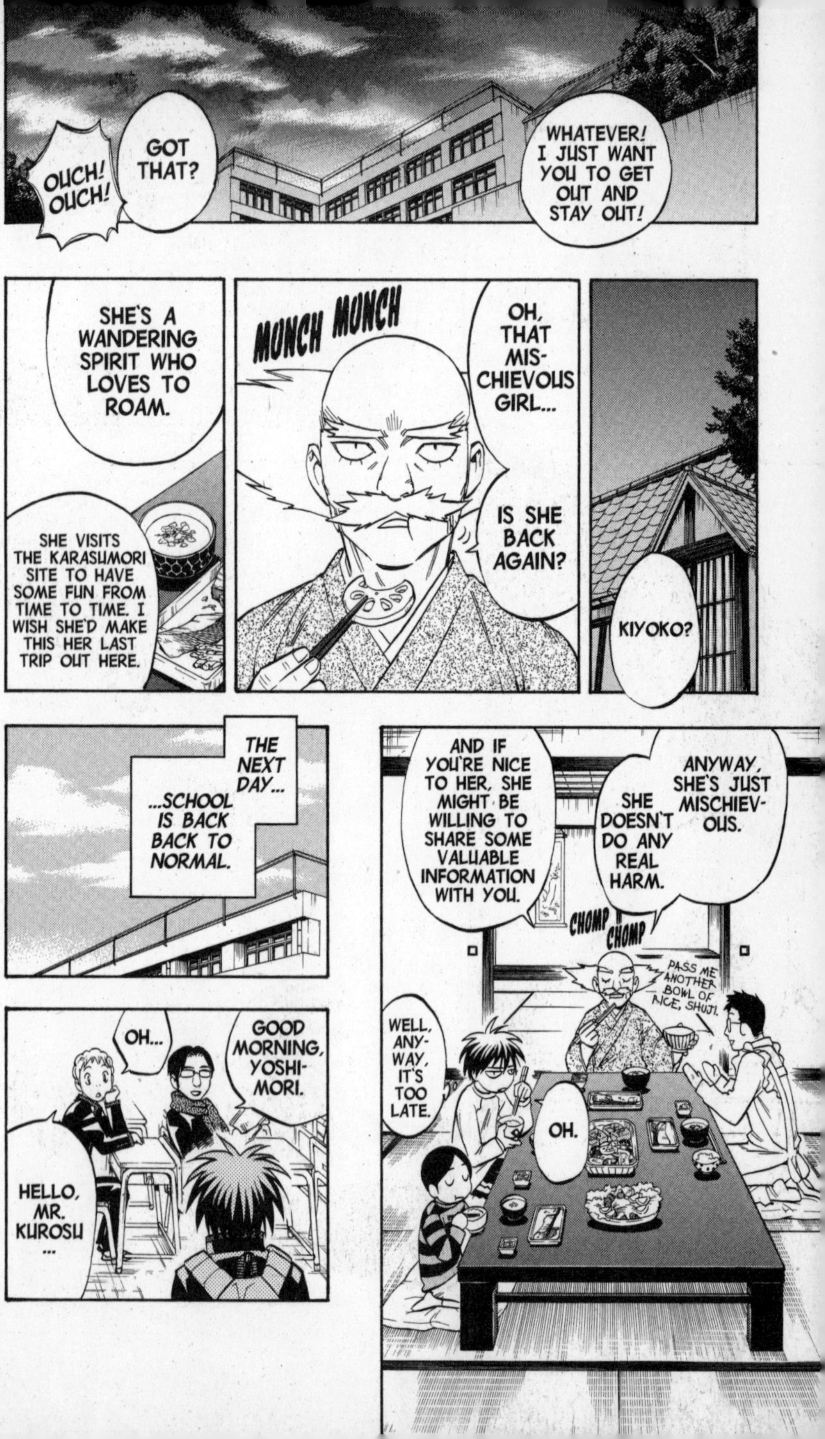
WHATEVER! I JUST WANT YOU TO GET OUT AND STAY OUT!
GOT THAT?
OUCH! OUCH!
KIYOKO?
OH, THAT MIS-CHIEVOUS GIRL...
IS SHE BACK AGAIN?
MUNCH MUNCH
SHE'S A WANDERING SPIRIT WHO LOVES TO ROAM.
SHE VISITS THE KARASUMORI SITE TO HAVE SOME FUN FROM TIME TO TIME. I WISH SHE'D MAKE THIS HER LAST TRIP OUT HERE.
ANYWAY, SHE'S JUST MISCHIEV-OUS.
SHE DOESN'T DO ANY REAL HARM.
AND IF YOU'RE NICE TO HER, SHE MIGHT BE WILLING TO SHARE SOME VALUABLE INFORMATION WITH YOU.
CHOMP CHOMP
PASS ME ANOTHER BOWL OF RICE, SHUJI.
WELL, ANYWAY, IT'S TOO LATE.
OH.
THE NEXT DAY...
...SCHOOL IS BACK BACK TO NORMAL.
GOOD MORNING, YOSHI-MORI.
OH...
HELLO, MR. KUROSU ...

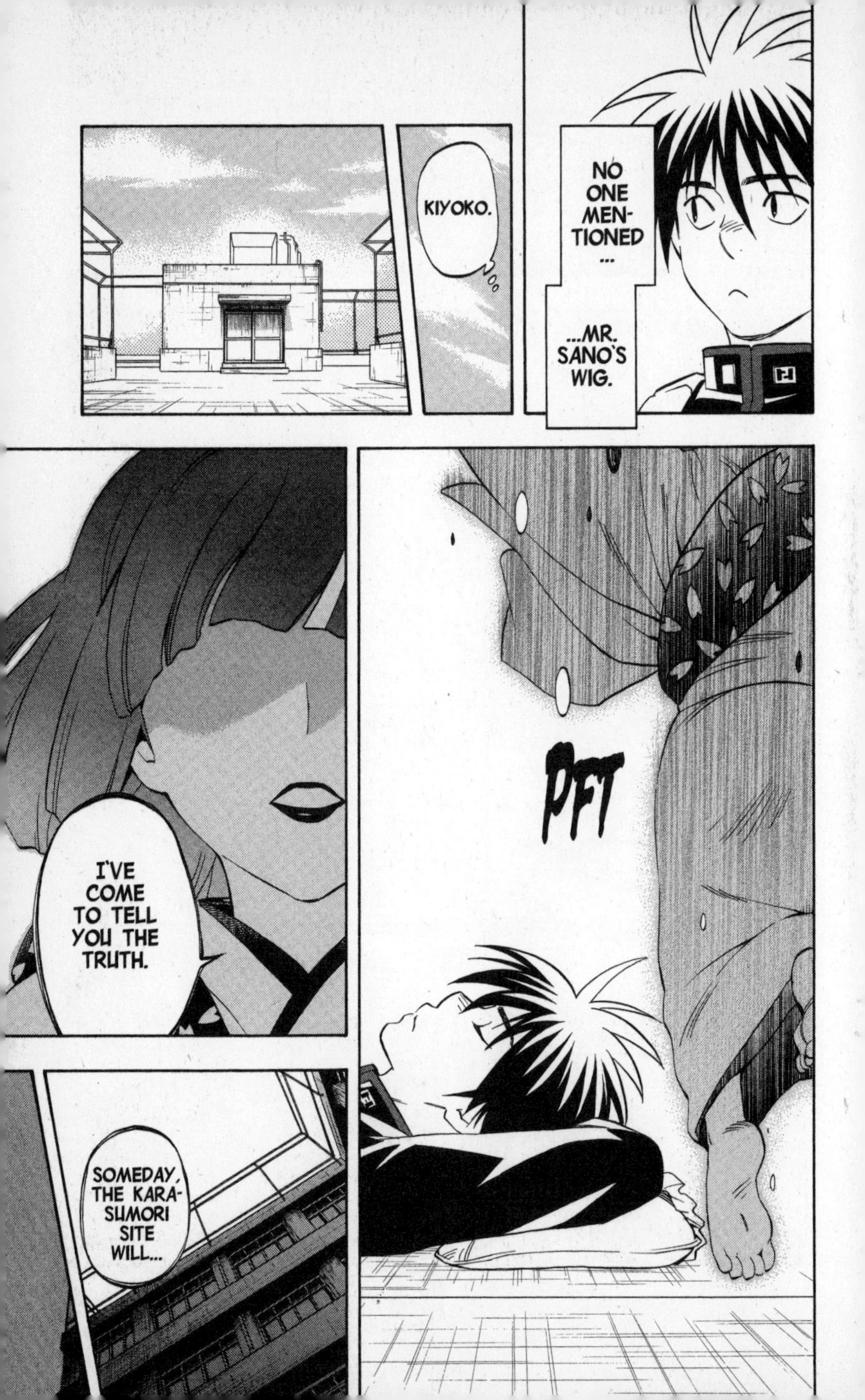
NO ONE MEN- TIONED ...
...MR. SANO'S WIG.
KIYOKO.
PFT
I'VE COME TO TELL YOU THE TRUTH.
SOMEDAY, THE KARA- SUMORI SITE WILL...

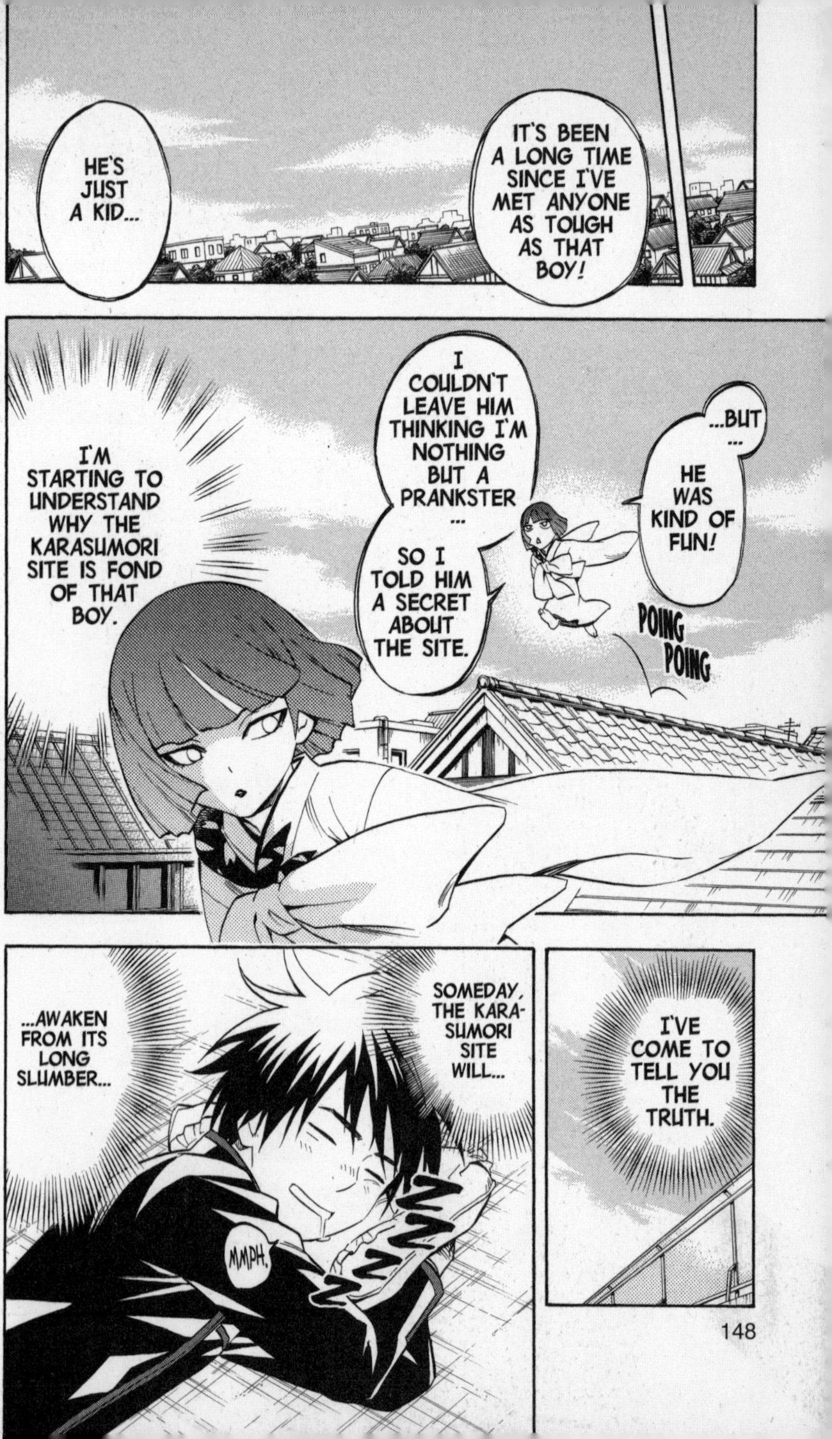
IT'S BEEN A LONG TIME SINCE I'VE MET ANYONE AS TOUGH AS THAT BOY!
HE'S JUST A KID...
...BUT ...
HE WAS KIND OF FUN!
POING POING
I COULDN'T LEAVE HIM THINKING I'M NOTHING BUT A PRANKSTER ...
SO I TOLD HIM A SECRET ABOUT THE SITE.
I'M STARTING TO UNDERSTAND WHY THE KARASUMORI SITE IS FOND OF THAT BOY.
I'VE COME TO TELL YOU THE TRUTH.
SOMEDAY, THE KARASUMORI SITE WILL...
...AWAKEN FROM ITS LONG SLUMBER...
MMPH.

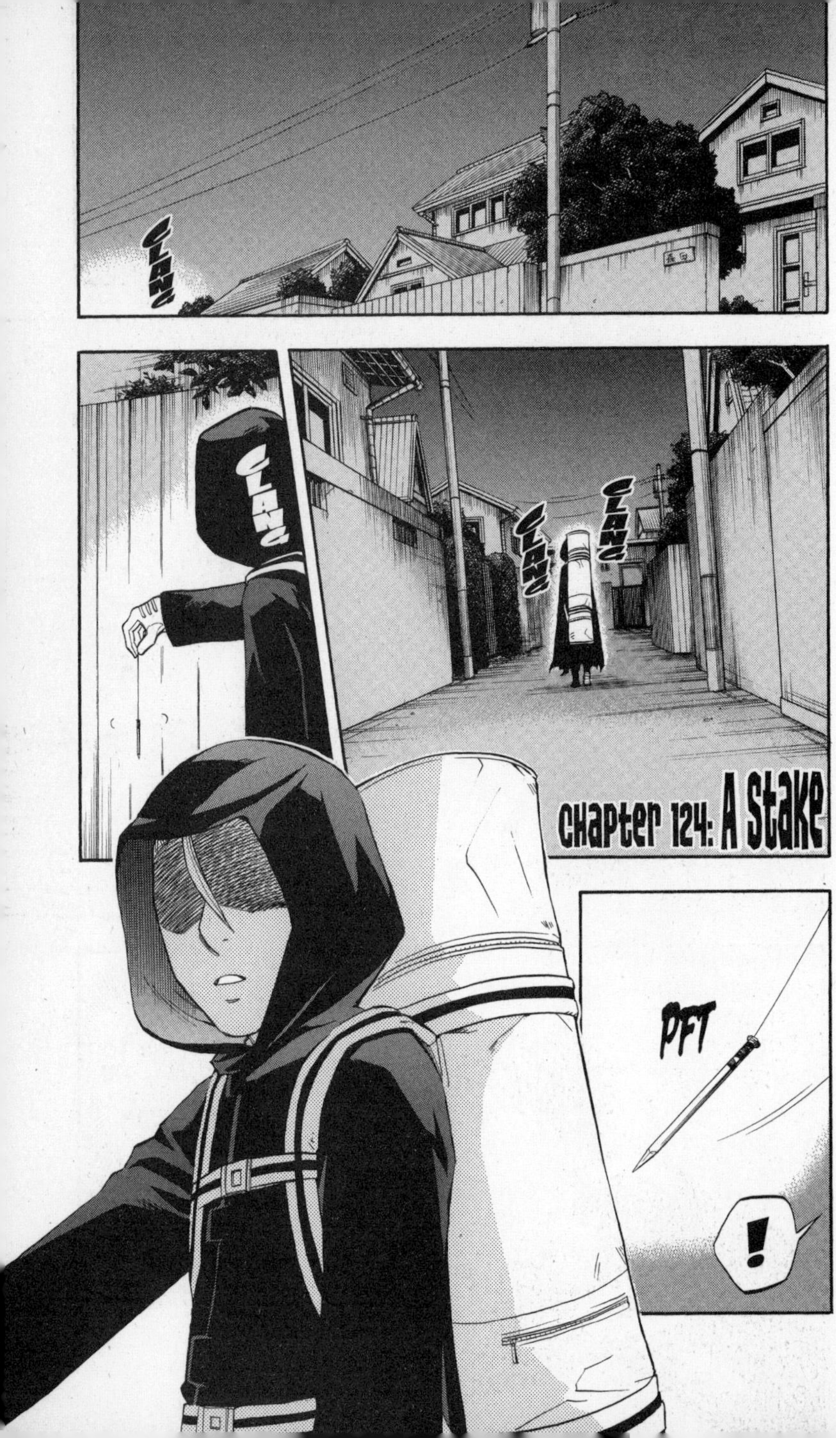
CLANG
CLANG
CLANG
CLANG
Chapter 124: A Stake
PFT
!

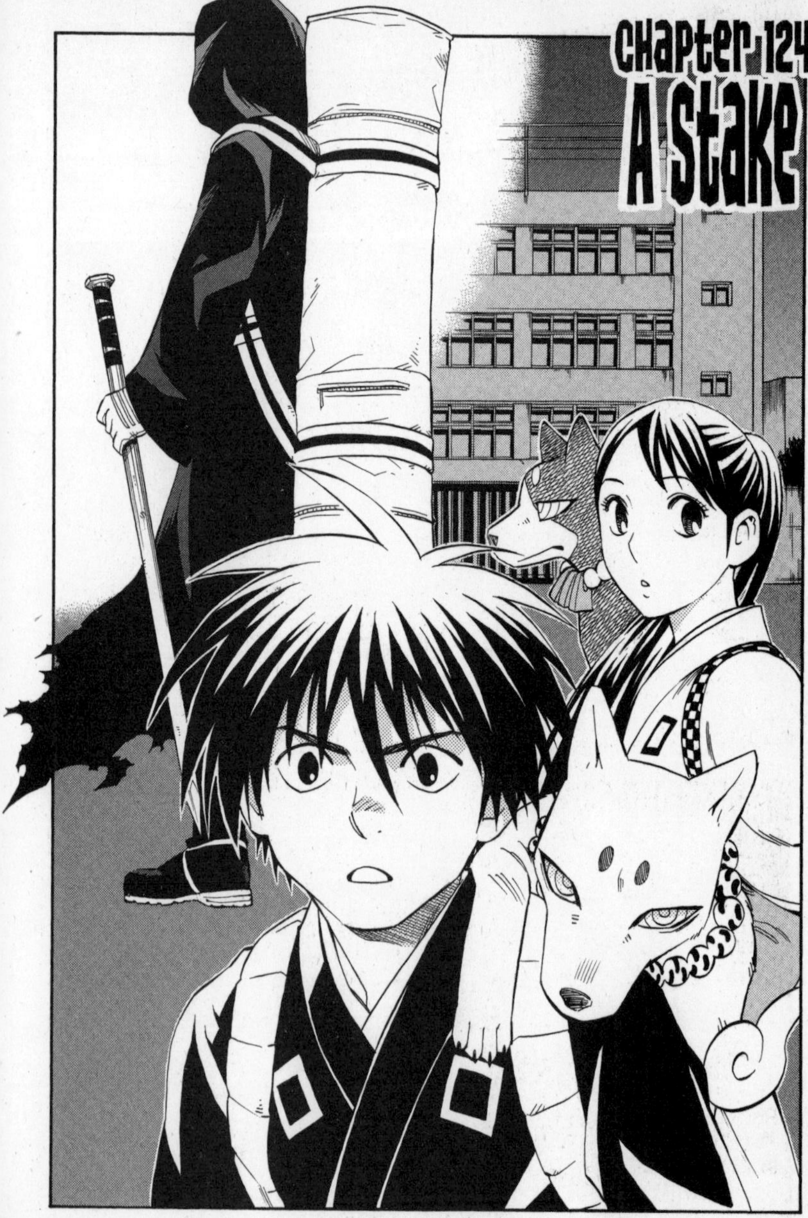
Chapter 124:
A Stake

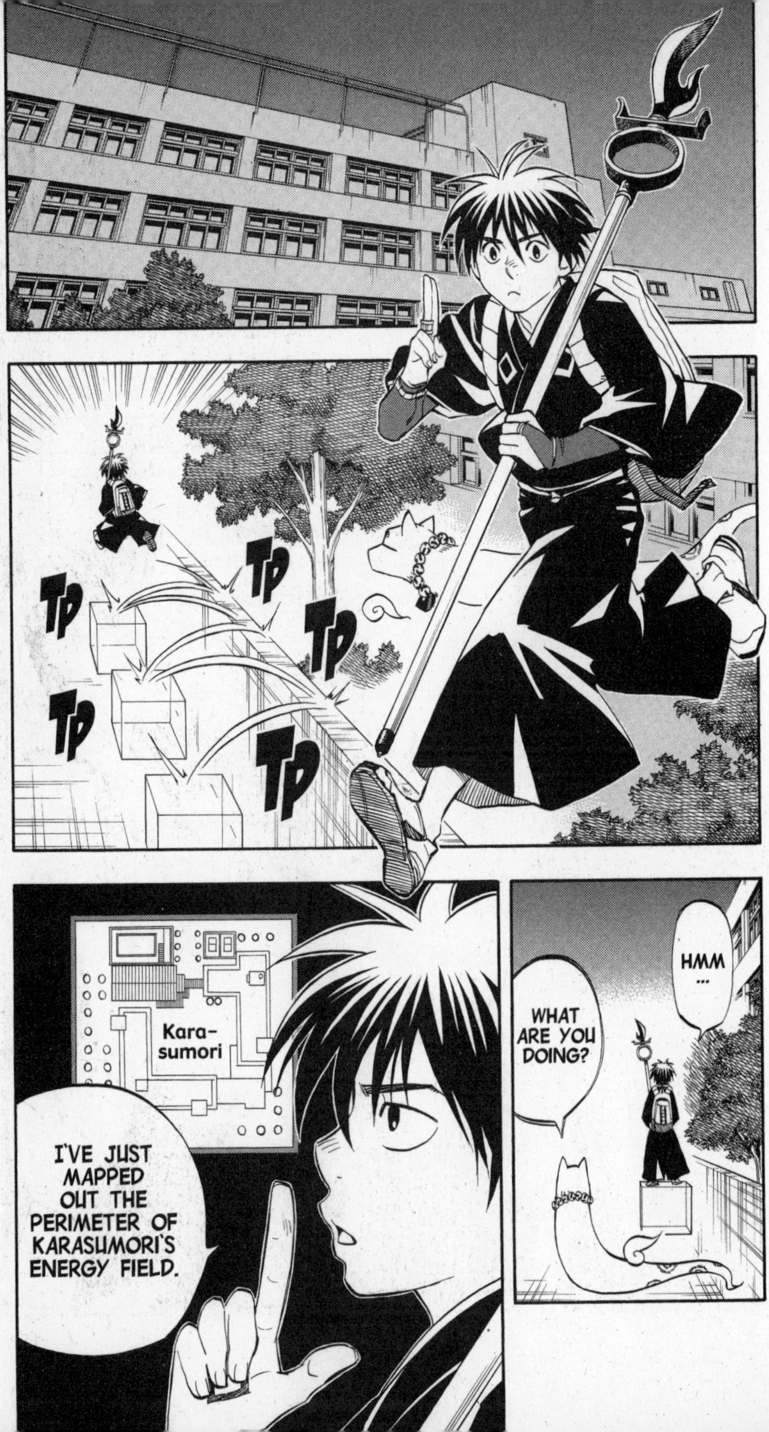
TP
TP
TP
TP
TP
HMM...
WHAT ARE YOU DOING?
Kara-
sumori
I'VE JUST MAPPED OUT THE PERIMETER OF KARASUMORI'S ENERGY FIELD.

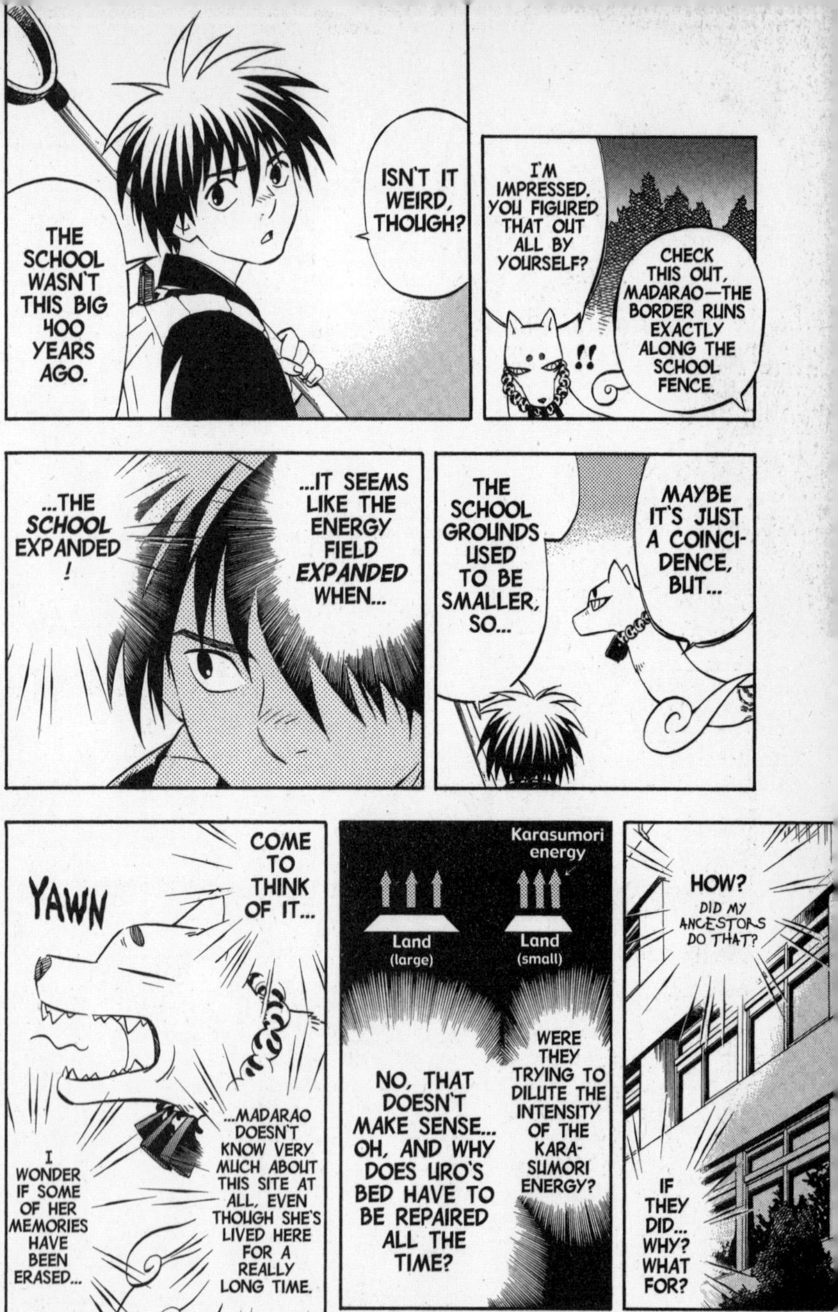
CHECK THIS OUT, MADARAO—THE BORDER RUNS EXACTLY ALONG THE SCHOOL FENCE.
!!
I'M IMPRESSED. YOU FIGURED THAT OUT ALL BY YOURSELF?
ISN'T IT WEIRD, THOUGH?
THE SCHOOL WASN'T THIS BIG 400 YEARS AGO.
MAYBE IT'S JUST A COINCIDENCE, BUT...
THE SCHOOL GROUNDS USED TO BE SMALLER, SO...
...IT SEEMS LIKE THE ENERGY FIELD *EXPANDED* WHEN...
...THE *SCHOOL* EXPANDED!
HOW? DID MY ANCESTORS DO THAT?
IF THEY DID... WHY? WHAT FOR?
Karasumori energy
Land (small)
Land (large)
WERE THEY TRYING TO DILUTE THE INTENSITY OF THE KARASUMORI ENERGY?
NO, THAT DOESN'T MAKE SENSE... OH, AND WHY DOES URO'S BED HAVE TO BE REPAIRED ALL THE TIME?
COME TO THINK OF IT...
YAWN
...MADARAO DOESN'T KNOW VERY MUCH ABOUT THIS SITE AT ALL, EVEN THOUGH SHE'S LIVED HERE FOR A REALLY LONG TIME.
I WONDER IF SOME OF HER MEMORIES HAVE BEEN ERASED...

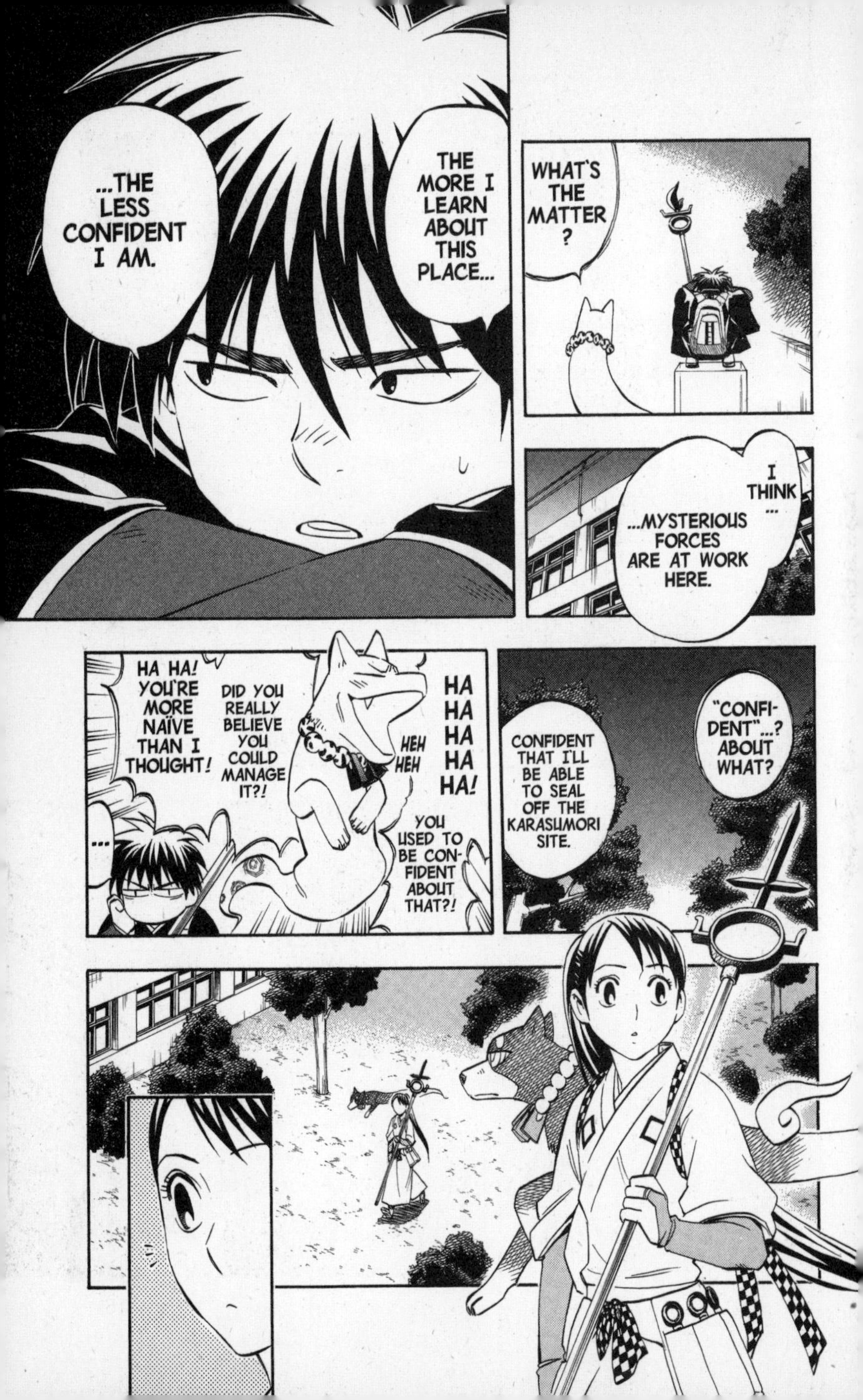
WHAT'S THE MATTER?
I THINK...
...MYSTERIOUS FORCES ARE AT WORK HERE.
THE MORE I LEARN ABOUT THIS PLACE...
...THE LESS CONFIDENT I AM.
"CONFI-DENT"...? ABOUT WHAT?
CONFIDENT THAT I'LL BE ABLE TO SEAL OFF THE KARASUMORI SITE.
HA HA HA HA HA!
HEH HEH
YOU USED TO BE CON-FIDENT ABOUT THAT?!
DID YOU REALLY BELIEVE YOU COULD MANAGE IT?!
HA HA! YOU'RE MORE NAÏVE THAN I THOUGHT!
...

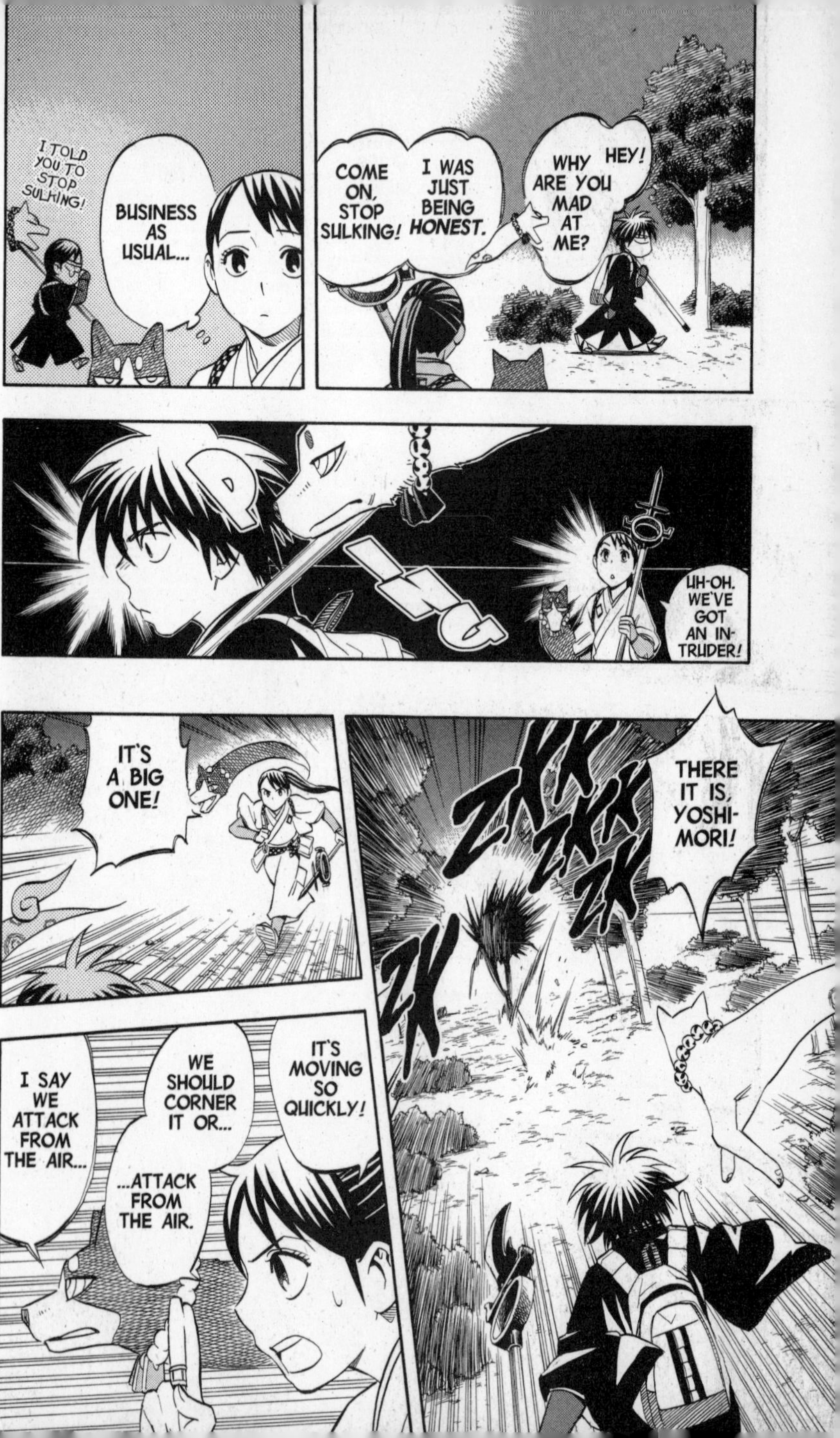
HEY! WHY ARE YOU MAD AT ME?
I WAS JUST BEING HONEST.
COME ON, STOP SULKING!
BUSINESS AS USUAL...
I TOLD YOU TO STOP SULKING!
UH-OH. WE'VE GOT AN IN-TRUDER!
THERE IT IS, YOSHI-MORI!
ZK ZK ZK ZK ZK
IT'S A BIG ONE!
IT'S MOVING SO QUICKLY!
WE SHOULD CORNER IT OR...
...ATTACK FROM THE AIR.
I SAY WE ATTACK FROM THE AIR...

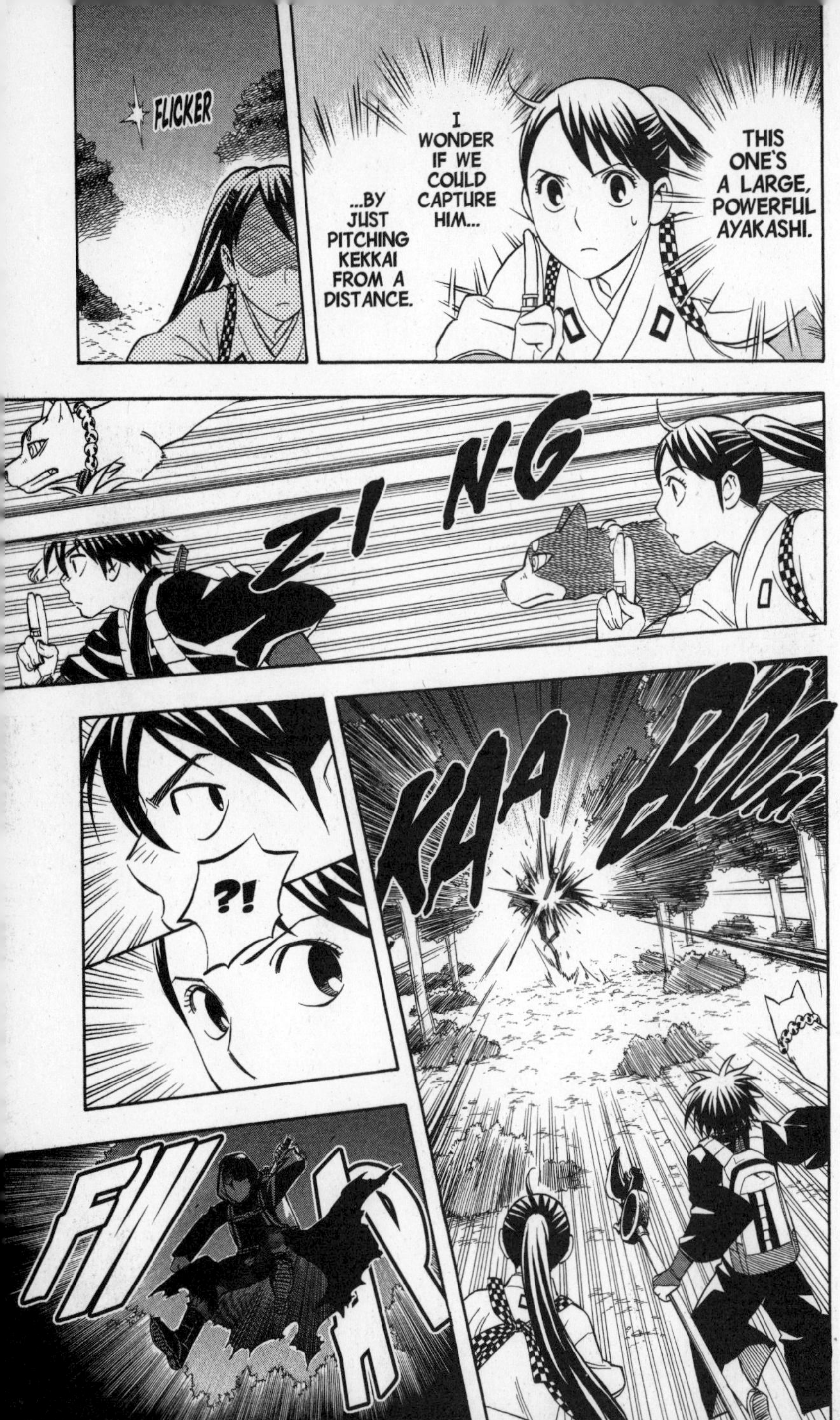
THIS ONE'S A LARGE, POWERFUL AYAKASHI.
I WONDER IF WE COULD CAPTURE HIM...
...BY JUST PITCHING KEKKAI FROM A DISTANCE.
FLICKER
ZING
KAABOOM
?!
FWHR

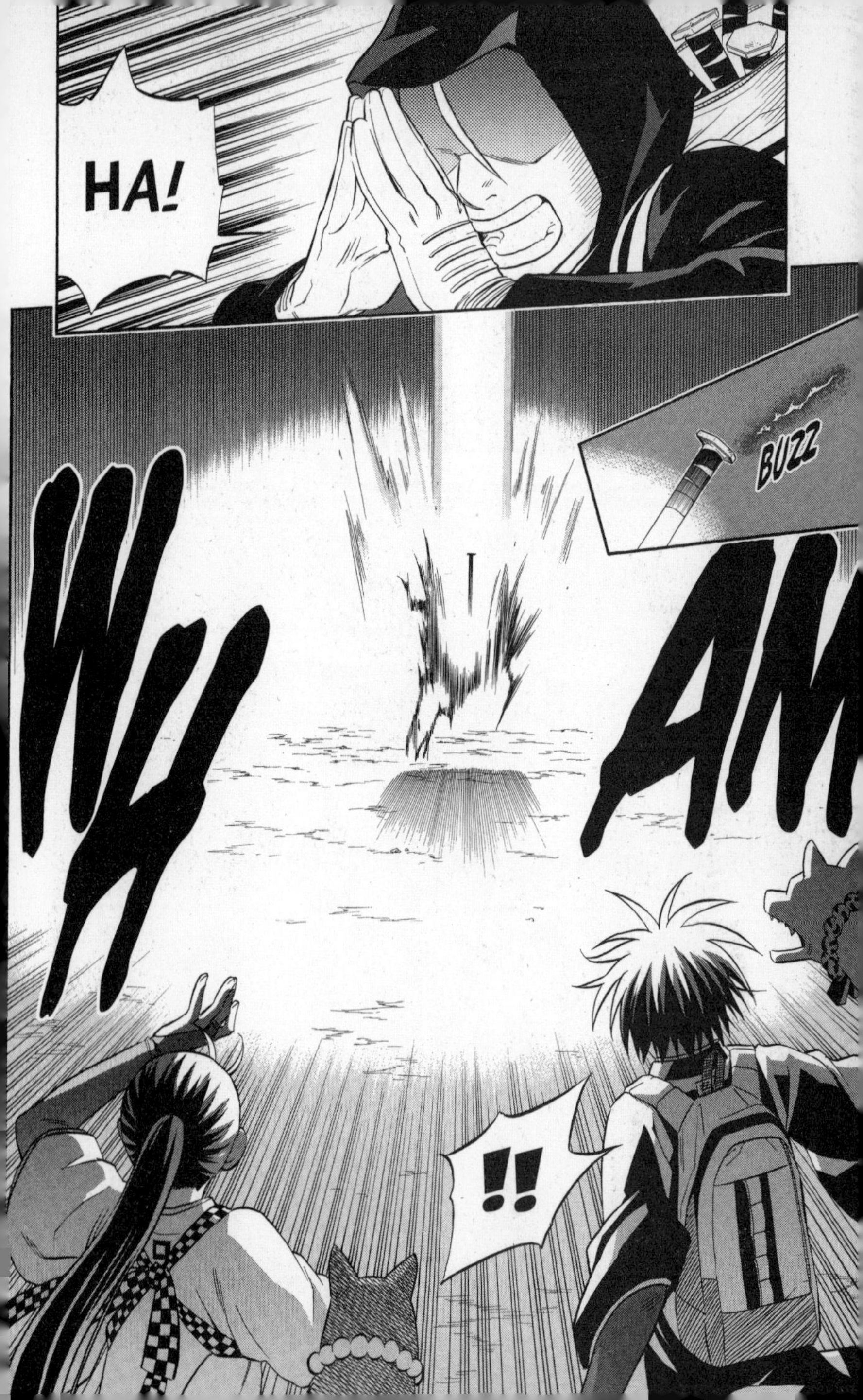
HA!
BUZZ
WHAM
!!

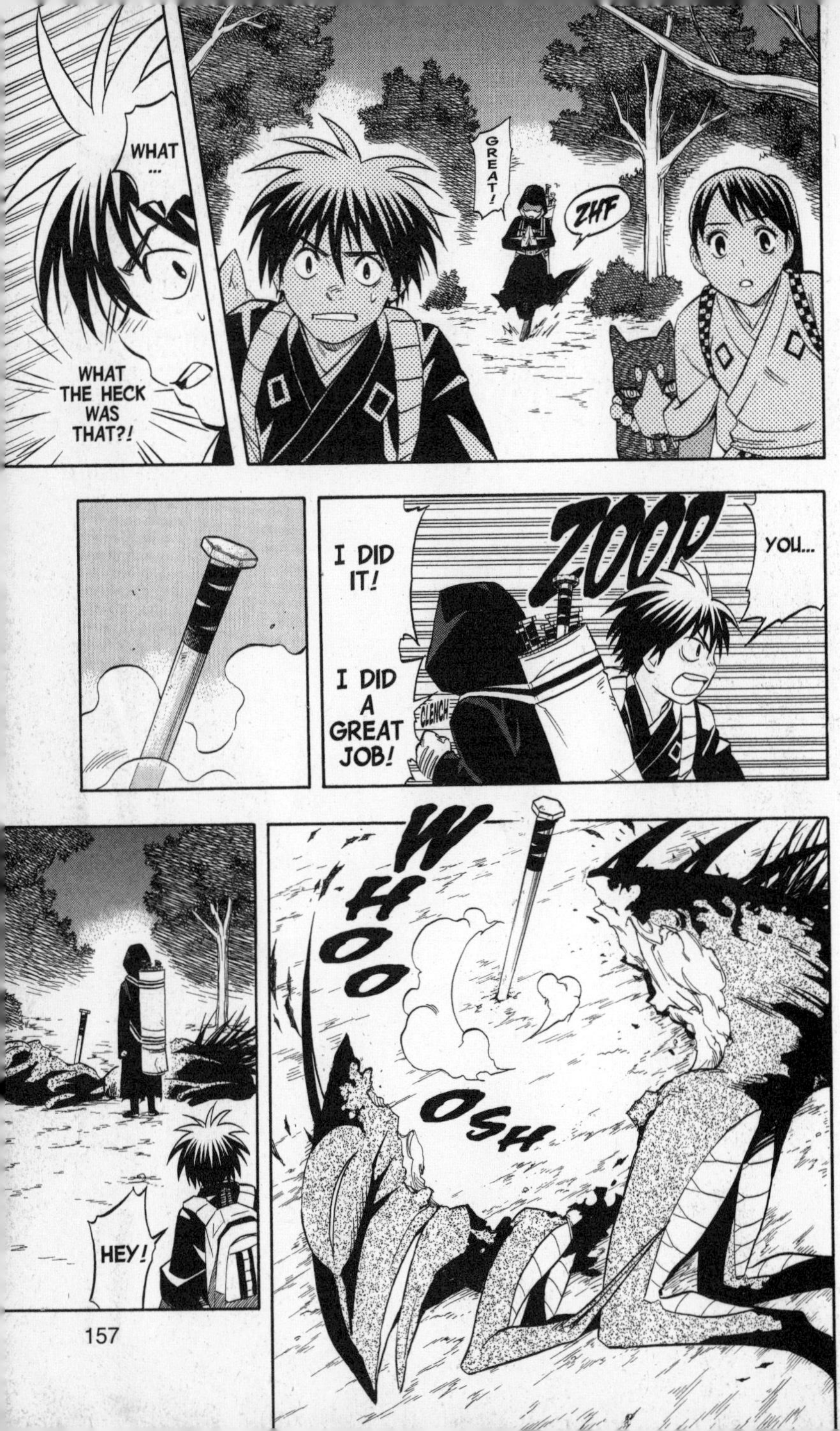
GREAT!
ZHF
WHAT ...
WHAT THE HECK WAS THAT?!
YOU...
ZOOP
I DID IT!
CLENCH
I DID A GREAT JOB!
WHOOOSH
HEY!

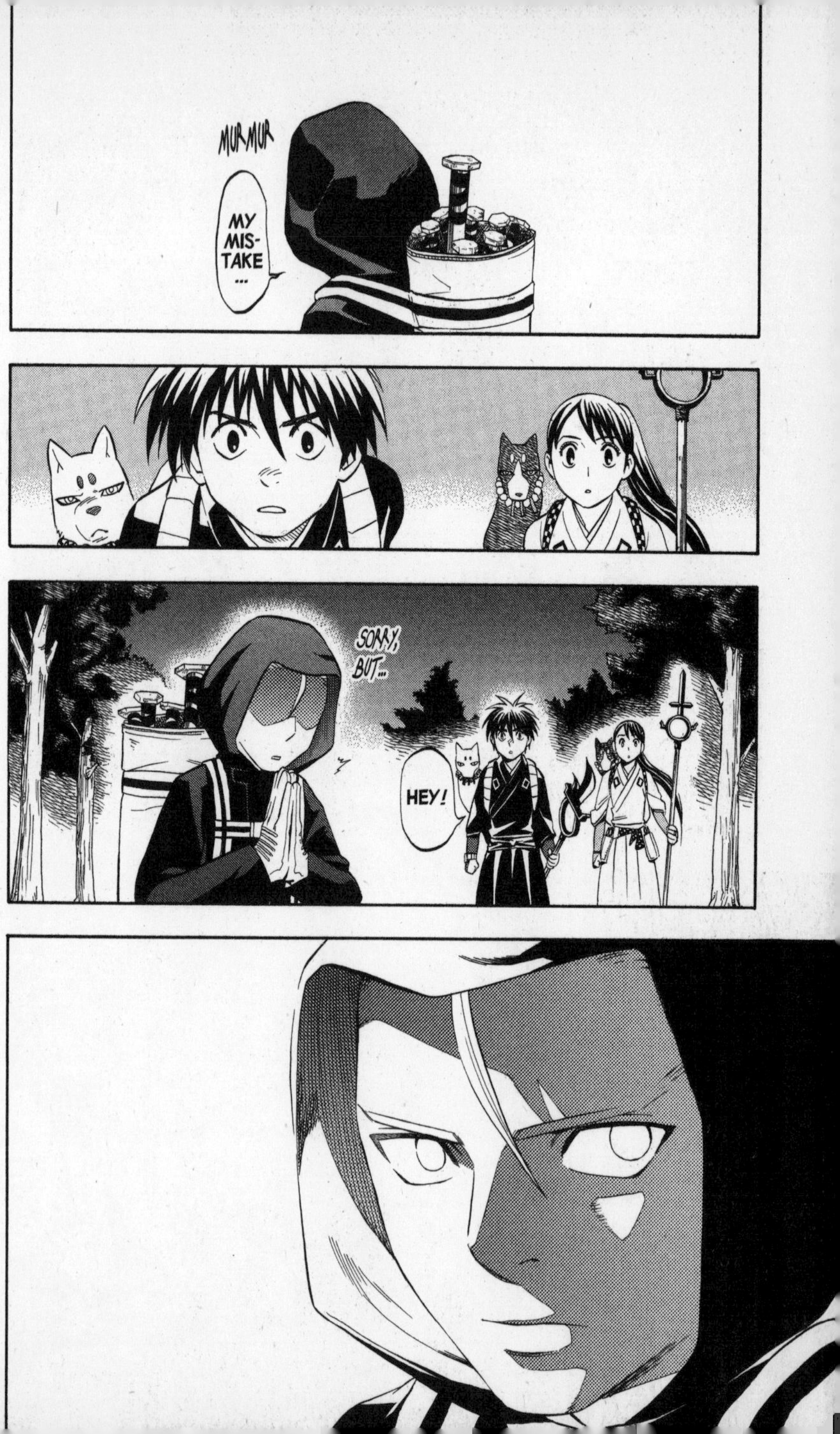
MURMUR
MY MIS-TAKE...
SORRY, BUT...
HEY!

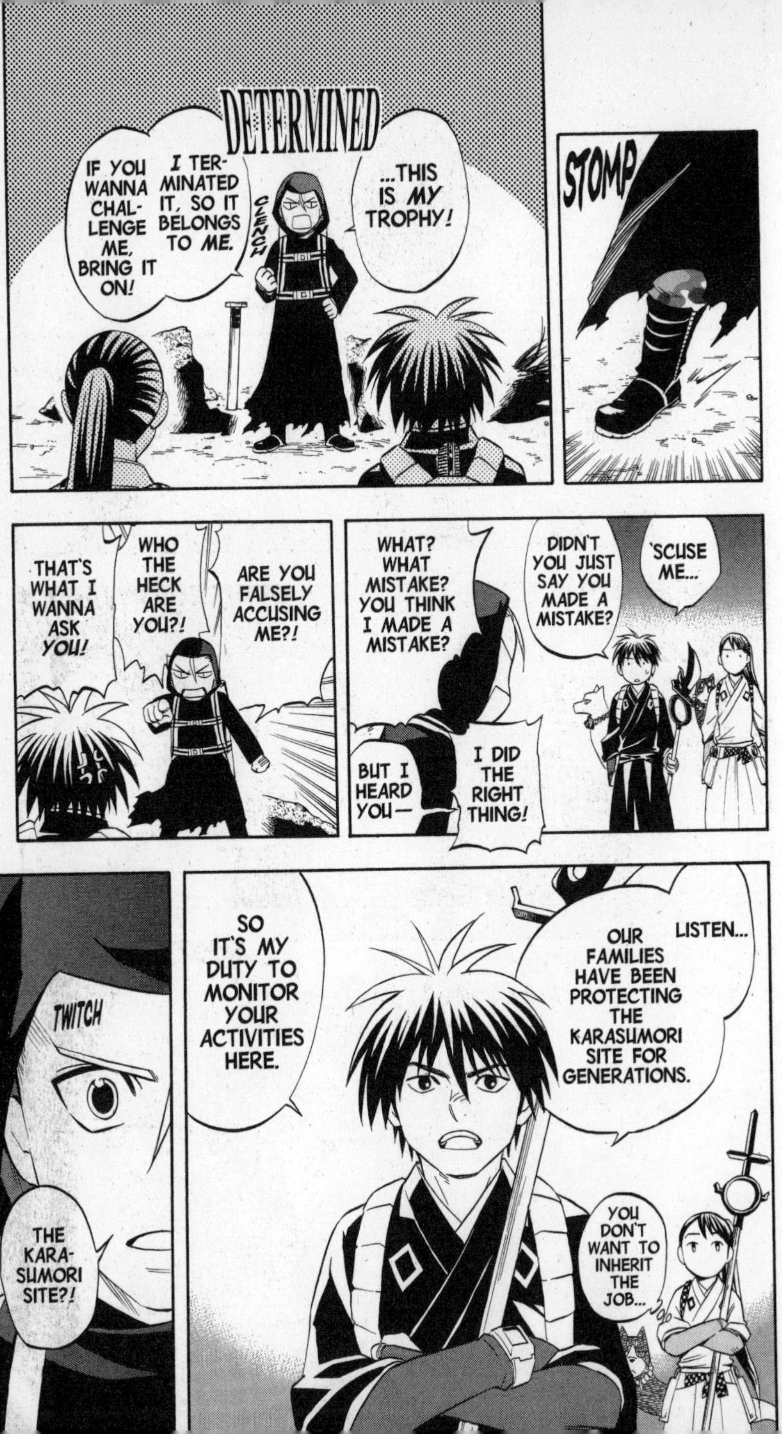
STOMP
...THIS IS MY TROPHY!
DETERMINED
CLENCH
I TERMINATED IT, SO IT BELONGS TO ME.
IF YOU WANNA CHALLENGE ME, BRING IT ON!
'SCUSE ME...
DIDN'T YOU JUST SAY YOU MADE A MISTAKE?
WHAT? WHAT MISTAKE? YOU THINK I MADE A MISTAKE?
I DID THE RIGHT THING!
BUT I HEARD YOU—
ARE YOU FALSELY ACCUSING ME?!
WHO THE HECK ARE YOU?!
THAT'S WHAT I WANNA ASK YOU!
LISTEN...
OUR FAMILIES HAVE BEEN PROTECTING THE KARASUMORI SITE FOR GENERATIONS.
SO IT'S MY DUTY TO MONITOR YOUR ACTIVITIES HERE.
YOU DON'T WANT TO INHERIT THE JOB...
TWITCH
THE KARASUMORI SITE?!

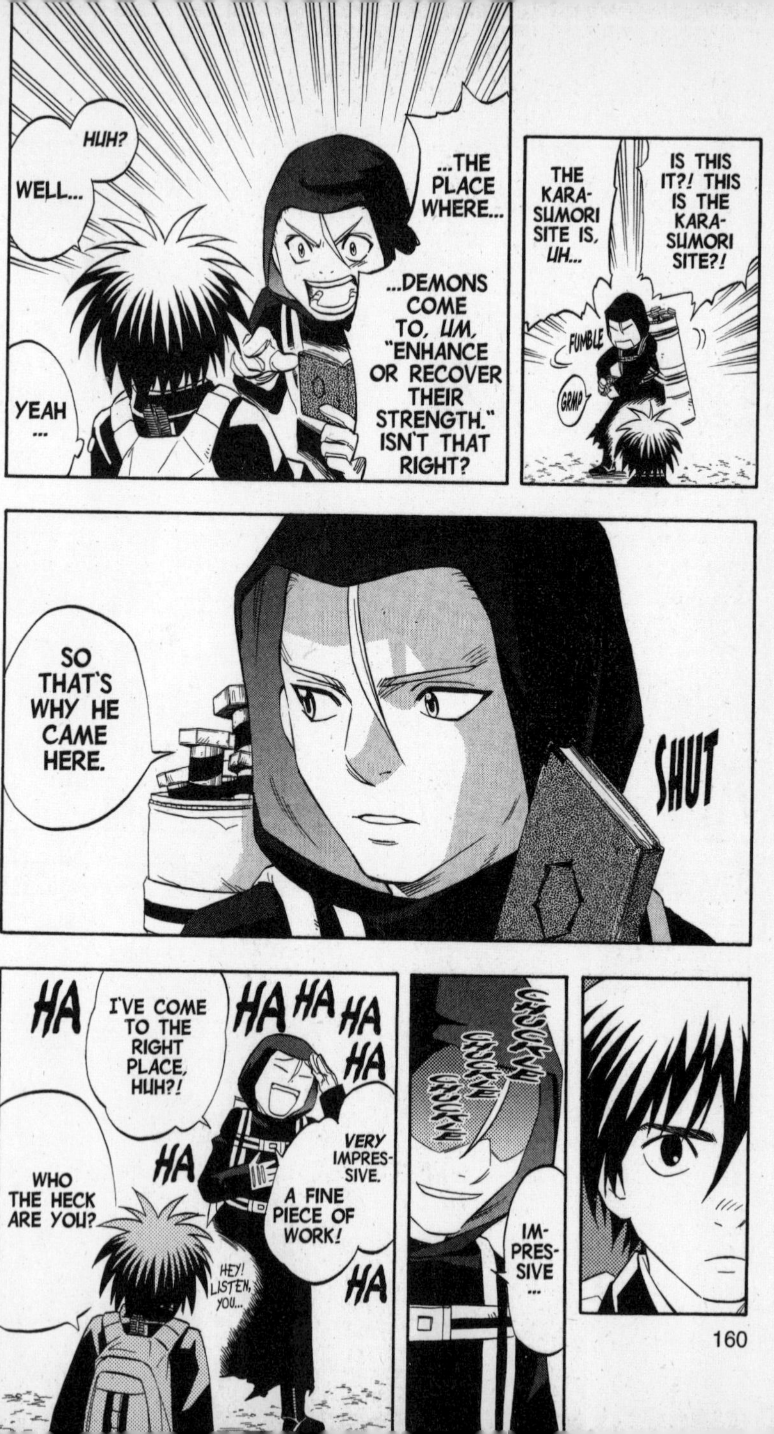
IS THIS IT?! THIS IS THE KARA-SUMORI SITE?!
THE KARA-SUMORI SITE IS, UH...
FUMBLE
GRMP
...THE PLACE WHERE...
...DEMONS COME TO, UM, "ENHANCE OR RECOVER THEIR STRENGTH." ISN'T THAT RIGHT?
HUH?
WELL...
YEAH ...
SHUT
SO THAT'S WHY HE CAME HERE.
CHUCKLE
CHUCKLE
CHUCKLE
IM-PRES-SIVE ...
HA HA HA HA HA
VERY IMPRES-SIVE. A FINE PIECE OF WORK!
HA
HA
I'VE COME TO THE RIGHT PLACE, HUH?!
HA
HEY! LISTEN, YOU...
WHO THE HECK ARE YOU?

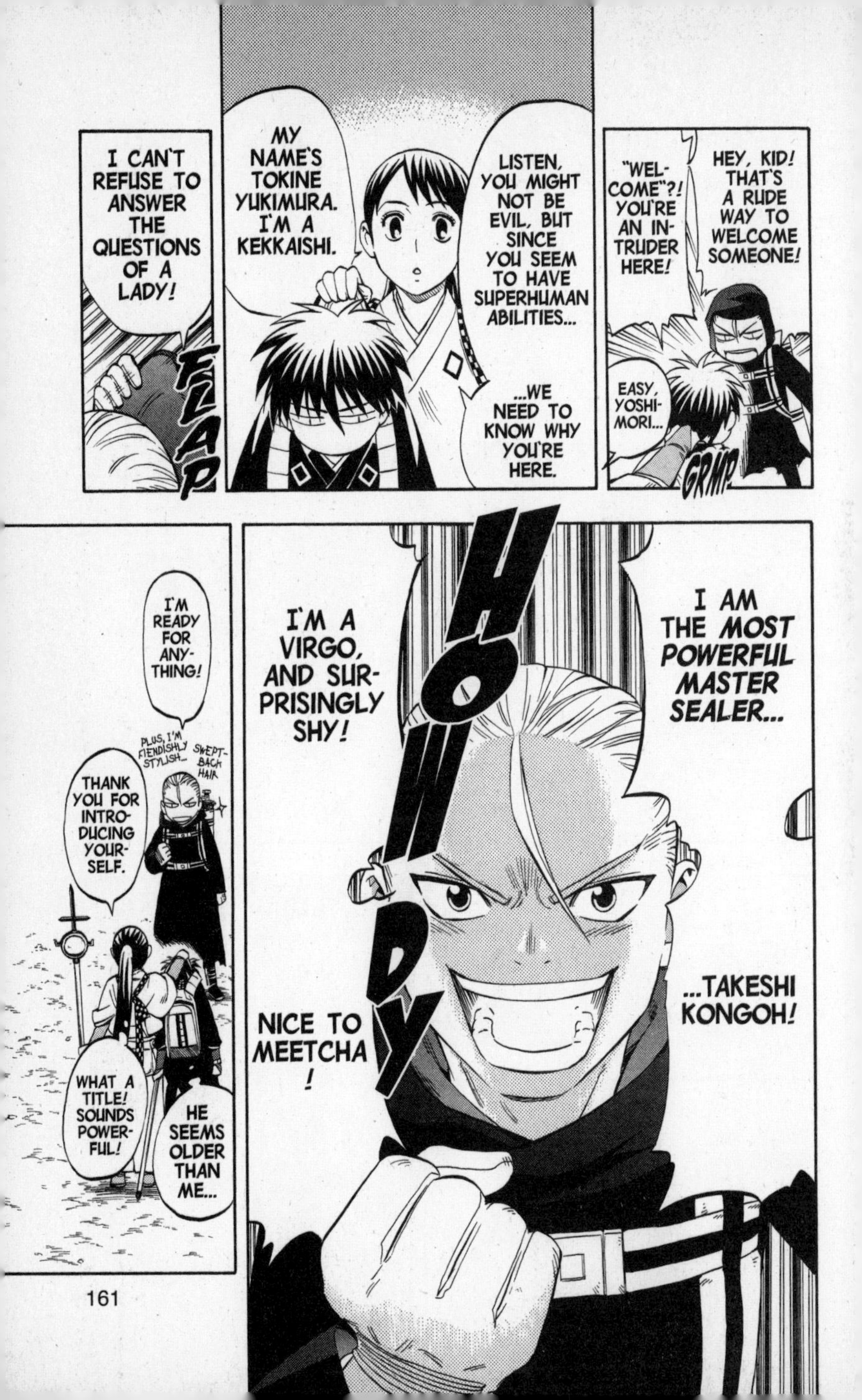
HEY, KID! THAT'S A RUDE WAY TO WELCOME SOMEONE!
"WEL-COME"?! YOU'RE AN IN-TRUDER HERE!
EASY, YOSHI-MORI...
GRMP
LISTEN, YOU MIGHT NOT BE EVIL, BUT SINCE YOU SEEM TO HAVE SUPERHUMAN ABILITIES...
...WE NEED TO KNOW WHY YOU'RE HERE.
MY NAME'S TOKINE YUKIMURA. I'M A KEKKAISHI.
I CAN'T REFUSE TO ANSWER THE QUESTIONS OF A LADY!
FLAP
I AM THE MOST POWERFUL MASTER SEALER...
I'M A VIRGO, AND SUR-PRISINGLY SHY!
HOWDY
...TAKESHI KONGOH!
NICE TO MEETCHA!
I'M READY FOR ANY-THING!
PLUS, I'M FIENDISHLY STYLISH...
SWEPT-BACK HAIR
THANK YOU FOR INTRO-DUCING YOUR-SELF.
WHAT A TITLE! SOUNDS POWER-FUL!
HE SEEMS OLDER THAN ME...

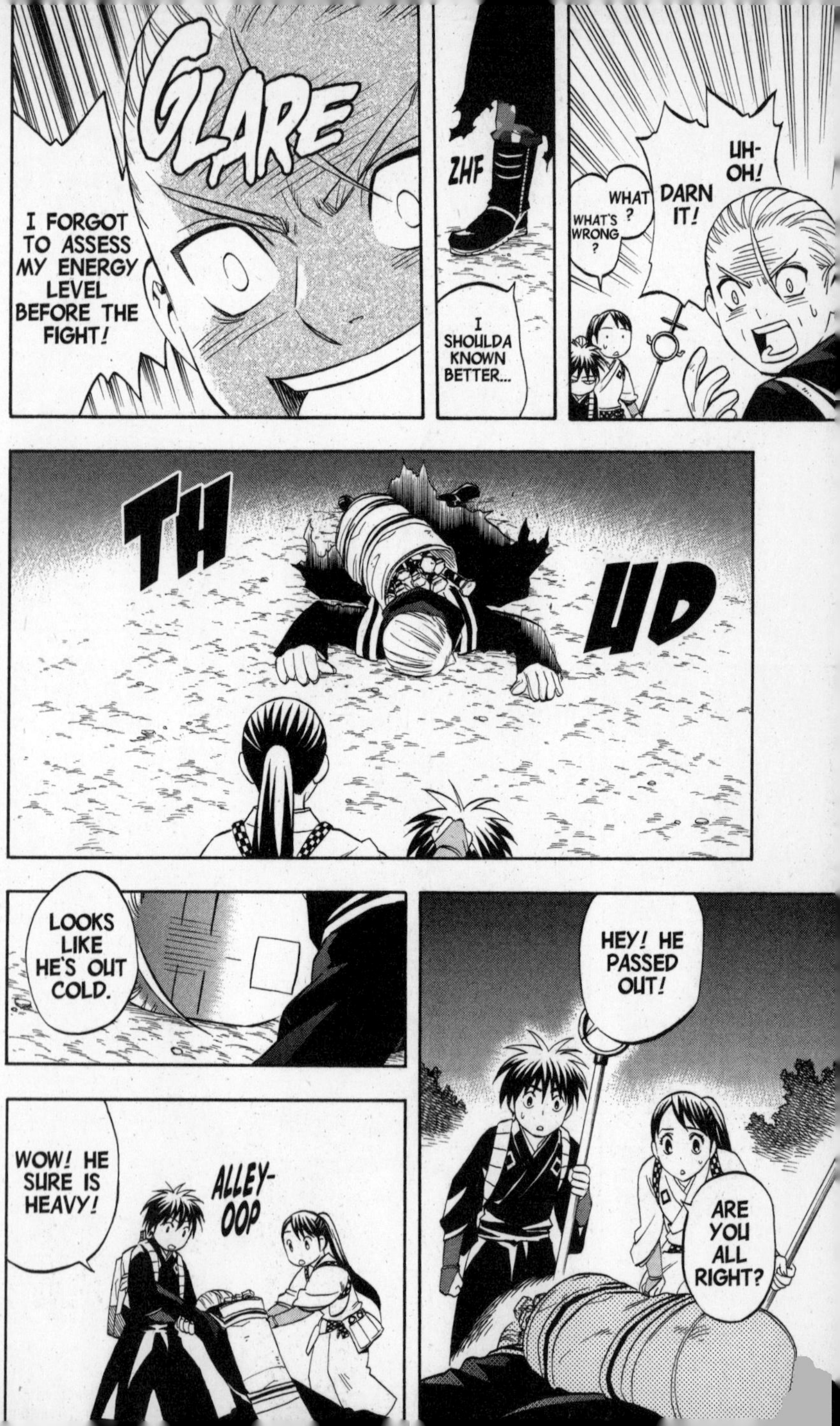
UH-OH!
DARN IT!
WHAT? WHAT'S WRONG?
ZHF
I SHOULDA KNOWN BETTER...
GLARE
I FORGOT TO ASSESS MY ENERGY LEVEL BEFORE THE FIGHT!
THUD
HEY! HE PASSED OUT!
ARE YOU ALL RIGHT?
LOOKS LIKE HE'S OUT COLD.
ALLEY-OOP
WOW! HE SURE IS HEAVY!

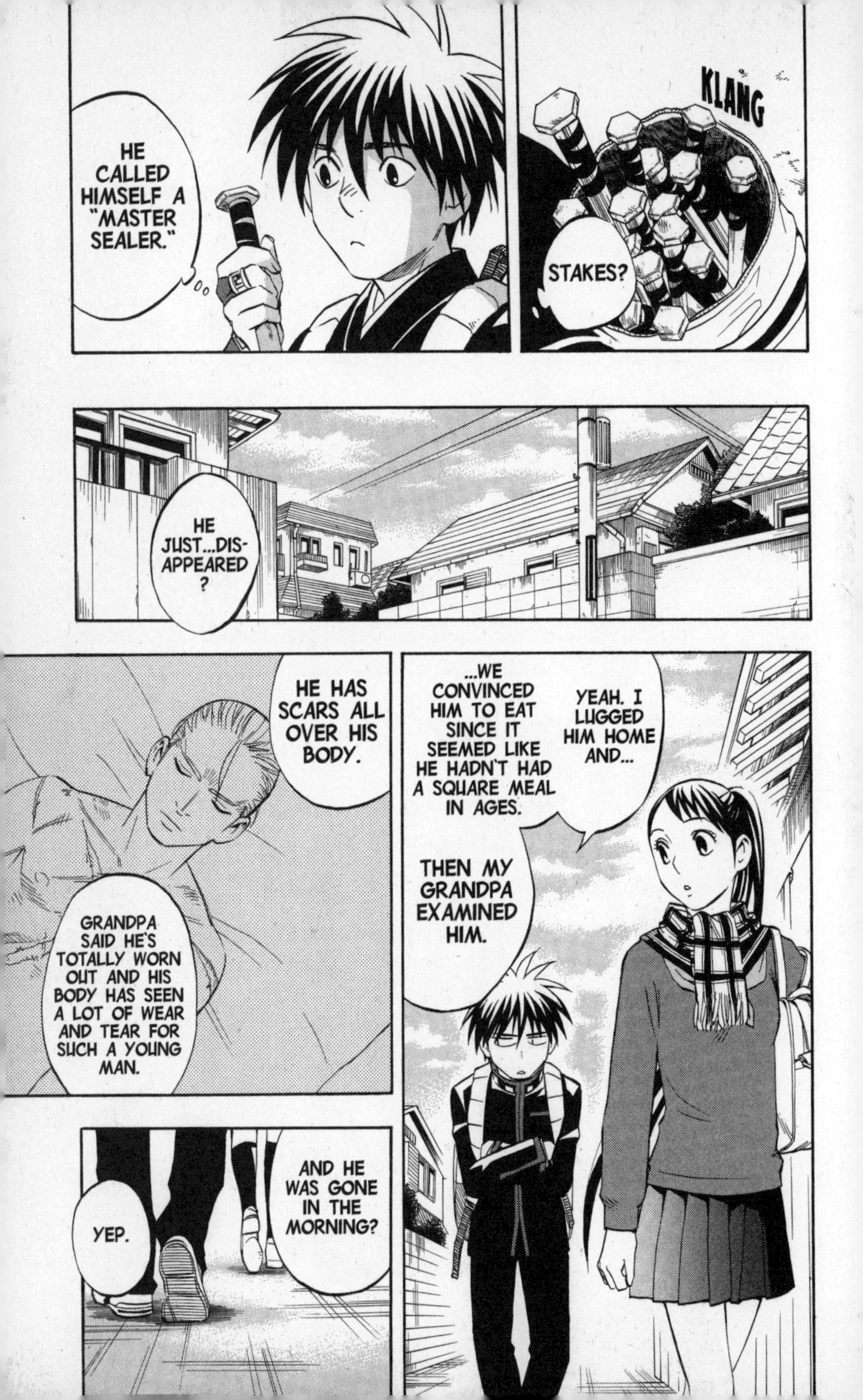
KLANG
STAKES?
HE CALLED HIMSELF A "MASTER SEALER."
HE JUST...DIS-APPEARED?
YEAH. I LUGGED HIM HOME AND...
...WE CONVINCED HIM TO EAT SINCE IT SEEMED LIKE HE HADN'T HAD A SQUARE MEAL IN AGES.
THEN MY GRANDPA EXAMINED HIM.
HE HAS SCARS ALL OVER HIS BODY.
GRANDPA SAID HE'S TOTALLY WORN OUT AND HIS BODY HAS SEEN A LOT OF WEAR AND TEAR FOR SUCH A YOUNG MAN.
AND HE WAS GONE IN THE MORNING?
YEP.

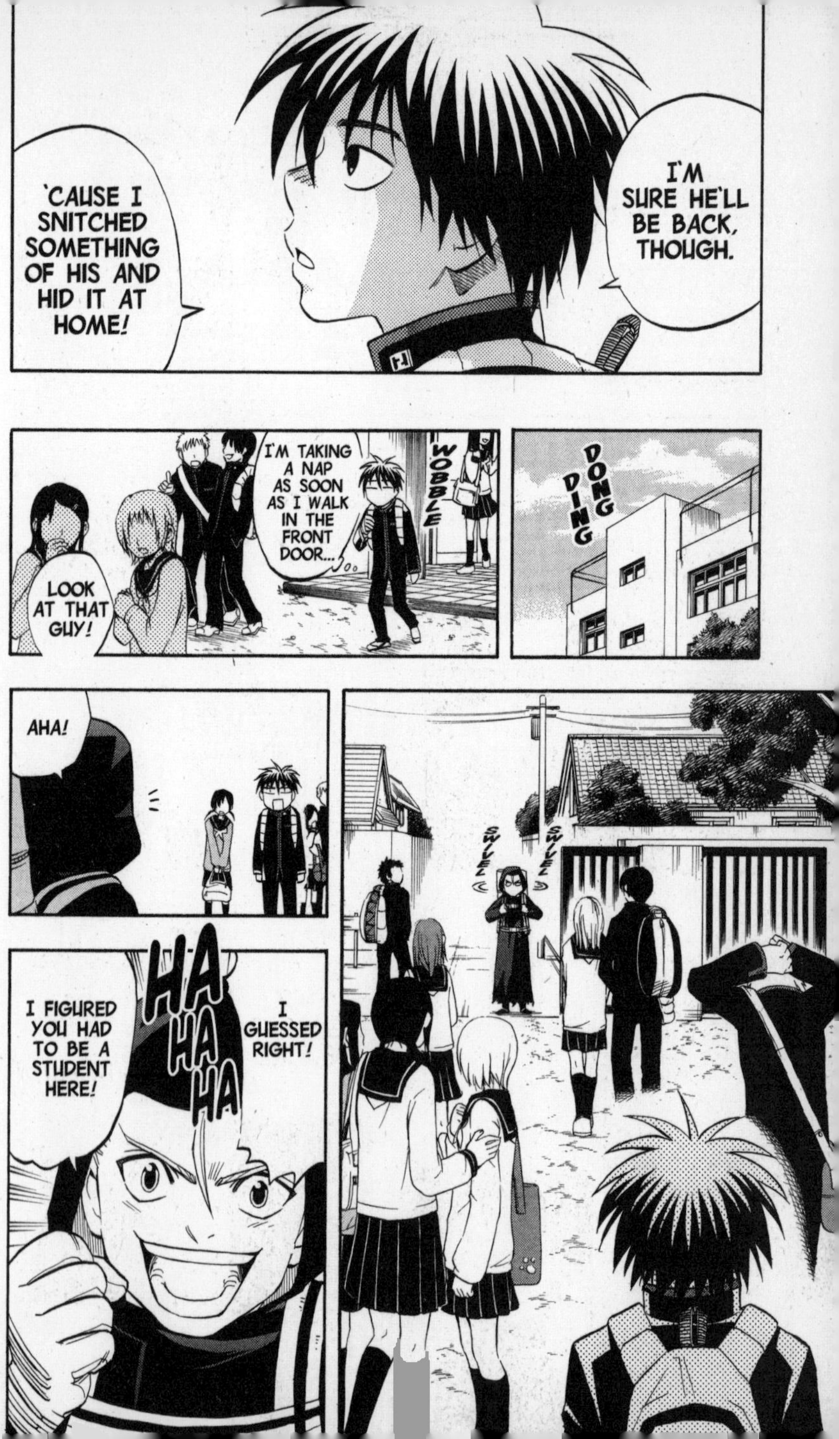
I'M SURE HE'LL BE BACK, THOUGH.
'CAUSE I SNITCHED SOMETHING OF HIS AND HID IT AT HOME!
DING DONG
WOBBLE
I'M TAKING A NAP AS SOON AS I WALK IN THE FRONT DOOR...
LOOK AT THAT GUY!
SWIVEL
SWIVEL
AHA!
HA HA HA HA
I GUESSED RIGHT!
I FIGURED YOU HAD TO BE A STUDENT HERE!

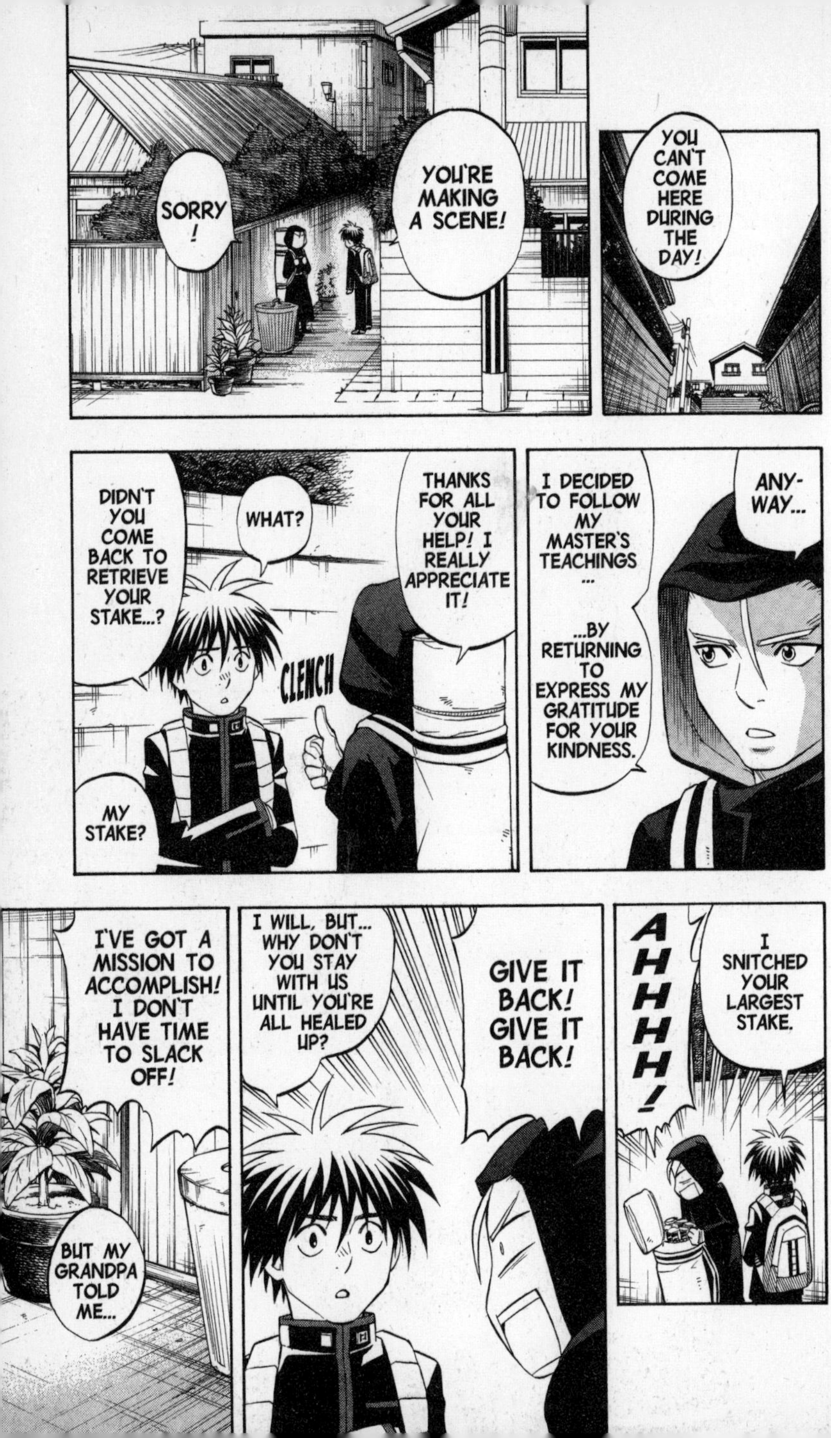
YOU CAN'T COME HERE DURING THE DAY!
YOU'RE MAKING A SCENE!
SORRY!
ANY-WAY...
I DECIDED TO FOLLOW MY MASTER'S TEACHINGS...
...BY RETURNING TO EXPRESS MY GRATITUDE FOR YOUR KINDNESS.
THANKS FOR ALL YOUR HELP! I REALLY APPRECIATE IT!
WHAT?
CLENCH
DIDN'T YOU COME BACK TO RETRIEVE YOUR STAKE...?
MY STAKE?
I SNITCHED YOUR LARGEST STAKE.
AHHHH!
GIVE IT BACK! GIVE IT BACK!
I WILL, BUT... WHY DON'T YOU STAY WITH US UNTIL YOU'RE ALL HEALED UP?
I'VE GOT A MISSION TO ACCOMPLISH! I DON'T HAVE TIME TO SLACK OFF!
BUT MY GRANDPA TOLD ME...

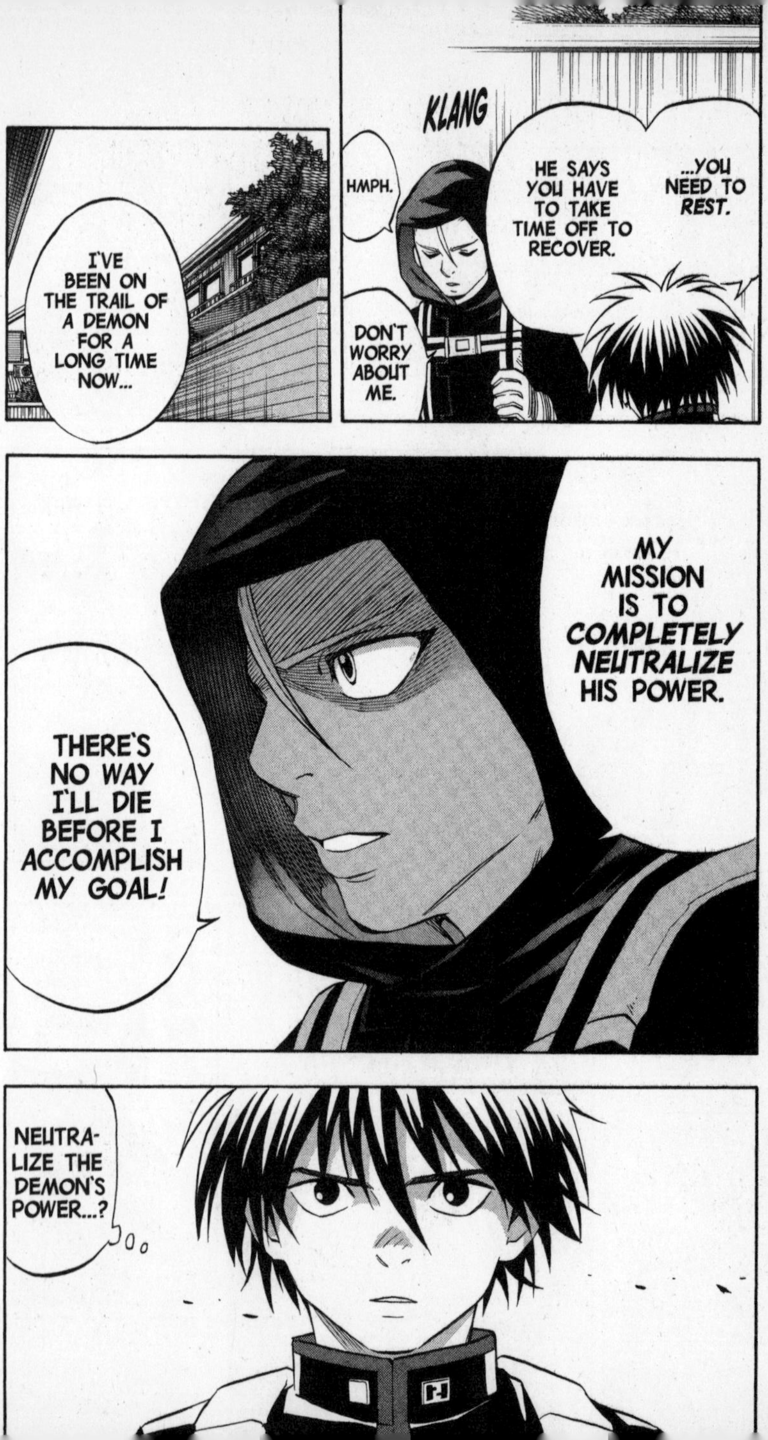
KLANG
...YOU NEED TO REST.
HE SAYS YOU HAVE TO TAKE TIME OFF TO RECOVER.
HMPH.
DON'T WORRY ABOUT ME.
I'VE BEEN ON THE TRAIL OF A DEMON FOR A LONG TIME NOW...
MY MISSION IS TO COMPLETELY NEUTRALIZE HIS POWER.
THERE'S NO WAY I'LL DIE BEFORE I ACCOMPLISH MY GOAL!
NEUTRA-LIZE THE DEMON'S POWER...?

Chapter 125: Master and Disciple

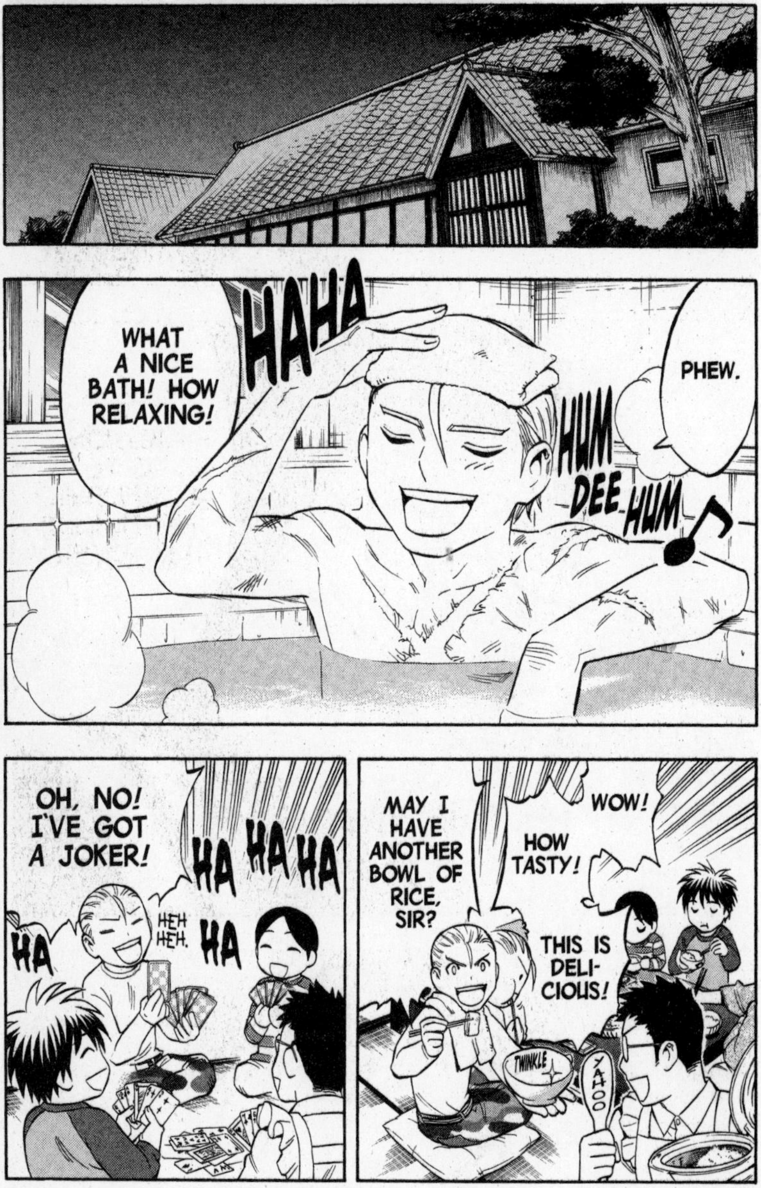
PHEW.
HUM DEE HUM
HAHA
WHAT A NICE BATH! HOW RELAXING!
WOW!
HOW TASTY!
MAY I HAVE ANOTHER BOWL OF RICE, SIR?
THIS IS DELICIOUS!
TWINKLE
YAHOO
HA HA HA
OH, NO! I'VE GOT A JOKER!
HEH HEH.
HA
HA

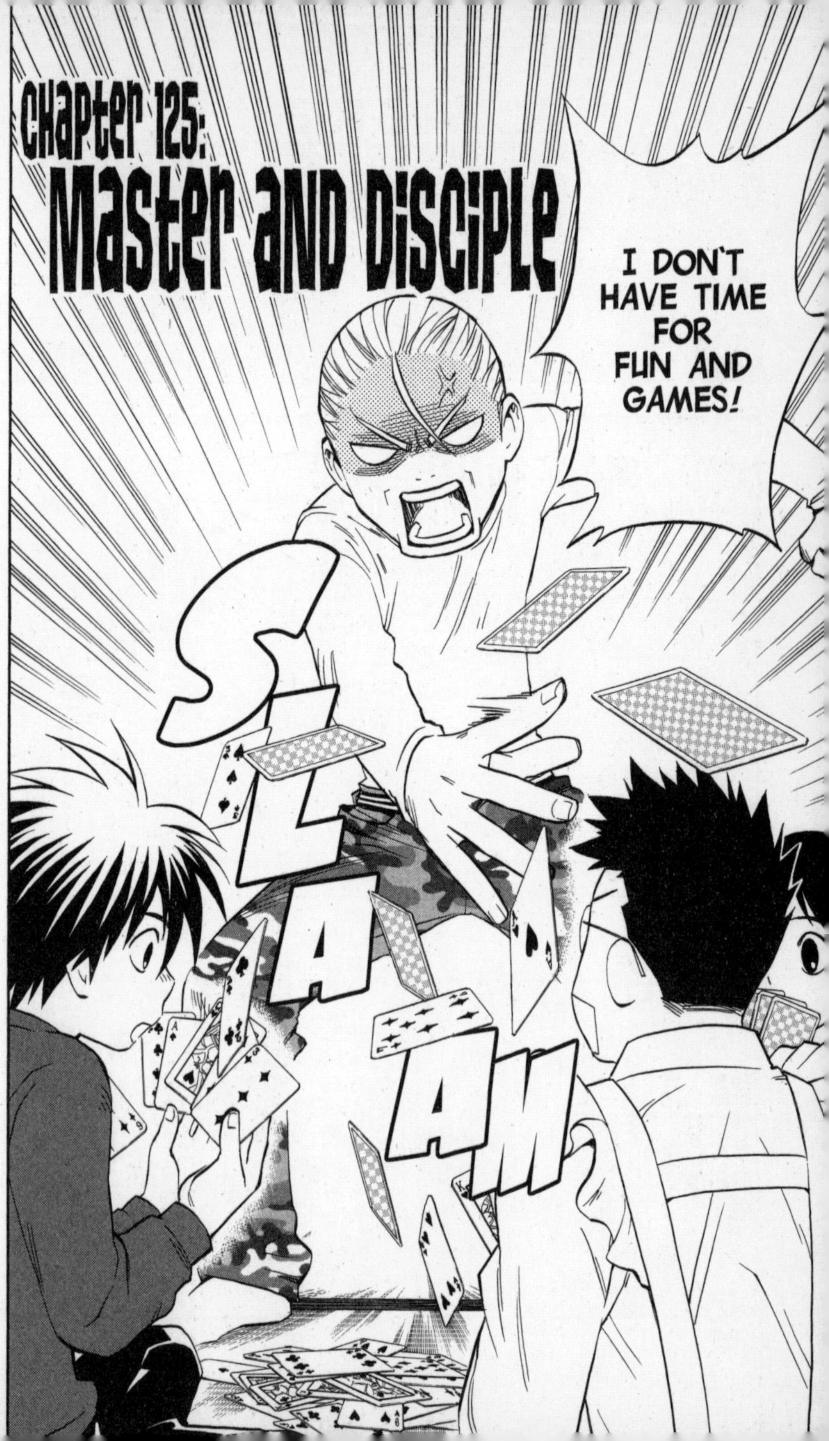
Chapter 125:
Master and Disciple
I DON'T HAVE TIME FOR FUN AND GAMES!
SLAAAM

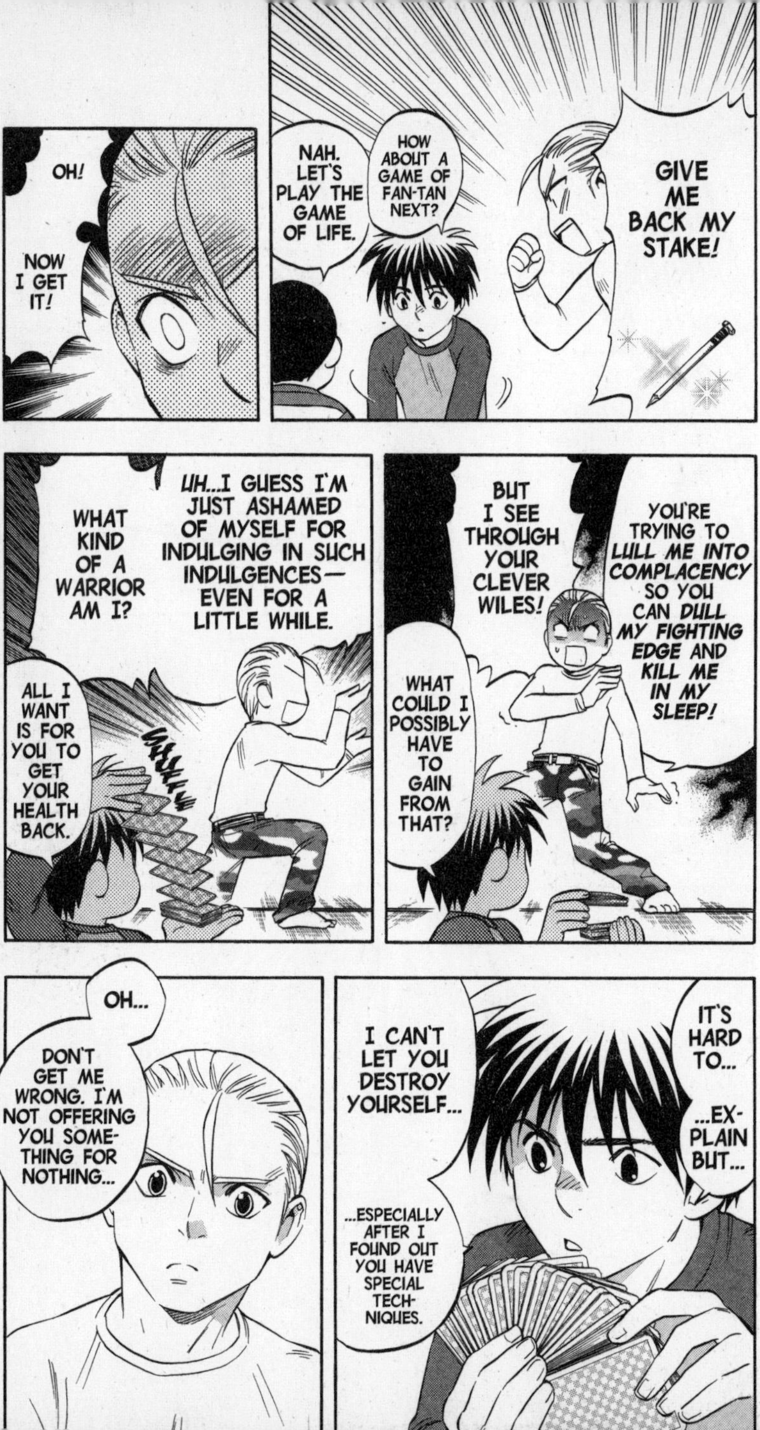
GIVE ME BACK MY STAKE!
HOW ABOUT A GAME OF FAN-TAN NEXT?
NAH. LET'S PLAY THE GAME OF LIFE.
OH!
NOW I GET IT!
YOU'RE TRYING TO LULL ME INTO COMPLACENCY SO YOU CAN DULL MY FIGHTING EDGE AND KILL ME IN MY SLEEP!
BUT I SEE THROUGH YOUR CLEVER WILES!
WHAT COULD I POSSIBLY HAVE TO GAIN FROM THAT?
UH...I GUESS I'M JUST ASHAMED OF MYSELF FOR INDULGING IN SUCH INDULGENCES—EVEN FOR A LITTLE WHILE.
WHAT KIND OF A WARRIOR AM I?
ALL I WANT IS FOR YOU TO GET YOUR HEALTH BACK.
IT'S HARD TO...
...EX-PLAIN BUT...
I CAN'T LET YOU DESTROY YOURSELF...
...ESPECIALLY AFTER I FOUND OUT YOU HAVE SPECIAL TECH-NIQUES.
OH...
DON'T GET ME WRONG. I'M NOT OFFERING YOU SOME-THING FOR NOTHING...

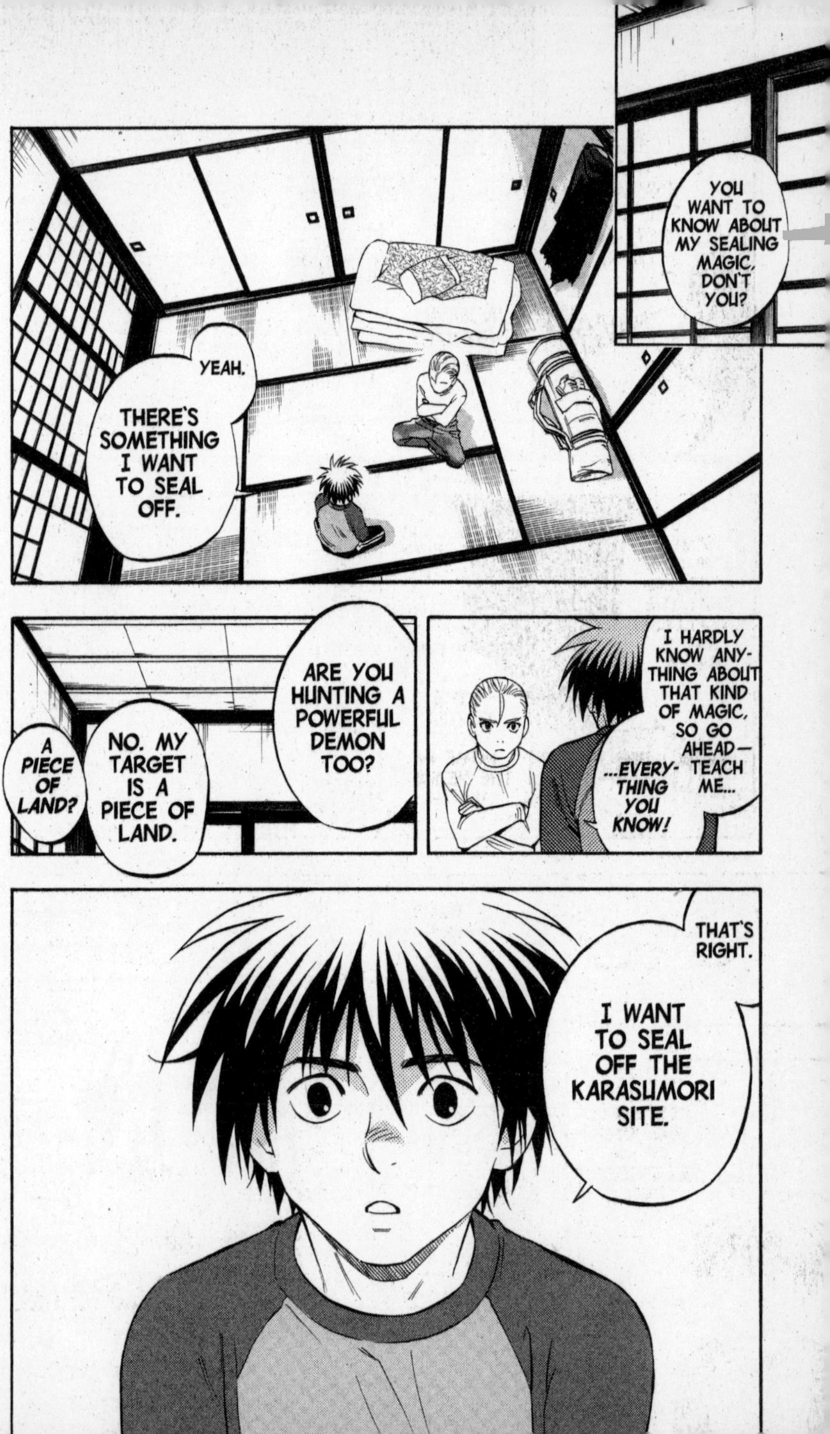
YOU WANT TO KNOW ABOUT MY SEALING MAGIC, DON'T YOU?
YEAH.
THERE'S SOMETHING I WANT TO SEAL OFF.
I HARDLY KNOW ANYTHING ABOUT THAT KIND OF MAGIC, SO GO AHEAD—TEACH ME...
...EVERYTHING YOU KNOW!
ARE YOU HUNTING A POWERFUL DEMON TOO?
NO. MY TARGET IS A PIECE OF LAND.
A PIECE OF LAND?
THAT'S RIGHT.
I WANT TO SEAL OFF THE KARASUMORI SITE.

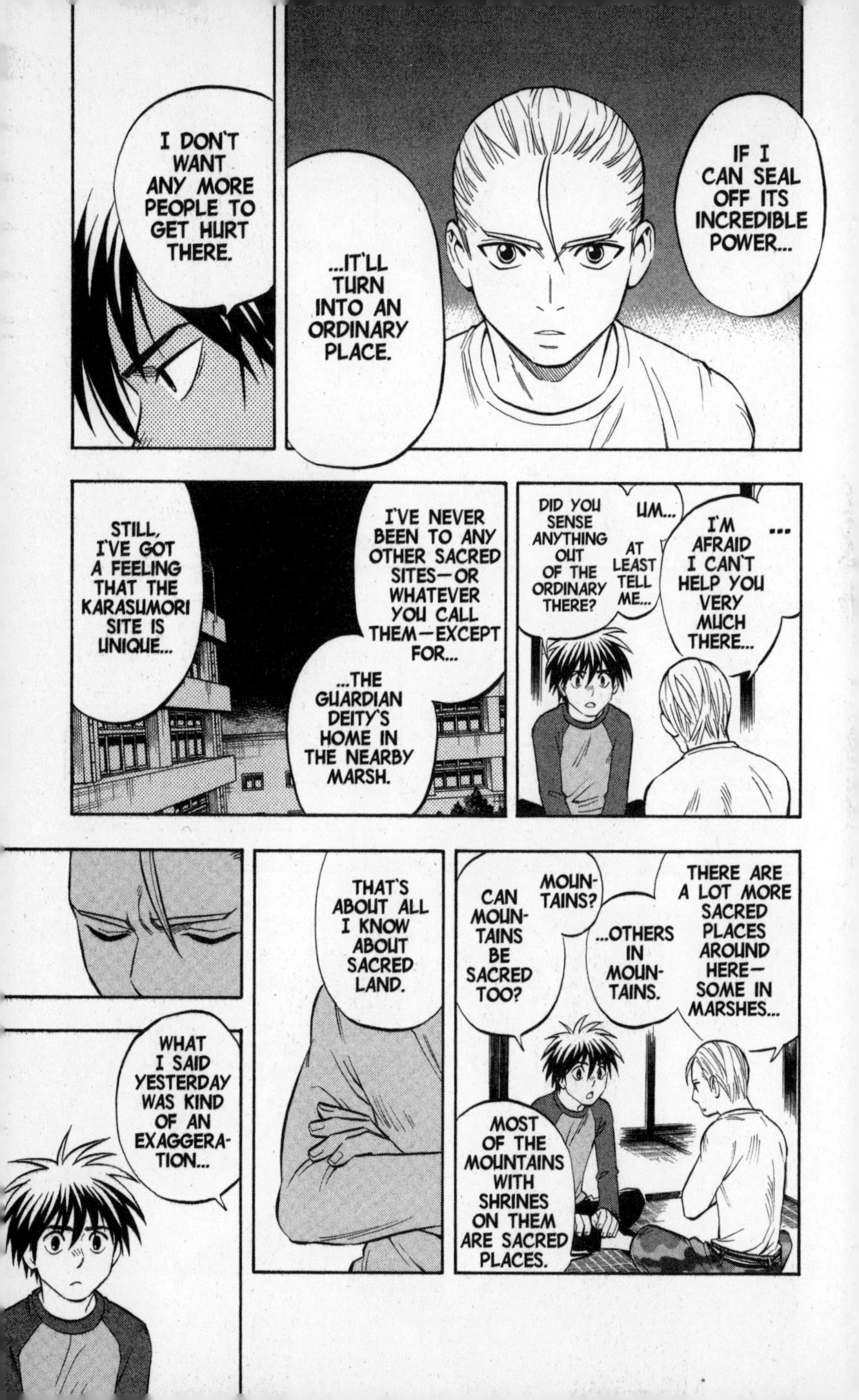
IF I CAN SEAL OFF ITS INCREDIBLE POWER...
...IT'LL TURN INTO AN ORDINARY PLACE.
I DON'T WANT ANY MORE PEOPLE TO GET HURT THERE.
UM...
AT LEAST TELL ME...
DID YOU SENSE ANYTHING OUT OF THE ORDINARY THERE?
...
I'M AFRAID I CAN'T HELP YOU VERY MUCH THERE...
I'VE NEVER BEEN TO ANY OTHER SACRED SITES—OR WHATEVER YOU CALL THEM—EXCEPT FOR...
...THE GUARDIAN DEITY'S HOME IN THE NEARBY MARSH.
STILL, I'VE GOT A FEELING THAT THE KARASUMORI SITE IS UNIQUE...
THERE ARE A LOT MORE SACRED PLACES AROUND HERE— SOME IN MARSHES...
...OTHERS IN MOUN-TAINS.
MOUN-TAINS?
CAN MOUN-TAINS BE SACRED TOO?
MOST OF THE MOUNTAINS WITH SHRINES ON THEM ARE SACRED PLACES.
THAT'S ABOUT ALL I KNOW ABOUT SACRED LAND.
WHAT I SAID YESTERDAY WAS KIND OF AN EXAGGERA-TION...

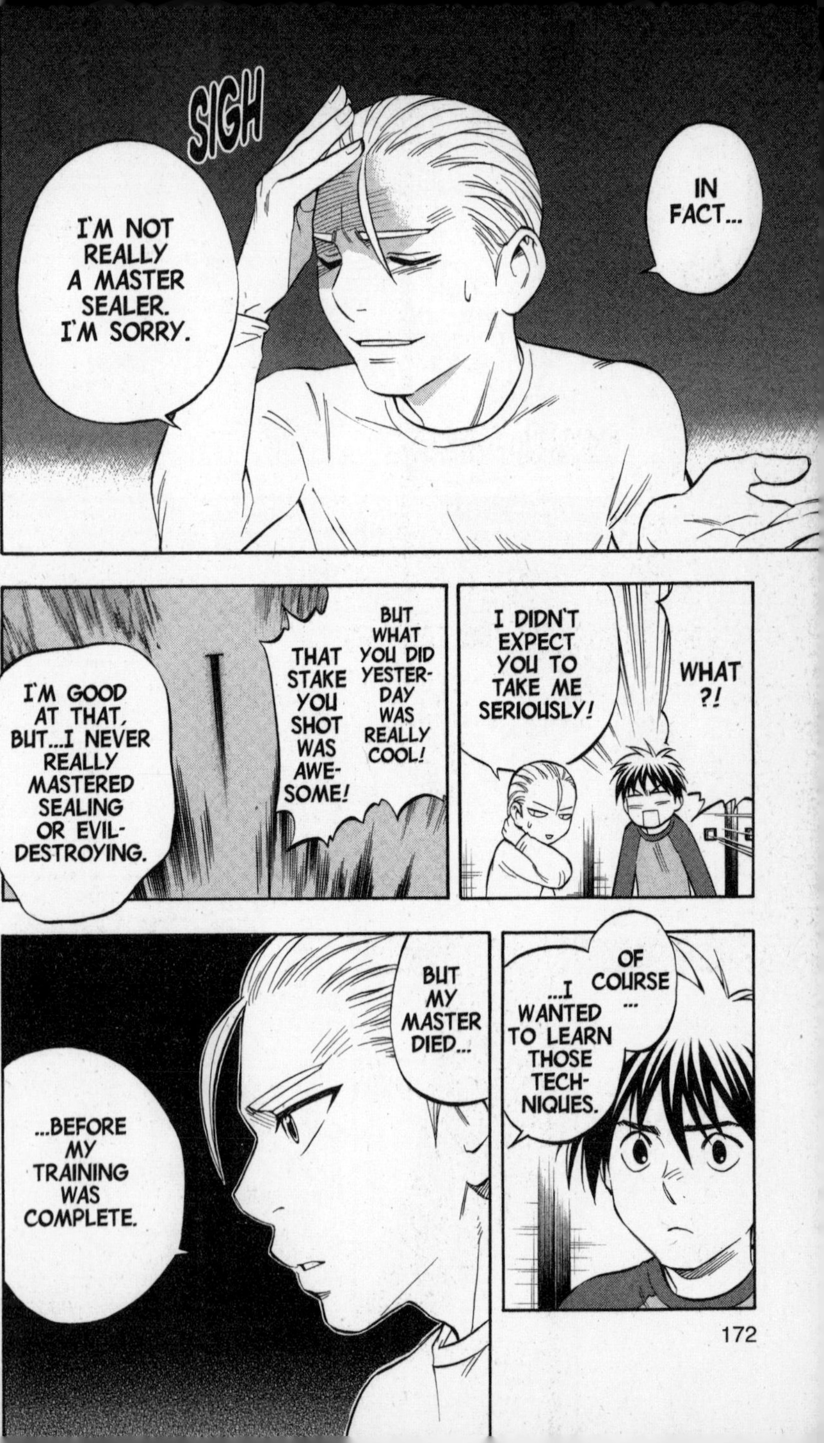
IN FACT...
SIGH
I'M NOT REALLY A MASTER SEALER. I'M SORRY.
WHAT?!
I DIDN'T EXPECT YOU TO TAKE ME SERIOUSLY!
BUT WHAT YOU DID YESTER-DAY WAS REALLY COOL!
THAT STAKE YOU SHOT WAS AWE-SOME!
I'M GOOD AT THAT, BUT...I NEVER REALLY MASTERED SEALING OR EVIL-DESTROYING.
OF COURSE...
...I WANTED TO LEARN THOSE TECH-NIQUES.
BUT MY MASTER DIED...
...BEFORE MY TRAINING WAS COMPLETE.

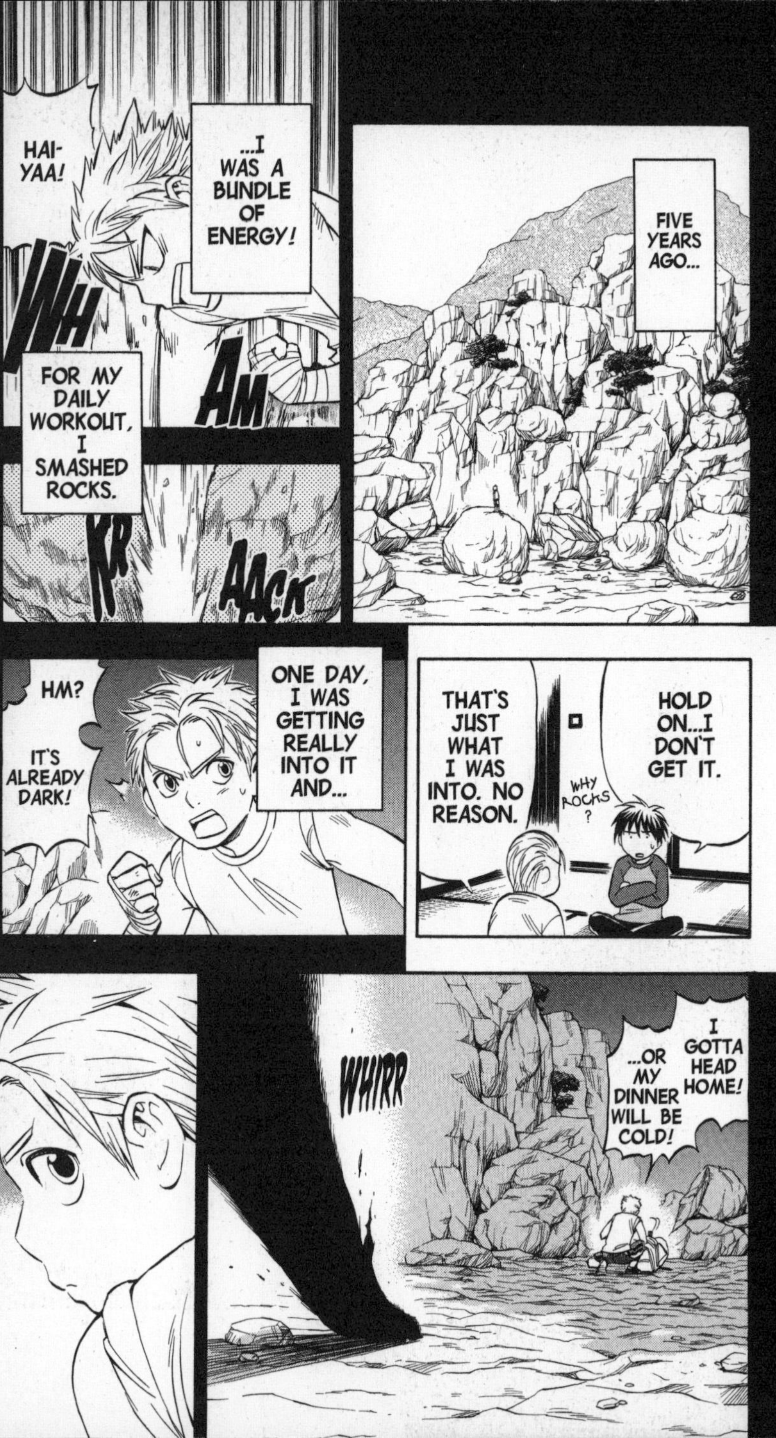
FIVE YEARS AGO...
...I WAS A BUNDLE OF ENERGY!
HAI-YAA!
WHAM
FOR MY DAILY WORKOUT, I SMASHED ROCKS.
KRAACK
HOLD ON...I DON'T GET IT.
WHY ROCKS?
THAT'S JUST WHAT I WAS INTO. NO REASON.
ONE DAY, I WAS GETTING REALLY INTO IT AND...
HM?
IT'S ALREADY DARK!
I GOTTA HEAD HOME!
...OR MY DINNER WILL BE COLD!
WHIRR

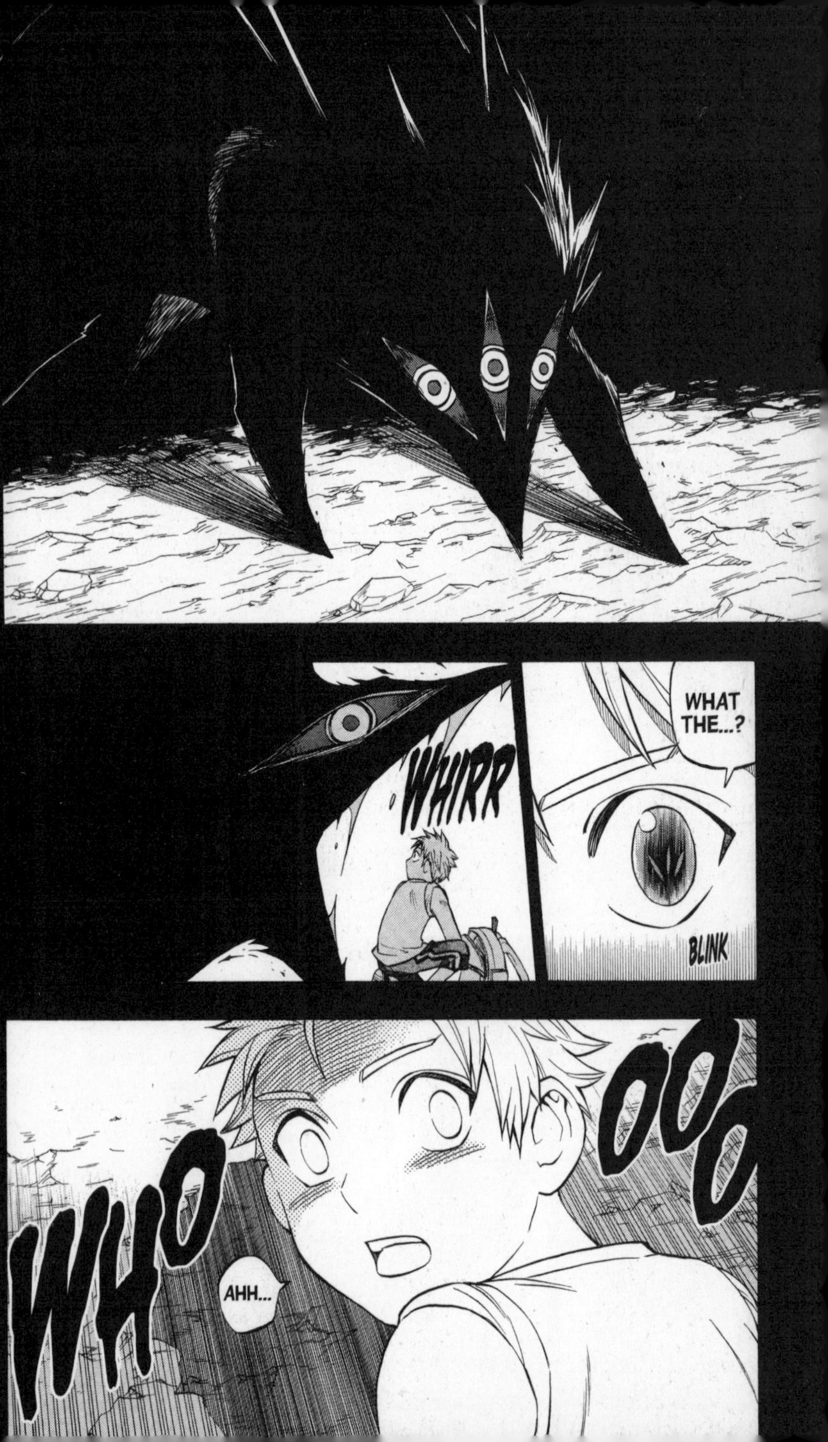
WHAT THE...?
BLINK
WHIRR
WHOOOO
AHH...

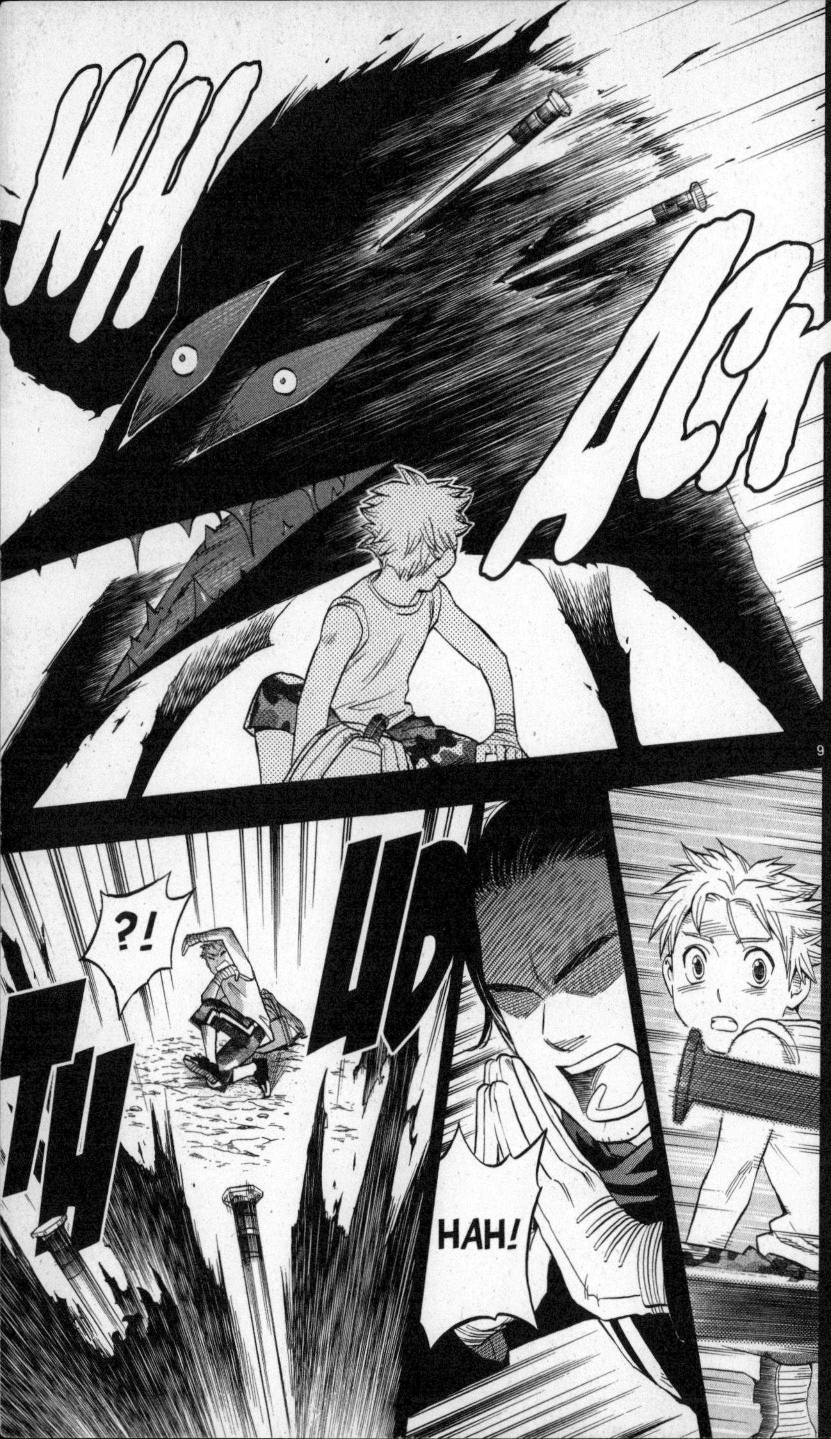
HAH!
?!

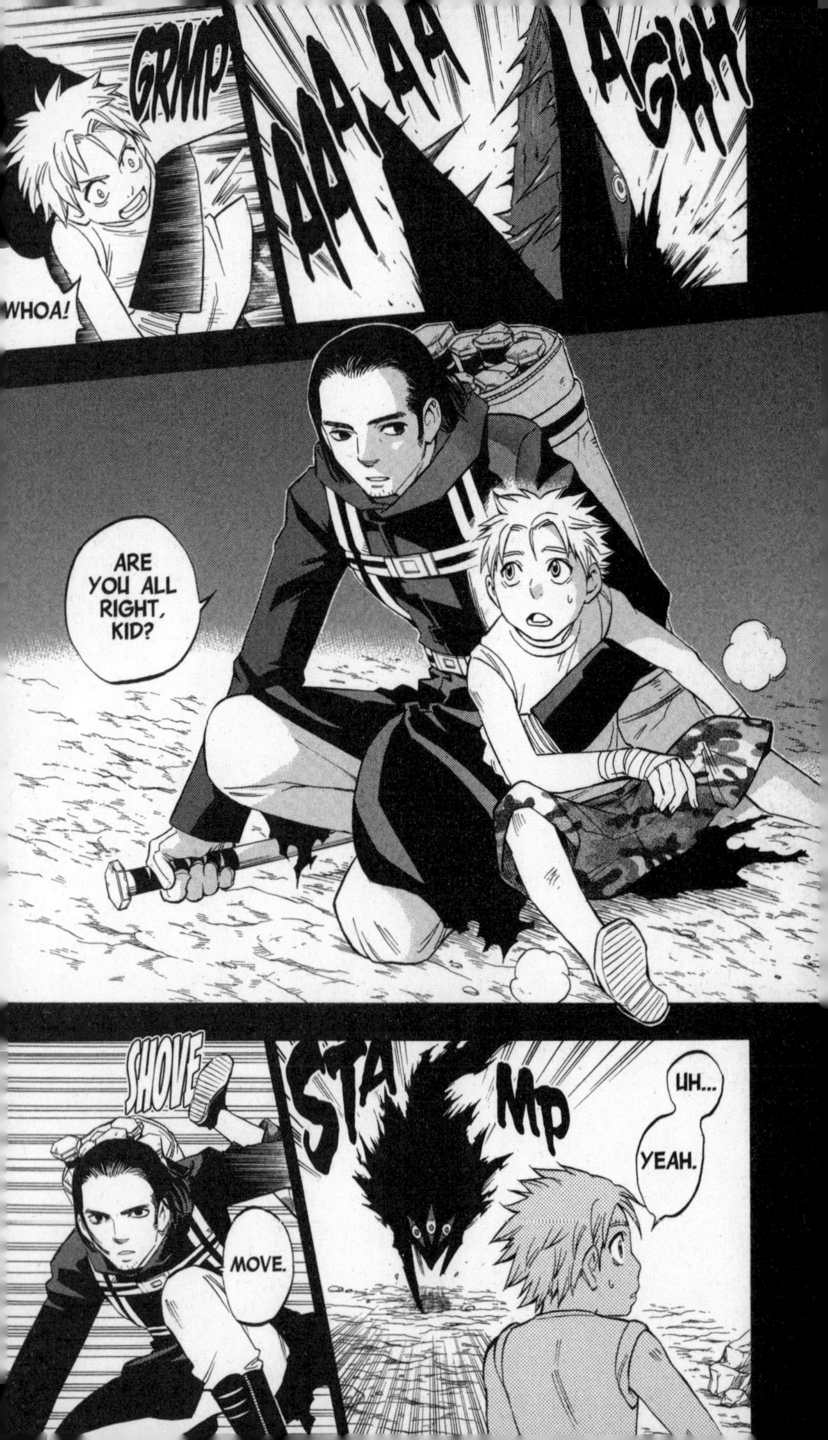
AAAAAA AGHH
GRMP
WHOA!
ARE YOU ALL RIGHT, KID?
STAMP
UH... YEAH.
SHOVE
MOVE.

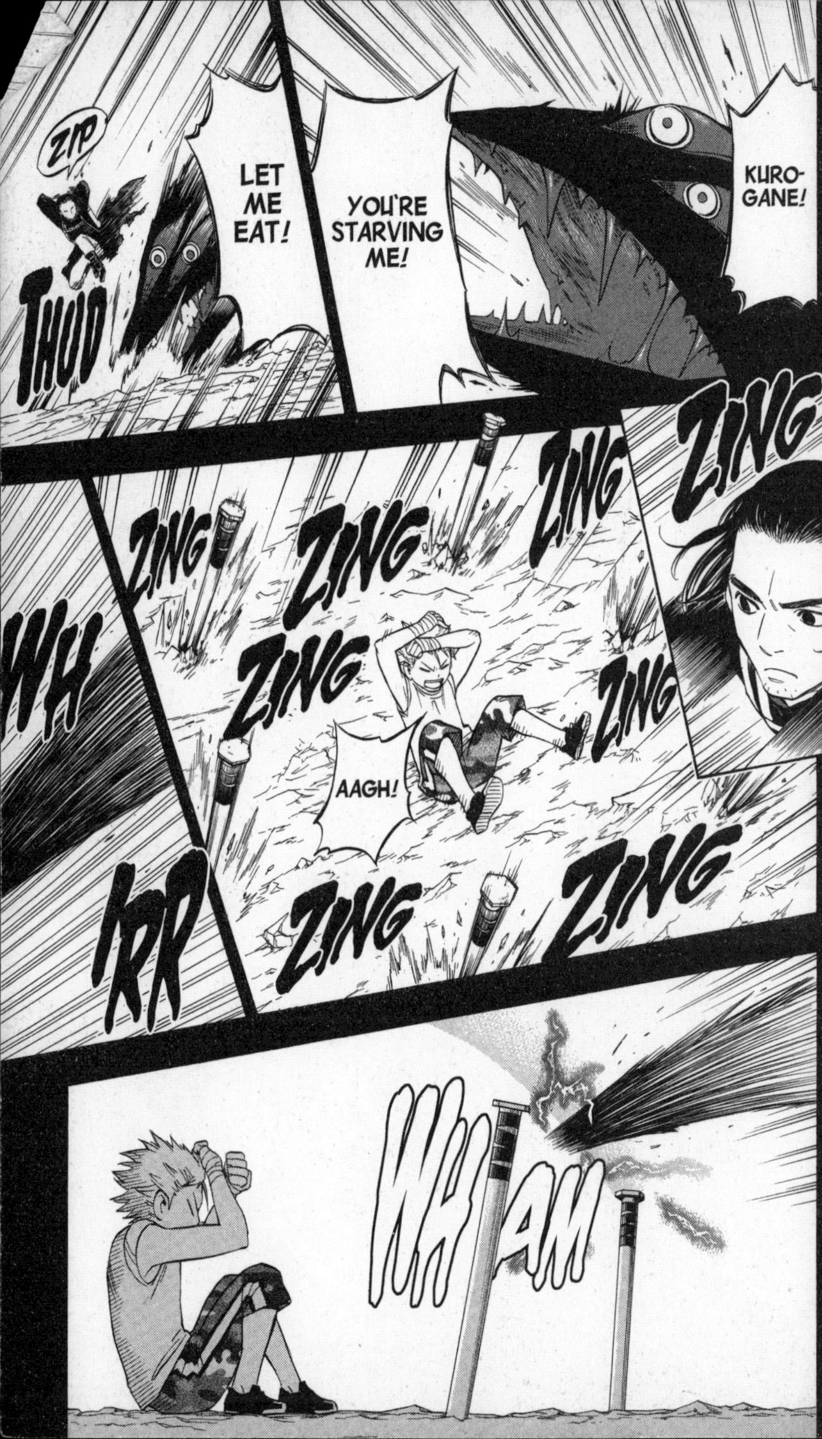

KURO-GANE!
YOU'RE STARVING ME!
LET ME EAT!
ZIP
THUD
ZING
ZING
ZING
ZING
ZING
ZING
AAGH!
ZING
ZING
WHIRR
WHAM

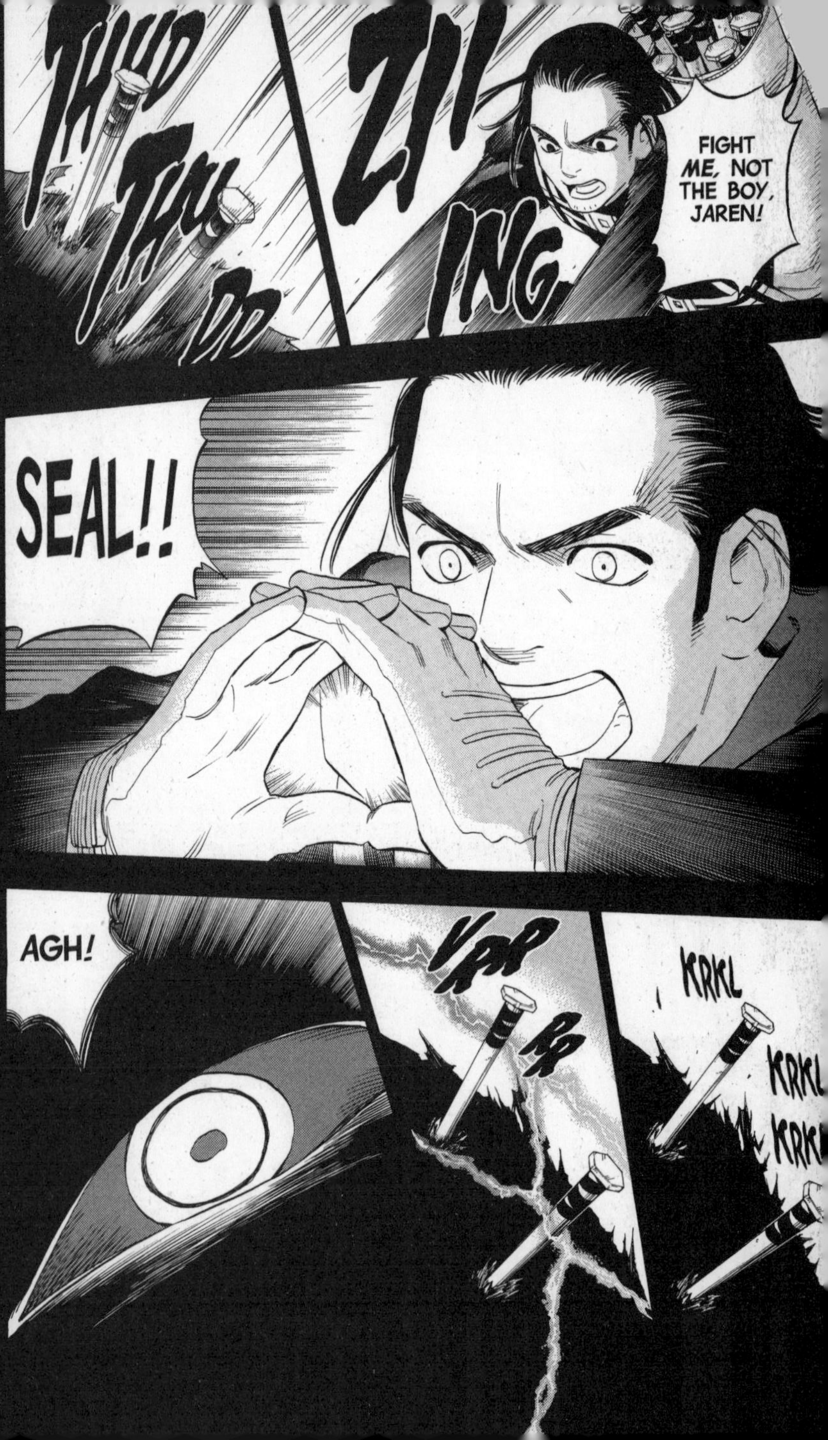
ZIING
FIGHT ME, NOT THE BOY, JAREN!
THUD
THU DD
SEAL!!
KRKL
KRKL KRK
VRR RR
AGH!

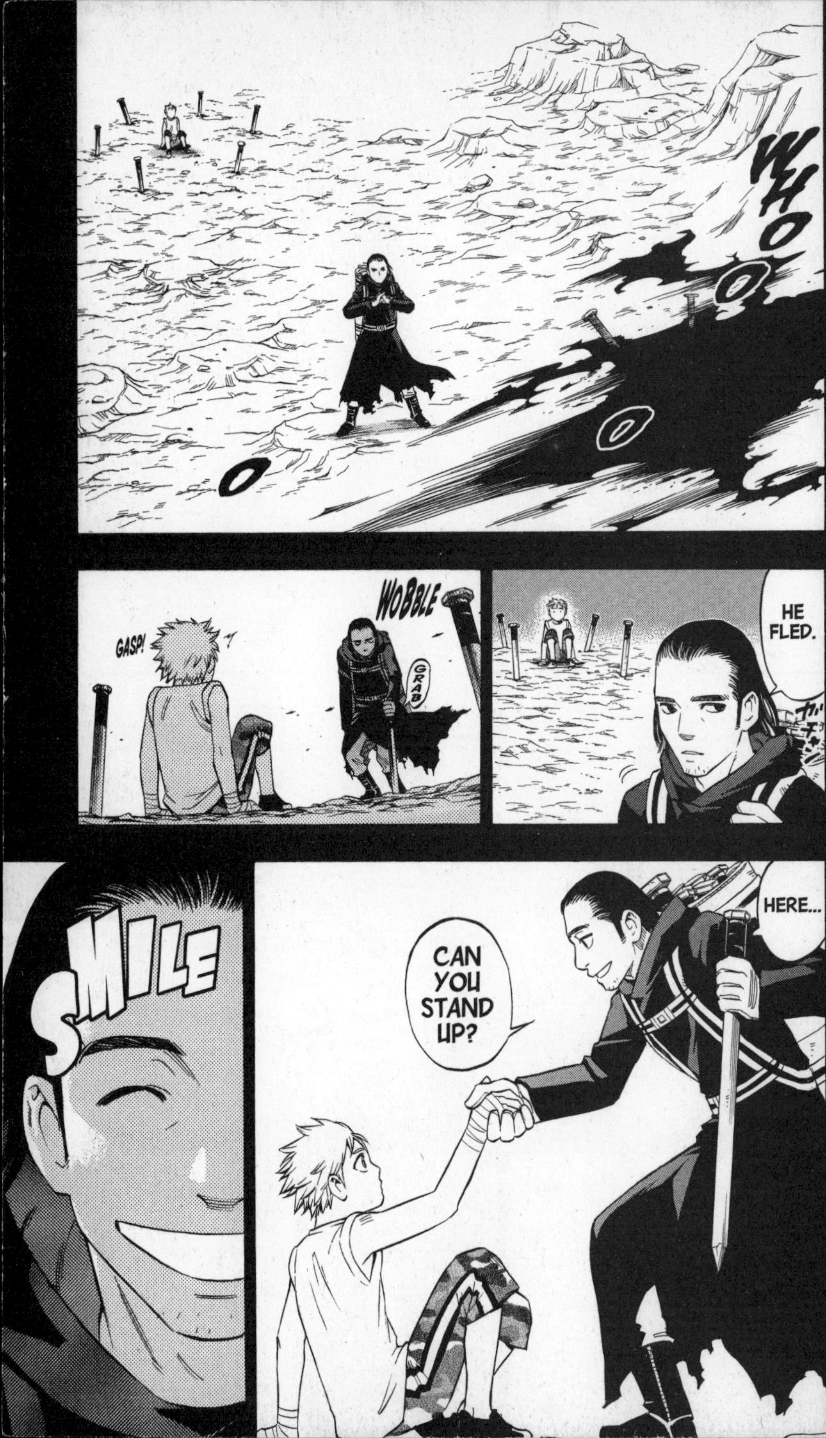
WHOOOO
HE FLED.
WOBBLE
GRAB
GASP!
HERE...
CAN YOU STAND UP?
SMILE

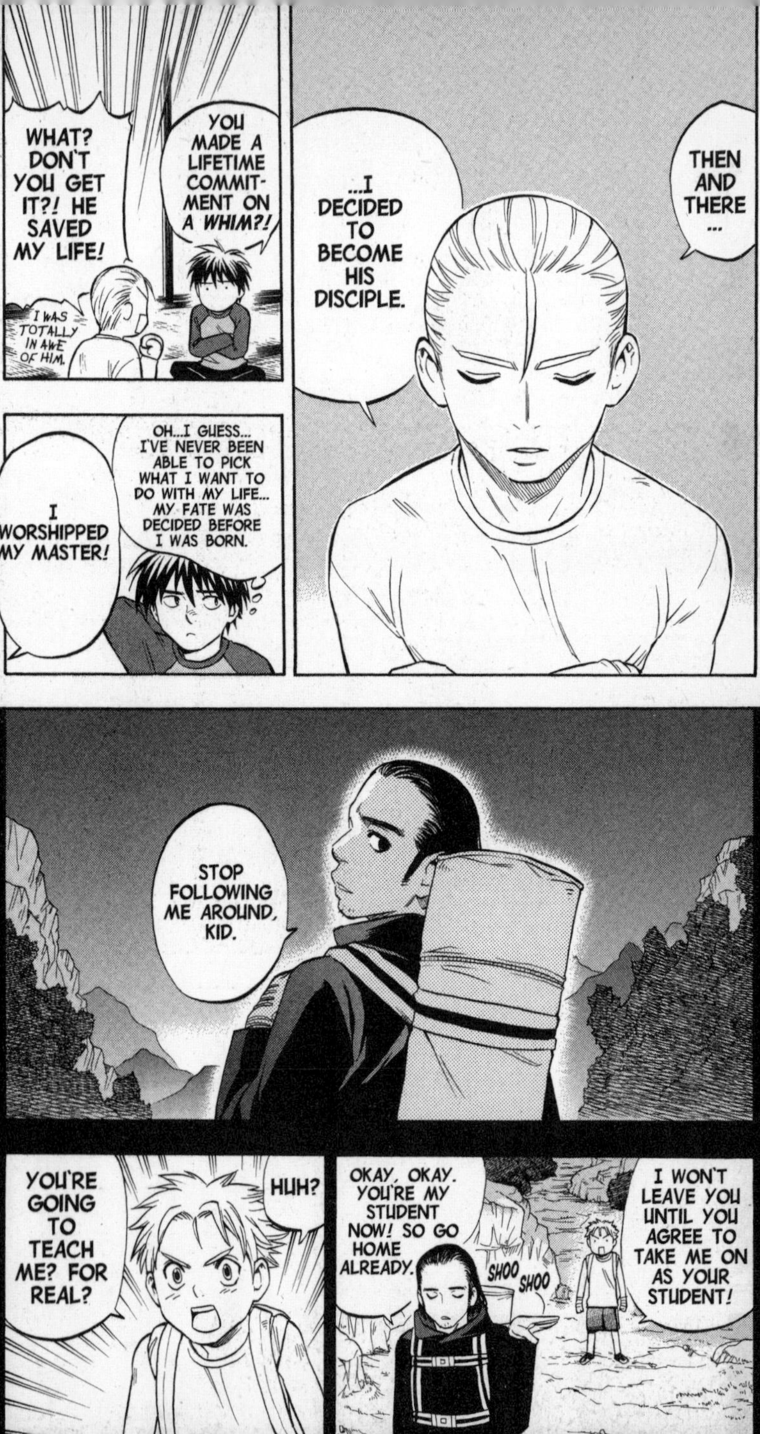
THEN AND THERE...
...I DECIDED TO BECOME HIS DISCIPLE.
YOU MADE A LIFETIME COMMITMENT ON A *WHIM*?!
WHAT? DON'T YOU GET IT?! HE SAVED MY LIFE!
I WAS TOTALLY IN AWE OF HIM.
OH...I GUESS... I'VE NEVER BEEN ABLE TO PICK WHAT I WANT TO DO WITH MY LIFE... MY FATE WAS DECIDED BEFORE I WAS BORN.
I WORSHIPPED MY MASTER!
STOP FOLLOWING ME AROUND, KID.
I WON'T LEAVE YOU UNTIL YOU AGREE TO TAKE ME ON AS YOUR STUDENT!
OKAY, OKAY. YOU'RE MY STUDENT NOW! SO GO HOME ALREADY.
SHOO SHOO
HUH?
YOU'RE GOING TO TEACH ME? FOR REAL?

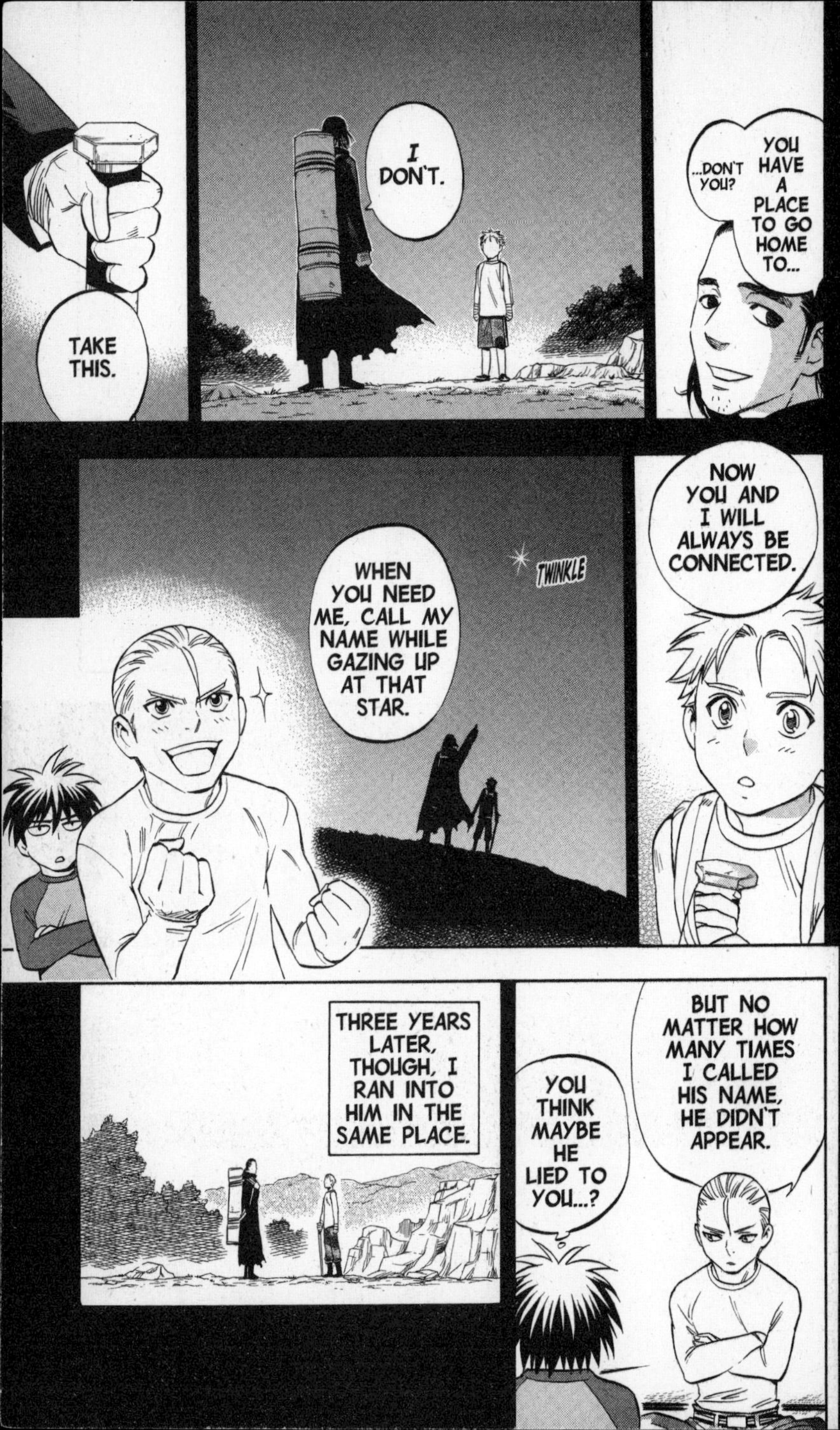
YOU HAVE A PLACE TO GO HOME TO...
...DON'T YOU?
I DON'T.
TAKE THIS.
NOW YOU AND I WILL ALWAYS BE CONNECTED.
TWINKLE
WHEN YOU NEED ME, CALL MY NAME WHILE GAZING UP AT THAT STAR.
BUT NO MATTER HOW MANY TIMES I CALLED HIS NAME, HE DIDN'T APPEAR.
YOU THINK MAYBE HE LIED TO YOU...?
THREE YEARS LATER, THOUGH, I RAN INTO HIM IN THE SAME PLACE.

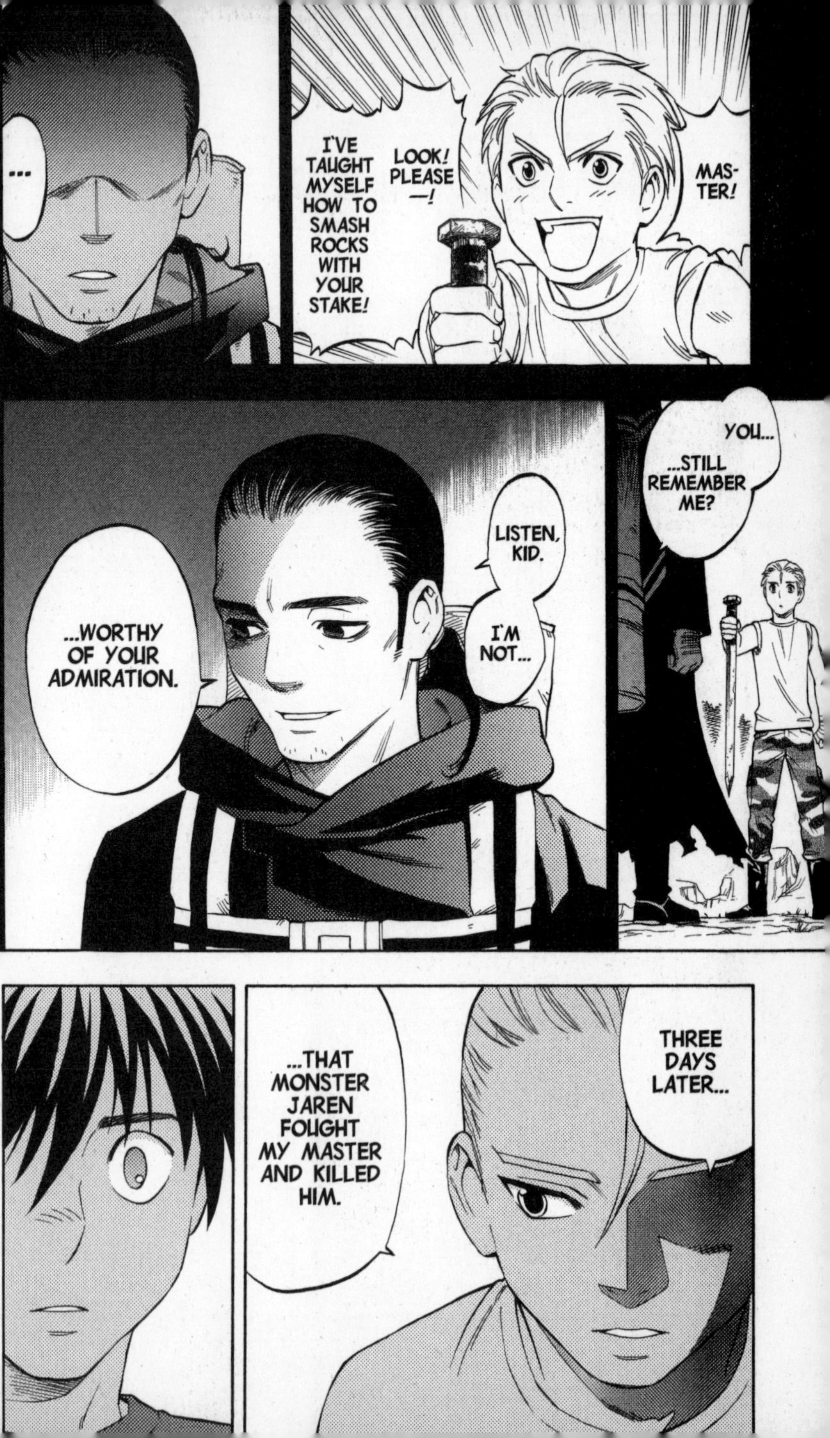
MAS-TER!
LOOK! PLEASE —!
I'VE TAUGHT MYSELF HOW TO SMASH ROCKS WITH YOUR STAKE!
...
YOU...
...STILL REMEMBER ME?
LISTEN, KID.
I'M NOT...
...WORTHY OF YOUR ADMIRATION.
THREE DAYS LATER...
...THAT MONSTER JAREN FOUGHT MY MASTER AND KILLED HIM.

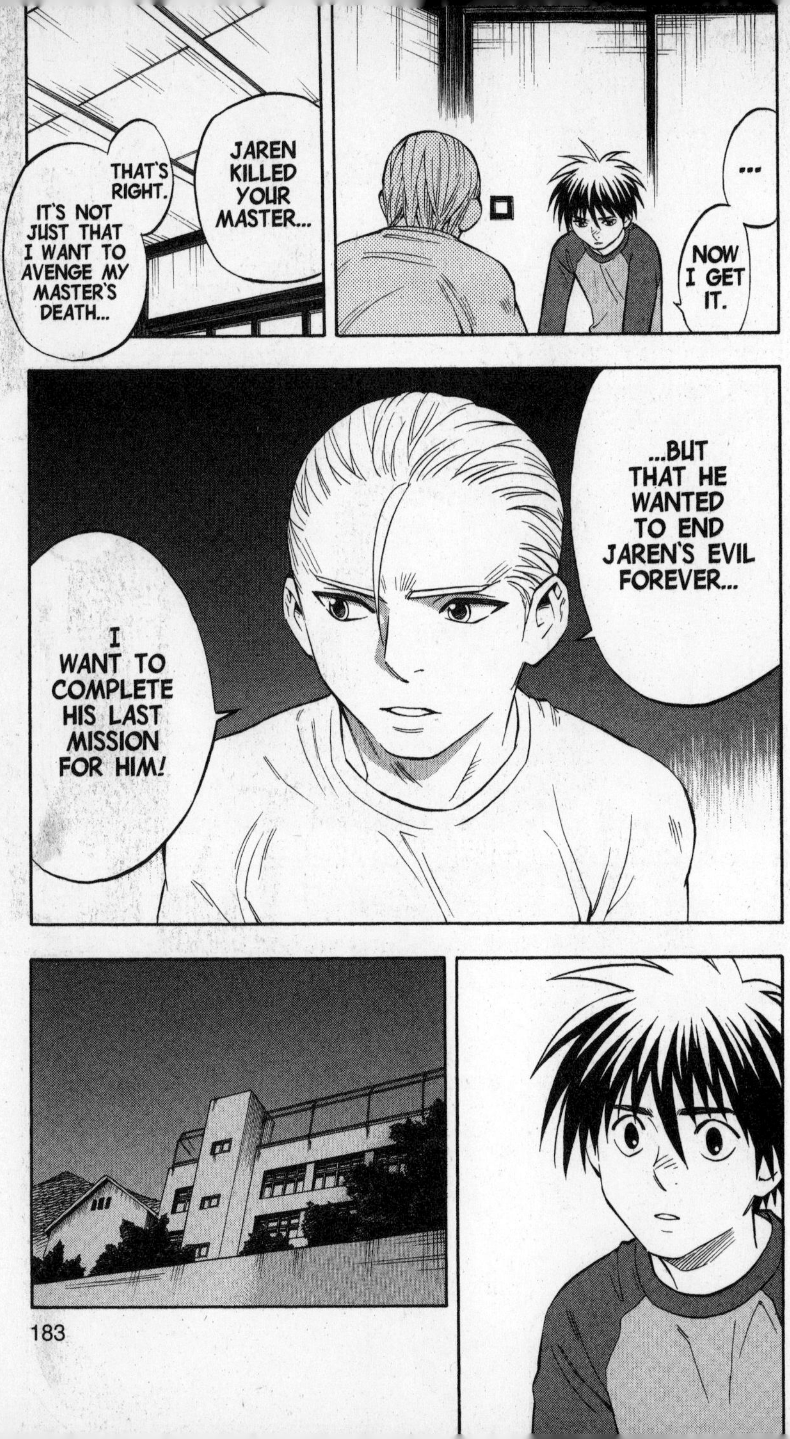
...
NOW I GET IT.
JAREN KILLED YOUR MASTER...
THAT'S RIGHT. IT'S NOT JUST THAT I WANT TO AVENGE MY MASTER'S DEATH...
...BUT THAT HE WANTED TO END JAREN'S EVIL FOREVER...
I WANT TO COMPLETE HIS LAST MISSION FOR HIM!

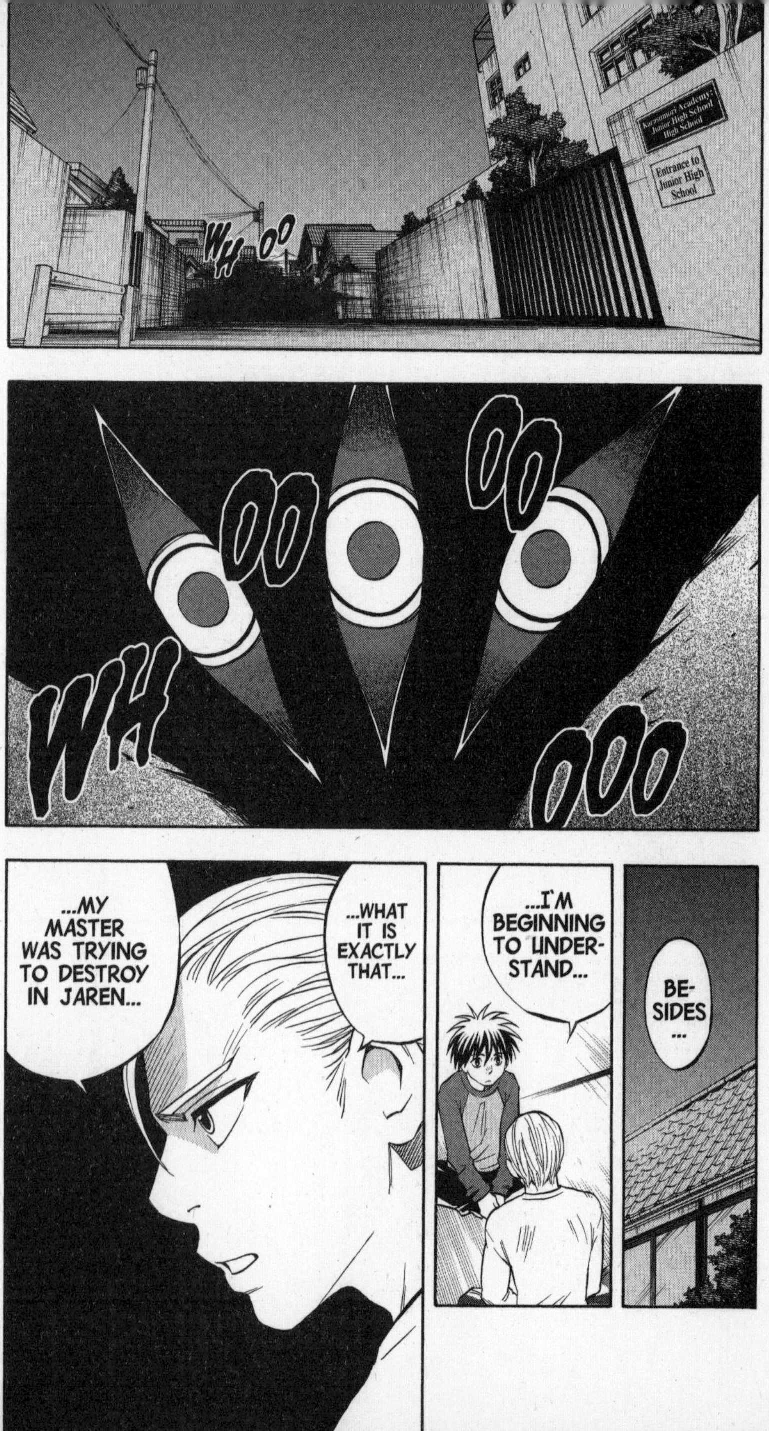
Karasumori Academy: Junior High School High School
Entrance to Junior High School
WH OO
WH OO OO OOO
BE-SIDES...
...I'M BEGINNING TO UNDER-STAND...
...WHAT IT IS EXACTLY THAT...
...MY MASTER WAS TRYING TO DESTROY IN JAREN...

SQUEEZE

結界師

MESSAGE FROM YELLOW TANABE

There are some foods I hated as a child but came to like as I grew up.
Eggplant is the first example that comes to mind.
Today I don't understand how I could ever have hated eggplant.
Maybe I was put off by its weird texture.
Now I love it. Eggplant is delicious!

KEKKAISHI

VOLUME 13

VIZ MEDIA EDITION

STORY AND ART BY YELLOW TANABE

Translation/Yuko Sawada
Touch-up Art & Lettering/Stephen Dutro
Cover Design & Graphic Layout/Izumi Evers
Editor/Annette Roman

Editor in Chief, Books/Alvin Lu
Editor in Chief, Magazines/Marc Weidenbaum
VP of Publishing Licensing/Rika Inouye
VP of Sales/Gonzalo Ferreyra
Sr. VP of Marketing/Liza Coppola
Publisher/Hyoe Narita

© 2006 Yellow TANABE/Shogakukan Inc. First published by
Shogakukan Inc. in Japan as "Kekkaishi." All rights reserved. The
stories, characters and incidents mentioned in this publication are
entirely fictional.

No portion of this book may be reproduced or transmitted in any form
or by any means without written permission from the copyright
holders.

The rights of the author(s) of the work(s) in this publication to be so
identified have been asserted in accordance with the Copyright,
Designs and Patents Act 1988. A CIP catalogue record for this book is
available from the British Library.

Printed in the U.S.A.

Published by VIZ Media, LLC
P.O. Box 77010
San Francisco, CA 94107

VIZ Media Edition
10 9 8 7 6 5 4 3 2 1
First printing, May 2008

PARENTAL ADVISORY
KEKKAISHI is rated T for Teen
and is recommended for ages 13
and up. It contains fantasy
violence.
ratings.viz.com

www.viz.com

store.viz.com

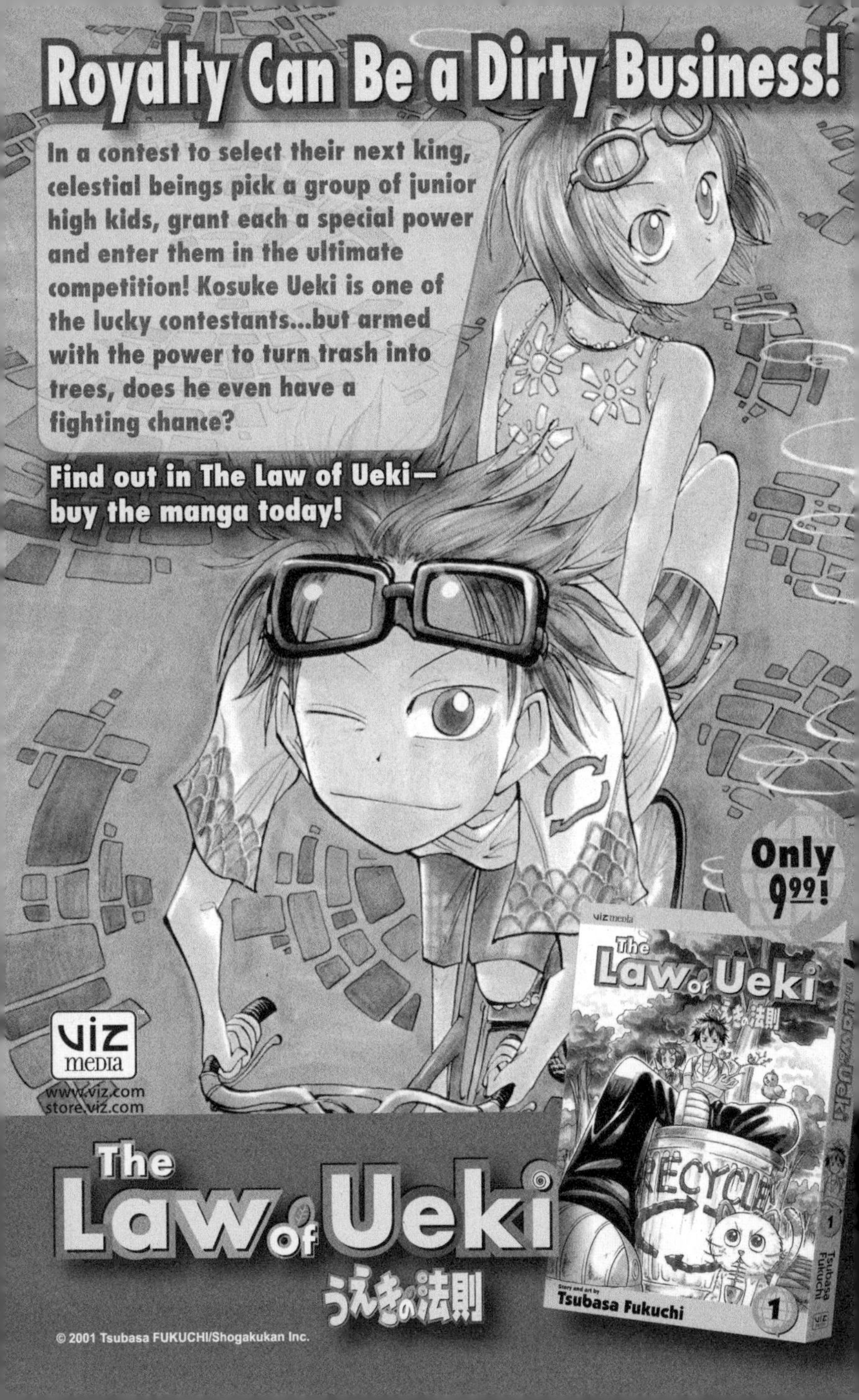
Royalty Can Be a Dirty Business!
In a contest to select their next king, celestial beings pick a group of junior high kids, grant each a special power and enter them in the ultimate competition! Kosuke Ueki is one of the lucky contestants...but armed with the power to turn trash into trees, does he even have a fighting chance?
Find out in The Law of Ueki— buy the manga today!
Only 9.99!
VIZ media
www.viz.com
store.viz.com
The Law of Ueki
うえきの法則
VIZ media
The Law of Ueki
うえきの法則
RECYCLE
Story and art by
Tsubasa Fukuchi
1
© 2001 Tsubasa FUKUCHI/Shogakukan Inc.

Embark on a Mystical Quest for ÄRM!

MÄRCHEN AWAKENS ROMANCE

An ordinary boy enters the land of his dreams!
Now part of Team MÄR, Ginta and Babbo must fight to save
the MÄR World. But will Ginta's mission be compromised by
his ally's secrets?

Find out in the MÄR anime—
own it on DVD today!

Watch it now at ToonamiJetstream.com

© Nobuyuki Anzai / 2005, 2007
Shogakukan, ShoPro, TV Tokyo
Cover art subject to change.

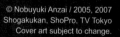

www.viz.com
store.viz.com

LOVE MANGA?
LET US KNOW WHAT YOU THINK!

OUR MANGA SURVEY IS NOW
AVAILABLE ONLINE. PLEASE VISIT:
VIZ.COM/MANGASURVEY

HELP US MAKE THE MANGA
YOU LOVE BETTER!

FULLMETAL ALCHEMIST © Hiromu Arakawa/SQUARE ENIX INUYASHA © 1997 Rumiko TAKAHASHI/Shogakukan Inc.
NAOKI URASAWA'S MONSTER © 1995 Naoki URASAWA Studio Nuts/Shogakukan Inc. ZATCH BELL! © 2001 Makoto RAIKU/Shogakukan Inc.

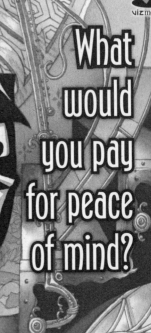

What would you pay for peace of mind?

YUMEKUI KENBUN

NIGHTMARE INSPECTOR

Suffer from nightmares? Meet Hiruko. He's more than a special kind of private investigator—he's a dream eater. And he'll rid you of your darkest visions…but at what price?

Find out in
Nightmare Inspector—
MANGA ON SALE NOW!

On sale at store.viz.com
Also available at your local bookstore and comic store.

© 2002 Shin Mashiba/SQUARE ENIX

RATED T+ FOR OLDER TEEN
ratings.viz.com

www.viz.com